THE FIRST AMENDMENT RECONSIDERED represents one of the very few recent efforts to focus on the meaning and theory of the First Amendment in the latter part of the twentieth century. It provides a special examination of the First Amendment at a time when economics and technology are forcing a reevaluation of traditional approaches to media freedom. Four prize-winning papers and three presentations by prominent First Amendment scholars and attorneys reassess the historical base for our current understanding of the First Amendment and suggest a variety of approaches to press freedom for the future.

The book opens with a foreword by a major legal scholar which examines how different research traditions and methodologies can be used to inform the legal process. The introduction is followed by a research paper which successfully challenges long-held assumptions about the role of the state courts in the development of First Amendment theory. Four papers critically evaluate the approach toward the First Amendment taken by the U.S. Supreme Court in recent years. In the final section, two papers discuss First Amendment issues in the light of a model democratic theory and in the light of developing media technologies.

LONGMAN SERIES
IN PUBLIC
COMMUNICATION

Series Editor: **Ray Eldon Hiebert**

Congress shall make no law respecting an establishment of religion, or prohibiting the free exercise thereof; or abridging the freedom of speech, or of the press; or the right of the people peaceably to assemble, and to petition the government for a redress of grievances.

THE FIRST AMENDMENT
RECONSIDERED
NEW PERSPECTIVES ON THE MEANING OF FREEDOM OF SPEECH AND PRESS

Edited by: Bill F. Chamberlin
University of North Carolina,
Chapel Hill

Charlene J. Brown
Indiana University

Longman
New York & London

The First Amendment Reconsidered
New Perspectives on the Meaning of Freedom of Speech and Press

Longman Inc., 19 West 44th Street, New York, N.Y. 10036
Associated companies, branches, and representatives
throughout the world.

Developmental Editor: Gordon T. R. Anderson
Editorial and Design Supervisor: Joan Matthews
Manufacturing and Production Supervisor: Anne Musso

Library of Congress Cataloging in Publication Data

Main entry under title:
The First Amendment Reconsidered.

    Includes index.
    1. Liberty of the press—United States—Addresses,
essays, lectures. 2. Liberty of speech—United
States—Addresses, essays, lectures. I. Chamberlin,
Bill F., 1944–   . II. Brown, Charlene J.
KF4774.A75F57   342.73'0853   81–15561
ISBN 0-582-28303-5   347.302853   AACR2

Manufactured in the United States of America
9 8 7 6 5 4 3 2 1

To Jeanne

To Trevor, Trevor L., and Leigh

Contents

Foreword

Marc A. Franklin*

On a day-to-day basis, First Amendment law is in the hands of the practitioners—journalists, attorneys, prosecutors, judges. They are the ones creating, arguing, and deciding the cases. Unfortunately, the daily pressures that engulf them give little opportunity for reflection.

Journalists want to know what their rights are, what their risks are, what will happen if they do this or that. After the deadline has passed, they may rail against the rules and the constraints on their First Amendment rights, but because of the pressures of deadlines, their primary concern is to know what those rules and constraints are and what might happen if they were disregarded.

Lawyers working on clients' problems on a daily basis also focus on very practical concerns: What are the relevant sources of law and scholarship? What are the clients' rights under these sources? How can the relevant materials be best used? Time for reflection on larger issues of First Amendment law or theory is a luxury available to few advocates.

Judges tend to focus on the specific case at bar. They generally view their task as a matter of deciding the case before them in conformity with related decisions. It is not common for judges, even in First Amendment areas, to write opinions springing from general theoretical bases.[1] Constrained by the accumulated body of cases and by the unpredictability of fact situations in future cases, chastened by the variety, randomness, and overwhelming number of cases appearing on their dockets, judges have few occasions to build theories or develop broad principles, even when they are so inclined. Further, there may be surprising dangers when judges do try to evolve their own theories.[2]

---

*Marc A. Franklin, widely recognized for his contributions in communications law, is the Frederick I. Richman Professor of Law at Stanford Law School, where he has taught for 20 years.

He has published five books, including *The First Amendment and the Fourth Estate: Communications Law for Undergraduates* (1981); *Injuries and Remedies: Cases and Materials on Tort Law and Alternatives* (1979); *Cases and Materials on Mass Media Law* (1982); *Dynamics of American Law* (1968); and *Biography of a Legal Dispute* (1968). Among his several law journal articles are "Suing Media for Libel: A Litigation Study" (*American Bar Foundation Research Journal*, 1981); "Winners and Losers and Why: A Study of Defamation Litigation" (*American Bar Foundation Research Journal*, 1980); "Reflections on *Herbert* v. *Lando*" (*Stanford Law Review*, 1979), "The Origins and Constitutionality of Limitations on Truth as a Defense in Tort Law" (*Stanford Law Review*, 1964) and "A Constitutional Problem in Privacy Protection: Legal Inhibitions on Reporting of Fact" (*Stanford Law Review*, 1963).

Franklin received his A.B. from Cornell University in 1953 and his LL.B. from Cornell Law School in 1956. He served as a law clerk to U.S. Supreme Court Chief Justice Earl Warren from 1958 to 1959. He taught at Columbia University School of Law before moving to Stanford. He also has been a Fellow at the Center for Advanced Study in Behavioral Sciences at Stanford and a Fulbright Research Scholar in New Zealand.

Of necessity, the opportunity and responsibility for broad analysis and reflection about the First Amendment belong to the scholars in law and journalism and related fields. To some extent, scholars do what practitioners do when they analyze, reorganize, and distinguish cases. But scholars have an opportunity to stand back and look at not only where a line of cases is going but why it is going there. What premises are the courts using? Why were these, rather than others, adopted? What legal theory underlies, implicitly or explicitly, the line of decisions? What peculiarities shape a particular body of law? How does that particular area square with its neighbors? Scholars need to ask these questions. And if they will take that broader look, they can contribute valuable empirical and theoretical insights to the resolution of First Amendment controversies.

Three major types of scholarly First Amendment research have emerged. The first is historical research, efforts to identify some past tradition or explain some process. How open were criminal trials in earlier days? What kinds of legal claims did litigants press? In addition to telling us more about our heritage, historical research helps us to understand current problems and may help point to sensible resolutions.

The second type of research can be called quantitative empirical research. Empirical research seeks to describe the realities of the day. Are jurors prejudiced by having been exposed to certain types of pretrial publicity? Do public figures really have access to media to respond to attacks on their reputations? How effective are the responses in such cases? How are particular litigation processes actually working—as distinct from theories about how a system should work?

The third type of scholarly research is normative theory-building that tells us how and why legal doctrines should change. The prescriptions tend to be philosophical and are based on views of what the country needs to be true to its founding spirit or to meet its contemporary situation. Unlike historical and empirical scholarship, theory-building tends to be sweeping in structure and to cut across traditional lines. Empirical research would be likely to study a problem already identified as belonging to the realm of libel, for example, but normative theory would probably sweep across all types of communication.[3]

Each type of reseach has a different relevance to the resolution of First Amendment disputes. One may be more suitable than another to legal and judicial use. Judges may be more skeptical, for example, of studies using complex quantitative methodologies.

Historical research is closest to the mainstream of judicial thought.[4] Judges regularly try to learn the context of legislation or how something functioned in earlier days.[5] An understanding of whether criminal trials were traditionally open to the public may have helped resolve a contemporary dispute.[6] What the framers meant by *speech* and *press* might be significant today.[7]

Historical research is readily understood and accepted when it is unchallenged,[8] though the Court may decide that in some cases historical developments must take a back seat to a more pressing consideration.[9]

Empirical research presents different considerations. Judges often are skeptical about complex methodologies, much as they are concerned about the impact of new technology.[10] Even when that deterrent is absent, quantitative arguments present a different problem. For example, much research has been done on the question of whether persons who have been exposed to extensive pretrial publicity will carry biases from that exposure into jury deliberations.[11] Initially there is the difficulty of creating an experimental design that will approximate the real trial process, but quantitative conclusions themselves present a problem. Suppose, for example, the conclusion is that 90 percent of jurors so exposed are able to put aside the earlier information and perform their jury tasks in the same way as persons who were not similarly exposed. Even if courts were to accept such a conclusion as valid, what should they do about the 10 percent of jurors who are influenced by pretrial publicity? Unless they could be identified and relieved from jury duty, courts would be unlikely to alter their current attitudes toward pretrial publicity.

The nature of the pretrial publicity dispute makes it a strong candidate for empirical study. If the lack of bias could be shown conclusively, there would be no apparent reason for controlling the speech of others or closing courtrooms.

But in many other areas, the resolution of empirical questions may only give rise to nonempirical questions. Even if, for example, courts were satisfied that the presence of television cameras at criminal trials did not affect the behavior of any of the participants, a remaining question would be whether showing the trials was comparable to mass public trials and antithetical to our traditional values.[12]

In the obscenity area, survey research might tell us much about what the public considered to be of "prurient interest" and "patently offensive," but we would still have to consider whether a community was entitled to establish a public tone that excluded certain types of activities.[13]

In another vein, research might disclose that in a particular state public officials are regularly able to respond to defamatory attacks in a variety of media, often including the newspaper in which the original attack occurred. This might induce the state courts to develop an absolute privilege for such defamations as a matter of state law, a protection that would go beyond the protection extended to media under federal law in a comparable situation.

In sum, then, empirical research can be extremely valuable in helping the court correctly understand the nature of the world in which it is functioning and in educating the courts about particular values, attitudes, and attributes of the citizenry. Sometimes this will be enough to swing the decision. At other times, it might lead a court to reconsider a decision that was based on something that now appears to be an incorrect assumption about the general situation or to frame a new and narrower rule to meet the problem.[14] At still other times, such research may sharpen the nature of the issues before a court by eliminating some concerns that have no basis in fact. This will push the decision on to other grounds and produce new arguments—however the case may come out.

Scholars who undertake normative theory-building in the First Amendment are least likely to see the results of their work affect decisions. There are several reasons for this. First, as noted, judges tend to orient their thinking to the cases before them and to earlier decisions in what are perceived to be neighboring areas. The search for consistency and for comparability—even in the First Amendment area—tends to deflect judges from grand theories. Second, since the cases come to the courts in no logical sequence, judges are aware that they may not be seeing the most typical problems. They tend to move slowly with early cases in an area until they are confident that they are seeing a range of cases typical of that area.[15]

There is some paradox here because judges are presumably least restrained by precedent—and thus most able to adopt new theoretical views—when there is little prior case law to have to distinguish or deal with. Yet, it is precisely in these early stages that judges are most reluctant to write large. Occasionally jurists seek to restructure areas after having experience with enough earlier cases to be persuaded that the earlier approach is so seriously flawed that it must be replaced.[16] A judge who does try to develop a First Amendment theory may distort cases to fit his predetermined pattern.[17]

Normative theories tend to sweep across conventional substantive lines. An approach based on one's view of the underlying nature of this country,[18] or on the needs of today's voters,[19] need not be concerned with acknowledging traditional areas of libel, privacy, national security, and the like.[20] The theorist's tendency to look at the world in such broad perspectives is antithetical to the judicial tendency to stress the special aspects of each case and area.

But even if judges have not completely accepted and applied the theories of Meiklejohn[21] and Emerson,[22] this does not mean that the efforts of these scholars have not been extraordinarily valuable—nor that they have had no discernible impact. In fact lawyers have adopted several of these approaches in appropriate cases. Judges have relied on these theorists in occasional cases[23] and, even when rejecting theoretical arguments, judges must address them and explain why they are being rejected.

Moreover, judges must decide cases within some framework. For some judges that framework is more fully developed than for others. But no judge is able to decide a case without having at least some operative framework. Although this framework reflects the judge's experiences and moral precepts, legal theory also has its impact. Although this influence may be indirect, it also may be most profound.

The basic assumption of this book, and of the contest that produced the book, is that research on First Amendment subjects should be encouraged. That assumption seems indisputable. Each of the three types of research sketched above has its place. Historical research is congenial and is likely to be incorporated into legal doctrine where relevant. Empirical research may well affect the outcome in certain types of cases and will certainly improve our understanding in others. Both historical and empirical research are likely to address relatively narrow self-contained areas and thus to be readily applicable to those areas. Theoretical scholarship, on the other hand, tends to approach problems more broadly, tends to stress generality rather than uniqueness, and, by virtue of its breadth, tends to alter the very nature of the basic questions being asked. Theoretical research may not sweep the field or control the outcomes of cases, but it is probably the most likely to have lasting impact in the literature and to shape the way future cases are analyzed.

No Foreword to this book would be complete without a statement of the enormous debt all readers owe to Charlene Brown and Bill Chamberlin. Some of their editorial work, such as the Introduction, can be spotted easily. But in fact their presence can be felt throughout the book. It might well have been easier for them to have written a book on First Amendment theory all by themselves rather than to have run a contest, arranged for several stages of judging, organized and edited the winning entries plus additional articles to achieve continuity and uniform style. This book is a tribute to them both.

Notes

1. See, e.g., Brandeis, J., concurring in Whitney v. California, 274 U.S. 357 (1927).
2. Consider, for example, the effort of Justice Stewart to develop a special approach to protection of the press, wanting to limit that protection to publishing and not extend it to gathering. Potter Stewart, "Or of the Press," *Hastings Law Journal* 26 (January 1975): 631–37. Although every other justice found First Amendment protection in a report that a judge was under investigation for misbehavior, Justice Stewart rejected such protection for a citizen who uttered those words but concurred with the judgment in the case because a newspaper had published the report. Landmark Communications, Inc. v. Virginia, 435 U.S. 829 (1978). Similarly, Justice Stewart analyzed the prison interview situation as involving a request for gathering information from government, when it might have been analyzed at least as easily as an attempt by a willing speaker and a willing gatherer to exchange information but with the impediment that the would-be speaker was in government custody. Treating this as government information fit neatly into Justice Stewart's forthcoming speech. Pell v. Procunier, 417 U.S. 817 (1974) and Saxbe v. Washington Post Co., 417 U.S. 843 (1974).
3. E.g., the action-expression distinction in Thomas I. Emerson's *The System of Freedom of Expression* (New York: Random House, Vintage Books, 1970) and the self-governance focus in Alexander Meiklejohn's *Free Speech and Its Relation to Self-Government* (New York: Harper & Brothers, 1948).
4. E.g., Margaret A. Blanchard, "Filling in the Void: Speech and Press in State Courts prior to *Gitlow*," infra, pp. 14–59 and David M. Rabban, "The First Amendment in Its Forgotten Years," *Yale Law Journal* 90 (January 1981): 514–95.
5. E.g., Nye v. United States, 313 U.S. 33 (1941). See Heydon's Case, 3 Coke's Rep. 7a, 76 Eng. Rep. 637 (1584), in which judges are told to identify "the mischief and defect for which the common law did not provide" in an effort to understand the goals of the statute that was passed to change the situation.
6. Richmond Newspapers, Inc. v. Virginia, 448 U.S. 555 (1980).
7. See Burger, C.J., concurring in First Nat'l Bank of Boston v. Bellotti, 435 U.S. 765 (1978).
8. But see the disputes about the development of freedom of expression in this country. Compare Zechariah Chafee, Jr., *Free Speech in the United States* (Cambridge, Mass.: Harvard University Press, 1941) with Leonard W. Levy, *Legacy of Suppression: Freedom of Speech and Press in Early American History* (Cambridge, Mass.: Belknap Press of Harvard University Press, 1960).
9. The Supreme Court was not impressed with the showing that entry into newspaper publishing had become much harder between the early days of this country and the mid-twentieth century, Miami Herald Publishing Co. v. Tornillo, 418 U.S. 241 (1974).
10. See, eg., Estes v. Texas, 381 U.S. 532 (1965) and Chandler v. Florida, 449 U.S. 560 (1981).
11. See, e.g., Alice M. Padawer-Singer and Allen H. Barton, "The Impact of Pretrial Publicity on Jurors' Verdicts," in *The Jury System in America: A Critical Overview*, ed. Rita James Simon (Beverly Hills, Calif.: Sage Publications, 1975), pp. 125–39 and Rita J. Simon, *The Jury: Its Role in American Society* (Lexington, Mass.: Lexington Books, D. C. Heath & Co., 1980), pp. 109–21.
12. See Warren, C. J., concurring in Estes v. Texas, 381 U.S. 532 (1965).
13. See Paris Adult Theatre I v. Slaton, 413 U.S. 49 (1973), quoting an argument by Yale Law School professor Alexander Bickel.
    On a related point, the Court has occasionally said that the reality of a situation may not be as important as its appearance. Thus, conduct intended to influence a judge may be punishable even if the judge was not influenced. "A State may protect against the possibility of a conclusion by the public . . . that the judge's action was in part a product of intimidation and did not flow only from the fair and orderly working of the judicial process." Cox v. Louisiana, 379 U.S. 559 (1965).

14. Consider the impact on *Gannett Co.* v. *DePasquale*, 443 U.S. 368 (1979), of a demonstration that the content of confessions is virtually never disclosed during suppression hearings—or that the content is never relevant in such hearings and could readily be excluded.

15. Consider the first case to impose federal limitations on state libel law, *New York Times Co.* v. *Sullivan*, 376 U.S. 254 (1964). The racial aspects of the case, the size of the award, and the flimsy defamation claim made the case a clear one for reversal. As Harvard University law professor Paul Freund put it in a speech to the Judicial Conference of the Third Circuit, "I dare say the problem before the Supreme Court was how to reverse." *Federal Rules Decisions* 42 (1966): 491. In addition, the case arose from a commercial advertisement rather than from editorial comment or a news report.

   Note also that the first *privacy* case involved false statements. Time, Inc. v. Hill, 385 U.S. 374 (1967).

   One of the few explicit comments about reluctance to draw broad lines in first cases was made by Justice Byron White, concurring in Nebraska Press Ass'n v. Stuart, 427 U.S. 539, 571 (1976): "It may be the better part of discretion, however, not to announce such a [general] rule in the first case in which the issue has been squarely presented here."

16. See Brennan, J., in Rosenbloom v. Metromedia, Inc., 403 U.S. 29 (1971) (attempting to reorganize the libel area) and in Paris Adult Theatre I v. Slaton, 413 U.S. 49 (1973) (attempting to reorganize the obscenity area).

17. See note 2 supra.

18. See Meiklejohn, *Free Speech.*

19. See John L. Hodge, "Democracy and Free Speech: A Normative Theory of Society and Government," infra, pp. 148–180.

20. But see Harry W. Stonecipher, "Safeguarding Speech and Press Guarantees: Preferred Position Postulate Reexamined," infra, pp. 89–128 and Gerald J. Baldasty and Roger A. Simpson. "The Deceptive 'Right to Know': How Pessimism Rewrote the First Amendment," infra, pp. 62–88.

21. See note 3 supra.

22. See note 3 supra.

23. See CBS, Inc. v. Democratic Nat'l Committee, 412 U.S. 94 (1973), quoting Meiklejohn approvingly.

Preface

This book is the culmination of a two-year project initiated by the Law Division of the Association for Education in Journalism (AEJ) to stimulate scholarship and interest in First Amendment theory. The project, which included a national First Amendment theory paper competition, a set of programs at the 1980 AEJ Convention held in Boston, and this book, was undertaken in cooperation with the Mass Communications Law Section of the Association of American Law Schools (AALS). The two associations are the professional organizations of journalism and law teachers in higher education.

The book brings together the winning papers from the First Amendment theory competition and a selection of complementary, significant presentations from the 1980 convention. It offers the opportunity both to recognize the scholarship and insights of the contributing authors and to challenge readers to reflect again on the meaning of freedom of speech and press.

The competition, which was held during the 1979–80 academic year, was publicized nationally and open to any interested scholar. The entries justified the sponsors' optimism that the competition would encourage significant scholarly activity. The competition, however, went beyond the sponsors' expectations by producing papers that focus on related issues from provocatively different perspectives.

The book is organized in what seemed to the editors as only one of several possible ways. Readers are encouraged to consider the contributions, both those generated by the competition and those invited for the convention, as a symposium. The pieces are particularly effective in increasing our understanding of the First Amendment because of the interaction of the ideas they present.

The authors winning recognition in the competition were:

First Prize:	Margaret A. Blanchard, School of Journalism, University of North Carolina at Chapel Hill
Second Prize:	John L. Hodge, Department of Philosophy, California State at Hayward
Third Prize:	Gerald J. Baldasty and Roger A. Simpson, School of Communications, University of Washington
Honorable Mention:	Harry W. Stonecipher, School of Journalism, Southern Illinois University at Carbondale.

The other contributions to the book come from noted media attorney Floyd Abrams, a partner in the New York law firm of Cahill Gordon &

Reindel; nationally recognized Burger Court scholar A. E. Dick Howard, White Burkett Miller Professor of Law and Public Affairs at the University of Virginia; and Douglas Watts, staff counsel of the American Newspaper Publishers Association. Abrams and Howard participated in a convention program entitled "The Burger Court and the First Amendment: Putting Ten Years into Perspective." Watts spoke on "A Major Issue of the 1980s—New Communication Tools" during a one-day symposium, "The First Amendment in the 1980s."

All contributions to the book have been revised for publication. The Baldasty/Simpson piece was rewritten and published in the *Washington Law Review* and is reprinted here without further revision.

The papers submitted in the competition were screened by Dwight L. Teeter, Jr., of the Department of Journalism at the University of Texas at Austin and by Kent R. Middleton of the School of Journalism and Mass Communication at the University of Georgia. The final selections were made by a panel of three judges: Marc A. Franklin of the Stanford University School of Law, Donald M. Gillmor of the School of Journalism and Mass Communication at the University of Minnesota, and Alfred T. Goodwin, judge for the U.S. Court of Appeals, Ninth Circuit. We are grateful not only for the time and effort these men gave to the judging process but also for their extensive comments, which were invaluable in the preparation of the manuscript for the book. The competition was administered by Jay B. Wright of the S. I. Newhouse School of Public Communications at Syracuse University. His care and attention to detail contributed greatly to the competition's success.

The editors are indebted to David M. Rice, chair of the AALS Mass Communications Law Section during 1979–80, and Michael Botein, chair of the section during 1978–79, for the support they and their organization provided for the entire First Amendment theory project. Both are members of the faculty of the New York Law School.

Those organizations which made the project possible through their grants were the Frank E. Gannett Newspaper Foundation, the *Boston Globe*, and the Philip Graham Fund. The American Newspaper Publishers Association Foundation provided supplies and organizational assistance.

The most valuable help in the book's preparation came from Jeanne M. Chamberlin, who essentially served as a third editor. She helped establish a uniform style for the diverse contributions and spent countless hours editing, typing, and proofreading. Her judgment was a crucial factor in most of the important decisions made during the editorial process. We are grateful, too, for her fine work on the index.

We also wish to express our gratitude to the staff of the Indiana University School of Law Library, particularly its director, Colleen K. Pauwels; Byron D. Cooper, associate director; Linda K. Fariss, public services librarian; and Keith A. Buckley, reference librarian. Our many questions were always cheerfully and patiently answered.

Also directly contributing to the publication were Mary Bulterman, Deborah Hirsch, Benjamin Justesen, and Carolyn Jack, master's students at the School of Journalism at the University of North Carolina in Chapel Hill. They helped with legal research, typing, and proofreading. We also want to thank Sue Jackson, a master's student at Indiana University, who helped by transcribing taped convention activities.

The editors especially appreciate the patience and guidance provided by Gordon T. R. Anderson, an executive editor at Longman Inc., who skillfully directed the publication of the book. His enthusiastic support from the time he first heard about the project was a vital element in the book's publication.

Bill F. Chamberlin
Chapel Hill, North Carolina

Charlene J. Brown
Bloomington, Indiana

About the Editors

Bill F. Chamberlin, a faculty member of the School of Journalism at the University of North Carolina, specializes in mass media law and media-government relations in both his teaching and his research.

Chamberlin has published articles about the regulation of broadcast programming by the Federal Communications Commission in the *Federal Communications Law Journal*, the *North Carolina Law Review*, and the *Journal of Broadcasting*. He also has published in *Popular Government, Journalism Quarterly*, and *Journalism History*.

Chamberlin received his doctorate in communications from the University of Washington in 1977. He received his bachelor's degree in journalism from the University of Washington and his master's degree in political science from the University of Wisconsin as a Russell Sage Social Science Writing Fellow.

Chamberlin began his teaching career at Central Washington State College in Ellensburg, Washington. At North Carolina, he is director of the honors program and coordinator of the master's program.

In 1981, Chamberlin was head of the Law Division of the Association for Education in Journalism and secretary of the Advisory Board. As associate head of the Law Division the year before, Chamberlin directed the First Amendment theory paper competition and symposium.

Chamberlin has worked for *Congressional Quarterly*, two daily newspapers, a weekly, a wire service, and two university information services. In North Carolina, he is a member of the News Media–Administration of Justice Council.

Charlene J. Brown is a member of the faculty of the School of Journalism at Indiana University, where she teaches communications law and news writing and reporting. She is a Danforth Associate and a Poynter Center Faculty Fellow. (The Poynter Center was established by Nelson Poynter, the late publisher of the *St. Petersburg Times* and *Congressional Quarterly*, for the study of American institutions.)

Her major areas of research interest are First Amendment law, media-government relations, and media performance, particularly coverage of federal regulatory agencies. She has published in *Journalism Quarterly* and in books, including *The Media and the People*, which she coauthored with Trevor R. Brown and William L. Rivers.

Brown has worked for *The Reader's Digest* and as a book editor. Her undergraduate degree from Stanford University is in political science and her master's degree, also from Stanford, is in communications–public affairs. She has taught at Stanford as a visiting faculty member.

Brown has been an active member of the Association for Education in Journalism, serving as an officer of the Law Division from 1977 to 1980 and as division head in 1979–80. She has also served on the board of the South African Institute of Race Relations.

Introduction

Charlene J. Brown and Bill F. Chamberlin

Congress shall make no law respecting an establishment of religion, or prohibiting the free exercise thereof; or abridging the freedom of speech, or of the press; or the right of the people peaceably to assemble, and to petition the government for a redress of grievances.

U.S. CONSTITUTION, AMENDMENT I (1791)

The freedom of speech and press protected in the First Amendment[1] to the U.S. Constitution has been remarkably durable through 200 years of enormous social, political, economic, and technological change, but its meaning has not been constant nor indeed ever fully agreed upon. Its durability may well have been the direct benefit of the sparse language its authors used: "Congress shall make no law...abridging the freedom of speech, or of the press...."[2] Although it can be argued that the use of the phrase *the freedom* defines freedom in the terms it was understood in America at the time the amendment was written, the men who wrote the Bill of Rights did not leave a clear account of the nature and the limits of the freedom the amendment was to protect.[3] The ambiguity of the phrasing has allowed later generations to shape its meaning to the needs and passions of their times.

For 200 years the Constitution has been the foundation of one of the world's most stable governments. That stability, however, belies the tension, turmoil, and change during those two centuries. In 1790, the country's population was almost four million.[4] Now it is more than 228 million.[5] The weak federation of thirteen states has become a strong national government involved directly in the lives of the citizens of fifty states, a national government shaping and sometimes dictating the activities of state and local governments. The vulnerable new country of the eighteenth century has become a major, although still vulnerable, world power. Large metropolitan areas dominate a nation once largely rural. Industry has replaced farming as the central preoccupation of the economy. Major corporations have replaced small businesses and family farms. A people who once relied on horses and ships to carry their messages now turn to cables and satellites.

The country has been tested by war, violence, political crime, economic disaster, racism, and its own fears, and yet its protections for freedom of speech and press have not only survived but also, in many ways, grown. That the growth has not always been steady and sure does not refute the fact that there is, in fundamental areas, more freedom for speech and press now than there was 200 years ago.[6]

In an essay in *The Federalist*, a collection of writings favoring adoption of the Constitution, Alexander Hamilton argued against a written guarantee for freedom of the press because any definition given that freedom would leave room for evasion. "Its security...," he said, "must altogether depend on public opinion, and on the general spirit of the people and of the government."[7] Our history, however, demonstrates that a written guarantee can help protect rights of expression and can educate the public to the value and nature of the freedom. The founding fathers left a legacy that must be explored and nurtured if it is to endure. No freedom can be won for all time; each generation must give it meaning. That the meaning changes with time is to be expected and should generally be appreciated.

Not every change is welcome, of course, and not every change should be accepted without reservation or resistance. Indeed, some observers in recent years have argued that the meaning of the First Amendment is not just changing but being eroded and that the changes that are being made are unpredictable and often made without reason or logic.[8] The challenge is to preserve the essence of the First Amendment while adapting its particulars to changing conditions. The problems are identifying and agreeing on what the essence is and figuring out how to protect and preserve it in an increasingly complicated world.

The pieces in this book approach the First Amendment from different perspectives and reach different and in some instances mutually exclusive conclusions. They are, nevertheless, bound together by a common concern to explore and understand the nature of and need for freedom of speech and press in a self-governing society. They challenge us to give fresh thought to old ideas and to test, if not accept, new ones. The book looks both backward to give a more complete account of our legal history and ahead to warn of the challenges to traditional First Amendment ideas being posed by the introduction of new technologies and the rearrangement of economic forces. It looks at what has been, at what some of the authors think should not have been, and at what some think ought to be. The differences in perspectives and in opinions give the reader no opportunity to be comfortable.

The Role of the States Reconsidered

While we do not know with certainty what the First Amendment meant to those who ratified it or quite why it was worded as it was, we do know that it left the states free for more than 130 years to protect and regulate speech and press according to their individual constitutions, statutes, and case law. What is generally overlooked is what the states actually contributed during that period to the concepts of freedom of speech and freedom of the press and to the legal history of the First Amendment.

The first paper in this volume, Margaret A. Blanchard's richly documented analysis of state court opinions in speech and press cases from 1787 to 1925, fills an important gap in our knowledge and gives us a fresh historical perspective on current First Amendment issues. For example, in the early nineteenth century, American political thinkers such as George Hay, Tunis Wortman, James Madison, and John Thomson constructed a new libertarian theory that came close to arguing an absolute freedom for speech and press,[9] but Blanchard's research shows us that their lead was not followed by the courts of the period. Indeed, Blanchard tells us that from the late eighteenth century to the early twentieth century state courts coupled freedom with responsibility and accepted willingly the idea that government could regulate speech and press to protect the general welfare. What is more, Blanchard tells us, when the U.S. Supreme Court decided to hold the states to a federal standard of protection for speech and press, it did not break with state law but drew heavily on the precedents state courts had generated. There was no abrupt change in direction but a continuation of an evolution already under way.

In an analysis of the Burger Court, A. E. Dick Howard makes the observation that an adequate course on press law could, with few exceptions, be taught on the basis of cases decided by the Supreme Court in the 1970s. While that is fundamentally true, many of the issues treated by the Court in the 1970s had already been addressed by the state courts in the nineteenth and early twentieth centuries: whether prior restraint, including gag orders on the press in fair trial situations, was legitimate; whether the use of the state's police power to restrict expression in the interests of national security or domestic tranquility was permissible; what distinction, if any, should be made between speech and press rights; whether the press deserved greater protection in libel law for government-related comment than for other material; whether subsequent punishment was as serious a threat to freedom of the press as prior restraint and whether civil action was as chilling as a criminal prosecution; whether journalists had the right to withhold the identity of a confidential source; whether the concept of *the press* should be expanded to cover developing technology; and so on. Even the perception of the press as immensely powerful and capable of inflicting as much harm as government itself was expressed by Americans in the nineteenth and early twentieth centuries.

The Twentieth-Century Search for the Meaning of Freedom of the Press

Throughout its history the First Amendment has been valued for its contribution to self-government. However, that value does not define the precise nature of the freedom or identify clearly who is to enjoy the right of free speech and press. Does the individual have an unconditional right to speak? Does the listener have a right to hear? Does the public have a right to know? What moral or legal responsibilities do the media have to inform the public? What role should the government play if the media fail the citizens or citizens fail their society by not seeking out the information they need to govern intelligently? Is the best test of truth "the power of the thought to get itself accepted in the competition of the market"?[10] What role should the government play if the economics of the marketplace put the individual who wishes to speak to fellow citizens and the individual who wishes to learn from them at the mercy of those with money?

Gerald Baldasty and Roger Simpson, in their critique of the right-to-know concept, argue that the First Amendment was meant to protect the right to speak. They warn that the emergence of the concern to protect the listener, the consumer, and the public's right to know is not only *not* serving the interests of a self-governing society but is also undermining the traditional rights of speakers, which do serve those interests. Tracing the origins of the right-to-know concept to ideas advanced in the years after World War II and to the government's experience with the regulation of broadcasting, Baldasty and Simpson argue that the Supreme Court's use in libel law of the *actual malice* rule,[11] which they see as a direct consequence of that concern, defines public speech too narrowly and lays bare the media's editorial processes to the scrutiny of government. They argue that in broadcast regulation the shift of First Amendment rights from the broadcaster to the listener has *deprived* the citizen of differing points of view. They argue that the extension of First Amendment rights to commercial speech, on the theory that the public has a right to know, threatens to weaken First Amendment protection for political speech. In addition, they argue, in cases treating the news-gathering function of the media, the right to know has not supported the right of the press to gather information but has strengthened the right of government to decide for itself what it shall reveal.

Baldasty and Simpson's arguments are based on a faith that the needs of citizens in a self-governing society will be better served by a freedom that protects speakers than by a system that *commands* the press to serve consumers responsibly and invites government to supervise or to participate directly in the marketplace of ideas. They see the right-to-know concept as a consequence of an erosion of faith in the citizen's ability to sort truth from falsehood, of a lack of confidence that the citizen will seek out the information necessary for intelligent decision making, and of a lack of confidence in the functioning of the marketplace itself.

Like Baldasty and Simpson, Harry W. Stonecipher is concerned to protect First Amendment freedoms so as to encourage and enhance free public discussion of governmental affairs. In his article on the preferred position doctrine, he expresses the concern of many contemporary journalists that the Burger Court's reliance on a balancing of interests approach is allowing justices' individual prejudices, as well as sound principles, to influence decisions and is seriously eroding First Amendment freedoms.

Unlike Baldasty and Simpson, who deplore the use of the actual malice rule, Stonecipher sees it as an expression of a preference for First Amendment freedoms that should be safeguarded. He shares their concerns but argues the overall effect of the constitutional libel privilege has been to give extra protection to political expression. He urges continued use of the *New York Times* malice rule to protect "uninhibited, robust, and wide-open" debate about matters of general and public concern[12] against defamation actions.

Recognizing that an absolutist approach to the First Amendment is unlikely to persuade either the members of the Supreme Court or the American public, Stonecipher seeks to encourage the use of an approach that will reaffirm the preference for freedom of speech and press that he finds in American political and legal history. He identifies three more essential safeguards in addition to the actual malice rule. The Court has used all four at one time or another. Stonecipher urges continued treatment of prior restraint as presumptively invalid with a heavy burden of proof placed on those seeking to overcome that presumption. He urges using the clear and present danger test, with the authority to determine whether the danger is present reserved for the courts and not for the legislatures. Finally he urges the maintenance of higher standards of procedural due process when First Amendment interests are at stake.

Stonecipher sees the preferred position postulate not only as an essential legal safeguard but also as a clear statement of faith in the democratic process. He warns, however, that whether or not the courts and the public grant such special protection will depend on whether those who seek to exercise those freedoms do so responsibly. He sees particularly the need for the media to commit themselves to maintaining a healthy and free marketplace of ideas.

The Burger Court

Despite the ambiguity of the First Amendment itself, there is a long-standing principle that the boundaries legislatures and courts set for freedom of speech and press must be clearly drawn because uncertainty chills the exercise of that freedom and encourages self-censorship.[13] As a practical matter, what the First Amendment means is what the Supreme Court says it means. Thus, it is imperative that the Court state its position clearly and adhere to that position with sufficient consistency that individuals and institutions can have a fair chance of predicting the legal consequences of their decisions and actions. The unpredictable outcome may be preferable to a certain loss, but in the long run both are destructive of freedom.

A. E. Dick Howard and Floyd Abrams look specifically at the performance of the Burger Court. Although a substantial foundation had already been laid by both state courts and the U.S. Supreme Court, many of the most important cases involving the press have been decided since 1969, when Warren E. Burger became chief justice.[14] Howard provides a discussion of the Court's treatment of constitutional law as a framework for Abrams's analysis of the treatment of press issues.

Howard describes the Burger Court's performance as episodic, almost random, and its treatment of many constitutional issues unpredicted and unpredictable. He notes the fluid voting pattern, the absence of cohesive voting blocs, and the lengthy, opaque, fractured opinions. He attributes the trouble the Court appears to be having with some issues to its realization that the questions are not as readily answered, the problems not as easily solved as the Warren Court[15] seemed to suggest. The Burger Court does not seem sure of its answers, and, Howard warns, no one can be sure of what the Court will say—indeed, what it has said—or what its view of the world is.

Certainly, the Burger Court has had difficulty in producing solid majorities[16] and clearly stated, carefully reasoned majority opinions[17] in First Amendment cases. Diversity is a valued First Amendment goal, but it is an unsettling characteristic to find in Supreme Court decision making.

While Howard finds the Burger Court unpredictable on constitutional issues, Abrams does see a pattern in the Court's treatment of press cases, which, in his view, justifies the concern the press has voiced about the Court. Abrams focuses on the common understanding that the Court's impact on the law is as much a consequence of its choice of cases to hear as of its decisions in those cases. While Howard finds the Court willing to take the cases as they come, Abrams finds the Court selecting press cases in ways that violate the tradition of the Court's own procedures and harm First Amendment freedoms. He offers evidence of the Court's insensitivity to First Amendment issues and describes a pattern in which the Court takes—even reaches—for cases the press has won in lower courts but refuses to consider cases the press has lost.

However, what is perhaps most striking in the Abrams piece—in no small part because it comes from such a prominent media attorney—is that he paints the brightest picture in the book of the current status of press freedom. "The American press," he writes, "has never been more free, never been more uninhibited, and—most important—never been better protected by law."[18] He concludes, however, that while that state of affairs is in part because of the Burger Court, it is also in part in spite of that Court.

The First Amendment in the 1980s

Howard describes the Burger Court's performance as episodic. John L. Hodge argues that we cannot expect clarity, consistency, or intellectual order in First Amendment law until the Court embraces [19] a carefully reasoned, clearly articulated theory of free speech. Hodge begins the task of building such a theory.

Hodge starts by constructing a normative theory of government that places the right of free speech in a prominent role. Drawing on the traditions and aspirations of the United States, Hodge identifies democracy as the primary goal and defines it as a system of government in which "the powers of government legitimately exist . . . only insofar as the citizens under that government delegate those powers to it, and . . . only when the powers of delegation are equally distributed among the citizens."[20] All rights flow directly from those two principles of delegation and equality. Not surprisingly, in Hodge's theory voting rights are basic to the functioning of his democracy principle, and government has the affirmative duty to remove all obstacles to the exercise of those rights. The right of free speech is also basic to his theory, and that right imposes on government a similar obligation to remove all obstacles to its exercise.

Unlike Baldasty and Simpson, who expect democracy to benefit if the right to speak is protected, Hodge argues the right of *voters* must be served if democracy is to function and that involves a recognition of the right of listeners as well as speakers. If the right to delegate power is to remain equally distributed among citizens, all must have access to the range of available information regarding ballot issues and government must work to ensure that access is real. Denying voters the right to information, in Hodge's view, denies their basic right to an equal voice in government.

Hodge does not share the fear and distrust of government that has fueled First Amendment thinking for so long. He defines government as the servant of the people, capable of exercising only those powers given it. In his system the majority cannot use the government to deprive others of their basic rights because the power of government may not be used to deny the principle of equal distribution of those rights. Also, the majority cannot use nongovernmental means to abridge those basic rights because government has an affirmative obligation to guarantee them.

Hodge acknowledges that he is describing what ought to be rather than what is, but he argues that his theory does not reach beyond what is possible. He also argues that traditional First Amendment theory is based on something that does not exist—a free marketplace of ideas—and ignores the reality of the threat private forces pose to freedom.

Both Hodge and Douglas R. Watts deal with what Thomas I. Emerson has called "the shift from the liberal laissez-faire to the mass technological society."[21] The premises and approaches of Hodge and Watts, however, are fundamentally different. Hodge dismisses the laissez faire marketplace of ideas concept as a dated, faulty analogy that serves only to shield from view the harm worked by unrestrained private forces. He seeks to construct a theory of government and free speech that takes account of the reality of the present communications system. Watts, by contrast, sees the preservation of the free marketplace as an important and still-valid First Amendment goal. Watts describes the emerging communications technologies and focuses on the First Amendment issues they raise. He argues that with the new technologies there is the potential to establish a truly open marketplace with greater opportunities for individuals both to send and to receive information than have ever existed before. For example, a viewdata system using the telephone network already in place can, he writes, give any individual, at relatively little cost, the opportunity to communicate with a mass audience. The economic, technological, and governmental barriers to entry into the older technologies of print and broadcasting do not need to restrict access to the new. With cable television, satellites, videotex, the reallocation of the broadcasting spectrum, and other changes, the limits on diversity are no longer imposed by technology and need not be imposed by economics or government. We may, he suggests, soon be limited only by our ability and willingness to make use of what is offered.

Watts identifies four categories of First Amendment issues likely to be raised by the new communications technologies: who shall own and control the new communications systems, who shall have access to them, what regulation of content will be needed or permitted, and how shall individuals' interest in the privacy of their use of the new systems be protected.

One of the factors in the evolution of First Amendment law and theory has been that different generations have asked different questions about freedom. The general issues Watts identifies are not new, but many of the specific questions are. Watts suggests that a significant First Amendment question for the 1980s is who owns the vertical blanking interval of an over-the-air television signal delivered by a cable television system. An explanation of why the question is significant depends on the detail Watts provides in his article, but it is worth pointing out the obvious here: the founding fathers did not give us the answer to that question. We are on our own to struggle to understand not only how the new technologies work but also what the consequences are of the decisions we and our government make now. One conclusion to be drawn from the Watts article is that current government regulation and Court doctrine do not begin to come to grips with the First Amendment issues created by the emerging technologies.

Values, Concepts, Precepts, and Distinctions

Vincent Blasi, a professor of law at the University of Michigan, speculated in a recent speech on the vitality and future of "values, concepts, precepts, and distinctions"[22] used in First Amendment theories over the years. His speculation was provocative, but in some respects the process was even more compelling than the predictions themselves. Anyone who cares about the First Amendment should force himself or herself to reexamine from time to time the watchwords on which we rely and which float so easily through our discussions.

Several values have been called fundamental to the First Amendment. Thomas I. Emerson, who is often quoted on this point, lists the values of self-fulfillment, self-government, attainment of truth, and the achievement of a balance in society between stability and change.[23] Blasi talked in his speech of the possibilities of the value of diversity, not because it leads to truth or stability, but because it enriches life, because it gives "a richer sense of possibilities."[24] Blasi has also written at length about the checking value, the use of freedom of speech and press to check the tyranny of government.[25] Are these the quintessential values that must be preserved even as society changes? Is one more important than others? How do we choose among them when they conflict?

Among the concepts on which Blasi speculated was the right to know, and it figures prominently in this book as well. The concept has a wide appeal; thus we need to explore whether it serves us well. Does the public have a right to know everything about government—even what the press chooses, at its discretion, not to report? What does the public have a right to know—and what not? Is there a line that can be drawn between the two clearly and consistently? The rhetorical imperative when transformed into practical terms demands an object—the right to know *what*—because clearly the public should not have a right to know everything.[26] When the rhetoric becomes a legal right or a moral right, against whom is it lodged? The government? The press?

Another concept that has come into question is the free marketplace of ideas. Is the marketplace an appropriate metaphor for the process by which we exchange and evaluate ideas? *Is* the best test of truth its ability to get itself accepted in the marketplace? Is that not a test that defines truth in terms of popularity, that, in effect, defines whatever is accepted in the marketplace as truth? Can we trust the marketplace to function as long as the hand of government is restrained?

A long-standing precept in First Amendment law is that the regulation of speech must never turn on its content.[27] Yet, the Supreme Court has long held that some categories of speech are so lacking in social utility that they deserve no First Amendment protection.[28] Hodge points out that the precept is not only not rigorously adhered to by the Court, it is not even consistently stated by it.

What of the precept that "under the First Amendment there is no such thing as a false idea"?[29] Obscenity is a category of speech that lacks social utility and is therefore excluded from the protection of the First Amendment,[30] yet Nazi doctrine is, it seems, as protected as the pledge of allegiance.[31] Is that a sign of the strength or the weakness of our thinking on the First Amendment?

Will we hold on to the distinction between print and broadcasting now made by the Court[32] if the bases for the distinction—the scarcity of the broadcast spectrum and the differences in the nature and functions of the media—do not hold?

What will come of the debate over whether the press clause represents a distinct and larger protection for the institutional press than the speech clause gives to individual citizens?[33] Blanchard reports that state courts in the nineteenth and early twentieth centuries enlarged freedom for the press—but never beyond that for the individual—as society's demands on and expectations of it grew. Does the pattern continue today? Is contemporary society well served by limiting the rights of the press to those that can be given to individuals as well—regardless of how our expectations of and demands on the press might change? Does the modern citizen's need to know about people and things beyond his or her reach justify special protection for the press as the representative of the citizen?[34] Does the public appreciate that its rights are at stake even as the focus of litigation has shifted from the concern for individual rights of expression to a preoccupation with the rights of the institutional press?

There are other important questions but none more fundamental than those that illuminate the role of government in the system of freedom. Blasi has suggested that the distinction between negative freedom and positive freedom—between the First Amendment as a restraint on government as opposed to the First Amendment as a command to government to enhance the communication process—is likely to survive and that the courts will continue to prefer the former and resist the latter.[35] He sees this as likely in part because of the difficulty of defining, limiting, and agreeing on the specific, affirmative actions we might have government take. Do we have greater faith in the consequences of unregulated private interest or of government-imposed public interest? Certainly, many citizens seem to be trying in other areas to disengage government from their lives. However, the public may well look to government for protection against the abuses of the media if the public has no sense of a community of interests with the media.

Asking questions, of course, is only the beginning of inquiry. Intelligent decisions cannot be made about traditional concerns or approaching problems without a conception of what principles are fundamental and a vision of a theoretical framework for freedom. Some choices have to be made, some answers given. The authors in this book seek not only to critique ideas they think have not worked or are not working but also to give us sounder information—both about our past and about our future—on which to build theory, to take at least the first steps toward building sound theories, and to encourage the reader to take the process still further.

Notes

1. The term *First Amendment* is used throughout the Introduction as a convenient shorthand for its speech and press clauses.
2. U.S., Constitution, Amend. 1.

3. See Margaret A. Blanchard, "Filling in the Void: Speech and Press in State Courts prior to *Gitlow*," infra, pp. 17–18 and esp. p. 45 n. 14 for a discussion of the period.
4. U.S., Department of Commerce, Bureau of the Census, *Historical Statistics of the United States Colonial Times to 1970* (Washington, D.C.: Government Printing Office, 1975), p. 8.
5. U.S., Department of Commerce, Bureau of the Census, *Estimates of the Population of the United States to February 1, 1981*, Current Population Reports Series P-25, no. 898, p. 2.
6. For example, the newly ratified First Amendment to the U.S. Constitution did not prevent the passage by Congress of the Sedition Act of 1798, which made certain criticisms of government criminal offenses. U.S., *Statutes at Large*, 1:596. The U.S. Supreme Court has since said "that prosecutions for libel on government have [no] . . . place in the American system of jurisprudence," New York Times Co. v. Sullivan, 376 U.S. 254, 291 (1964), quoting City of Chicago v. Tribune Co., 307 Ill. 595, 601, 139 N.E. 86, 88 (1923), and has said that although the Sedition Act was never tested in the Court, history has found it invalid, New York Times Co. v. Sullivan, 376 U.S. at 276. The Court has also said public officials, public figures, and even private persons seeking punitive damages must, when bringing libel actions, prove by clear and convincing evidence that the defendant acted with knowledge of falsity or reckless disregard for the truth. Gertz v. Robert Welch, Inc., 418 U.S. 323 (1974).

   As a more general example, the phrasing of the First Amendment explicitly prohibits the *Congress* of the United States from *making any law* abridging the freedom of speech or of the press. The Supreme Court, however, has interpreted the First Amendment prohibition as applying to any activity of any branch of government abridging speech and press freedom, Watkins v. U.S., 354 U.S. 178, 188 (1957), and has held that the protections of the First Amendment are incorporated in the due process clause of the Fourteenth Amendment and are thus applicable against state as well as federal government, Near v. Minnesota ex rel. Olson, 283 U.S. 697, 707 (1931).
7. Alexander Hamilton, John Jay, and James Madison, *The Federalist*, ed. Paul L. Ford (New York: Henry Holt and Co., 1898), pp. 574–75.
8. See, e.g., A. E. Dick Howard, "A Framework," infra, pp. 131–36; Floyd Abrams, "An Analysis," infra, pp. 139–42; and John L. Hodge, "Democracy and Free Speech: A Normative Theory of Society and Government," infra, pp. 161–71.
9. Leonard W. Levy, ed., *Freedom of the Press from Zenger to Jefferson* (Indianapolis: Bobbs-Merrill Co., 1966), pp. lxx–lxxix.
10. Abrams v. United States, 250 U.S. 616, 630 (1919) (Holmes, J., dissenting).
11. The *actual malice* rule requires that the plaintiff prove the defamatory statement was made "with knowledge that it was false or with reckless disregard of whether it was false or not." New York Times Co. v. Sullivan, 376 U.S. at 280.
12. Ibid. at 270. Justice William J. Brennan, Jr., in his opinion for the Court, noted "a profound national commitment to the principle that debate on public issues should be uninhibited, robust, and wide-open, and that it may well include vehement, caustic, and sometimes unpleasantly sharp attacks on government and public officials." Ibid.
13. See, e.g., Nebraska Press Ass'n v. Stuart, 427 U.S. 539, 568 (1976); Hynes v. Mayor of Oradell, 425 U.S. 610, 620 (1976); Baggett v. Bullitt, 377 U.S. 360, 372 (1964); Smith v. California, 361 U.S. 147, 151 (1959); Winters v. New York, 333 U.S. 507, 509–10, 517, 518 (1948); Herndon v. Lowry, 301 U.S. 242, 259 (1937); Near v. Minnesota ex rel. Olson, 283 U.S. at 712–13.
14. See, e.g., CBS, Inc. v. FCC, 101 S.Ct. 2813 (1981); Chandler v. Florida, 101 S.Ct. 802 (1981); Richmond Newspapers, Inc. v. Virginia, 448 U.S. 555 (1980); Gannett Co. v. DePasquale, 443 U.S. 368 (1979); Herbert v. Lando, 441 U.S. 153 (1979); Wolston v. Reader's Digest Ass'n, 443 U.S. 157 (1979); FCC v. Pacifica Foundation, 438 U.S. 726 (1978); Houchins v. KQED, Inc., 438 U.S. 1 (1978); Zurcher v. Stanford Daily, 436 U.S. 547 (1978); Landmark Communications, Inc. v. Virginia, 435 U.S. 887 (1978); Zacchini v. Scripps-Howard Broadcasting Co., 433 U.S. 562 (1977); Nebraska Press Ass'n v. Stuart, 427 U.S. 539 (1976); Time, Inc. v. Firestone, 424 U.S. 448 (1976); Cox Broadcasting Corp. v. Cohn, 420 U.S. 469 (1975); Gertz v. Robert Welch, Inc., 418 U.S. 323 (1974); Miami Herald Publishing Co. v. Tornillo, 418 U.S. 241 (1974); CBS, Inc. v. Democratic Nat'l Comm., 412 U.S. 94 (1973); Branzburg v. Hayes, 408 U.S. 665 (1972); New York Times Co. v. United States, 403 U.S. 713 (1971); Rosenbloom v. Metromedia, Inc., 403 U.S. 29 (1971).

15. Earl Warren served as chief justice of the U.S. Supreme Court from 1953 to 1969.
16. See, e.g., Richmond Newspapers, Inc. v. Virginia, 448 U.S. 555 (1980); Gannett Co. v. DePasquale, 443 U.S. 368 (1979); Houchins v. KQED, Inc., 438 U.S. 1 (1978); Young v. American Mini Theatres, Inc., 427 U.S. 50 (1976); CBS, Inc. v. Democratic Nat'l Comm., 412 U.S. 94 (1973); Branzburg v. Hayes, 408 U.S. 665 (1972); New York Times Co. v. United States, 403 U.S. 713 (1971) (This may not be a strong example because the case was handed down just six days after it was taken to the Court, but evident in the six separate opinions from the six justices in the majority are significant differences on fundamental issues, differences that more time probably would not have erased.); Rosenbloom v. Metromedia, Inc., 403 U.S. 29 (1971). In his analysis of the Burger Court's treatment of freedom of expression cases, Archibald Cox also remarks on the fragmentation of the Court. "Foreword: Freedom of Expression in the Burger Court," *Harvard Law Review* 94 (November 1980): 72.
17. See, e.g., Snepp v. United States, 444 U.S. 507 (1978); Time, Inc. v. Firestone, 424 U.S. 448 (1978); Miami Herald Publishing Co. v. Tornillo, 418 U.S. 241 (1974).
18. Abrams, "An Analysis," infra, p. 143.
19. Hodge does not charge the Court with the responsibility for *creating* the theory but looks to scholars to do so. Indeed, the Court as an institution seems ill suited to such a task.
    Henry M. Hart, Jr., said of the Court in a 1959 *Harvard Law Review* article that has since been much discussed:

    > The Court is predestined in the long run not only by the thrilling tradition of Anglo-American law but also by the hard facts of its position in the structure of American institutions to be a voice of reason, charged with the creative function of discerning afresh and of articulating and developing impersonal and durable principles of constitutional law and impersonal and durable principles for the interpretation of statutes and the resolution of difficult issues of decisional law.

    "Foreword: The Time Chart of the Justices," *Harvard Law Review* 73 (November 1959): 99.
    Even Hart, however, found the Court of his day unable to measure up to his model. He saw its work load as a major obstacle to the thoughtful, time-consuming deliberation the law and the country deserved. (By his calculation, the nine justices had dealt with an average of 1,540 cases a year in the mid-1950s. Ibid., p. 86. In the 1979 term the same number of justices disposed of 3,812 cases. "The Supreme Court, 1979 Term," *Harvard Law Review* 94 [November 1980]: 292.)
    There are many factors which work against the "maturing of collective thought" (Hart, "Time Chart of the Justices," p. 100) and the Court's functioning as the source of a theoretical framework or soundly reasoned, durable principles of constitutional law: the pressures of the volume, variety, and complexity of cases the Court confronts; the confines of precedent and procedure; the differences in the abilities and perspectives of justices; the nature of the deliberative process which requires a consensus among at least five justices for the Court to speak as an institution; the shifting alliances brought about in part by changes in the personnel of the Court; the deference shown other branches of government; the Constitutional requirement that the Court focus on *cases* and *controversies*; the erratic order in which cases appear before the court; and so on.
20. Hodge, "Democracy and Free Speech," infra, p. 154.
21. Thomas I. Emerson, *The System of Freedom of Expression* (New York: Random House, Vintage Books, 1970), p. 728.
22. "First Amendment Theory in the 1980s," speech delivered at the annual meeting of the Association for Education in Journalism, Boston, Mass., August 10, 1980.
23. Emerson, *Freedom of Expression*, pp. 6–9.
24. Blasi, "First Amendment Theory in the 1980s."
25. Vincent Blasi, "The Checking Value in First Amendment Theory," *American Bar Foundation Research Journal* 1977 (Summer 1977): 521–649.
26. There are few who would not concede *something* ought to be withheld—perhaps a private citizen's income tax returns, academic grades, medical files, or the identity of a reporter's confidential source.
27. See, e.g., Hudgens v. NLRB, 424 U.S. 507, 520 (1976); Erznoznik v. Jacksonville, 422 U.S. 205, 207 (1975); Police Dep't of Chicago v. Mosley, 408 U.S. 92, 95–96 (1972); Niemotko v. Maryland, 340 U.S. 268, 272 (1951). But see, e.g., FCC v. Pacifica Founda-

tion, 438 U.S. at 744–48 (Stevens, J., with two justices concurring); Young v. American Mini Theatres, Inc., 427 U.S. at 63–71 (Stevens, J., with three justices concurring).

28. See, e.g., Central Hudson Gas & Electric Corp., v. Public Service Comm'n of New York, 447 U.S. 557, 563–64, 566 (1980); Gertz v. Robert Welch, Inc., 418 U.S. at 340; Miller v. California, 413 U.S. 15, 20–21 (1973); Chaplinsky v. New Hampshire, 315 U.S. 568, 571–72 (1942).

29. Gertz v. Robert Welch, Inc., 418 U.S. at 339.

30. E.g., Miller v. California, 413 U.S. at 20–21.

31. See, e.g., Police Dep't of Chicago v. Mosley, 408 U.S. at 95; Terminiello v. Chicago, 337 U.S. 1, 4 (1949); Collin v. Smith, 447 F.Supp. 676, 686–87 (N.D. Ill. 1978), affm'd 578 F.2d 1197 (7th Cir. 1978), cert. denied 439 U.S. 916 (1978).

32. See, e.g., CBS, Inc. v. FCC, 101 S.Ct. 2813 (1981); FCC v. Pacifica Foundation, 438 U.S. 726 (1978); CBS, Inc. v. Democratic Nat'l Comm., 412 U.S. 94 (1973); Red Lion Broadcasting Co. v. FCC, 395 U.S. 367 (1969).

33. For discussion of the issue, see, e.g., First Nat'l Bank of Boston v. Bellotti, 435 U.S. 765, 797–802 (1978) (Burger, C. J., concurring); Potter Stewart, "Or of the Press," *Hastings Law Journal* 26 (January 1975): 631–37; Margaret A. Blanchard, "The Institutional Press and the First Amendment Privileges," in *Supreme Court Review 1978*, ed. Philip B. Kurland and Gerhard Casper (Chicago: University of Chicago Press, 1978), pp. 225–96; David Lange, "The Speech and Press Clauses," *U.C.L.A. Law Review* 23 (October 1975): 77–119; Melville B. Nimmer, "Introduction—Is Freedom of the Press a Redundancy: What Does It Add to Freedom of Speech?" *Hastings Law Journal* 26 (January 1975): 639–58; and William W. Van Alstyne, "The Hazards to the Press of Claiming a 'Preferred Position,'" *Hastings Law Journal* 28 (January 1977): 761–70.

34. In a concurring opinion in *Houchins* v. *KQED*, Justice Stewart accepted the principle that the press was not entitled to greater access to jail facilities than other members of the public in the sense that it had no right to see areas from which the public was excluded. He argued, however, that because the press served as the representative of the public, it should have been given more flexible and frequent access than the general public and should have been permitted to use its cameras and recording equipment. 438 U.S. at 16–19.

35. Blasi, "First Amendment Theory in the 1980s."

PART I

The Role of the States Reconsidered

CHAPTER 1

Filling in the Void: Speech and Press in State Courts prior to *Gitlow*

Margaret A. Blanchard*

Students of journalism history may trace the development of that field on the North American continent fairly easily. The antecedents of the profession that exists today are clearly visible in the writings of numerous scholars; the path it took from past to present is fairly clear; the trends in its development are easy to find. The same may be said of the development of American constitutional history. Its roots can be found in the colonies, and its evolution is clearly outlined in the revolutionary period, the constitutional era, and the years when the three branches of government began giving meaning to the U.S. Constitution. What is not so easy to trace, however, is the development of the constitutional history of journalism—the evolution of efforts to give meaning to the phrase *freedom of the press*.

Most journalism historians, as well as most legal historians, believe that there was no activity of any consequence on speech and press issues in all of American history prior to the early twentieth century—except, of course, the trial of John Peter Zenger, the ratification of the First Amendment, and the experiment with the Alien and Sedition Acts of 1798. Most scholars who take this view toward the development of free speech and free press values in American society are looking at the problem from a purely legal perspective.

---

*Margaret Ann Blanchard, a faculty member at the School of Journalism at the University of North Carolina since 1974, has concentrated her research in the study of the legal history of the First Amendment and press freedom and responsibility. Her article, "The Institutional Press and Its First Amendment Privileges," was a comprehensive examination of the Supreme Court's relative treatment of the terms *free speech* and *free press*. The article was published in the *Supreme Court Review* in 1978. She has also published articles in *Journalism Quarterly*, *Journalism History*, and *Journalism Monographs*.

Blanchard's doctoral dissertation, completed in 1981, focuses on the interpretation of the First Amendment by news professionals from 1946 to 1952. Her Ph.D. program at the University of North Carolina at Chapel Hill focused on American constitutional history. She received her bachelor's and master's degrees from the College of Journalism and Communications at the University of Florida at Gainesville.

Blanchard worked as a reporter for the *Palm Beach Post-Times* and then as a reporter and a women's editor for the *Miami Herald*. She began teaching journalism at East Carolina University in Greenville, North Carolina. Her specialties are the history of the First Amendment, communications history, communications law, news editing, and feature writing. She has been active in many professional journalism organizations, including the Society of Professional Journalists, Sigma Delta Chi and Women in Communications, Inc.

Blanchard expresses appreciation to Dr. John Semonche, professor of history at the University of North Carolina, for his advice and encouragement in the research and writing of this article.

Some scholars recognize that issues such as abolitionism, censorship during the Civil War, and the persecution of the radical labor movement in the late nineteenth and early twentieth centuries had a significant impact on the social and political content of speech and press.[1] While acknowledging this, however, both historians and legal scholars seem equally sure that a constitutional meaning of freedom of speech and freedom of the press did not exist during these years. After all, the U.S. Supreme Court, the ultimate arbiter of constitutional meaning, did not find the values of speech and press within its purview until the early twentieth century. Then, confronted with cases arising from the Sedition Act of 1918 during World War I, the justices were forced, beginning with *Schenck* v. *United States*,[2] to give an interpretation of freedom of speech. Even then, the justices did not believe that they had an unrestricted mandate to give meaning to freedom of speech and of the press in the United States. The Court's early encounters with these freedoms originated only when federal law was challenged as potentially infringing upon First Amendment freedoms. It was not until 1925 when, with what was almost an offhanded comment in *Gitlow* v. *New York*,[3] the justices launched themselves into extending their interpretations of the contents of First Amendment freedoms to the state level; and it was not until 1931, with *Near* v. *Minnesota*,[4] that the Court began using this new authority with any degree of vigor.

If traditional interpretations are correct, legal thinking about speech and press issues stopped after the Alien and Sedition Acts. This would mean that the Supreme Court faced a significant problem because its decisions in this area of the law were written on a blank slate. There would be—according to this view—no precedents to draw upon, no legal treatises to read for guidance, no signposts as to what kind of cases the justices might expect to encounter in this new area of litigation.

This traditional notion is supported by legal researchers of the caliber of Yale law professor Thomas I. Emerson, who wrote, "The basic theory underlying the legal framework [of free speech and press] has remained substantially unchanged since its development in the seventeenth and eighteenth centuries."[5] To bolster his statement that nothing of importance happened during those years, Emerson said that the legal system in the nineteenth century had a "relatively narrow" view of "protecting freedom of expression," adding: "The main business of the courts was with property relations.... Freedom of expression was more the by-product of the economic and political system than the result of deliberate articulation and enforcement of legal doctrine by the courts."[6] From Emerson's vantage point, the notion that freedom of speech and of the press was held in a state of suspended animation for over 100 years seems entirely valid.

Harvard law professor Zechariah Chafee, Jr., emerges with a similar belief in a great void in this area of legal thought. He first, however, tantalizes his readers by suggesting that the scholar, in searching for the meaning of freedom of speech and of the press, should look at those guarantees as they appear in both the U.S. Constitution *and* individual state constitutions.[7] Yet, Chafee quickly makes it clear that he is willing to do no more than take note of the state constitutional guarantees and that he will do that only for historical grounding. Additional research in this direction, he claims, is fruitless, for

> There were practically no satisfactory judicial discussions before 1917 about the
> meaning of the free speech clauses. The pre-war courts in construing such clauses
> did little more than place obvious cases on this side or that side of the line....
> when we asked where the line actually ran and how they knew on which side of it
> a given utterance belonged, we found little answer in their opinions.[8]

Why, Chafee seems to be asking, would anyone want to try to find a historical basis for the development of free speech and free press in the American
legal system? Such a basis did not exist and a search for it would be a waste
of time, he said, as he put forth his belief in the great void between the
period of constitution making and the period of Supreme Court interpretation of free speech values.

The question, then, is: Are Emerson and Chafee and others who follow
this line of thinking correct? One chorus of no votes would come, most likely,
from the justices of the U.S. Supreme Court who wrote those early twentieth-
century decisions in speech and press cases. As it will be demonstrated, the
Court found ample precedent from state courts throughout the nineteenth
and early twentieth centuries to cite in its later interpretations of the speech
and press clauses. If this is the case, the next question becomes: Why has the
development at the state court level of a rationale for dealing with speech and
press cases been denigrated or ignored? One reason comes from the focus of
scholars on the national level in general and on the Supreme Court in particular as the only places where valid constitutional interpretations can be
made. This ignores the federal nature of the union and the fact that it has
only been with the onset of the twentieth century and with the growing complexity of society that attention has been focused on the national level of government as the only level which matters. A second possible reason is that a
study of activities relating to speech and press issues during the nineteenth
and early twentieth centuries means an immersion into a morass of state
court decisions which are unwieldy and have the potential of being unprofitable.

Because the development of speech and press values on the state level
during the nineteenth and early twentieth centuries has been ignored, the student
of these constitutional guarantees has been robbed of a vital link in the evolution of these privileges. In order to understand the foundation upon which
the U.S. Supreme Court built its First Amendment interpretations beginning
in 1919, a look at what the founding fathers said about freedom of speech
and of the press at the time of the ratification of the Bill of Rights is not
enough. The system of values that gave meaning to these freedoms developed
almost daily throughout the nineteenth and early twentieth centuries in city
and town and state. The Supreme Court drew from these ongoing interactions when it began hearing claims involving speech and press issues. In fact,
a look at state court and Supreme Court decisions in these areas shows several common denominators: the discovery and use of a common heritage from
English history upon which to base these freedoms, the establishment first of
the parameters of these freedoms for the individual and then the extension of
these freedoms to the press, the conscious decision to make these rights bend
to the needs of the public welfare, and the requirement that those—both individuals and press—seeking to exercise these freedoms do so responsibly.*

---

* See the appendix for an annotated list of the state court cases used by Margaret Blanchard in the preparation of this chapter. —Ed.

Only when the artificial void that has plagued this specialized area of history is filled and only when the contributions of state court jurists over the nineteenth and early twentieth centuries are acknowledged will the full richness of the American heritage of freedom of speech and of the press be understood. Only then will an accurate evaluation of the evolution of First Amendment guarantees and the place accorded them in American society be possible.

The Beginning: Concern for a Free and Responsible Press

Any discussion of the way in which freedom of speech and of the press developed within the individual states of the union must begin, strangely enough, on the national level. It was the Continental Congress that issued the first official document making reference to the position in which Americans placed freedom of speech and freedom of the press, the Address to the Inhabitants of Quebec, in 1774.[9] It was an order from the Continental Congress in 1776 that told the colonies to become states and, as part of that process, to draft constitutions. Residents of those new states included bills of rights in their new constitutions, and most of the bills of rights contained specific guarantees of freedom of speech and of the press, in addition to other civil liberties, for residents of those states. It was the new federal constitution and the process of its ratification in 1787 and 1788 that stirred residents of various states to think about the lack of protection for individual liberties in that document, to talk and to write about the importance of such guarantees, and to demand the addition of a bill of rights as a condition for ratification.[10]

With James Madison's efforts to advance the Bill of Rights through the new federal congress, we find even more signs that both the states and the federal government were involved in the protection of these rights. Madison proposed at least two separate amendments to the U.S. Constitution concerning freedom of speech and freedom of the press. The first would have guaranteed that "the people shall not be deprived or abridged of their right to speak, to write, or to publish their sentiments; and the freedom of the press, as one of the great bulwarks of liberty, shall be inviolable."[11] In his second proposal, Madison showed some concern over the possibility that state action could possibly impinge upon these freedoms, when he suggested that the Constitution be amended to include: "No State shall violate the equal rights of conscience, or the freedom of the press, or the trial by jury in criminal cases."[12] There is no indication of why Madison tried to include a prohibition on state action as part of his proposals to safeguard civil liberties. The Bill of Rights, as it emerged from the Senate and as it was presented to the states for ratification, carried only the injuction that "Congress shall make no law ... abridging the freedom of speech, or of the press...."[13]

Gone were Madison's comments about the press being one of the bulwarks of liberty and about the need to protect the press from state action. The omission of the latter provision was understandable. Congress was in the midst of creating a strong federal government, an action which many Americans, so recently freed from the central government of Great Britain, mistrusted. Every effort was made to keep the new government from seeming to invade the rights of the states. Consequently, the idea that the Constitution would require the states to behave in a certain way on speech and press matters ran contrary to prevailing political wisdom. Because there are no records of the debate on the Bill of Rights in the Senate and only very sketchy records of the debate in the House, there is no way to prove these suppositions.[14] It is likely, however, that members of Congress actually felt that speech and press were within those things left to state protection and regulation.[15] In any event, both the protection of the freedom of speech and of the press and its regulation were left to the individual states.

The free press and free speech provisions found in the new state constitutions varied. The constitution of Georgia, in its 1789 form, resembled the Madison proposal which would have combined freedom of the press and protection of trial by jury when it said, "Freedom of the press and trial by jury shall remain inviolate."[16] The North Carolina constitution of 1776 offered language similar to that which appeared in Madison's second proposed amendment related to freedom of the press: "The freedom of the press is one of the great bulwarks of liberty, and therefore ought never to be restrained."[17] The Virginia constitution of 1776, in addition to finding freedom of the press a bulwark of liberty, added that such freedom "can never be restrained but by despotic governments."[18] The Pennsylvania constitution of 1790 provided an indication of the way in which states would eventually combine the guarantee of freedom of the press with its responsible exercise when it said, "The free communication of thoughts and opinions is one of the invaluable rights of man; and every citizen may freely speak, write, and print on any subject, being responsible for the abuse of that liberty."[19] The relationship between such freedom and its responsible use was also stated in the constitution of Delaware, adopted in 1792: "The press shall be free to every citizen who undertakes to examine the official conduct of men acting in a public capacity; and any citizen may print on any subject, being responsible for the abuse of that liberty."[20]

In all, nine of the original thirteen states had constitutions that included free speech and/or free press provisions in place prior to or coincidental with the ratification of the Bill of Rights to the U.S. Constitution.[21] Of these early provisions, only two forecast the emphasis of the future—that the freedoms be exercised responsibly.[22] By the 1840s, each of the original thirteen states had constitutional provisions pledging free speech and/or free press. By that time, the most prevalent approach was a variation of the New York guarantee: "Every citizen may freely speak, write, and publish his sentiments on all subjects, being responsible for the abuse of that right; and no law shall be passed to restrain or abridge the liberty of speech, or of the press."[23] These constitutional protections offered to speech and press showed not only that the states perceived the need for explicit guarantees for freedom of speech and press in their fundamental laws, but that many also perceived these freedoms had to be limited by requiring the responsible exercise of the rights promised.

The move of the original thirteen states toward linking freedom of the press with its responsible exercise was adopted in other parts of the country. This type of provision appeared regularly in the constitutions ratified by the members of the Confederacy as a condition for readmission to the Union during Reconstruction.[24] The requirement that freedom of speech and freedom of the press be exercised responsibly also appeared in the vast majority of constitutions ratified as new states from the West were added to the Union.[25]

The movement toward this freedom-and-responsibility standard cannot be termed accidental. The same language appeared in far too many state constitutions to be happenstance. The state court rulings upholding this standard from the earliest years of the Republic up through the 1920s support the contention that the inclusion of these constitutional provisions was the result of purposeful action, not of indiscriminate copying.

So vital did this linkage of freedom and responsibility seem that state court judges often felt constrained to explain how responsibility was implicit in the state constitutional provisions of freedom of speech and press—even if it was not explicitly mentioned in the document. The first Pennsylvania constitution, for example, a liberal document drafted in 1776, contained only the broad statement, "That the people have a right to freedom of speech, and of writing, and publishing their sentiments; therefore the freedom of the press ought not to be restrained."[26] In explaining this in 1788, a Pennsylvania jurist said the constitutional guarantee of freedom of the press "is amply secured by permitting every man to publish his opinion." But, "the peace and dignity of society" required, he said, an inquiry into the "motives of such publications... to distinguish between those which are meant for use and reformation, and with an eye solely to the public good, and those which are intended merely to delude and defame." He said that when a judicial inquiry found the publications belonged in the latter category, a judge was allowed to impose punishment because it was "impossible that any good government should afford protection and immunity" to such affronts to society.[27] Interestingly enough, when the conservative faction regained control of the Pennsylvania political structure, a new constitution was drafted. This document, mentioned above, was ratified in 1790 and put some of the concerns of the Pennsylvania judge into fundamental law by holding that citizens may freely express themselves as long as they were responsible for "abuse of that liberty."[28]

It seemed to be widely accepted that a freedom of the press which placed the press "wholly beyond the reach of the law" would be, as James Kent of the New York state supreme court put it in 1804, "the source of every evil." Kent, who would later write a leading treatise on the development of American constitutional law, used the 1804 opinion as a vehicle for tracing the constitutional history of the young American nation. He found nothing in his survey to indicate that the press could not be regulated to make it compatible "with the existence and good order of civil society."[29]

These two early cases found state court judges writing their decisions in the speech and press areas without much formal written guidance in the way of precedents, treatises, or laws. Apparently, the decisions were based only on what the judges intuitively believed was the place freedom of speech and freedom of the press held in society. In the Pennsylvania court decision mentioned above, for instance, there was no guidance from the 1776 state constitution. That document had imposed no standard of responsibility upon the person who exercised freedom of the press. As this case was being heard, the ninth state was ratifying the new national constitution. Even if that document had been in effect, however, it would have offered no guidance on press-related issues because it as yet contained no bill of rights. Thus, the Pennsylvania court was creating the first of many precedents that would govern speech and press cases for decades as it deliberated on just what freedom of the press entailed. Significantly, the court was not the only participant in the suit breaking new ground. The defendant, publisher of a newspaper which carried anonymous stories about the character of the master of a girls' school in Philadelphia, claimed that the law of libel was incompatible with liberty and freedom of communication in a free country, thus offering a novel interpretation of the type of society the new constitution was designed to create. The Pennsylvania court ignored this ingenious and forward-looking argument as it ruled that abuse of the privilege of a free press was punishable.

The New York court also was drawn into a situation requiring path breaking when it found itself in the middle of a political fray. Its 1804 case dealt with a libel of then-President Jefferson by a defendant who was represented by Alexander Hamilton. James Kent, the man whose written opinion would have a great impact on libel law in New York and elsewhere during this formative period in American jurisprudence, was philosophically in favor of holding the press responsible for any abuses that might stem from its free exercise. He was swayed, however, by arguments presented by Hamilton that urged the court to widen the area of permissible comment about public officials and other matters. The court was evenly split and upheld the lower decision in favor of Jefferson and against Hamilton's client. Kent's written opinion, however, became "the foundation on which the state's law of freedom of the press was subsequently built."[30] Kent's words also established the foundation upon which other state courts would base many of their decisions. "Liberty of the press," he wrote, "consists of the right to publish, with impunity, truth, with good motives, and for justifiable ends, whether it respects government, magistracy, or individuals."[31]

The vociferous party press, active during the early 1800s, inspired the latter case, but the decision endured much longer than this violent form of journalism. In fact, these two cases from Pennsylvania and New York became keys to the rapidly developing freedom-and-responsibility standard. So engrained did that standard become that, fifty years later, an Arkansas court could remark that "the distinction between the constitutional freedom, and licentious abuse of the press, is now . . . well understood in this country."[32]

Thus, state courts in the early years of the Republic were trying to provide a meaning and substance for freedom of speech and of the press that would stand the test of time. The judges involved in these early cases used the only resource available to them: history. Consequently, state courts carefully sought out historical landmarks in the development of freedom of speech and of the press. In incorporating this material into decisions, the courts usually began with the introduction of the printing press to Great Britain, moved through the addition of the First Amendment to the U.S. Constitution, and on into the individual state's own constitutional experience. The progression was the same from place to place and from time to time.[33]

"The struggle for freedom of speech has marched hand in hand in the advance of civilization," one Illinois judge wrote. "History teaches that human liberty cannot be secured unless there is freedom to express grievances. As civilization advanced and as the means for expressing grievances multiplied, the struggle between the people and their despotic rulers became more bitter."[34]

Such a struggle resulted in the licensing and prosecution of editors, according to a New York judge. When refusing a request for an injunction to stop publication of a libel in 1839, he detailed how the "star chamber in England once exercised the power of cutting off the ears, branding the foreheads, and slitting the noses of the libellers of important personages." The star chamber court was abolished, said the judge, "and I believe no judge or chancellor from that time to the present has attempted to follow that precedent."[35]

Efforts to invoke English precedents to curtail free expression in America were uniformly rejected by state courts. A California judge in 1893 commented that he was "aware of the fact that there are English precedents for holding that the courts possess and exercise the power to prohibit in all cases the publication of their proceedings." But, he asserted, there was "no decision in this country upholding the right of a court to make such a prohibition, except where the publication tended to interfere with the proceedings before the court."[36] A Washington state court agreed in 1898 that "the arbitrary rule existing in England before the American revolution was thus abrogated in this country."[37]

The guarantee of speech and press had a direct relationship to freedom from government oppression in the eyes of these judges. As a Montana court said in 1891, "It was not ordinary talk and publication, which was to be disenthralled from censorship, suppression, and punishment" but "a species of talk and publication which had been found distasteful to governmental powers and agencies."[38] A New Jersey court, in an opinion written in 1919, looked at 1787, the year in which American political leaders joined together to supplant the Articles of Confederation with the Constitution, and determined, "The men who framed our present national government . . . necessarily opposed and condemned, and in no uncertain terms, the then existing government of the confederation." Quieting their speech "would have been monstrous then as now."[39]

Attempts by the British to control freedom of expression in the colonies were well understood by the constitution makers of early America and by the judges who interpreted those constitutions in later years. As one Nebraska court said in 1916, "The evils calling for a different attitude toward printing were fresh in the public mind when the first American Constitutions were framed."[40] The court added that the importance of the press "in the evolution of just and efficient government" was well understood when Nebraska and other states included provisions dealing with freedom of the press in their fundamental laws.[41]

Through such historical excursions, judges showed their grasp of the background of the free speech and press guarantees. With this perspective, they not only developed a series of guidelines for dealing with free speech and free press claims, but they also developed an understanding that the ultimate meaning of freedom of speech and press was an evolutionary one, with the process still under way. As one Kansas judge, writing in 1908, put it:

> The constitutional guaranty clearly means that the press shall be free from previous government license, and the decisions are quite uniform, but not unanimous, that it shall be free from court censorship through injunctions against publication. Early writers on constitutional law and early cases say that it means no more, but later commentators and later decisions maintain that it does mean more.[42]

The reader of this decision could infer that the opinion writer knew the positions of other courts in other states on free speech and press matters and that he was cognizant of the views of legal commentators in the field as well. This opinion, taken with others, shows that judges in various states quoted extensively from the same materials and cited similar authorities.[43] The common bond between state courts, established through a similar view of the American heritage of freedom of speech and of the press, continued to grow through the use of such common authorities. Repeated references to them also kept the judges aware of the current status of American thinking on speech and press topics.

Despite this growth of an obviously American rationale in speech and press cases, twentieth-century American writers in the field often seem more inclined to credit English jurist William Blackstone as having an influence on the development of American thought in this area than they are to acknowledge the impact of American writings.[44] Although Blackstone's contributions in the area of prior restraint[45] are important, the writers of opinions in state courts on speech and press issues seem far more influenced by the views of a trio of American legal scholars—James Kent, Joseph Story, and Thomas M. Cooley—than by Blackstone. From these three men came the basic principles which the state courts either supported or rebutted in speech and press decisions.

In the section of Kent's legal treatise, *Commentaries on American Law*, that dealt with speech and press issues, Kent discussed actions for slander and libel. The importance of these actions, he explained, was obvious because "the preservation of every person's good name from the vile arts of detraction" was included in the "laws of the ancients, no less than those of modern nations."[46] With this importance acknowledged, Kent was quick to admonish his readers:

> But though the law be solicitious to protect every man in his fair fame and character, it is equally careful that the liberty of speech, and of the press, should be duly preserved. The liberal communication of sentiment, and entire freedom of discussion, in respect to the character and conduct of public men, and of candidates for public favor, is deemed essential to the judicious exercise of the right of suffrage, and of that control over their rulers, which resides in the free people of these United States. It has, accordingly, become a constitutional principle in this country, that "every citizen may freely speak, write, and publish his sentiments, on all subjects, being responsible for the abuse of that right, and that no law can rightfully be passed to restrain or abridge the freedom of speech, or of the press."[47]

This summarized the position afforded speech and press in the states during the first quarter of the nineteenth century. Protection of character was balanced against freedom of speech and press, creating a careful freedom-and-responsibility equilibrium that tipped slightly toward freedom when comments about the government and those who ran it were at issue. Kent, however, in summarizing various court actions on the subject, noted that control of "the malicious abuse or licentiousness of the press . . . is the most effectual way to preserve its freedom in the genuine sense of the constitutional declarations on the subject."[48] A conservative on speech and press freedoms by twentieth-century standards, Kent, writing in 1818, said he believed that the nation was too concerned with maintaining and promoting freedom of discussion and not concerned enough with protecting individual character from the abuse of that freedom.[49]

Sharing Kent's belief in the need for limits to free speech and press was U.S. Supreme Court Justice Joseph Story, whose writings on the U.S. Constitution were liberally cited in state court rulings. Referring to the First Amendment, Story wrote, "That this amendment was intended to secure to every citizen an absolute right to speak, or write, or print, whatever he might please, without any responsibility, public or private therefor, is a supposition too wild to be indulged by any rational man."[50] The amendment, he concluded, "imports no more than that every man shall have a right to speak, write, and print his opinion upon any subject whatsoever, without any prior restraint, so always, that he does not injure any other person[,] ... disturb the public peace, or attempt to subvert the government."[51] Story maintained that this doctrine, derived from state libel law, saved the privilege of freedom of the press from becoming a scourge on society.

Justice Story found most of his materials for his discussion of freedom of speech and press at the state level, both in case law and in constitutional provisions. As he examined this fund of information, Justice Story, a moderate Republican appointee to the High Bench, asked whether "liberty of the press is so much more valuable than all other rights in society, that the public safety ... [or] the existence of government itself, is to yield to it?"[52] He answered his own question in the negative, believing that to give free rein to the press would be the height of irresponsibility and a sure sign that the government was about to fall.[53]

The commentaries of Chancellor Kent and Justice Story reflected, in part, the tempestuous political environment of the late eighteenth and early nineteenth centuries.[54] Party factionalism was great, finding expression not only in the partisan journals of the day but also in the courts, where the Federalists and the Republicans were battling for control of the judiciary.[55] The extent to which these political controversies affected these writings on freedom of speech and of the press is not known. Regardless of any political influences, however, the commentaries produced by Kent and Story, because of the stature of the authors, immediately influenced American legal thought. Both men had a significant effect on the development of thinking about speech and press in this country.

The freedom-and-responsibility standard was also accepted by the third of the leading writers in the field, Thomas M. Cooley, although he did not display the fear of the press evident in the writings of Kent and of Story. Cooley, a one-time professor of law and American history at the University of Michigan, sat on the Michigan state supreme court and wrote his commentaries on constitutional and other legal issues in the latter third of the nineteenth century. His work recognized that the First Amendment was not the sole resource for protection of freedom of speech and press. The states, he said, put provisions "of similar import" to the First Amendment in their constitutions "with a jealous care of what is almost universally regarded a sacred right, essential to the existence and perpetuity of free government."[56] The purpose of these provisions, he said,

> has evidently been to protect parties in the free publication of matters of public concern, to secure their right to a free discussion of public events and public mea-

sures, and to enable every citizen at any time to bring the government and any person in authority to the bar of public opinion by any just criticism upon their conduct in the exercise of the authority which the people have conferred upon them.[57]

The liberty of speech and press, then, implied to Cooley "a right to freely utter and publish whatever the citizen may please." Within this freedom, he said, the citizen was "protected against any responsibility for so doing, except so far as such publications, from their blasphemy, obscenity, or scandalous character, may be a public offence, or as by their falsehood and malice they may injuriously affect the standing, reputation, or pecuniary interests of the individuals."[58]

From his vantage point in the 1870s and 1880s, Cooley saw the newspaper in a perspective not available to Kent or to Story. Newspapers had brought news of the Civil War to readers, and many organs of the press had served the public's interest in a time of great political corruption. The press had moved with society—industrializing and urbanizing—and had reported these changes to the American people. Therefore, Cooley decided that "among the inventions of modern times, by which the world has been powerfully influenced, and from which civilization has received a new and wonderful impulse, must be classed the newspaper."[59] He believed, however, that the newspaper's relationship with society was not yet firmly established. Society levied such demands on a publisher, until, in order to succeed, he must "daily spread before his readers a complete summary of the events transpiring in the world, public or private, . . . and he who does not comply with this demand must give way to him who will." Also, perhaps because of a willingness to accede to society's demands, "the publisher of the daily paper occupies to-day the position in the courts that the village gossip and retailer of scandal occupied two hundred years ago, with no more privilege and no more protection."[60]

Cooley showed considerable insight by including these factors in the consideration of free speech and free press matters. Among the legal commentators on the subject, he was the leading and, perhaps, at the time, the only advocate of putting the public's expectations of the press into the freedom-and-responsibility equation. He wrote:

> The public demand[s] and expect[s] accounts of every important meeting, of every important trial, and of all events which have a bearing upon trade and business, or upon political affairs. It is impossible that these shall be given in all cases without matters being mentioned derogatory to individuals; . . . it might be worthy of inquiry whether some line of distinction could not be drawn which would protect the publisher when giving in good faith such items of news as would be proper, if true, to spread before the public, and which he gives in the regular course of his employment, in pursuance of a public demand, and without any negligence, as they come to him from the usual and legitimate sources, which he has reason to rely upon; at the same time leaving him liable when he makes his columns the vehicle of private gossip, detraction, and malice.[61]

Cooley's writings show a shift in the views of legal commentators concerning the role of the press in society. Much of the earlier legal writing on the topic had focused on the licentiousness of the press, as had many of the early court decisions, which were products, no doubt, of the times. From the middle of the nineteenth century onward, however, as the court cases show, there seemed to be a greater realization that a significant question in such litigation was whether the role society had awarded the press carried any special safeguards along with it. Some state courts faced that question and decided it in the affirmative, some faced it and decided it negatively, and some state courts ignored it altogether. The process of reasoning, however, was fairly uniform, regardless of the decision. As court cases and treatises became more plentiful, state court decisions relied upon American precedent and scholarship in the area of speech and press cases.

Promoting the General Welfare

By 1925 state court opinions had established a series of basic propositions regarding the speech and press guarantees that were generally followed in decision making. The key to these propositions was that freedom and responsibility had to be coupled in the exercise of these rights. Almost of equal importance was the idea that courts should look at how the contested exercise of these rights would affect the general welfare. Although the courts differed on just what constituted the general welfare, broad outlines of permitted activities were discernible from state to state. Also apparent was that courts would allow the regulation, under the state's police power, of speech and press perceived as detrimental to the general welfare.[62]

Exploration of the meaning of free speech–free press clauses in state constitutions continued to play an important role in this decision making. Courts found that the meaning of such provisions was "much misunderstood,"[63] particularly if a litigant tried to use those rights to repulse a libel action. The guarantee, according to the state courts, had a simple meaning. As a Pennsylvania tribunal explained in 1805, "Publish as you please in the first instance without control; but you are answerable both to the community and the individual, if you proceed to unwarrantable lengths."[64] Added a Michigan court in 1868, the "law favors the freedom of the press, so long as it does not interfere with private reputation or other rights entitled to protection."[65]

Although measures of the general welfare were central in determining free speech–free press issues, the courts came close to outlawing all attempts to impose prior restraint.[66] Such decisions were also often based on the public welfare, at least insofar as the public needed access to information from differing points of view.

Freedom from prior restraint of expression was seen by most courts as fundamental to free speech and free press guarantees, but sustaining this protection did not always please state court judges. Indicative of this unhappiness was the repeated suggestion to individuals that postpublication punishment was a viable alternative to prior restraint under state constitutions. Typical of such decisions was one by a Texas court in 1909 which said that the state constitution and "the jurisprudence of the United States" prohibited the issuance of an injunction to "restrain the publication of a libel." The only "remedy for the abuse of this right conferred by the Constitution...[is] an action at law for damages or a criminal proceeding by indictment or information."[67]

When it came to prior restraints imposed by a governmental body on the dissemination of information, however, the state courts generally had little patience. The courts, apparently, were fearful of the effect such power placed in the hands of government would have on the availability of information in the society. If such prior restraints were allowed to stand, said one New York court in 1918, "our greatest newspapers and other organs of information and discussion would be at the mercy of little groups of local officials here and there, and would be permitted to reach the people or not, according as such groups approved or disapproved the particular news of such publications."[68]

Even so, the protection afforded the right to speak or print was quite relative during the nineteenth and early twentieth centuries. This was especially true when the attempted prior restraint involved state or municipal efforts to restrict the spreading of ideas advocating a violent change in government. Self-preservation of government ranked high on the list of priorities for state courts, and jurists had no difficulty writing decisions which curtailed advocacy of change. They generally held that the constitutional privilege could not be interpreted to protect so blatant an abuse. Such decisions, however, had to be carefully explained.

Often the courts took a carrot-and-stick approach in writing these decisions. Judges said, on the one hand, how important freedom of expression was to the maintenance of a democratic way of life. On the other hand, the courts issued the very explicit warning that freedom of expression most certainly did not include the right to express the opinion that the existing government needed to be overthrown.

"Every intelligent person recognizes that one of the greatest rights secured to the citizens of this country is that of free and fearless discussion of public questions including even the merits and shortcomings of our government," a New York jurist explained in 1922, adding that "it would be intolerable to think that any attempt could be successfully made to impair such right." On the other hand, the judge said, any person who advocates the destruction of government "by means which are abhorrent to the entire spirit of our institutions" may be silenced by the legislature. Legislatures acting under these circumstances, the opinion continued, cannot be accused of infringing an individual's freedom of speech.[69] A California judge writing in 1921 had taken the same approach: "The right of free speech was guaranteed to prevent legislation which would by censorship, injunction, or other method prevent the free publication by any citizen of anything that he deemed it was necessary to say or publish.... [but] the right of free speech does not include the right to advocate the destruction or overthrow of government or the criminal destruction of property."[70]

The New York state constitution, according to a 1902 state court opinion, placed "no restraint upon the power of the legislature to punish the publication of matter which is injurious to society.... It does not deprive the state of the primary right of self-preservation."[71] Seeking to buttress the decision still further, the opinion continued, "All courts and commentators contrast the liberty of the press with its licentiousness, and condemn as not sanctioned by the constitution of any state, appeals designed to destroy the reputation of the citizen, the peace of society, or the existence of the government."[72] Yet another state, Iowa, acknowledged in 1920 that although the state constitution did protect freedom of speech and press, the constitutional proviso included the notion that the person exercising freedom of expression bore the responsibility for its abuse: "The constitutional guaranty itself qualifies the immunity, by a plain indication that, while the right is given, the abuse of that right is not to be tolerated. The framers of our Constitution were laboring for the good of the commonwealth. They did not intend to protect what might destroy the state."[73]

Occasionally, state courts would find that the person charged with advocating the overthrow of the existing government was, for some reason, not guilty of the offense.[74] In most cases, however, courts joined with citizens bent upon the suppression of dissent. Convictions involving trade unionists,[75] Socialists,[76] anarchists,[77] Communists,[78] antiwar activists,[79] and aliens expressing disapproval of the government[80] were upheld, most of them routinely. In many cases, the courts did not deal with free speech or free press claims, for the general welfare obviously dictated that the guilty verdict be upheld.[81]

Although the state courts alluded to the possible role of freedom of speech and of the press in these cases, most of the decisions were not based on these grounds. The state courts had not yet begun to face the speech and press challenge as the sole basis for argument and decision making in such instances. The state's police power or ability to regulate certain activities in the interest of the citizen's health, safety, and moral well-being formed the core of decision making in advocacy cases. The state's police power was also the basis for the regulation of obscenity and motion pictures.[82] Where counsel was ingenious enough to develop arguments on speech and press grounds, the state courts turned a deaf ear, just as the same jurists had ignored similar claims in advocacy cases. Decisions in cases involving the regulation of obscenity and motion pictures were made, almost uniformly, on the basis of the state's need to protect the public from contamination by these two sources of corruption. The modern observer might not be able to see the regulation of obscenity and the regulation of motion pictures as having much common ground, but to the state courts around the turn of the century, obscenity and motion pictures were seen as almost identical evils. Both obscenity[83] and motion pictures were discussed in terms of indecency. The courts found that the state's police power was sufficient to suppress obscene or indecent materials and to allow the licensing of motion pictures prior to showing.

Opinions rendered in cases involving indecent materials may have included a brief acknowledgment of the existence of a free speech claim if one was offered, but the decisions quickly moved beyond that point. A Connecticut court, writing in a 1900 case involving a man charged with selling a newspaper dominated by crime news, said, "Immunity [through freedom of speech] in the mischievous use is as inconsistent with civil liberty as prohibition of the harmless use."[84] The court reasoned that "the liberty protected is not the right to perpetuate acts of licentiousness, or any act inconsistent with the peace or safety of the State."[85] Among the things that could be punished without violating constitutional guarantees were libel and obscenity, said a Missouri court in an 1896 opinion. The judge added that a particular statute was valid even though it was designed to "suppress a class of so-called newspapers which are mainly filled with obscene matter and salacious scandals thoroughly calculated to exercise a most corrupting and depraving influence not only upon the youth of the commonwealth but upon adults, save those of firm and stable minds."[86] Legislation to "prevent the publication and sale of newspapers especially devoted to the publication of scandals and accounts of lecherous and immoral conduct"[87] presented no problems, explained the Kansas bench in 1895, because "the legislature has power to suppress this class of publications, without in any manner violating the constitutional liberties of the press."[88]

Court opinions in cases involving motion picture regulation were based on the same feelings of protectiveness toward society that lay behind the obscenity decisions. An Illinois court opinion written in 1909 said, "The audiences [of motion pictures] include those classes whose age, education and situation in life specially entitle them to protection against the evil influence of obscene and immoral representations." The court added, "The welfare of society demands that every effort of municipal authorities to afford such protection shall be sustained, unless it is clear that some constitutional right is interfered with."[89]

Although the state courts based their decisions on the police power, many of the challenges to governmental actions were brought on the ground of infringement of the freedom to conduct a business.[90] The constitutional basis for the complaint was the protection of property. In one case, however, a free speech–free press claim was made by a manufacturer of motion picture newsreels who wanted his productions placed in the same legal category as newspapers. A New York court, writing in 1922, decided against such a classification because "the motion picture attracts the attention so lacking with books, or even newspapers, particularly so far as children and the illiterate are concerned."[91] Clearly show business, said the court, was different from the newspaper business because "those who engage in the show business are none too likely to confine their productions to the things which are just, pure, and of good report; but, in order to continue to attract patrons, many would cast discretion and self-control to the winds, without restraint, social or moral."[92] Because of such a possibility, the courts of the nation approved the exercise of a state's police power with regard to motion pictures.

The willingness of courts to sanction the use of the state's police power to protect the general welfare was just as apparent in cases dealing with the more unorthodox methods of spreading information such as unauthorized parades in the public streets, picketing by labor unions, speaking in public parks on unpopular subjects, or distributing circulars. In general, the state courts found that public property was designed for the use of the entire public and not for the use of disgruntled minorities seeking to upset the peace of mind and the ease of transit of majorities.

A standard response to contentions that free speech was abridged by the requirement that permits be obtained for the use of public streets was provided by a New York court in 1921: "The ordinance merely concerns the use of public streets and is not directed against or concerned with free speech generally. The people have many constitutional rights, the exercise of which on the public streets may be prohibited."[93] A New Jersey court, writing in 1922, elaborated on this point: "The constitutional guaranty of liberty of speech no more authorizes a citizen to appropriate to his own use the public property of a community for the purpose of exercising that guaranty than it permits him to occupy *in invitum* [without invitation] the private property of a fellow citizen for the same purpose."[94] To the person claiming access to the streets, a Pennsylvania court responded in 1920 that such a person "would hardly admit that others would have the right so to do in his house, without his consent; and doubtless would concede the same to all other citizens."[95] There was a growing concern in some courts, however, that access to the streets depended on the social acceptability of the ideas promoted. Even though this realization was developing, state courts in the early twentieth century usually approved the exercise of municipal discretion in granting permits.[96]

Attempts by labor unions to show their displeasure with certain businesses by picketing were usually classified as another of those socially unacceptable messages that the state could curtail. Very few of the cases involving picketing were argued on the basis of infringement upon a person's right to speak or publish. When this argument was presented, the courts attempted to deal with it, although the decisions often permitted the restraining of union activity. An Idaho court, writing in 1922, exemplified the tone for decision making in this area when it said, "We do not think the right of free speech guaranteed by sec. 9, art. 1, of our constitution, is directly involved. We are concerned only with the abuse of the freedom of speech."[97] In 1924, an Indiana court agreed that the rights of free speech, assembly, and the use of the public streets "are all subject to such reasonable regulations as the governing body of the government may make for the general good, and, as we deem the ordinance in question to be reasonable and one within the power of the council to adopt, it does not infringe upon any of the constitutional rights of appellants."[98] The curtailment of picketing, said a Texas tribunal in 1921, did not destroy the right of free speech as contended by a labor union. Such a regulation merely assumed "you must respect the rights of others, which are as sacred as yours, and which must be protected."[99]

The free speech contentions of unions often were looked upon as spurious. When a 1920 Missouri majority opinion did not deal with the free speech issue when enjoining picketing, a concurrence stressed that such a claim was "a 'straw man' erected by astute counsel for defendants, with the view that this court would spend its force knocking it down, to the exclusion of the real issue"[100] which, in this instance, was considered to be a conspiracy to destroy property rights. In dissent, another justice found such attitudes about freedom of speech disturbing: "If the court can, under our Bill of Rights, close the mouth of the individual by injunction, it can, as well, lay its restraining hand upon the newspaper."[101] Few state court justices, however, had such a sensitive perception of the interrelated nature of speech activities during the nineteenth and early twentieth centuries, or at least such views were not apparent when such emotional issues as picketing were before the courts.

The distribution of circulars also held a very precarious place in the hierarchy of free speech values, and municipal regulation of such distribution was generally permitted. Here too, though, state court judges were beginning to find some protection. When the distribution was allowed, the court justified it by finding that the material involved was socially acceptable. A New

York court recognized this in 1920 when it allowed the National Association for the Advancement of Colored People to invoke the state constitutional protections of speech and press for its distribution of circulars against a motion picture favorable to the Ku Klux Klan. Said the court, "It would be a dangerous and un-American thing to sustain an interpretation of a city ordinance which would prohibit the free distribution by a body of citizens of a pamphlet setting forth their views against what they believe to be a movement subversive to their rights as citizens." The court here found that the ordinance against distribution of such material was designed to "prevent the littering of streets with commercial advertising, such as a merchant or shopkeeper might send forth for the purpose of aiding the sale of purchaseable commodities."[102] The NAACP literature was not in that category and hence could be distributed.

The balance that the New York court tried to find between the rights of speech and press and the general welfare was one long sought by state courts across the nation. The balance was a delicate one, and although it tipped from time to time in the direction of speech and press rights, more often it preferred the general welfare.

Equating the Press and the Public

The general welfare often clashed violently with freedom of speech and of the press when state courts considered libel cases, one of the areas most obviously connected with these freedoms during the nineteenth and early twentieth centuries. Although most of the court rulings on libel dealt with what behavior could be termed libelous[103] or whether the truth could be introduced as evidence,[104] there were other cases that evoked great soul-searching on the parts of the judges. These cases forced the state courts to deal directly with the role of the press in society and with how much latitude the press should be given to meet society's needs and expectations as opposed to how much protection should be given to an individual reputation.

If there was any consensus on this role for the press, it was that the rights of the press were an extension of the individual's right to free speech. As one Michigan court explained in 1889, "The liberty of the press . . . is only a more extensive and improved use of the liberty of speech which prevailed before printing became general; . . . the law recognizes no distinction in principle between a publication by the proprietor of a newspaper and a publication by any other person."[105] State constitutions, with their tendency to protect the citizen's right to "freely speak, write, and publish his sentiments on all subjects,"[106] almost necessitated this interpretation, and the state courts were very willing to provide it. Courts also found it important to stress, as did Kentucky's in 1889, that by the constitutional guarantee of "the 'freedom of the press,' it was simply intended to secure to the conductors of the press the same rights and immunities that are enjoyed by the public at large."[107] If the ordinary citizen had the "right and duty," as one Virginia court put it in 1912, "to criticise public officers and candidates for public office" with "no liability unless express malice be shown," then it followed that "the press enjoys no special privilege or immunity, but stands in all respects, before the law, upon the same footing as the great body of citizens."[108] A Maryland court, writing in 1882, said: "No one denies the right of the defendants [a newspaper] to discuss and criticise boldly and fearlessly the official conduct of the plaintiff [a state senator]. It is a right which, in *every* free country[,] belongs to the citizen."[109]

The reason for this right of both public and press to comment was equally clear to all state courts: full discussion of matters of public concern was essential to the governing process.[110] Such comments, explained an 1882 Maryland decision, afford "some protection at least against official abuse and corruption."[111] The citizen, said a Kentucky court a few years later, "has the right to criticise the acts of government, provided it is with the good motive of correcting what he believes to be existing evils or defects and of bringing about a more efficient or honest administration of government."[112] An eighteenth-century Pennsylvania opinion said the state constitutional provisions "give to every citizen a right of investigating the conduct of those who are intrusted with the public business."[113]

Should such comments by either an individual or the press transgress the boundaries of what the courts conceived as appropriate, there was recourse to the damages of a libel suit. Explained a Louisiana court in 1873:

> Public journalists, like everybody else, are held to an observance of the proprieties of social life. While the utmost latitude is accorded to them in the discussion of all subjects, and they may freely comment upon the acts and conduct of men as individuals, to say nothing of the wide expanse of authority to speak faithfully and boldly in the interests of the people regarding public measures and questions of all kinds that concern the community at large, still there is a limit beyond which this freedom becomes license. It is upon the confines of these that responsibility begins.[114]

Another court, this time in West Virginia, expressed the fear in 1878 that the "terms 'freedom of the press' and 'liberty of the press' have misled some to suppose, that the proprietors of a newspaper had the right to publish that with impunity, for the publication of which others would have been held responsible."[115]

Several problems existed when it came to applying libel rules to newspapers. One difficulty came when the courts tried to balance their beliefs in freedom of the press with their beliefs that reputation was something that should be protected. In Pennsylvania, an 1878 court decision found the judges granting that "the liberty of the press should at all times be justly guarded and protected; but so should the reputation of an individual against calumny," adding, "the right of each is too valuable to be encroached on by the other."[116] Consequently, said the court, the state constitutional protection of the right to freely speak, write, and print had to be balanced against a section in the state's declaration of rights guaranteeing property and reputation. "A good reputation," said the Pennsylvania court, "is too valuable to admit of its being falsely assailed without the law giving some redress to the person injured. The general liberty of the press must be construed in subordination to the right of any person calumniated thereby, to hold it responsible for an abuse of that liberty."[117] An Ohio court, writing in 1860, however, said it could not understand what all the confusion was about in this area of litigation. After all, it said, "the liberty of the press, properly understood, is not . . . inconsistent with the protection due to private character."[118]

Another problem facing courts in newspaper libel cases concerned the increasing importance of the newspaper in society. State judiciaries, although repeatedly stressing that newspaper rights were equivalent to individual rights in their decisions, could not avoid a growing awareness that newspapers were far more powerful than individuals. "The press is the most important single psychological influence in our civilization and determines, at least in part, the conscious thinking and will and conduct of a great multitude of people,"[119] said an Illinois court in 1920. A Michigan court, writing in 1868, said that because the newspaper was "one of the necessities of civilization, the conditions under which it is required to be conducted should not be unreasonable or vexatious." But that same court also said that "since an injurious statement inserted in a popular journal does more harm to the person slandered than can possibly be wrought by any other species of publicity, the care required of such journals must be such as to reduce the risk of having such libels creep into their columns."[120] This greater harm from newspapers was created by "the greater extent of circulation [which] makes . . . libels more damaging, and imposes special duties as to care to prevent the risk of such mischief, proportioned to the peril,"[121] said another Michigan court a decade later. If this greater level of care was not evident, the state courts upheld decisions for the victims of libelous publications.

The courts found it difficult to establish one rule for all libel offenses. If the freedoms of speech and press were designed to help the public keep a check on government, then it seemed the courts had to allow a greater range of permissible comment on government-related issues. State courts, however, found that the idea of a two-tier standard, with one tier for government-related comment and one for anything else, divided them more deeply than any other free speech or press issue. What emerged were liberal and conservative positions on the issue, with the dividing line drawn on the ability to comment on the private character of public officials or on the standard of truth required in such reports.[122]

Court decisions became essays on the role of the press in a democratic society. "It is not only the privilege, but the duty, of the public press to discuss before the electors the fitness and qualification of candidates for public office conferred by election of the people,"[123] said an Oregon court in 1893. The court added, "When a man becomes such a candidate, he must be considered as putting his character in issue so far as respects his fitness and qualification for the office." Such a decision by the candidate means that "every person who engages in the discussion, whether in private conversation, in public speech, or in the newspapers, may, while keeping within proper limits and acting in good faith, be regarded and protected as one engaged in the discharge of a duty."[124]

This privilege often extended to commenting on material which could not be confirmed. Such an extension was necessary, said a Pennsylvania court in 1886, because "if the voters may not speak, write or print anything but such facts as they can establish with judicial certainty, the right does not exist, unless in such a form that a prudent man would hesitate to exercise it."[125] Public policy required "that free discussion, especially upon political topics and candidates, shall not be so hampered, as to make its exercise dangerous."[126]

In 1818, a South Carolina court said that public scrutiny of a candidate could be an ordeal, but "it is the result of that freedom of speech, which is the necessary attribute of every free government, and is expressly guaranteed to the people of this country by the Constitution."[127] This privilege of discussion could be carried to extremes, the court admitted, but "it is the only conceivable method by which the characters of public men can be developed and their qualifications for office made known."[128]

Exposure to such comment, a Massachusetts court said in 1890, was permitted because it was "one of the infelicities of public life, that a public officer is thus exposed to critical and often to unjust comments; but these, unless they pass the bounds of what the law will tolerate, must be borne for the sake of maintaining free speech."[129]

From this protection of critical statements about public officials and candidates for public office, it was inevitable that the courts would be asked to protect the purveyor of falsehood about a public official from the rigors of libel law. Some of the state courts were willing to move in that direction.

"What are the limitations upon the right of a newspaper to discuss the official character and conduct of a public official who is a candidate for reelection by popular vote to the office which he holds?"[130] asked a Kansas court in 1908. The court found no answer from either the history of freedom of the press in England or the history of press freedom in America because "the press as we know it to-day is almost as modern as the telephone and the phonograph" and "judicial interpretation must take cognizance of these facts."[131] Freedom of the press, according to the court, included freedom from prior restraint but allowed prohibitions against advocacy of overthrow of the government and allowed exercise of the police power to protect the morals of the people.[132] The justices from Kansas decided, however, to depart from these traditional views on freedom of the press and ruled that it was time to permit broader comment about the qualifications of candidates for office:

> It is of the utmost consequence that the people should discuss the character and qualifications of candidates for their suffrages. The importance to the state and to society of such discussions is so vast, and the advantages derived are so great, that they more than counterbalance the inconvenience of private persons whose conduct may be involved, and occasional injury to the reputations of individuals must yield to the public welfare, although at times such injury may be great. The public benefit from publicity is so great, and the chance of injury to private character so small, that such discussion must be privileged.[133]

Members of the Kansas court realized that such an interpretation of its state's constitutional guarantee gave the press more freedom to comment on public officials than had been granted by other state courts. Newspaper publishers sought such a "liberal indulgence," said the court, because of changing conditions "which govern the collection of news items, and the insistent popular expectation that newspapers will expose, and the popular demand that they shall expose, actual and suspected fraud, graft, greed, malfeasance and corruption in public affairs and questionable conduct on the part of public men and candidates for office."[134] The public approved of such behavior, according to the court, because judges had discovered that juries "do not, and the people do not, hold a newspaper publisher guilty...if in an effort in good faith to discharge his moral duty to the public he oversteps"[135] the boundaries of traditional libel rules.

Thus Kansas, with its willingness to allow the press greater freedom in commenting about government and public officials, added a new factor to the consideration of libel cases involving public officials. Although most other states ignored this new approach to libel, four additional states had adopted this new path by 1923.[136] In giving its assent to this new standard, a California court ruled that protection for public comment by a newspaper "does not arise from the fact that the publication is made in a newspaper." Rather, "it is based on the fact that the official conduct of public officers, especially in a government by the people, is a matter of public concern of which every citizen may speak in good faith and without malice."[137] The court stressed the idea that newspapers were no different from other citizens in possessing this ability to comment, and it noted, as did the Kansas court, that this right of comment was not universally recognized. Freedom to speak even that which was not true and to comment about appointed officials had to be considered privileged unless malice could be proved, according to the California court.

An Illinois court took this new approach to libel cases one step further in a 1923 case involving an admittedly false report in the *Chicago Tribune* that the city of Chicago was bankrupt. The court approached the matter by finding, "If this action can be maintained against a newspaper it can be maintained against every private citizen who ventures to criticise the ministers who are temporarily conducting the affairs of his government."[138] It was clear to the court that "a civil action [a libel suit] is as great, if not a greater, restriction"[139] on freedom of speech than a criminal libel prosecution would be. "A despotic or corrupt government can more easily stifle opposition by a series of civil actions [libel suits] than by criminal prosecutions.... It follows, therefore, that every citizen has the right to criticise an inefficient or corrupt government without fear of civil [libel] as well as criminal prosecution."[140] To prevent such problems, the Illinois court was willing to tolerate intentional falsehood in the press:

> By its demurrer appellee admits it published malicious and false statements regarding the city of Chicago with intent to destroy its credit and financial standing, and assuming that there was a temporary damage to the city and a resultant increase in taxes, it is better that an occasional individual or newspaper that is so perverted in judgment and so misguided in his or its civic duty should go free than that all of the citizens should be put in jeopardy of imprisonment or economic subjugation if they venture to criticise an inefficient or corrupt government. We do not pass upon the truth or falsity of the publications nor the merits of the political controversy between the parties. We consider the question solely from the standpoint of public policy and fundamental principles of government. For the same reason that members of the legislature, judges of the courts and other persons engaged in certain fields of the public service or in the administration of justice are absolutely immune from actions, civil or criminal, for libel for words published in the discharge of such public duties, the individual citizen must be given a like privilege when he is acting in his sovereign capacity. This action is out of tune with the American spirit and has no place in American jurisprudence.[141]

State courts may have shown a willingness to allow newspapers greater latitude to criticize public officials, but that increased freedom was from libel actions and involved officials other than judges. Actions for contempt of court were perhaps the second most numerous category of cases involving free speech and free press in the nineteenth and early twentieth centuries. These contempt decisions, as might be expected, dealt with the effect of publications on pending cases,[142] with the dignity of the court,[143] and with criticism of judicial personages.[144] Most included suggestions for alternative courses of action for judges deprived, because of circumstances, of resort to the contempt power.[145]

In contempt cases, state constitutional provisions guaranteeing the freedom of speech and press were pitted against constitutional, statutory, or common law provisions for contempt of court citations.[146] The sanctity of the court was usually stressed in contempt decisions, for although judges may have favored robust criticism of public officials and candidates for public office, they tended to find their offices too fragile to bear the brunt of such commentary. "If courts of justice may be publicly assailed by libel and slander or otherwise threatened and traduced in respect to causes, civil or criminal, pending before them for hearing or trial, then, indeed, no one's rights are any longer safe, and life, liberty, and property are held by a feeble tenure,"[147] said a Colorado court in 1893.

An Illinois court nearly two decades earlier proclaimed that freedom of the press was "indispensable to the preservation of the freedom of the people." The court then added that such a belief did not stop it from rebuffing any effort by the press to "control the administration of justice or influence the decision of pending cases."[148] A Missouri court in 1903 suggested that the press practice a form of enlightened self-interest: "There is no species of property and no class of people, that need the protection of the law as much as newspapers and editors, and they would feel the loss of such protection more speedily and more acutely than any one else." This need, said the court, should "induce them not to impair the power or authority of the courts."[149]

The opinions generally, however, were careful to say that courts and their judges were not shielded from press comment just because of their place in the judicial system. It was only when press comment adversely affected a pending case that contempt citations were seen as appropriate. "Judicial officers, like other public servants, must answer for their official actions before the chancery of public opinion; they must make good their claims to popular esteem by excellence and virtue, by faithful and efficient service, and by righteous conduct,"[150] said a Nebraska court in 1900.

This disclaimer notwithstanding, the wall of protection built around courts by the judges themselves was almost impenetrable throughout the nineteenth and early twentieth centuries. This was especially true when the contempt citation was handed down by the state supreme court itself, as many of them were.[151] Even so, in the area of contempt, as in libel, there was a division of opinion among the jurisdictions. Some states did grant the press more freedom to comment about the judiciary than others, but the freedom was always limited.[152] Courts should be open to newspaper criticism, said a California court in 1890: "If a public supervision and censure, through the press or otherwise, is necessary to suppress corruption, and keep the channels of justice pure and untainted, the right to exercise such supervision, and to censure and expose wrong-doing, should be and must be upheld by the courts."[153] Such criticism had to be allowed, wrote a Wisconsin court in 1897, because permitting the judge to halt comments at will was dangerous: "If there can be any more effectual way to gag the press, and subvert freedom of speech, we do not know where to find it."[154] Considering the elective nature of the judiciary, an 1875 Illinois court opinion had said, "There is, therefore, the same responsibility, in theory, in the judicial department, that exists in the legislative and executive departments to the people, for the diligent and faithful discharge of all duties."[155] If such was the case, "the same necessity exists, for public information, with regard to the conduct and character of those intrusted to discharge those duties, in order that the elective franchise shall be intelligibly exercised, as obtains in regard to the other departments of the government."[156] A Montana court determined in 1922 that it could not "believe that the legislature ever intended to denounce as a crime [under contempt statutes] every false or grossly inaccurate report concerning causes finally determined, when no public interest can suffer as a consequence of the publication."[157] With the removal of such an extensive contempt power, the next step seemed logical: "When such a digression becomes too flagrant to be disregarded, a prosecution for libel is usually the most appropriate and effective remedy."[158]

Thus, in cases of libel and contempt of court, the two areas most directly involved in free press litigation during these years, the courts attempted to build rationales for their decisions out of commonly accepted principles: freedom and responsibility in the exercise of freedom of speech and press and the need to protect the general welfare. From these, a third standard developed, one which held that the rights of the press were equal to and no greater than the rights of the individual. Even with this common core of beliefs, state court judges interpreted the standards liberally or conservatively, granting more or less freedom of expression to those seeking it, as seemed reasonable for their particular jurisdictions. Regardless of whether the interpretation given these common standards was conservative or liberal in nature, however, all state court judges relied on the same set of authorities to buttress their opinions. The conservative judge may have seen his liberal colleague as bending precedent out of shape to reach a liberal decision, and vice versa, but the same basic ingredients, as discussed above, appeared in most state court decisions by the end of the nineteenth century and the beginning of the twentieth century. Thus, a solid core of precedent on speech- and press-related issues was established at the state court level. It was possible to take almost any situation involving a speech or a press claim and find several state courts that had heard similar cases and had written decisions on the matter. Perhaps even more important, the state courts provided two distinct lines of decisions interpreting free speech and free press claims. One line would allow judges to use precedent to rule conservatively on these claims, restricting the exercise of them. The other set laid the foundation for a more liberal, or freeing, interpretation of speech and press matters. When the Supreme Court of the United States moved into this area of litigation, it found alternatives for action clearly outlined in state opinions.

Moving to the Supreme Court

Further development of the rights of freedom of speech and freedom of the press first became a matter before the Supreme Court of the United States in 1919 with the Court's discovery of meaning in the First Amendment through its decision in *Schenck* v. *United States*.[159] Over the next six years, the Court debated the applicability of the First Amendment to the states through the due process clause of the Fourteenth Amendment.[160] Then, in 1925, the First Amendment was determined to be binding on the states via the Court's opinion in *Gitlow* v. *New York*.[161] Yet another six years passed before the Court overturned any state statute with this new authority.[162]

The movement of decisions about free speech and free press issues from the state supreme courts to the U.S. Supreme Court was hardly a revolutionary step. When the Supreme Court used its newly found authority to decide challenges to state actions under the First Amendment, the reasoning it used to support its decisions was indistinguishable from that used by state courts for many years. Not only were the principles used in Supreme Court decisions on speech and press issues familiar to state courts, but the precedents used to buttress those conclusions came directly from the state courts themselves. The state courts had established such a rich foundation of decision making in the area that, in the years after 1925, it would become difficult to find a U.S. Supreme Court opinion in speech or press cases without an antecedent, either explicit or implicit, in these early state court decisions.[163]

This use of state court rulings relating to speech and press matters to support similar U.S. Supreme Court decisions began in the mid-nineteenth century. In 1848, the Court cited an 1808 Massachusetts libel decision involving a public official[164] as it examined a subject "most intimately connected with the rights and happiness of individuals, as it is with the quiet and good order of society,"[165] the ability of citizens to comment on public officials. The Court, after a fairly extensive discussion, sent the case back for reconsideration based upon the standards of truth and malice developed over the years by state courts and legal commentators.[166]

State court decisions involving interpretations of state constitutional provisions guaranteeing speech and press rights appeared in at least one U.S. Supreme Court case before 1907.[167] The first substantial use of opinions from the state level was in the 1907 case, *Patterson* v. *Colorado*.[168] Here, Justice Oliver Wendell Holmes, Jr., in dismissing Patterson's attempt to have a contempt of court citation reviewed by the High Court, noted with apparent approval the existence of state libel laws and contempt of court provisions and endorsed various state court decisions on these subjects.[169]

The use of state court decisions relating to speech and press continued as the U.S. Supreme Court heard cases involving labor problems[170] and sundry prosecutions for sedition.[171] However, it was not until the U.S. Supreme Court invalidated a Minnesota statute on the grounds that it was an impermissible prior restraint and thus moved fully into the superintending of state court action through its new interpretation of the First Amendment that state court citations appeared in Supreme Court opinions in any great number.

The Court's opinion in *Near* v. *Minnesota*[172] was written by Chief Justice

Charles Evans Hughes. In leading a five-man majority, the Chief Justice cited various state court decisions which supported the action taken by the High Court on prior restraint issues and related subjects. Chief Justice Hughes's survey of the status of free speech and free press as of 1931 repeatedly stressed a long-held belief: "It is recognized that punishment for the abuse of the liberty accorded to the press is essential for the protection of the public." He repeatedly referred to state court decisions in recognizing the validity of contempt citations against the press, on the one hand,[173] and the impermissibility of prior restraints on the press, on the other.[174]

The U.S. Supreme Court's specific citation of state court decisions in the free speech and press area would continue over the ensuing decades as the Court's case load in the free speech and free press areas increased and diversified. Although state court decisions were not cited as extensively after *Near*, the Court did regularly find appropriate precedent on the state court level—precedent established before 1925—to support decisions. From this early period, the Court could substantiate its statement in *Lovell* v. *Griffin*[175] that "the liberty of the press is not confined to newspapers and periodicals. It necessarily embraces pamphlets and leaflets.... The press in its historic connotation comprehends every sort of publication which affords a vehicle of information and opinion."[176] Support for its refusal to find protection for obscenity was also found in state court decisions. Thus in *Roth* v. *United States*,[177] Justice William J. Brennan, Jr., conducted a brief excursion into the past:

> The guaranties of freedom of expression in effect in 10 of the 14 States which by 1792 had ratified the Constitution, gave no absolute protection for every utterance. Thirteen of the 14 States provided for the prosecution of libel, and all of those States made either blasphemy or profanity, or both, statutory crimes.[178]

Based upon this historical research, Justice Brennan, agreeing with earlier state court action in the area, said, "The unconditional phrasing of the First Amendment was not intended to protect every utterance."[179]

State court action before 1925 also foreshadowed some of the Court's more controversial decisions of the 1960s and the 1970s. The Court's decisions on libel, for example, starting in 1964 with *New York Times Co.* v. *Sullivan*,[180] were presaged by the liberal interpretation of libel rules developed by the state courts. The Court's 1964 opinion acknowledged that support for its decision to broaden the range of acceptable comment about public officials came from "an oft-cited statement of a like rule, which has been adopted by a number of state courts,... found in the [1908] Kansas case of *Coleman* v. *MacLennan*."[181] Further support for this interpretation was garnered from the *Chicago Tribune* case. Indeed, the Supreme Court adopted specific language from that opinion: "What a State may not constitutionally bring about by means of a criminal statute is likewise beyond the reach of its civil law of libel. The fear of damage awards under [such] a rule...may be markedly more inhibiting than the fear of prosecution under a criminal statute."[182]

All the precedents provided by early state court actions, however, did not increase the scope of freedom of speech or press in U.S. Supreme Court rulings. The two-track system of state court decision making, which produced both liberal and conservative rulings on the issue, offered like options to those on the Supreme Court writing opinions. State court judges practiced a discriminating use of precedent, picking and choosing among state court decisions. A similar exercise of judicial discretion in picking precedent by the U.S. Supreme Court justices should come as no surprise.

In some areas, however, the U.S. Supreme Court could find a remarkably consistent line of precedent to support its conclusions. A very early example of this can be found in the Court's conclusion in *Mutual Film Corp.* v. *Ohio Industrial Commission*[183] that state courts were correct in assuming that the police power was involved in regulation of motion pictures and that such restrictions in no way involved freedom of speech. As Justice Joseph McKenna reviewed such state regulation, he wrote approvingly that "it seems not to have occurred to anybody in the cited cases that freedom of opinion was repressed in the exercise of the power which was illustrated. The rights of property were only considered as involved."[184] The Supreme Court saw the issue from the same perspective.

A similar line of rulings was found when the U.S. Supreme Court sought state precedent for its decision in *Branzburg* v. *Hayes*,[185] the case in which newsmen sought constitutional protection to keep the identities of their sources confidential. Justice Byron R. White, in writing for the Court, found it

> not surprising that the great weight of authority is that newsmen are not exempt from the normal duty of appearing before a grand jury and answering questions relevant to a criminal investigation. At common law, courts consistently refused to recognize the existence of any privilege authorizing a newsman to refuse to reveal confidential information to a grand jury.[186]

In none of the four pre-1925 cases cited did the state court reach the question of whether freedom of speech or of the press was involved, and apparently, in none of the cases did the newsmen involved offer freedom of the press per se as a defense.[187] In another case, not cited in *Branzburg*, a North Dakota court did discuss the application of free speech and free press to a newsman's attempt to conceal his source.[188] The court found that no such rights were involved and that the newsman would be found in contempt of court if he did not reveal his source.

Although the U.S. Supreme Court cited state court precedent when dealing with certain areas of the law, it left untapped state precedent that clearly anticipated other areas. State courts, for instance, had explored the relationship between free speech and political rights,[189] supported nondiscriminatory business regulation of newspapers,[190] dealt with questions of symbolic speech,[191] heard cases involving the question of anonymous speech,[192] determined matters involving union membership and the use of dues to support political causes,[193] dealt with offensive language,[194] decided cases dealing with limitations on political contributions,[195] and probed problems of free press–fair trial, including the validity of gag rules.[196] When the U.S. Supreme Court moved into each of these areas later, it was breaking no new ground.

It is true that all these cases will not be found listed under the free speech–free press heading in legal indices. Many of the cases which became free speech–free press cases at the U.S. Supreme Court level after 1925 were argued on other grounds in the state courts. For example, regulation of motion pictures was challenged in state courts prior to 1925 under the taxing power and the right to use property without interference. It should be remembered, however, that the U.S. Supreme Court did not place motion pictures under the wings of the First Amendment until 1952 in *Joseph Burstyn Inc.* v. *Wilson*[197] and since then it has been wary of completely removing films from the censor's watchful eye. In another example, prior to 1925, labor unions asked the state courts to protect picketing, with these cases usually brought in terms of freedom of contract and protection of property. Unions won First Amendment protection for their picketing for a brief time after *Senn* v. *Tile Layers Union*[198] in 1937. Court decisions on the state level that might have formed precedent for the U.S. Supreme Court's development of the commercial speech doctrine were also based on contractual and police power grounds.[199]

State courts were not unwilling to hear free speech and free press issues; many of the cases described above carried a challenge based on these grounds, and the justices on the state benches dealt with that challenge. In many other cases, however, such a challenge was not made. Prior to 1925, when the First Amendment was applied to the states via the Fourteenth, the law had not evolved sufficiently to give these guarantees substantial legal weight. The legal community was not yet attuned to issues involving civil liberties; that would come after 1937. Thus, in cases involving motion pictures, picketing, and the use of public streets, the viable body of law dealt with contracts, the right to uninhibited use of property, or the proper exercise of police power. The issues which would later give rise to free speech and free press litigation were nevertheless present, and although the bases for decisions varied, opinions rendered following arguments not related to speech or press issues prior to 1925 mesh remarkably well with those rendered on such grounds after 1925.

Apparently there was no long scream of protest from the state courts about Supreme Court usurpation of an area of litigation traditionally seen as under state control. Several factors could account for what might be termed acquiescence by the state courts. The nature of free speech and free press litigation had changed dramatically by the early twentieth century. Although state courts still heard a variety of traditional speech and press cases such as those involving libel, the main constitutional challenge in the states now dealt with the advocacy of ideas designed to overthrow the existing government. The U.S. Supreme Court had not yet ruled that state laws regulating such advocacy were preempted by federal legislation,[200] but the first High Court decisions giving vitality to the First Amendment were brought on the basis of federal law on sedition and espionage.[201] The case that served as the vehicle for nationalizing the First Amendment guarantees of speech and press involved a state criminal anarchy statute.[202] The Supreme Court was giving much-needed relief and assistance to the state courts as more and more of these cases were heard by the High Court.

Not only did the Supreme Court relieve the state courts of final judgment in an increasingly troublesome area of litigation, but its early decisions on speech and press issues were highly supportive of state court interpretations on these same matters. Indeed, the Court had been supportive of state court decisions in this area long before 1925. A number of state court decisions in this area had been heard by the High Court on various grounds by then. Of the 250 state court cases studied by this author, eleven had appeared on the Court's docket for decisions or dismissal by 1925.[203] Only five[204] had resulted in decisions by the Supreme Court by 1925, and in each of those cases, the state court ruling had been affirmed.[205] The only case which resulted in the overturning of a conviction based on First Amendment rights prior to 1931, *Fiske* v. *Kansas*,[206] originated before 1925 but was not decided until 1927. The grounds for overturning that conviction were not threatening to state law; that law was sustained while the particular conviction was found faulty. Even when the Supreme Court began overturning state statutes, as with *Stromberg* v. *California*[207] and *Near*,[208] both decided in 1931, it did not stray far from the path outlined by numerous state supreme courts.

Still another factor contributing to the ease with which free speech and free press issues moved from the state supreme courts to the U.S. Supreme Court was the apparent assumption by some state courts that the First Amendment to the U.S. Constitution might have some application on the state level. Throughout this discussion, it has been pointed out that state courts and the U.S. Supreme Court operated on the same basic principles and assumptions and arrived at much the same conclusions. That the state constitutions contained guarantees of free speech and press and that some of those guarantees had portions sounding much like the free speech and press clause of the First Amendment add to this general impression of sameness.[209] Thus it should not be surprising, *Barron* v. *Baltimore*[210] notwithstanding, that state courts would discuss the application of First Amendment guarantees to state cases.

Many of the state courts referred to the First Amendment to the U.S. Constitution as they recited the grounds upon which a case was brought to the state court's attention, and then they proceeded to rule in terms of state constitutional law.[211] Other state courts commented briefly on the place of the First Amendment guarantees in society. A Washington state court said in 1898, "The constitutional liberty of speech and the press and the guaranties against its abridgment are found in the laws of all the American states, and the federal constitution, and undoubtedly primarily grew out of the censorship of articles intended for publication by public authority."[212] A later Washington court, writing in 1912, said, "While the constitutions of the United States and of this state guarantee the right to freely speak, write and publish upon all subjects, it is not meant thereby that persons may with impunity advocate disregard of the law."[213] A New York court in 1922 commented, "The First Amendment to the United States Constitution and section 8 of article I of the New York State Constitution, which secure the freedom and liberty of speech and of the press, do not protect the violation of this liberty or permit attempts to destroy that freedom which the Constitutions have established."[214]

Some courts did point out that the First Amendment did not apply to the states. Said a Maine court in a 1921 blasphemy case, "The constitutional guaranties found in Article 1 of the amendments to the Federal Constitution have no application to the constitutionality of our statute . . . for it there provided only that Congress shall make no law restraining religious freedom or freedom of speech." Such a restraint, the court stressed, applied only to the federal congress, which had not passed the blasphemy statute. "The Federal Declaration of Rights not only restrains Congress from enacting any statute restraining religious freedom or freedom of speech but, by necessary implication, leaves those matters to be dealt with by the sovereign power of the several States."[215]

Other jurisdictions, probing for meaning in the First Amendment, came up with a different conclusion: that the First Amendment was to be reckoned with in state decision making. A California court, looking at its state constitutional provision as well as that of the federal constitution in 1896, wrote:

> This provision of the constitution as to freedom of speech varies somewhat from that of the constitution of the United States, and also more or less from the provisions of many state constitutions treating of this question; but it there is a material difference in the various provisions, it works no harm to this petition, for the provision here considered is the broader.[216]

Some state courts apparently were willing to invoke whichever provision granted the most protection. Other courts directly explored the application of the First Amendment to the states via the Fourteenth Amendment. In Minnesota that exploration ended in 1918 without resolution: "To what extent this amendment takes from the states the power to place legislative restrictions upon the freedom of speech and the freedom of the press is still a mooted question; but conceding that it protects this right from abridgment by the states, the freedom secured thereby is not an unlimited license."[217]

Thus, state courts had arrived at the point of questioning whether the First Amendment applied to the states at about the same time the U.S. Supreme Court decided that it was applicable. The new relationship thus established was not earthshaking for either court system. More importantly, the state court sytem before 1925 had laid very firm foundations for later U.S. Supreme Court activity.

Conclusion

Although often ignored or belittled by scholars, it is clear that state court decisions of the nineteenth and early twentieth centuries had a significant impact on the development of freedom of speech and press in America.

State courts before 1925 were continually asked to grant the press special privileges. By the late nineteenth century, newspapers were available to more people and they had a far greater potential influence upon the society. The state courts recognized this reality and struggled valiantly to balance the needs of the press with the needs of the public. Although some courts may have allowed the press a little more latitude in reporting about public officers or candidates for public office because of the importance such material had for society as a whole, generally the state courts held the press to a rather rigorous standard of rights and responsibilities. The U.S. Supreme Court, in contending with media representatives, has usually adhered to the earlier state court model of measuring such claims against the public need and of considering the rights and responsibilities of the press in light of the rights and responsibilities of individuals under similar circumstances.

The state court judges also discussed the need for a malleable interpretation of speech and press guarantees, for they had seen the changes that technology had brought to their way of life and could see the challenge that technological change would bring to the future. At times they seemed ready to expand the meaning of speech and press to include alternative means of communication such as picketing and the distribution of literature on the public streets. Sometimes these hints of a willingness to accommodate the products of technology came in an offhanded way, as in a comment in an unrelated case, but the seed was planted. The U.S. Supreme Court, when it started hearing cases in this area, adopted the same stance and has, over the years, widened the meaning of the terms *speech* and *press* in the First Amendment to cover more and more forms of communication.

That some state courts were dealing with the First Amendment to the U.S. Constitution in some of their rulings on speech and press is also of importance. In some cases, this was perhaps indicative of a certain sloppiness in opinion writing, but in other instances, the First Amendment is discussed quite carefully. This use of the U.S. Constitution by the state courts brings the long-accepted notion that the Bill of Rights guarantees were not applicable to the states into question. Could the statement by Chief Justice John Marshall in *Barron* v. *Baltimore* have been seen as only applying to the Fifth Amendment guarantees which were the subject of that particular case? Were states willing to consider the First Amendment binding on them—with or without the Fourteenth Amendment—even though the U.S. Supreme Court was not willing to impose it? Were the First Amendment guarantees and the protections for speech and press provided in the state constitutions seen as so identical as to allow the use of both in state decision making? The answers to these questions are not yet apparent, but it is clear that old assumptions in this area can no longer be considered automatically true.

State court decisions on free speech and free press issues should also not be dismissed from study because they were argued in terms of property rights or sanctity of contracts. The evolutionary status of the law must be taken into account here. State courts did hear some constitutional challenges on free speech and free press grounds. The incidence of such cases is significant, although such arguments were not as common before 1925 as they have become today. The appearance of such cases brings several questions not within the scope of this study to the fore. What situations gave rise to these confrontations with speech and press rights? What kind of laws were challenged on speech and press grounds? Did state court approaches to speech and press questions vary within individual states over time? If so, how?

The need for additional research in this area is great, for these questions only skim the surface of the possible areas for investigation. One thing is certain, however. Assumptions about the inapplicability of state court rulings to a study of the development of the freedoms of speech and press are invalid. It was through state court decisions that the American people became accustomed to having speech and press issues litigated. It was through state court decisions that basic assumptions upon which Supreme Court decisions were constructed are found. Truly, then, it must be said that the state courts played an important role in laying the foundations for a modern-day understanding of freedom of speech and of the press.

Notes

1. See Nat Hentoff, *The First Freedom: The Tumultuous History of Free Speech in America* (New York: Delacorte Press, 1980) and John Lofton, *The Press as Guardian of the First Amendment* (Columbia, S.C.: University of South Carolina Press, 1980).
2. 249 U.S. 47 (1919).
3. 268 U.S. 652 (1925). In upholding the right of the state of New York to enact laws designed to protect itself from overthrow, the Court opened the door to decades of future challenges of state laws in the federal courts on First Amendment grounds. Wrote Justice Edward T. Sanford, "For present purposes we may and do assume that freedom of speech and of the press—which are protected by the First Amendment from abridgment by Congress—are among the fundamental personal rights and 'liberties' protected by the due process clause of the Fourteenth Amendment from impairment by the States...." Ibid. at 666. The Court was anxious to establish this principle so that it could go on to say:

   > It is a fundamental principle, long established, that the freedom of speech and of the press which is secured by the Constitution, does not confer an absolute right to speak or publish, without responsibility, whatever one may choose, or an unrestricted and unbridled license that gives immunity for every possible use of language and prevents the punishment of those who abuse this freedom.

   Ibid.

   Charles Warren, author of a three-volume history of the Supreme Court, writing shortly after the *Gitlow* decision, traced the now-merged paths of the incorporation theory of the Bill of Rights and the freedom of speech.

   > The *Gitlow* case, therefore, affords an illuminating example of the manner in which our constitutional law grows; . . . No one who read Judge Sanford's opinion would imagine that, for over fifty years, counsel had, time and again, attempted to get the Court to hold that rights similar to the right of freedom of speech were protected by the Fourteenth Amendment against infringement by State legislation, and that in every instance the Court had declined so to hold. Yet, in this *Gitlow* case, without even mentioning these previous cases, the Court assumes, without argument, that this right of free speech is so protected by the Fourteenth Amendment. Thus, by one short sentence, rights, the protection of which have hitherto been supposed to be within the scope of the State Courts alone, are now brought within the scope of Federal protection and of the United States Supreme Court.

   "The New 'Liberty' under the Fourteenth Amendment," *Harvard Law Review* 39 (February 1926): 432–33.
4. Near v. Minnesota ex rel. Olson, 283 U.S. 697 (1931).
5. Thomas I. Emerson, *The System of Freedom of Expression* (New York: Random House, Vintage Books, 1971), p. 5.
6. Thomas I. Emerson, *Toward a General Theory of the First Amendment* (New York: Random House, Vintage Books, 1966), pp. 35–36. Emerson added:

   > The mechanisms of communications were left to the operation of the general system of laissez-faire. The federal government had no occasion to restrict individual expression except in a military emergency, and here its powers were seldom contested in the courts. Federal authority did not extend to control over most state, local or nongovernmental interference. The state legal systems were entrusted with protection of speech against violent interference by private persons, a task not always adequately performed, but otherwise were seldom called upon to deal with issues of individual expression.

   Ibid., p. 36.
7. Zechariah Chafee, Jr., *Free Speech in the United States* (New York: Atheneum, 1969), p. 7.
8. Ibid., pp. 14–15. Chafee explained that the state courts

   > told us, for instance, that libel and slander were actionable, or even punishable, that indecent books were criminal, that it was contempt to interfere with pending judicial proceedings, and that a permit could be required for street meetings; and on the other

hand, that some criticism of the government must be allowed, that a temperate examination of a judge's opinion was not contempt, and that honest discussion of the merits of a painting caused no liability for damages.

Ibid., p. 15.

9. The address told the Canadians:

The last right we shall mention, regards the freedom of the press. The importance of this consists, besides the advancement of truth, science, morality, and arts in general, in its diffusion of liberal sentiments on the administration of Government, its ready communication of thoughts between subjects, and its consequential promotion of union among them, whereby oppressive officers are shamed or intimidated, into more honourable and just modes of conducting affairs.

Bernard Schwartz, *The Bill of Rights: A Documentary History*, 2 vols. (New York: Chelsea House Publishers, 1971), 1:223.

10. Schwartz provides a sampling of the pamphlet literature written by the Federalists and anti-Federalists during the ratification controversy and also provides the highlights of state ratifying conventions. Ibid., 1:443–2:980.

The best known of the material written in support of the Constitution is grouped under the title *The Federalist*. In one of the most famous of these essays, No. 84, Alexander Hamilton relates the view of freedom of the press held by many of those favoring the ratification of the Constitution without adding a bill of rights:

On the subject of the liberty of the press, as much has been said, I cannot forbear adding a remark or two: In the first place, I observe that there is not a syllable concerning it in the constitution of this state [New York], and in the next, I contend that whatever has been said about it in that of any other state, amounts to nothing. What signifies a declaration, that "the liberty of the press shall be inviolably preserved?" What is the liberty of the press? Who can give it any definition which would not leave the utmost latitude for evasion? I hold it to be impracticable; and from this, I infer, that its security, whatever fine declarations may be inserted in any constitution respecting it, must altogether depend on public opinion, and on the general spirit of the people and of the government.

Ibid., 1:581–82.

11. U.S., Congress, House, *Annals of Congress*, 1st Cong., 1st sess., 1789, 1:434.

12. Ibid., p. 435. *Speech* was added to the original Madison proposal. Ibid., p. 755. Prior to the amendment's being sent to the Senate for consideration, the proposal was reworded to reflect a positive statement and a slight change in emphasis: "The equal rights of conscience, the freedom of speech or of the press, and the right of trial by jury in criminal cases, shall not be infringed by any State." Ibid.

13. U.S., *Constitution*, Amend. 1.

14. Tracing congressional reaction to Madison's proposals regarding freedom of speech and press is most difficult. The records kept in those days were spotty at best for the House and almost nonexistent in the Senate. Apparently, though, there was not much debate on the measures in either house. Madison is virtually the only one who is recorded as having spoken on the matter, and many of his comments were made in an attempt to get the attention of his colleagues away from the pressing business of making a new government work and onto the promised Bill of Rights. There are no records of debate in the Senate on the various parts of the Bill of Rights. The proposals simply entered the Senate and emerged from the Senate, adding to the mystery of congressional intent surrounding all these measures. For a concentrated documentary history of the entire Bill of Rights, see Schwartz, *Bill of Rights*, 2:983–1167.

15. Leonard Levy says supporters of the First Amendment in Congress "did not repudiate the concept of seditious libel and did not deny the power of the *states* [emphasis added] to control speech and press." *Freedom of Speech and Press in Early American History: Legacy of Suppression* (New York: Harper & Row, 1963), p. 264. See also Walter F. Berns, *The First Amendment and the Future of American Democracy* (New York: Basic Books, 1976), pp. 80–146.

16. Georgia, *Constitution of 1789*, Art. IV, sec. 3, quoted in Francis Newton Thorpe, comp.

and ed., *The Federal and State Constitutions, Colonial Charters, and Other Organic Laws of the States, Territories, and Colonies Now or Heretofore Forming the United States of America*, 7 vols. (Washington, D.C.: Govt. Printing Office, 1909), 2:789 (hereinafter cited as *Constitutions and Charters*).

17. North Carolina, *Constitution of 1776*, Declaration of Rights, &C., Art. XV, quoted in Thorpe, *Constitutions and Charters*, 5:2788.

18. Virginia, *Constitution of 1776*, Bill of Rights, sec. 12, quoted in Thorpe, *Constitutions and Charters*, 7:3814.

19. Pennsylvania, *Constitution of 1790*, Art. IX, sec. 7, quoted in Thorpe, *Constitutions and Charters*, 5:3100.

20. Delaware, *Constitution of 1792*, Art. 1, sec. 5, quoted in Thorpe, *Constitutions and Charters*, 1:569.

21. Two of these states, Connecticut and Rhode Island, continued using colonial charters, adopted as constitutions, until 1818 and 1842 respectively. When new constitutions were adopted, they carried the freedom-and-responsibility standard for freedom of speech and press. Connecticut, *Constitution of 1818*, Art. I, Declaration of Rights, sec. 5, quoted in Thorpe, *Constitutions and Charters*, 1:537; Rhode Island, *Constitution of 1842*, Art. I, Declaration of Certain Constitutional Rights and Principles, sec. 20, quoted in Thorpe, *Constitutions and Charters*, 6:3224. The states of New York and New Jersey used constitutions adopted in 1776 until they were revised in 1821 and 1844 respectively. The older constitutions, adopted in the hurry of events surrounding independence, set up a form of government but did little in the way of a guarantee of rights. When the new constitutions were adopted in these states, the freedom-and-responsibility standard for speech and press guarantees was used. New York, *Constitution of 1821*, Art. VII, sec. 8, quoted in Thorpe, *Constitutions and Charters*, 5:2648; New Jersey, *Constitution of 1844*, Art. I, Rights and Privileges, sec. 5, quoted in Thorpe, *Constitutions and Charters*, 5:2599.

22. Pennsylvania, *Constitution of 1790*, in Thorpe, *Constitutions and Charters*, 5:3100, and Delaware, *Constitutions of 1792*, in Thorpe, *Constitutions and Charters*, 1:569.

23. New York, *Constitution of 1821*, in Thorpe, *Constitutions and Charters*, 5:2648.

24. The provision in the North Carolina constitution of 1868 is indicative of the free speech—free press guarantees adopted at this time: "The freedom of the press is one of the great bulwarks of liberty, and, therefore, ought never to be restrained, but every individual shall be held responsible for the abuse of the same." North Carolina, *Constitution of 1868*, Art. I, Declaration of Rights, sec. 20, quoted in Thorpe, *Constitutions and Charters*, 5:2802.

25. See generally, free speech and free press guarantees in Thorpe, *Constitutions and Charters*. For the constitutions of Oklahoma, New Mexico, and Arizona, all of which entered the union after Thorpe's compilation, see Columbia University, Legislative Drafting Research Fund, *Constitutions of the United States: National and State*, 3d cum. supp., 2 vols. (Dobbs Ferry, N.Y.: Oceana Publications, 1969).

26. Pennsylvania, *Constitution of 1776*, A Declaration of Rights of the Inhabitants of the Commonwealth, or State of Pennsylvania, Art. XII, quoted in Thorpe, *Constitutions and Charters*, 5:3083.

27. Respublica v. Oswald, 1 Dall. (Pa.) 319, 325 (1788).

28. Pennsylvania, *Constitution of 1790*, in Thorpe, *Constitutions and Charters*, 5:3100.

29. People v. Croswell, 3 Johns. Cas. (N.Y.) 337, 393 (1804).

30. Berns, *First Amendment*, p. 130. For a general discussion of the Croswell case, see Berns, pp. 128–43. A discussion of Hamilton's role in shaping this episode in the development of freedom of the press may be found in Julius Goebel, Jr., ed., *The Law Practice of Alexander Hamilton: Documents and Commentary*, 2 vols. (New York: Columbia University Press, 1964), 1:775–848.

31. 3 Johns. Cas. (N.Y.) at 393–94. The inability of the state court to accept truth as evidence in this libel case prompted the New York legislature, the following year, to enact a statute so providing. See James Kent, *Commentaries on American Law*, 5th ed., 2 vols. (New York: Printed for the Author by James Van Norden & Co., 1844), 2:23.

The New York state constitution of 1821 put the heart of Kent's statement into fundamental law:

In all prosecutions or indictments for libel, the truth may be given in evidence to the jury; and if it shall appear to the jury that the matter charged as libellous is true, and was published with good motives and for justifiable ends, the party shall be acquitted; and the jury shall have the right to determine the law and the fact.

New York, *Constitution of 1821*, in Thorpe, *Constitutions and Charters*, 5:2648. Similar provisions may be found in a variety of state constitutions, including the New Jersey constitution of 1844 and the Connecticut constitution of 1818. New Jersey, *Constitution of 1814*, in Thorpe, *Constitutions and Charters*, 5:2599 and Connecticut, *Constitution of 1818*, Art. I, Declaration of Rights, sec. 7, quoted in Thorpe, *Constitutions and Charters*, 1:537.

32. State v. Morrill, 16 Ark. 384, 406 (1855).
33. For a general treatment of the evolution of English practices relating to freedom of the press and its relationship to American development in the area, see Henry Schofield, "Freedom of the Press in the United States," *Essays on Constitutional Law and Equity and Other Subjects*, 2 vols. (Boston: Published for Northwestern Law School by The Chipman Law Publishing Co., 1921), 2:510.
34. City of Chicago v. Tribune Co., 307 Ill. 595, 599 (1923).
35. Brandreth v. Lance, 8 Paige Ch. (N.Y.) 24, 27 (1839).
36. In re Shortridge, 99 Cal. 526, 534 (1893).
37. State v. Tugwell, 19 Wash. 238, 250 (1898).
38. In re MacKnight, 11 Mont. 126, 138 (1891).
39. State v. Tachin, 92 N.J.L. 269, 273 (1919).
40. Howell v. Bee Publishing Co., 100 Neb. 39, 41 (1916).
41. Ibid. at 41–42.
42. Coleman v. MacLennan, 78 Kan. 711, 718–19 (1908).
43. See, e.g., Sweeney v. Baker, 13 W. Va. 158 (1878); Upton v. Hume, 24 Or. 420 (1893); Bee Pub. Co. v. Shields, 68 Neb. 750 (1903); State ex rel. Attorney General v. Circuit Court of Eau Claire County, 97 Wis. 1 (1897).
44. Zechariah Chafee, Jr., in *Free Speech in the United States*, spends several portions of his first chapter discussing the relevance of Blackstone to the development of American principles of freedom of speech and of the press. Ibid., pp. 3–35. In the same chapter, he makes a number of references to Thomas M. Cooley, but the references are fewer in number and in less detail than those involving Blackstone. Justice Joseph Story is quoted in reference to a particular case later in the book. Ibid., pp. 254–56. James Kent receives no mention.

    Neither of Thomas I. Emerson's works cited above makes reference to Kent, Story, or Cooley—nor, for that matter, to Blackstone.
45. Wrote Blackstone:

    The liberty of the press is indeed essential to the nature of a free state: but this consists in laying no *previous* restraints upon publications, and not in freedom from censure for criminal matter when published. Every freeman has an undoubted right to lay what sentiments he pleases before the public: to forbid this, is to destroy the freedom of the press: but if he publishes what is improper, mischievous, or illegal, he must take the consequence of his own temerity.

    Commentaries on the Laws of England, with notes and additions by Edward Christian, 4 books (Boston: T. B. Wait and Sons, 1818), 4:151–52.
46. Kent, *Commentaries on American Law*, 2:15.
47. Ibid., p. 17.
48. Ibid., p. 21.
49. Kent believed "the tendency of measures in this country has been to relax too far the vigilance with which the common law surrounded and guarded character, while we are animated with a generous anxiety to maintain freedom of discussion." Ibid., p. 23.
50. *Commentaries on the Constitution of the United States*, 2d ed., 2 vols. (Boston: Little and Brown, 1851), 2:597.
51. Ibid., pp. 597–98.
52. Ibid., p. 603.
53. Story's own view of the dangers presented by the press comes through in his analysis of how European leaders felt about the press:

    It is not an uncommon opinion among European statesmen, of high character and extensive attainments, that the liberty of the press is incompatible with the permanent existence of any free government; nay, of any government at all. That, if it be true that free governments cannot exist without it, it is quite as certain that they cannot exist with it. In short, that the press is a new element in modern society; and likely, in a great measure, to control the power of armies, and the sovereignty of the people. That it works with a silence, a cheapness, a suddenness, and a force, which may break up, in an instant, all the foundations of society, and move public opinion, like a mountain torrent, to a general desolation of every thing within its reach.

Ibid., p. 605.

Story's solution for the problem posed by the press apparently would have been the passage of restrictive legislation. In reference to the Alien and Sedition Acts of 1798, he points out that "it is well known, that the opinions then deliberately given by many professional men, and judges, and legislatures, in favor of the constitutionality of the law, have never been retracted." Ibid., p. 606.

54. See also William Rawle, *A View of the Constitution of the United States of America*, 2d ed. (1829; reprint ed., New York: DaCapo Press, 1970). Rawle found that without freedom of speech and press, "life is indeed of little value. The foundation of a free government begins to be undermined when freedom of speech on political subjects is restrained; it is destroyed when freedom of speech is wholly denied." He said that because such liberties might be abused, "remedies will always be found while the protection of individual rights and the reasonable safeguards of society itself form parts of the principles of our government." Rawle also feared the power of the press and agreed with his contemporaries, Kent and Story, that liberty of the press did not mean an absence of punishment for abuse of that liberty. Ibid., pp. 123–24.

55. Both Kent, a Federalist, and Story, a moderate Republican, were leaders in the legal community of the time and, sporadically, were targets of political opposition. See Richard E. Ellis, *The Jeffersonian Crisis: Courts and Politics in the Young Republic* (New York: Oxford University Press, Norton Library, 1974).

56. Thomas M. Cooley, *A Treatise on the Constitutional Limitations Which Rest upon the Legislative Power of the States of the American Union*, 2d ed. (Boston: Little, Brown, and Co., 1871), p. 414.

57. Ibid., pp. 421–22.

58. Ibid., p. 422.

59. Ibid., p. 451.

60. Ibid., p. 452.

61. Ibid., pp. 454–55.

62. Legal commentators generally agreed that a careful exercise of the state's police power to keep the use of speech and press rights from intruding on the rights of other persons was acceptable. See Christopher G. Tiedeman, *A Treatise on State and Federal Control of Persons and Property in the United States*, Foundations of Criminal Justice Series, 2 vols. (1900; reprint ed., New York: AMS Press, 1975), vol. 1, sec. 23, p. 61 and Ernst Freund, *The Police Power: Public Policy and Constitutional Rights* (Chicago: Callaghan & Co., 1904), secs. 471–79.

63. Runkle v. Meyer, 3 Yeates (Pa.) 518, 520 (1803). See also Commonwealth v. Blanding, 20 Mass. (3 Pick.) 304 (1825).

64. Respublica v. Dennie, 4 Yeates (Pa.) 267, 269 (1805).

65. Detroit Daily Post Co. v. McArthur, 16 Mich. 447, 451–52 (1868).

66. Problems occurred when prior restraint was applied to the regulation of theatrical performances and motion pictures. Compare Dailey v. Superior Court of City and County of San Francisco, 112 Cal. 94 (1896) with Commonwealth v. McGann, 213 Mass. 213 (1913). The California court found a theatrical performance to fall within the meaning of its state constitutional protection of freedom to speak, write, and publish. In Massachusetts, the state constitution was found to protect only the freedom of the press, and the question of protecting motion pictures was avoided. Other difficulties arose with questions stemming from union boycotts. Compare Marx & Haas Jeans Clothing Co. v. Watson, 168 Mo. 133 (1902) with Jordahl v. Hayda, 1 Cal. App. 696 (1905). In Missouri, the right of free speech was found to prevail; in California, free speech, when balanced against the right to own property, was found to be misused and was enjoined. See also Lindsay & Co. v. Montana Federation of Labor, 37 Mont. 264 (1908) and Empire Theatre Co. v. Cloke, 53 Mont. 183 (1917). But a newspaper's free press claim raised in

defense of publishing a description of an execution in violation of a state law expressly forbidding the press to cover such events was not found to immunize the press from what was seen as a permissible prior restraint. See State v. Pioneer Press Co., 100 Minn. 173 (1907).

67. Mitchell v. Grand Lodge Free and Accepted Masons, 121 S.W. (Tex.) 178, 179 (1909). See also Brandreth v. Lance, 8 Paige Ch. (N.Y.) 24 (1839); Life Ass'n of America v. Boogher, 3 Mo. App. 173 (1876); N.Y. Juvenile Guardian Society v. Roosevelt, 7 Daly (N.Y.) 188 (1877); Flint v. Hutchinson Smoke Burner Co., 110 Mo. 492 (1892); Marlin Firearms Co. v. Shields, 171 N.Y. 384 (1902); Strang v. Biggers, 252 S.W. (Tex.) 826 (1923).
68. Star Co. v. Brush, 170 N.Y.S. 987, 992 (1918). Before the New York courts finished with this episode, a total of four decisions, all but one basically along the same lines, would be rendered. See Star Co. v. Brush, 172 N.Y.S. 320 (1918); Star Co. v. Brush, 172 N.Y.S. 661 (1918); Star Co. v. Brush, 172 N.Y.S. 851 (1918). A New Jersey court reached the same result without touching the free speech–free press issue in New Yorker Staats–Zeitung v. Nolan, 89 N.J. Eq. 387 (1918). See also Ex parte Neill, 22 S.W. (Tex.) 923 (1893); Ulster Square Dealer v. Fowler, 111 N.Y.S. 16 (1908); New Yorker Staats-Zeitung v. Brush, 170 N.Y.S. 993 (1918).
69. People v. Gitlow, 234 N.Y. 132, 151 (1922) (Hiscock, C. J., concurring).
70. People v. Steelik, 187 Cal. 361, 375 (1921).
71. People v. Most, 171 N.Y. 423, 431–32 (1902).
72. Ibid. at 432.
73. State v. Gibson, 189 Iowa 1212, 1217 (1919).
74. See In re Hartman, 182 Cal. 447 (1920); Ex parte Meckel, 220 S.W. (Tex.) 81 (1920); State v. Diamond, 27 N.M. 477 (1921); Ex parte Campbell, 64 Cal. App. 300 (1923); State v. Gabriel, 95 N.J.L. 337 (1921).
75. See State v. Boyd, 86 N.J.L. 75 (1914); State v. Laundy, 103 Or. 443 (1922); State v. Fiske, 117 Kan. 69 (1924); People v. Cox, 66 Cal. App. 287 (1924); People v. Wagner, 65 Cal. App. 704 (1924); Berg v. State, 233 P. (Okla.) 497 (1925).
76. See In re Lithuanian Workers' Literature Society, 187 N.Y.S. 612 (1921).
77. See Spies v. People, 122 Ill. 1 (1887).
78. See People v. Taylor, 187 Cal. 378 (1921); People v. Ruthenberg, 229 Mich. 315 (1924).
79. See State v. Holm, 139 Minn. 267 (1918); State v. Kahn, 56 Mont. 108 (1919); State v. Tachin, 92 N.J.L. 269 (1919).
80. See Goldman v. Reyburn, 36 Pa. Co. 581 (1909); State v. Sinchuk, 96 Conn. 605 (1921).
81. At least two cases which have since found their way into the history of First Amendment decision making by the U.S. Supreme Court fall into this category. See State v. Gilbert, 141 Minn. 263 (1919); People v. Whitney, 207 P. 698 (1922).
82. Some arguments about the constitutionality of obscenity regulations were being unsuccessfully raised during these years. See Theodore A. Schroeder, *"Obscene" Literature and Constitutional Law* (1911; reprint ed., New York: DaCapo Press, 1972), and Theodore A. Schroeder, *Constitutional Free Speech Defined and Defended*, Civil Liberties in American History Series (1919; reprint ed., New York: DaCapo Press, 1970).
83. The term *obscenity* had a broad meaning in the nineteenth and early twentieth centuries. Some of the cases decided by state courts dealt with issues still confronted in the 1960s and the 1970s. See Commonwealth v. Buckley, 200 Mass. 346 (1909); Williams v. State, 130 Miss. 827 (1922); People v. Seltzer, 203 N.Y.S. 809 (1924); Halsey v. N.Y. Society for the Suppression of Vice, 234 N.Y. 1 (1922); In re Worthington Co., 30 N.Y.S. 361 (1894); People v. Muller, 96 N.Y. 408 (1884); Commonwealth v. Holmes, 17 Mass. 336 (1821). Obscenity included indecent language. See State v. Warren, 113 N.C. 683 (1893). It also included blasphemy. See Commonwealth v. Kneeland, 37 Mass. (20 Pick.) 206 (1838) and State v. Mockus, 120 Me. 84 (1921). Publishers of detailed accounts of sensational criminal trials could face prosecution for obscenity, as in the case of Kentucky newspapers carrying stories on the Harry K. Thaw murder trial. See Commonwealth v. Herald Publishing Co., 128 Ky. 424 (1908). Special licensing fees for publications in the latter category were permitted, as in the case of a Texas $500-per-county fee for newspapers featuring crime. See Thompson v. State, 17 Tex. Crim. App. 253 (1884).
84. State v McKee, 73 Conn. 18, 28 (1900).
85. Ibid. at 29.

86. State v. Van Wye, 136 Mo. 227, 239 (1896).

87. In re Banks, 56 Kan. 242, 243 (1895).

88. Ibid. at 243–44.

89. Block v. City of Chicago, 239 Ill. 251, 258 (1909).

90. Court challenges involving motion pictures included protests over the amount of the license fee, required safety equipment or personnel, alleged denial of property right, alleged unconstitutional use of the taxing power, possibility of judicial review of censors' decisions, and license removal. See City of Duluth v. Marsh, 71 Minn. 248 (1898); Higgins v. LaCroix, 119 Minn. 145 (1912); City of Chicago v. Weber, 246 Ill. 304 (1910); State v. Loden, 117 Md. 373 (1912); Vitagraph Corp. of America v. City of Chicago, 209 Ill. App. 591 (1918); State ex rel. Brewster v. Ross, 101 Kan. 377 (1917); People v. Schuettler, 209 Ill. App. 588 (1918); In re Franklin Film Mfg. Corp., 253 Pa. 422 (1916); In re Goldwyn Distributing Corp., 265 Pa. 335 (1919); Fox Amusement Corp. v. McClellan, 114 N.Y.S. 594 (1909); McKenzie v. McClellan, 116 N.Y.S. 645 (1909).

91. Pathé Exchange, Inc. v. Cobb, 195 N.Y.S. 661, 665 (1922).

92. Ibid. at 666.

93. People ex rel. Doyle v. Atwell, 232 N.Y. 96, 101 (1921). Most courts dealing with the matter followed the model of *Atwell* and simply said that certain activities were prohibited in the streets. In Fitts v. City of Atlanta, 121 Ga. 567 (1905), one court was far more specific:

> Every citizen has a right to lawfully acquire and hold personal property; but he has no right, constitutional or otherwise, to insist on storing his possessions in the street. Every man has the inalienable right to sleep and eat (if he has the edibles), but he has no constitutional right to make his bed or set his table in the street. Every man has not only the right to, but he should, bathe and cleanse himself, and change his raiment, if he has a change. This is a duty imposed by his individual constitution, if not by that of his country. But there is no constitutional right on his part to perform his ablutions or exercise the most necessary demands of his nature in the public streets. At proper times and in proper places, one may make loud noises, or shoot a gun, or test his lung power vocally to a considerable extent, without offending against any law; but there is no right, inherent or constitutional, to make vociferous outcries or practice gunnery in the street.

Ibid. at 570–71. See also Barker v. Commonwealth, 19 Pa. 412 (1852).

94. Harwood v. Trembley, 97 N.J.L. 173, 176 (1922).

95. City of Duquesne v. Fincke, 269 Pa. 112, 118 (1920).

96. See People v. Burman, 154 Mich. 150 (1908); Commonwealth v. Karvonen, 219 Mass. 30 (1914); City of Louisville v. Lougher, 209 Ky. 299 (1925); In re Frazee, 63 Mich. 396 (1886). In People ex rel. Doyle v. Atwell, 232 N.Y. 96 (1921), two justices questioned whether political affiliation was related to being granted a permit to use public property, thereby at least casting doubts on the wisdom of allowing unbridled municipal authority in the area. The point of municipal discretion was raised by counsel in City of Buffalo v. Till, 182 N.Y.S. 418 (1920), but was rejected by the court.

97. Robison v. Hotel and Restaurant Employees Local 782, 35 Idaho 418, 430 (1922).

98. Thomas v. City of Indianapolis, 195 Ind. 440, 450 (1924).

99. Cooks', Waiters' and Waitresses' Local Union v. Papageorge, 230 S.W. (Tex.) 1086, 1088 (1921).

100. Hughes v. Kansas City Motion Picture Machine Operators Local 170, 282 Mo. 304, 329–30 (1920) (Graves, J., concurring).

101. Ibid. at 350 (Blair, J., dissenting).

102. People v. Johnson, 191 N.Y.S. 750, 751 (1921). See also Ex parte Campbell, 64 Cal. App. 300 (1923).

103. See Martin L. Newell, *The Law of Libel and Slander in Civil and Criminal Cases as Administered in the Courts of the United States of America*, 2d ed. (Chicago: Callaghan & Co., 1898); John Townshend, *A Treatise on the Wrongs Called Slander and Libel, and on the Remedy by Civil Action for Those Wrongs*, 2d ed. (New York: Baker, Voorhis & Co., 1872); Thomas M. Cooley, *A Treatise on the Law of Torts or the Wrongs Which Arise Independent of Contract*, 2d ed. (Chicago: Callaghan & Co., 1888), pp. 193–221.

104. See People v. Croswell, 3 Johns. Cas. (N.Y.) 337 (1804); Territory v. Nugent, 1 Mart. (La.) 108 (1810); State v. Lehre, 2 S.C.L. 214 (2 Brev. 446) (1811); Commonwealth v. Morris, 1 Va. Cas. (3 Va.) 176 (1811); Hotchkiss v. Oliphant, 2 Hill (N.Y.) 510 (1842); Rowand v. DeCamp, 96 Pa. 493 (1880); Castle v. Houston, 19 Kan. 417 (1887).

105. McAllister v. Detroit Free Press Co., 76 Mich. 338, 357 (1889). See also Smart v. Blanchard, 42 N.H. 137 (1860); Aldrich v. Press Printing Co., 9 Minn. 123 (1864); Palmer v. City of Concord, 48 N.H. 211 (1868); Express Printing Co. v. Copeland, 64 Tex. 354 (1885); Bronson v. Bruce, 59 Mich. 467 (1886); Owen v. Dewey, 107 Mich. 67 (1895); Arnold v. Sayings Co., 76 Mo. App. 159 (1898); Van Lonkhuyzen v. Daily News Co., 203 Mich. 570 (1918).

106. New York, *Constitution of 1821*, in Thorpe, *Constitutions and Charters*, 5:2648.

107. Riley v. Lee, 88 Ky. 603, 612 (1889).

108. Williams Printing Co. v. Saunders, 113 Va. 156, 181 (1912).

109. Negley v. Farrow, 60 Md. 158, 176 (1882) (Maryland court's emphasis).

110. "The freedom of the press was undoubtedly intended to be secured on public grounds, and the general purpose may be said to be, to preclude those in authority from making use of the machinery of the law to prevent full discussion of political and other matters in which the public are concerned." Cooley, *Law of Torts*, p. 217. See also John Ordronaux, *Constitutional Legislation in the United States: Its Origin, and Application to the Relative Powers of Congress, and of State Legislatures* (Philadelphia: T. & J. W. Johnson & Co., 1891), pp. 236–40.

111. Negley v. Farrow, 60 Md. at 177.

112. Riley v. Lee, 88 Ky. at 612.

113. Respublica v. Oswald, 1 Dall. (Pa.) at 325.

114. Perret v. New Orleans Times Newspaper, 25 La. Ann. 170, 178 (1873).

115. Sweeney v. Baker, 13 W. Va. at 182.

116. Barr v. Moore, 87 Pa. 385, 392 (1878).

117. Ibid. at 393. See also Giddens v. Mirk, 4 Ga. 364 (1848). In a slander case the Georgia court said:

> Among the rights of personal security, are those of character. Character is as essential to the happiness and success of the citizen as any thing else. It is that which gives value to all other rights. It is sacred in proportion to the public appreciation of it. Hence in highly civilized and highly moral communities, the abhorrence of the vile arts of the slanderer is as it ought to be, extreme.

4 Ga. at 366.

118. Cincinnati Gazette Co. v. Timberlake, 10 Ohio St. 548, 555 (1860). See also Commonwealth v. Blanding, 20 Mass. (3 Pick.) 304 (1825).

119. Cooper v. Illinois Publishing and Printing Co., 218 Ill. App. 95, 101 (1920).

120. Detroit Daily Post Co. v. McArthur, 16 Mich. at 452.

121. Foster v. Scripps, 39 Mich. 376, 380 (1878). The courts lamented the lack of responsibility shown by the press.

> The article in question, grossly libellous as it is, is of a kind lamentably frequent in the columns of American newspapers. There is probably no other country in the civilized world where private character has so little security against newspaper assault. The conductors of the press are neither better nor worse than other men, but they are singularly reckless in the exercise of their great power. The anonymous mode of its exercise blunts the sense of personal responsibility.

Storey v. Wallace, 60 Ill. 51, 57 (1871). See also Fitzpatrick v. Daily States Publishing Co., 48 La. Ann. 1116 (1896).

122. See Atwater v. Morning News Co., 67 Conn. 504 (1896); Commonwealth v. Clap, 4 Mass. 163 (1808).

123. Upton v. Hume, 24 Or. at 428–29.

124. Ibid. at 429. See also Belknap v. Ball, 83 Mich. 583 (1890).

125. Briggs v. Garrett, 111 Pa. 404, 417 (1886).

126. Ibid. at 419.

127. Mayrant v. Richardson, 10 S.C.L. 140, 141, 1 Nott & McC. 347, 350 (1818).

128. Ibid. at 141, 1 Nott & McC. at 351.
129. Sillars v. Collier, 151 Mass. 50, 54 (1890).
130. Coleman v. MacLennan, 78 Kan. at 715.
131. Ibid. at 718.
132. Ibid. at 720.
133. Ibid. at 724.
134. Ibid. at 725.
135. Ibid. at 741. The coming of *Coleman* was not a surprise. In 1884, the Kansas court has said something similar:

> Generally, we think a person may in good faith publish whatever he may honestly believe to be true, and essential to the protection of his own interests or the interests of the person or persons to whom he makes the publication, without committing any public offense, although what he publishes may in fact not be true and may be injurious to the character of others. And we further think that every voter is interested in electing to office none but persons of good moral character, and such only as are reasonably qualified to perform the duties of the office.

State v. Balch, 31 Kan. 465, 472 (1884).
136. See McLean v. Merriman, 42 S.D. 394 (1920); Snively v. Record Publishing Co., 185 Cal. 565 (1921); City of Chicago v. Tribune Co., 307 Ill. 595 (1923); Salinger v. Cowles, 195 Iowa 873 (1923).
137. Snively v. Record Publishing Co., 185 Cal. at 571.
138. City of Chicago v. Tribune Co., 307 Ill. at 606.
139. Ibid. at 607.
140. Ibid. at 607–608.
141. Ibid. at 610.
142. See Stuart v. People, 4 Ill. (3 Scam.) 395 (1842); Cooper v. People ex rel. Wyatt, 13 Colo. 337 (1889); State ex rel. Phelps v. Judge of Civ. Dist. Ct., 45 La. Ann. 1250 (1893); McDougall v. Sheridan, 23 Idaho 191 (1913); State v. New Mexican Printing Co., 25 N.M. 102 (1918).
143. See Dunham v. State, 6 Iowa 245 (1858); In re Cheeseman, 49 N.J.L. 115 (1886); In re Shannon, 11 Mont. 67 (1891); Field v. Thornell, 106 Iowa 7 (1898); State ex rel. Metcalf v. Dist. Ct., 52 Mont. 46 (1922).
144. See State v. Morrill, 16 Ark. 385 (1885); State v. Frew & Hart, 24 W. Va. 416 (1884); Ex parte Barry, 85 Cal. 603 (1890); Burdett v. Commonwealth, 103 Va. 838 (1904); Boorde v. Commonwealth, 134 Va. 625 (1922).
145. See Ex parte Hickey, 12 Miss. (4 S. & M.) 751 (1844); Foster v. Commonwealth, 8 Watts & Serg. (Pa.) 77 (1844); Cheadle v. State, 110 Ind. 301 (1887); Myers v. State, 46 Ohio St. 473 (1889).
146. An overview of contempt by publication is provided by legal commentator Stewart Rapalje, who conceded that freedom of the press had an impact on court action in this area: "The force of public opinion in this country, in favor of freedom of the press, has restrained the free exercise of the power to punish this class of contempts, and in many jurisdictions statutes have been enacted depriving the courts of the power to punish them." *A Treatise on Contempt Including Civil and Criminal Contempts of Judicial Tribunals, Justices of the Peace, Legislative Bodies, Municipal Boards, Committees, Notaries, Commissioners, Referees and Other Officers Exercising Judicial and Quasi-Judicial Functions* (New York: L. K. Strouse & Co., 1884), sec. 56, p. 71.
147. People ex rel. Connor v. Stapleton, 18 Colo. 568, 585 (1893).
148. People v. Wilson, 64 Ill. 195, 214 (1872).
149. State ex inf. Crow v. Shepherd, 177 Mo. 205, 257 (1903).
150. State v. Bee Publishing Co., 60 Neb. 282, 296 (1900).
151. See In re Hughes, 8 N.M. 225 (1895); State ex rel. Haskell v. Faulds, 17 Mont. 140 (1895); State v. Rosewater, 60 Neb. 438 (1900); People ex rel. Attorney General v. News-Times Publishing Co., 35 Colo. 253 (1906); In re Egan, 24 S.D. 301 (1909); McDougall v. Sheridan, 23 Idaho 191 (1913); In re Hayes, 72 Fla. 558 (1916).
152. See Cooper v. People ex rel. Wyatt, 13 Colo. 337 (1889); In re Egan, 24 S.D. 301 (1909).
153. Ex parte Barry, 85 Cal. at 608.
154. State ex rel. Attorney General v. Circuit Court of Eau Claire County, 97 Wis. at 12.

155. Storey v. People, 79 Ill. 45, 52 (1875).
156. Ibid. at 52–53.
157. State ex rel. Metcalf v. Dist. Ct., 52 Mont. at 54.
158. Cheadle v. State, 110 Ind. at 313.
159. 249 U.S. 47 (1919).
160. In Gilbert v. Minnesota, 254 U.S. 325 (1920), Justice Joseph McKenna seemed to accept a
limited application of First Amendment freedoms to the states, noting that Gilbert had
"asserted that the right of free speech is a natural and inherent right, and that it, and the
freedom of the press, were 'regarded as among the most sacred and vital possessed by mankind, when this nation was born, when its constitution was framed and adopted.' " Ibid.
at 332. For the Court, Justice McKenna added:

> But without so deciding or considering the freedom asserted as guaranteed or secured
> either by the Constitution of the United States or by the constitution of the State, we
> pass immediately to the contention and for the purposes of this case may concede it,
> that is, concede that the asserted freedom is natural and inherent, but that it is not
> absolute, it is subject to restriction and limitation.

Ibid. A direct refusal to apply the First Amendment to the states via the Fourteenth
came in 1922 when Justice Mahlon Pitney wrote:

> The cases cited . . . place material dependence upon provisions of the several state con-
> stitutions guaranteeing freedom of speech, from which is deduced by contrast a right
> of privacy called the "liberty of silence"; . . . But, as we have stated, neither the Four-
> teenth Amendment nor any other provision of the Constitution of the United States
> imposes upon the States any restrictions about "freedom of speech" or the "liberty of
> silence."

Prudential Insurance Co. of America v. Cheek, 259 U.S. 530, 542–43 (1922).
The Court's assumption in *Gitlow* that the First Amendment guarantees of speech and
press applied to the states still did not set up firm guidelines on the extent of Supreme
Court review in the area, and the debate over the extent of the protection continued for
over a decade. See, e.g., Herbert v. Louisiana, 272 U.S. 312 (1926); Whitney v. Califor-
nia, 274 U.S. 357 (1927); Fiske v. Kansas, 274 U.S. 380 (1927).
Justice John Marshall Harlan, the elder, began the campaign to extend the protection
of the First Amendment to the states via the Fourteenth in his dissent in Patterson v.
Colorado, 205 U.S. 454 (1907). In response to the majority opinion written by Justice
Oliver Wendell Holmes, Justice Harlan wrote:

> As the First Amendment guaranteed the rights of free speech and a free press against
> hostile action by the United States, it would seem clear that when the Fourteenth
> Amendment prohibited the States from impairing or abridging the privileges of citizens
> of the United States it necessarily prohibited the States from impairing or abridging
> the constitutional rights of such citizens to free speech and a free press. But the court
> announces that it leaves undecided the specific question whether there is to be found
> in the Fourteenth Amendment a prohibition as to the rights of free speech and a free
> press similar to that in the First. It yet proceeds to say that the main purpose of such
> constitutional provisions was to prevent all such "*previous* restraints" upon publications
> as had been practiced by other governments, but not to prevent the subsequent
> punishment of such as may be deemed contrary to the public welfare. I cannot assent
> to that view, if it be meant that the legislature may impair or abridge the rights of a
> free press and of free speech whenever it thinks that the public welfare requires that to
> be done. The public welfare cannot override the constitutional privileges, and if the
> rights of free speech and of a free press are, in their essence, attributes of national
> citizenship, as I think they are, then neither Congress nor any State since the adoption
> of the Fourteenth Amendment can, by legislative enactments or by judicial action, im-
> pair or abridge them. In my judgment the action of the court below was in violation
> of the rights of free speech and a free press as guaranteed by the Constitution.
>   I go further and hold that the privileges of free speech and a free press, belonging
> to every citizen of the United States, constitute essential parts of every man's liberty,
> and are protected against violation by that clause of the Fourteenth Amendment for-

bidding a State to deprive any person of his liberty without due process of law. It is, I think, impossible to conceive of liberty, as secured by the Constitution against hostile action, whether by the Nation or by the States, which does not embrace the right to enjoy free speech and the right to have a free press.

Ibid. at 464–65.
161. 268 U.S. 652 (1925).
162. See Stromberg v. California, 283 U.S. 359 (1931); Near v. Minnesota, 283 U.S. 697 (1931).

The U.S. Supreme Court, using this newly found application of the First Amendment to the states via the Fourteenth in 1927, reversed a conviction under a Kansas syndicalism act. The Court found that there was no evidence to suggest that the organization to which the defendant Fiske belonged was engaged in any activity prohibited by the act. Thus the conviction was overturned; the law itself was found constitutional. Fiske v. Kansas, 274 U.S. 380 (1927).

163. There is no intention to argue here the correctness of U.S. Supreme Court usage of state court and other historical precedent. For one such discussion, see Charles A. Miller, *The Supreme Court and the Uses of History* (New York: Simon & Schuster, 1972), pp. 71–99.
164. Commonwealth v. Clap, 4 Mass. 163 (1808). In discussing the vulnerability to criticism of persons seeking or holding public office, the Massachusetts court said:

When any man shall consent to be a candidate for a public office conferred by the election of the people, he must be considered as putting his character in issue, so far as it may respect his fitness and qualifications for the office. And publications of the truth on this subject, with the honest intention of informing the people, are not a libel. For it would be unreasonable to conclude that the publication of truths, which it is in the interest of the people to know, should be an offense against their laws.

Ibid. at 169. But the court added, "The publication of a falsehood and calumny against public officers or candidates for public offices, is an offence most dangerous to the people, and deserves punishment, because the people may be deceived, and reject the best citizens, to their great injury, and it may be to the loss of their liberties." Ibid. at 169–70.
165. White v. Nicholls, 44 U.S. (3 How.) 266, 291 (1845). This case, Justice Peter Daniel wrote:

involves this issue, so important to society, viz: How far, under an alleged right to examine into the fitness and qualifications of men who are either in office or are applicants for office—or, how far, under the obligation of a supposed duty to arraign such men either at the bar of their immediate superiors or that of public opinion, their reputation, their acts, their motives or feelings may be assailed with impunity—how far that law, designed for the protection of all, has placed a certain class of citizens without the pale of its protection?

Ibid. at 285.
The case, which involved a letter asking the removal of the collector of the District of Columbia port from office, found the justice questioning how great a latitude could be given to such communications.
166. The Court decried that in view of state court actions in this area and the writings of legal authorities such as Chancellor Kent, whom it quoted, "the rule of evidence, as to such cases, is accordingly so far changed as to impose it on the plaintiff... to bring home to the defendant the existence of malice as the true motive of his conduct." Ibid. at 291. A lower court could decide whether the plaintiff had succeeded.
167. United States ex. rel. Turner v. Williams, 194 U.S. 279 (1904), citing People v. Most, 171 N.Y. 423 (1902). The New York court turned back arguments based on its state constitutional provision that legislation regulating seditious publications was invalid. The U.S. Supreme Court, searching the First Amendment guarantees, found no bar to congressional enactments forcing the deportation of those termed alien anarchists.
168. Patterson v. Colorado ex rel. Attorney General, 205 U.S. 454 (1907). *Patterson* originated as People ex rel. Attorney General v. News-Times Publishing Co., 35 Colo. 253 (1906).
169. Libel decisions cited from the state court level included Respublica v. Oswald, 1 Dall.

(Pa.) 319 (1788) and Commonwealth v. Blanding, 20 Mass. (3 Pick.) 304 (1825). Cited as maintaining the contempt power on the state court level was State v. Frew & Hart, 24 W. Va. 416 (1884).

170. See, e.g., Gompers v. Bucks Stove & Range Co., 221 U.S. 418 (1911), citing Beck v. Railway Teamsters' Protective Union, 118 Mich. 497 (1898) and Sherry v. Perkins, 147 Mass. 212 (1888); American Foundries v. Tri-Cities Central Trades Council, 257 U.S. 184 (1921), citing *Beck*; Truax v. Corrigan, 257 U.S. 312 (1921), citing *Beck*, *Sherry*, Lindsay & Co. v. Montana Federation of Labor, 37 Mont. 264 (1908), Empire Theatre Co. v. Cloke, 53 Mont. 183 (1917), and Marx & Haas Jeans Clothing Co. v. Watson, 168 Mo. 133 (1902); Prudential Ins. Co. of America v. Cheek, 259 U.S. 530 (1922), citing Wallace v. Georgia, C. & N. Rwy., 94 Ga. 732 (1894), Atchison, T. & S. F. Ry. v. Brown, 80 Kan. 312 (1909), and St. Louis Southwestern Rwy. v. Hixon, 126 S.W. (Tex.) 338 (1910); Chicago, R. I. & P. Ry. v. Perry, 259 U.S. 548 (1922), citing *Brown*, *Wallace*, St. Louis Southwestern Ry. v. Griffin, 106 Tex. 477 (1914), and Cheek v. Prudential Ins. Co., 192 S.W. (Mo.) 387 (1916).

171. See, e.g., Gilbert v. Minnesota, 254 U.S. 325 (1920), citing State v. Holm, 139 Minn. 267 (1918) and Ex parte Meckel, 220 S.W. (Tex.) 81 (1920); Whitney v. California, 274 U.S. 357 (1927), citing People v. Steelik, 187 Cal. 361 (1921), State v. Laundy, 103 Or. 443 (1922) and People v. Ruthenberg, 229 Mich. 315 (1924); Gitlow v. New York, 268 U.S. 652 (1925), citing State v. Boyd, 86 N.J.L. 75 (1914), State v. Tachin, 92 N.J.L. 269 (1919), State v. McKee, 73 Conn. 18 (1900), People v. Most, 171 N.Y. 423 (1902), *Steelik*, and *Holm*.

172. 283 U.S. 697 (1931).

173. Ibid. at 715. See Respublica v. Oswald, 1 Dall. (Pa.) 319 (1788); People v. Wilson, 64 Ill. 195 (1872); Storey v. People, 79 Ill. 45 (1875); Cooper v. People ex rel. Wyatt, 13 Colo. 337 (1889); State ex rel. Attorney General v. Circuit Court of Eau Claire County, 97 Wis. 1 (1897); State v. Tugwell, 19 Wash. 238 (1898); State v. Rosewater, 60 Neb. 438 (1900).

174. Ibid. at 719. See Respublica v. Oswald, 1 Dall. (Pa.) 319 (1788); Respublica v. Dennie, 4 Yeates (Pa.) 267 (1805); Commonwealth v. Blanding, 20 Mass. (3 Pick.) 304 (1825); Brandreth v. Lance, 8 Paige Ch. (N.Y.) 24 (1839); N.Y. Juvenile Guardian Society v. Roosevelt, 7 Daly (N.Y.) 188 (1877); Sweeney v. Baker, 13 W. Va. 158 (1878); State ex rel. Liversey v. Judge of Civ. Dist. Ct., 34 La. Ann. 741 (1882); Jones, Varnum & Co. v. Townsend's Adm'x., 21 Fla. 431 (1885); Ex parte Neill, 22 S.W. (Tex.) 923 (1893); Dailey v. Superior Court of City and County of San Francisco, 112 Cal. 94 (1896); Lindsay & Co. v. Montana Federation of Labor, 37 Mont. 264 (1908); Ulster Square Dealer v. Fowler, 111 N.Y.S. 16 (1908); Mitchell v. Grand Lodge Free and Accepted Masons, 121 S.W. (Tex.) 178 (1909); Howell v. Bee Publishing Co., 100 Neb. 39 (1916); Star Co. v. Brush, 170 N.Y.S. 987 (1918); Star Co. v. Brush, 172 N.Y.S. 320 (1918); Star Co. v. Brush, 172 N.Y.S. 851 (1918); New Yorker Staats-Zeitung v. Nolan, 89 N.J. Eq. 387 (1918).

175. 303 U.S. 444 (1938).

176. Ibid. at 452. See Star Co. v. Brush, 172 N.Y.S. 851 (1918); Ex parte Campbell, 64 Cal. App. 300 (1923).

177. 354 U.S. 476 (1957).

178. Ibid. at 482.

179. Ibid. at 483. See Commonwealth v. Kneeland, 37 Mass. (20 Pick.) 206 (1838). Also see Commonwealth v. Buckley, 200 Mass. 346 (1909), for a development of the standards of obscenity listed at 354 U.S. at 489.

180. 376 U.S. 254 (1964). See Coleman v. MacLennan, 78 Kan. 711 (1908); McLean v. Merriman, 42 S.D. 394 (1920); Snively v. Record Publishing Co., 185 Cal. 565 (1921); City of Chicago v. Tribune Co., 307 Ill. 595 (1923); Salinger v. Cowles, 195 Iowa 873 (1923).

181. 376 U.S. at 280. The Court detailed why it considered *Coleman* v. *MacLennan* appropriate:

The State Attorney General, a candidate for reelection and a member of the commission charged with the management and control of the state school fund, sued a newspaper publisher for alleged libel in an article purporting to state facts relating to his official conduct in connection with a school-fund transaction. The defendant pleaded

privilege and the trial judge, over the plaintiff's objection, instructed the jury that
> where an article is published and circulated among voters for the sole purpose of
> giving what the defendant believes to be truthful information concerning a
> candidate for public office and for the purpose of enabling such voters to cast
> their ballot more intelligently, and the whole thing is done in good faith and
> without malice, the article is privileged, although the principal matters con-
> tained in the article may be untrue in fact and derogatory to the character of
> the plaintiff; and in such a case the burden is on the plaintiff to show actual
> malice in the publication of the article.

In answer to a special question, the jury found that the plaintiff had not proved actual
malice, and a general verdict was returned for the defendant. On appeal the Supreme
Court of Kansas, in an opinion by Justice Burch, reasoned as follows (78 Kan., at
724, 98 P., at 286):
> It is of the utmost consequence that the people should discuss the character and
> qualifications of candidates for their suffrages. The importance to the state and
> to society of such discussions is so vast, and the advantages derived are so great,
> that they more than counterbalance the inconvenience of private persons whose
> conduct may be involved, and occasional injury to reputations of individuals
> must yield to the public welfare, although at times such injury may be great.
> The public benefit from publicity is so great, and the chance of injury to private
> character so small, that such discussions must be privileged.

The court thus sustained the trial court's instruction as a correct statement of the law,
saying:
> In such a case the occasion gives rise to a privilege, qualified to this extent: any
> one claiming to be defamed by the communication must show actual malice or
> go remediless. This privilege extends to a great variety of subjects, and includes
> matters of public concern, public men, and candidates for office. (78 Kan., at
> 723, 98 P., at 285.)

376 U.S. at 280–82.
182. 376 U.S. at 277.
183. 236 U.S. 230 (1915). See Block v. City of Chicago, 239 Ill. 251 (1909); McKenzie v.
McClellan, 116 N.Y.S. 645 (1909); Higgins v. LaCroix, 119 Minn. 145 (1912).
184. 236 U.S. at 244.
185. 408 U.S. 665 (1972).
186. Ibid. at 685. See Ex parte Lawrence, 116 Cal. 298 (1897); Plunkett v. Hamilton, 136 Ga.
72 (1911); In re Grunow, 84 N.J.L. 235 (1913); Joslyn v. People, 67 Colo. 297 (1919).
187. In Ex parte Lawrence, 116 Cal. 298 (1897), the newsman simply claimed the information
given him was privileged, with no apparent attempt to base his claim on the state constitutional protections of speech and press. The court denied his claim. The reporter in
Plunkett v. Hamilton, 136 Ga. 72 (1911), told the court demanding his sources that

> he believed he would forfeit the respect and confidence of the community at large if he
> divulged the name of his informant, and that to do so would subject him to ridicule
> and contempt. In answer to a question by his counsel, as to what would be the effect
> of his answering the last question propounded, so far as his occupation as a newspaper
> reporter was concerned, he answered, "It would ruin me in my business; it would
> cause me to lose my position as a newspaper reporter for the Augusta Herald, and
> would prevent my ever engaging in the occupation of a newspaper reporter again."

Ibid. at 81. The newsman in In re Grunow, 84 N.J.L. 235 (1913), told the court his
reason for not revealing his sources:

> "I declined to give the sources of my information or the names of any person or per-
> sons who gave me any information about it and gave as my reason for such refusal
> that I was a newspaper reporter and therefore could not give up my sources of
> information."

Ibid. at 236. Replied the court:

> In effect he pleaded a privilege which finds no countenance in the law. Such an im-
> munity, as claimed by the defendant, would be far reaching in its effect and de-

trimental to the due administration of law. To admit of any such privilege would be to shield the real transgressor and permit him to go unwhipped of justice.

Ibid. In response to a request from a Colorado court that he reveal his sources, another newsman replied, "'I decline to answer that question for the reason it is private, confidential and personal business.'" Joslyn v. People, 67 Colo. 297, 300 (1919). He was held in contempt.

188. In discussing the impact on free speech and free press of compelling testimony, a North Dakota court said:

Much has been said of the sacred rights of free speech. It is always conceded that the right is sacred, but at times such sacred right[s] must give way to others even more sacred. It has never been claimed that it will protect a man in invading a church and interrupting the sermon with his free speech. The free right of speech will not protect a man in obstructing the streets of a crowded city; the free right of speech may not be used to interrupt even social gatherings or political meetings. Should it, then, be allowed to interrupt the courts of justice? Surely there must come a time when the rights of the free speaker are overshadowed by the rights of other men to unhampered justice. The right of free speech and the freedom of the press are as sacred to the members of this court as they are to the defendant, and, we dare say, will be longer upheld by them than by him; but such rights must not be considered unbridled license to vilify and scandalize. It is as much a crime to assert charges which one knows to be untrue as it is to remain silent if he believes some offense to have been committed. When given an opportunity to prove the truth of the article which he published, the defendant Nelson remained silent. When asked to state any reason, weak or strong, why he had even believed such an article to be true, he replies that he must not tell because to do so would violate a confidential relation. In this he merely imitates the thief who, caught with the goods upon him, insists that he has purchased them from "a tall, light-complexioned stranger."

State v. Nelson, 29 N.D. 155, 162–63 (1914).

189. See United Public Workers of America v. Mitchell, 330 U.S. 75 (1947), citing McAuliffe v. City of New Bedford, 155 Mass. 216 (1892). Oliver Wendell Holmes, Jr., then sitting on the Massachusetts bench, set the tone for future discussion when he wrote, "The petitioner may have a constitutional right to talk politics, but he has no constitutional right to be a policeman." 155 Mass. at 220.

190. Although Justice George Sutherland used no state court precedent in writing Grosjean v. American Press Co., 297 U.S. 233 (1936), state court support for that decision can be traced back to a Louisiana case of 1859 in which the court found a state tax which touched newspapers was not invalid under the free speech and free press clause. City of New Orleans v. Crescent Newspaper, 14 La. Ann. 804 (1859). See also In re Jager, 29 S.C. 438 (1888); Cowan v. Fairbrother, 118 N.C. 406 (1896); City of Norfolk v. Norfolk Landmark Publishing Co., 95 Va. 564 (1898).

191. In the opinion announced in Stromberg v. California, 283 U.S. 359 (1931), handed down about two weeks before Near v. Minnesota, 283 U.S. 697 (1931), Chief Justice Hughes did not delve into state court cases for historical commentary on the use of symbols, in particular red flags, in political discussion. State courts had heard at least two cases in this area and had decided that although political rights were involved, the state's police power was sufficient to regulate the use of banners such as the red flag. Neither of these cases was appealed to the Supreme Court. See People v. Burman, 154 Mich. 150 (1908); Commonwealth v. Karvonen, 219 Mass. 30 (1914).

192. The U.S. Supreme Court, in Talley v. California, 362 U.S. 60 (1960), determined: "Anonymous pamphlets, leaflets, brochures and even books have played an important role in the progress of mankind. Persecuted groups and sects from time to time throughout history have been able to criticize oppressive practices and laws either anonymously or not at all." Ibid. at 64. Two state court decisions, Ex parte Harrison, 212 Mo. 88 (1908) and State v. Babst, 104 Ohio St. 167 (1922), provided support for both the allowing and the disallowing of such anonymous speech, with the Missouri court supporting the notion that names could be left off political material.

193. In a series of decisions beginning with Railway Employees' Department, American Fed-

eration of Labor v. Hanson, 351 U.S. 225 (1956), the Supreme Court began investigating the relationship between union membership and lobbying for certain goals. The Supreme Court upheld the required membership under union shop provisions and determined that payment of dues and subsequent use of that money for political purposes, "on the present record . . . is no . . . infringement or impairment of First Amendment rights." Ibid. at 238. In Spayd v. Ringing Rock Lodge, 270 Pa. 67 (1921), however, the state court determined that a union could not expel a member who actively lobbied against the union's position, and in People ex rel. Clifford v. Scannell, 77 N.Y.S. 704 (1902), the state court determined that a union member could not campaign against the announced policy of his public employer.

194. The Supreme Court's encounter with offensive language and subsequent problems of breach of peace has ranged from the fighting words of Chaplinsky v. New Hampshire, 315 U.S. 568 (1942), through Cohen v. California, 403 U.S. 15 (1971), and beyond, with the Court's tolerance of indecent language varying according to the language's content and the conditions under which it was uttered. State court actions in cases such as State v. Warren, 113 N.C. 683 (1893), and Watters v. City of Indianapolis, 191 Ind. 671 (1922), also followed social standards of the time and, in these instances, curtailed expression.

195. In dealing with challenges to the Federal Election Campaign Act of 1971, the U.S. Supreme Court, in Buckley v. Valeo, 424 U.S. 1 (1976), wove its way through a complex maze of limitations on campaign contributions, upholding some while disallowing others as impermissible restraints on expression. State court actions in Adams v. Lansdon, 18 Idaho 483 (1910), and State v. Pierce, 163 Wis. 615 (1916), trod the same path some sixty years before.

196. For a preview of Sheppard v. Maxwell, 384 U.S. 333 (1966), see Herald-American Publishing Co. v. Lewis, 42 Utah 188 (1913). In that case, the newspaper involved claimed the state constitutional protections provided the press a shield from a contempt citation handed down for publishing material which made it difficult to obtain an impartial jury or a fair trial. The contempt citation stood. See also Globe Newspaper Co. v. Commonwealth, 188 Mass. 449 (1905). State courts allowed most gag rules to stand but voided some because of their unreasonable nature. Compare State ex rel. Dorrien v. Hazeltine, 82 Wash. 81 (1914) and Tate v. State ex rel. Raine, 132 Tenn. 131 (1915) with In re Shortridge, 99 Cal. 526 (1893) and Ex parte Foster, 71 S.W. (Tex.) 593 (1903).

197. 343 U.S. 495 (1952).

198. 301 U.S. 468 (1937).

199. See, e.g., Commonwealth v. Boston Transcript Co., 249 Mass. 477 (1924).

200. See Hines v. Davidowitz, 312 U.S. 52 (1941). Such duplication of state and federal laws was not found in other areas falling under free speech and free press litigation, such as libel and contempt of court.

201. See, e.g., Schenck v. United States, 249 U.S. 47 (1919).

202. Gitlow v. New York, 268 U.S. 652 (1925).

203. See Spies v. People, 122 Ill. 1 (1887) at 123 U.S. 131 (1887); Commonwealth v. Davis, 162 Mass. 510 (1895) at 167 U.S. 43 (1897); People ex rel. Attorney General v. News-Times Publishing Co., 35 Colo. 253 (1906) at Patterson v. Colorado ex rel. Attorney General, 205 U.S. 454 (1907); State v. Fox, 71 Wash. 185 (1912) at 236 U.S. 273 (1915); Cheek v. Prudential Ins. Co. of America, 192 S.W. (Mo.) 387 (1916) at 252 U.S. 567 (1920) and 223 S.W. (Mo.) 754 (1920) at 259 U.S. 530 (1922); State v. Tachin, 92 N.J.L. 269 (1919) at 254 U.S. 662 (1920); Dickinson v. Perry, 75 Okla. 25 (1919) at Chicago, R. I. & P. Ry. v. Perry, 259 U.S. 548 (1922); Hughes v. Kansas City Motion Picture Machine Operators Local 170, 282 Mo. 304 (1920) at 254 U.S. 632 (1920) and 257 U.S. 621 (1922); People ex rel. Doyle v. Atwell, 232 N.Y. 96 (1921) at 261 U.S. 590 (1923); People v. Gitlow, 234 N.Y. 132 (1922) at 268 U.S. 652 (1925); People v. Ruthenberg, 229 Mich. 315 (1924) at 273 U.S. 782 (1927).

204. Davis v. Massachusetts, 167 U.S. 43 (1897), aff'g, 162 Mass. 510 (1895); Fox v. Washington, 236 U.S. 273 (1915), aff'g, 71 Wash. 185 (1912); Chicago, R. I. & P. Ry. v. Perry, 259 U.S.. 548 (1922), aff'g, 75 Okla. 25 (1919); Prudential Ins. Co. of America v. Cheek, 259 U.S. 530 (1922), aff'g, 223 S.W. (Mo.) 754 (1920); Gitlow v. New York, 268 U.S. 652 (1925), aff'g, 234 N.Y. 132 (1922).

205. Although the justices did not rule on state court decisions in Wallace v. Georgia, C. & N. Rwy., 94 Ga. 732 (1894), Atchison, T. & S. F. Ry. v. Brown, 80 Kan. 312 (1909), or St. Louis Southwestern Ry. v. Griffin, 106 Tex. 477 (1914), they used the majority opinion in Chicago, R. I. & P. Ry. v. Perry, 259 U.S. 548 (1922) to indicate their disapproval of those state court decisions. The state court decisions had found that a "liberty of silence" existed as an opposite to freedom of speech and thus said that employers could not be required to give service letters to those no longer in their employ. In *Perry* and in Prudential Ins. Co. of America v. Cheek, 259 U.S. 530 (1922), the Court upheld the state's ability to require a service letter from employers by saying that such a requirement was not a deprivation of property without due process.

206. 274 U.S. 380 (1927).

207. 283 U.S. 359 (1931).

208. 283 U.S. 697 (1931).

209. Zechariah Chafee, Jr., in discussing the development of the free speech guarantees, recognizes the presence of such guarantees in state constitutions and then, though his discussion is aimed at the federal guarantees, slips back and forth in his writing between guarantee and guarantees, clause and clauses, constitution and constitutions. See Chafee, *Free Speech in the United States*, pp. 3–35.

210. In discussing a case in which a Fifth Amendment protection from state action was sought, Chief Justice John Marshall wrote:

> The constitution was ordained and established by the people of the United States for themselves, for their own government and not for the government of the individual States. Each State established a constitution for itself, and, in that constitution, provided such limitations and restrictions on the powers of its particular government as its judgment dictated. The people of the United States framed such a government as they supposed best adapted to their situation, and best calculated to promote their interests. The powers they conferred on this government were to be exercised by itself; and the limitations on power, if expressed in general terms, are naturally, and, we think, necessarily applicable to the government created by the instrument. They are limitations of power granted in the instrument itself; not of distinct governments, framed by different persons and for different purposes.
>
> If these propositions be correct, the 5th amendment must be understood as restraining the power of the general government, not as applicable to the States.

Barron v. City Council of Baltimore, 32 U.S. (7 Pet.) 243, 247 (1833).

Some state courts, however, may have believed that the Fifth Amendment had some application despite John Marshall. See Meredith Lang, *Defender of the Faith: The High Court of Mississippi 1817–1875* (University, Miss.: University of Mississippi Press, 1977), pp. 97, 101.

211. See State ex rel. Liversey v. Judge of Civ. Dist. Ct., 34 La. Ann. 741 (1882); Louthan v. Commonwealth, 79 Va. 196 (1884); Cincinnati Gazette Co. v. Timberlake, 10 Ohio St. 548 (1860); Riley v. Lee, 88 Ky. 603 (1889); State ex rel. Attorney General v. Circuit Court of Eau Claire County, 97 Wis. 1 (1897); Sillars v. Collier, 151 Mass. 50 (1890); Stuart v. Press Publishing Co., 82 N.Y.S. 401 (1903); Fitts v. City of Atlanta, 121 Ga. 567 (1905); Pavesich v. New England Life Ins. Co., 122 Ga. 190 (1905); State v. Boyd, 86 N.J.L. 75 (1914); Howell v. Bee Publishing Co., 100 Neb 39 (1916); State v. Pierce, 163 Wis. 615 (1916); People v. Steelik, 187 Cal. 361 (1921); In re Hickey, 149 Tenn. 344 (1923); Berg v. State, 233 P. (Okla.) 497 (1923).

212. State v. Tugwell, 19 Wash. at 250.

213. State v. Fox, 71 Wash. at 186.

214. People v. Gitlow, 234 N.Y. at 136. See also Denis v. Leclerc, 1 Mart. (La.) 297 (1811); Dickinson v. Perry, 75 Okla. 25 (1919).

215. State v. Mockus, 120 Me. at 97. See also State v. Kahn, 56 Mont. 108 (1919).

216. Dailey v. Superior Court of City and County of San Francisco, 112 Cal. at 97–98.

217. State v. Holm, 139 Minn. at 275.

PART II

The Twentieth-Century Search for the Meaning of Freedom of the Press

CHAPTER 2

The Deceptive "Right to Know": How Pessimism Rewrote the First Amendment*

Gerald J. Baldasty[†] and Roger A. Simpson [‡]

In the decade of the 1940s, particularly in the years just after World War II, freedom of the press, which had been newly elevated and protected by the Supreme Court in the 1930s, began to suffer the corrosive effects of doubt about the strength of the American political system. Among the devastations of war was the failure of the intellectuals' confidence in the mettle of the American citizenry. By the mid-1960s, one consequence was clear: the First Amendment no longer meant that the American press was expected to speak

*This article originally appeared in its present form (except for adjustments in style) in *Washington Law Review* 56:3, 365–395. Copyright © 1981, Washington Law Review. Reprinted by permission.

†Gerald J. Baldasty is a member of the faculty of the School of Communications at the University of Washington, where he teaches history of communication and mass media law. He is a member of the advisory board of the Washington Journalism Education Association and of the editorial board of *Journalism History*.

In his research he has shown special interest in media and political history in the United States prior to 1850 and has published in several scholarly journals, including *Journalism Quarterly* and *Communications Research*. Among his articles are "Criticism of Public Officials and Government in the New Nation" (with Mary Ann Yodelis-Smith), published in *Journal of Communication Inquiry*, and "Toward an Understanding of the First Amendment: Boston Newspapers, 1782–91" in *Journalism History*. In 1974 and 1976 he won the Warren Price Award for historical research, an award given annually by the History Division of the Association for Education in Journalism.

Baldasty earned his undergraduate degree in communications at the University of Washington, graduating *magna cum laude*, and was named a member of Phi Beta Kappa. He holds a master's degree in journalism from the University of Wisconsin and a doctorate from the University of Washington.

He has worked as a journalist for the Spokane *Spokesman-Review* and the Portland *Oregonian*.

‡Roger A. Simpson, a member of the faculty of the School of Communications at the University of Washington, teaches journalism and the history, law, and economics of the mass media. He also directs the Business and Economics Journalism Program at Washington and serves on the editorial board of *Journalism History*.

His research has paralleled his teaching interests but has dealt particularly with labor questions. His book, *Unionism or Hearst: The Seattle Post-Intelligencer Strike of 1936* (with William E. Ames) was published in 1978.

Simpson holds a bachelor's degree in journalism and a doctorate in communications from the University of Washington. His master's degree in journalism was earned at the University of Wisconsin.

Simpson has worked as a journalist for four daily newspapers, including the *Wall Street Journal* and the *Detroit Free Press*.

freely; it had begun to mean that much of what the press said had to be re-sponsive to assumptions about those who might receive the communication. The idea of a public "right to know" had begun to undermine the solid found-ations of press freedom.

Since 1964, the Court has elevated the idea of a right to know to such an extent that the traditional imperative of a right to speak, developed so exten-sively by the Supreme Court in the 1930s, can no longer be confidently assumed. Hollow rights have been advanced on behalf of consumers to justify governmental controls on press content. This article shows the origins of this wrongheaded theory of the First Amendment in the intellectual ferment of the years immediately after World War II. It examines the evolution of Court thinking in three areas of press law: libel, broadcast regulation, and commer-cial speech.[1]

Free Expression: 1919–39

Under Chief Justice Charles Evans Hughes, the Court began in 1931 to build a durable framework for freedom of the press.[2] Government restraint prior to publication was held to be unconstitutional.[3] The freedom to publish was elaborated into a freedom to distribute the products of publication.[4] More-over, the protection was held to include pamphlets and leaflets, the medium characteristic of society's dissidents, as well as the newspapers, books, and magazines of the commercial media.[5] The imposition of taxes to punish pub-lishers was deemed as abhorrent as outright government censorship.[6] Moreover, the Court proceeded steadily on the assumption it had made first in 1925, in *Gitlow* v. *New York*,[7] that liberty of the press was among the clus-ter of liberties protected from invasion by the states under the Fourteenth Amendment.

The radical speech cases in World War I had forced the Supreme Court to concentrate on finding a workable test of the limits of government power to punish speech. Dissenters fell victim to stiff antisedition legislation, en-forced willingly in the courts. However, in distinction to the widespread punishment of radical speech, the Supreme Court moved away in its delib-erations from the "reasonable tendency" test,[8] which one scholar termed "capable of ensnaring the most innocent speech,"[9] to the "clear and present danger test" enunciated by Justice Holmes in *Schenck* v. *United States*: "The question in every case is whether the words used are used in such circum-stances and are of such a nature as to create a clear and present danger that they will bring about the substantive evils that Congress has a right to prevent."[10] The test was to prove far more circumscribed than its libertarian admirers expected, but it did clearly credit a presumption of a right to speak to the voices of the day.

The spirit of freedom conveyed by the test and by its eloquent declara-tions by the Court was muted by zealous suppression of speech in the period.[11] The Court, unfortunately, consistently followed its declaration in *Gitlow* v. *New York*: "This freedom does not deprive a State of the primary and essential right of self-preservation; which so long as human governments endure, they cannot be denied."[12]

The events of the day obscure the steadiness of the Court's view of the political role of the press. In 1927, Justice Brandeis articulated the assumptions which he contended underlay First Amendment interpretations by the Court in that decade: "Those who won our independence believed that the final end of the State was to make men free to develop their faculties; and that in its government the deliberative forces should prevail over the arbitrary."[13] The freedom to "think as you will and to speak as you think" was essential to the search for political truth. Freedom of speech necessarily churned some falsity and error into the public discussion, but that did not warrant government efforts to prevent or punish falsity. "If there be time to expose through discussion the falsehoods and fallacies, to avert evil by the processes of education, the remedy to be applied is more speech, not enforced silence."[14] Brandeis argued that suppression took its greatest toll on the individual, and then, as a consequence, on the society:

> [The founders of the nation] knew that order cannot be secured merely through fear of punishment for its infraction; that it is hazardous to discourage thought, hope and imagination; that fear breeds repression; that repression breeds hate; that hate menaces stable government; that the path of safety lies in the opportunity to discuss freely supposed grievances and proposed remedies; and that the fitting remedy for evil counsels is good ones. Believing in the power of reason as applied through public discussion, they eschewed silence coerced by law—the argument of force in its worst form. Recognizing the occasional tyrannies of governing majorities, they amended the Constitution so that free speech and assembly should be guaranteed.[15]

The Court applied the First Amendment unevenly in the decade after the war, but its view was fixed consistently on the claims of speakers for protection under the Constitution.

Free Expression in the Postwar Years

In the years after World War II, troublesome.new ideas about the relationship of press and citizen took form outside the Court and worked their way into judicial consciousness. By the 1960s, these ideas were shaping Court responses in significant areas of First Amendment interpretation.

Of the many currents of intellectual change in the postwar years, four sources are examined here. Each contributes some germ of the ideas manifest in the recent Supreme Court free press decisions. No single idea or theory has been adopted wholesale, but the influence is evident nevertheless. The first source is the significant reconception of the role of the press completed by the Commission on Freedom of the Press in 1947.[16] What the commission propounded essentially as a warning to the press was developed in a parallel legal theory at the same time by the teacher and philosopher Alexander Meiklejohn. His extraordinarily influential lectures, published as *Free Speech and Its Relation to Self-Government*,[17] are the second source. Third, ideas about relative rights of the press and its audience were emerging from administrative experience in the one realm of the press where the government had unchallenged freedom to regulate—broadcasting. Finally, the Court itself in the postwar years began to speak differently about the listener in this society and his place in the scheme of the First Amendment.

In its formal report, the commission presented standards of performance for the press and warned that the value of an adequately informed citizenry was so great that the government would be justified in meeting needs not adequately served by the press itself. The call was temperate; it simply urged the media to offset the adverse consequences of their great economic power by showing greater social responsibility. The commission's proposal for government involvement was little more than recognition of the changes in government activities in the depression and war years:

> Nor is there anything in the First Amendment or in our political tradition to prevent the government from participating in mass communications: to state its own case, to supplement private sources of information and to propose standards for private emulation. Such participation by government is not dangerous to the freedom of the press.[18]

Press irritation at this apparent endorsement of the government's developing relationship to the media distracted attention from the underlying reason for the proposal. It was the malaise of the citizenry that alarmed the commission. The rational man of the Enlightenment was an unrealistic model for the confused and self-interested citizen of the postwar years, wrote William Hocking in a commission document:[19] "The democracy of mental participation by the people in the main lines of public action runs shallow."[20] The times demanded the citizen's active interest, Hocking wrote, but the citizen was unwilling to engage in difficult thinking. Moreover, the institutions of family, school, church, and the press had failed to give Americans the support "needed for carrying out their citizen duties. When these free authorities are weak or absent, the weaker truth-seekers may so far flounder as to set up a prima facie case for a reversion to authoritative control, to the loss of that mental power on which social progress depends."[21] Zechariah Chafee, Jr., was as pessimistic at the outset of his review of First Amendment law, *Government and Mass Communications*:

> Today there is reason to suppose that the self-correcting process, although commonly considered to function fully, does not in fact function, to our danger.... There are no such natural harmonies and balances in a community as democratic theory used to assume.... Our people have put too much trust in the automatic tendencies of our society to right itself. We have found that we cannot depend on unmanaged processes, whether in economics or in communications.[22]

The commission exhorted the media to improve their performance and considered ways that government might inspire, but not enforce, such improvement. Despite its doubts about the political system, the commission kept its faith that freedom of speech and press had to be assured. "Valuable ideas may be put forth first in forms that are crude, indefensible, or even dangerous. They need the chance to develop through free criticism as well as the chance to survive on the basis of their ultimate worth. Hence the man who publishes ideas requires special protection."[23] Then the commission pondered how the government was to act toward speaker and listener. Both, after all, shaped the public discourse and served the ends of a vital community. The conclusion was artful: "Hence it is that, although there are these two direct interests, *only one of them in simple conditions, needs protection*. To protect the freedom of the issuer is to protect the interest of the consumer and in general that of the community also."[24] If changing conditions warranted some degree of interest in the consumer, the commission suggested encouragement of greater access to the press. It did not propose framing new First Amendment rights around the interests of listeners and readers.

Hocking, disillusioned about the malaise of the citizens, leaned further than the commission toward shaping mass communication to compensate for that indifference. "With the rights of editors and publishers to express themselves there must be associated a right of the public to be served with a substantial and honest basis of fact for its judgments of public affairs."[25]

The phrase, "right of the public," was ill chosen. Hocking's zest for a new approach to political communication had led him to infer from the 1945 Supreme Court decision in *Associated Press* v. *United States*[26] that the Court had set about to create a new level of protection for consumers of news. The decision, which upheld an antitrust prosecution of the Associated Press news service cooperative, had concluded only that the First Amendment did not bar such regulation of the press.

But Hocking wondered if much more could be read into the decision. "It is not clear from the opinions in this case how far the Court is prepared to go beyond this somewhat negative obligation of government to restrain restraints on the free flow of ideas. *Is it prepared to uphold positive standards of performance?* [Emphasis added.]"[27] As Hocking, the philosopher, interpreted the law, public welfare assumed a place of such importance that the idea of free speech must yield. "Originally, freedom of speech and press were liberties which chiefly concerned individuals who had opinions to utter; today their readers and hearers, the consumers of opinion, are equally concerned."[28] Detached from the practicalities of both journalism and the courts, Hocking was unable to sense the difficulties should the courts ever try to uphold "positive standards of performance" for the press.

Alexander Meiklejohn also sensed the forces reshaping the postwar conception of freedom and conceived a philosophical retreat that brilliantly answered the pessimism of the Commission on Freedom of the Press. He argued for absolute protection of speech that contributed to self-governance. Unlike Hocking, whose tolerance for free speech did not include calculated falsehoods, Meiklejohn wanted no such curb on political speech, whatever its motive or nature.

> Shall we give a hearing to those who hate and despise freedom, to those who, if they had the power, would destroy our institutions? Certainly, yes! Our action must be guided, not by their principles, but by ours. We listen, not because they desire to speak, but because we need to hear. If there are arguments against our theory of government, our policies in war or in peace, we the citizens, the rulers, must hear and consider them for ourselves. That is the way of public safety. It is the program of self-government.[29]

It was the need of the voter for information and discussion that warranted the state's protection of speakers. The protection was not for the speaker, but for political ideas, and this more than anything else reflected the new philosophical basis of the First Amendment. "What is essential is not that everyone shall speak, but that everything worth saying shall be said."[30]

The advocacy of absolute freedom in political matters camouflaged Meiklejohn's interest in controlled political discussion. He used the model of the town meeting approvingly to show how actions of a moderator, including the setting of agendas, prevention of redundant speeches, and balancing of presentations, contributed to the quality of discussion. Such interventions were warranted, he said, because "the point of ultimate interest is not the words of the speakers, but the minds of the hearers. The final aim of the meeting is the voting of wise decisions."[31] To make the "wise decisions" that were the essence of self-government, the voter had to hear all possible ideas and opinions. If state action denied him any ideas pertinent to his political duty, that action was proscribed by the First Amendment. But that amendment posed no barrier to the state playing a moderator's role. It was necessary for the state to so act if communication was to serve "the thinking process of the community."[32]

Meiklejohn's desire to protect political speech in the interests of self-governance was warranted at the time and is today. His choice of the town meeting analogy was hopeful, but unrealistic. The process by which Americans informed themselves of their world, punctuated as it was by occasional trips by some of them to polling places, was in no sense equivalent to the structured political participation of persons in a town meeting. Yet, Meiklejohn argued that the mass communication system should respond to the one as though it were the other.

Speech that did not contribute to governance was private and merited a different order of protection. "The First Amendment has other work to do," Meiklejohn wrote.[33] "It has no concern about the 'needs of many men to express their opinions.'"[34] Those needs were private matters, and the resulting speech could be denied on occasion, as long as due process was satisfied.[35] Yet, did not self-governance depend simply on the "needs of many men to express their opinions"?

Meiklejohn rightly distinguished kinds of speech according to the degree of protection each should be accorded. "The constitutional status of a merchant advertising his wares, of a paid lobbyist fighting for the advantage of his client, is utterly different from that of a citizen who is planning for the general welfare."[36]

But it was not clear how political speech was to be distinguished from those purely private kinds of expression, a confusion that Meiklejohn created in subsequent commentaries. In the original presentation of his theory, the voter was at the center of his view of political communication, but the realm of communication that was protected was obviously much broader than matters that pertained to pending elections. What was protected, he said in 1948, was discussion of public issues. But in 1961, when a student of Meiklejohn's philosophy asserted that "novels or dramas or paintings or poems" were not relevant to the political process,[37] Meiklejohn objected: "The people do need novels and dramas and paintings and poems, 'because they will be called upon to vote.'"[38] In theory, then, political speech might encompass much of what is communicated to the public, a broad definition that would free courts from making difficult decisions. But Meiklejohn's own waffling on the breadth of speech that merited absolute protection was reflected in, if not a cause of, the Supreme Court's own wide-ranging application of the First Amendment in subsequent libel decisions.

The Meiklejohnian heritage includes both a reverence for political speech and the harmful notion that mass communication should be regulated in order to give the citizen information to prepare him for the task of voting. That preparation had previously been assumed to be the consequence of a society in which citizens spoke freely; Meiklejohn encouraged those architects of the brave new world who felt that the survival of the nation could not be left to chance.

The idea of regulated mass communication was more than a philosophical exercise in the late 1940s, however. Within a year after Meiklejohn's lectures first were published, the Federal Communications Commission appeared to be applying his town meeting analogy to the nation's commercial broadcasting system. In 1949, the FCC reversed its 1941 prohibition of licensee editorial advocacy and formulated its two-pronged "fairness doctrine."

> This requires that licensees devote a reasonable percentage of their broadcasting time to the discussion of public issues of interest in the community served by their stations and that such programs be designed so that the public has a reasonable opportunity to hear different opposing positions on the public issues of interest and importance in the community.[39]

Although concern for the "public interest" was expressed as early as 1927 in the Federal Radio Act,[40] the FCC articulated that interest in terms remarkably similar to those used by Meiklejohn. Although the right of free speech was not to be impaired by FCC regulation, broadcasters were told that the publicly owned airwaves were dedicated to helping citizens form opinions on public issues. With approval and emphasis, the commission quoted from a congressional debate on passage of the Radio Act: "If enacted into law, the broadcasting privilege will not be a right of selfishness. It will rest upon an assurance of public interest to be served."[41] Of course, it was alarm about commercial selfishness that motivated the act and the subsequent actions of the FCC, but the commission, in justifying its fairness requirements, paid little attention to the value of selfish opinions or ideas. "The needs and interests of the general public . . . can only be satisfied by making available to them for their consideration and acceptance or rejection, of varying and conflicting views held by responsible elements of the community."[42]

But even as the commission instituted its version of a Meiklejohnian mass communication system, the philosopher himself was despairing of the futility of the effort, at least in radio.

> But never was a human hope more bitterly disappointed. The radio as it now operates among us is not free. Nor is it entitled to the protection of the First Amendment. It is not engaged in the task of enlarging and enriching human communication. It is engaged in making money. And the First Amendment does not intend to guarantee men freedom to say what some private interest pays them to say for its own advantage. It intends only to make men free to say what, as citizens, they think, what they believe, about the general welfare.[43]

The government, however, was trying to compensate for the obvious faults of a private system by enforcing standards of conduct intended to serve an idealized voter. The experiment demonstrated the considerable difference between the conduct of a closely knit corporate body of the type described by Meiklejohn in his discussion of town meetings and that disparate, divided, partially disinterested body called the nation.

Listener interests also attracted the attention of the Supreme Court in the 1940s, but without any substantial reduction in the protection afforded to speakers. The Court acknowledged that the right to speak implied there was a listener. But the justices joined the spirit of the times in finding new interests and value in those previously unrecognized listeners.

Cases in point are two Jehovah's Witnesses decisions of the mid-1940s. In *Martin* v. *City of Struthers*,[44] the Court reaffirmed the right to distribute religious literature by invalidating an Ohio ordinance that forbade knocking, ringing doorbells, or otherwise summoning occupants of a house to the door. Without further comment, Justice Black wrote that the freedom to distribute literature "necessarily protects the right to receive it."[45] Two years later, in *Marsh* v. *Alabama*, Justice Black, again writing for the majority, elaborated: "And we have recognized that the preservation of a free society is so far dependent upon the right of each individual citizen to receive such literature as he himself might desire that a municipality could not [prohibit door-to-door distribution]."[46]

The decisions served to exalt the speaking rights of the Jehovah's Witnesses and thus echoed traditional First Amendment values. Yet, the protection was linked to previously unconsidered rights to receive information, and the door was opened to elaboration and confusion of that idea.

The cases asserted simply that the "right to receive information" implied no limit of any kind on the speaker or publisher of the information; it was a derivative right appropriately encompassed by the First Amendment.[47] The Court reasoned similarly when it invalidated a state law requiring registration of union organizers: the law abridged both kinds of rights, the organizers' rights to speak and the rights of the workers to hear what organizers had to say.[48] At issue was a vote for union representation, a problem analogous to that advanced by Meiklejohn as the most obvious sort of protected speech, and the Court affirmed the workers' rights to "discuss and be informed concerning this choice."[49]

But did the right to be informed imply any control on the speaker, any responsibility to speak in a certain way or to speak truthfully? Justice Jackson said emphatically that it did not:

> But it cannot be the duty, because it is not the right, of the state to protect the public against false doctrine. The very purpose of the First Amendment is to foreclose public authority from assuming a guardianship of the public mind through regulating the press, speech, and religion. In this field every person must be his own watchman for truth, because the forefathers did not trust any government to separate the true from the false for us.... As I read their intentions, this liberty was protected because they knew of no other way by which *free* men could conduct representative democracy.[50]

The legacy of the 1940s was the emergence of an idea that one element in the constitutional theory of freedom of the press is the interest of the public or the citizen in receiving information. The Supreme Court had begun to express this troublesome doctrine as it listened to influential legal and philosophical arguments of the time. Moreover, a federal agency entrusted with authority over an increasingly powerful medium of public communication was using a concept of listener rights as the basis for mandating the airing of balanced political opinions.

The Refereed Debate of the 1960s and 1970s

The intellectual ferment of the 1940s, and the discovery of First Amendment rights (albeit vague ones) for listeners, influenced a series of important Supreme Court decisions in the 1960s and 1970s. The justices gave legal life to concepts heretofore strictly philosophical and in so doing changed or extended the original form of the ideas. More important, the law developed in at least two directions, which will be referred to here as the *Debate Model* and the *Right-to-Know Model*. In these years, members of the Court fashioned two interpretations of First Amendment rights which are not only widely divergent but, indeed, totally incompatible with one another. These interpretations stand as monuments to "the dangers that beset us when we lose sight of the First Amendment itself, and march forth in blind pursuit of its 'values.'"[51]

The Debate Model

Meiklejohn's concern for a properly informed electorate surfaced most clearly in the Supreme Court's 1964 decision *New York Times Co.* v. *Sullivan*.[52] Meiklejohn himself praised the case, saying, "It is an occasion for dancing in the streets."[53] Like Meiklejohn, Justice Brennan stressed the need and value of debate of public issues to produce an informed populace and electorate. In 1964, the Court sought to safeguard that debate by providing extensive—but not absolute—legal protection from defamation actions for those disseminating information and opinion about public officials.

The case evolved from a 1960 advertisement in the *New York Times*, which charged that the Rev. Dr. Martin Luther King, Jr., faced harassment, imprisonment, and perhaps even death because of his crusade for black civil rights. A number of Southern officials sued the *New York Times* for libel, and L. B. Sullivan, one of Montgomery, Alabama's three city commissioners, won $500,000 against the *Times* in Alabama, a verdict upheld by that state's supreme court.[54] The Supreme Court overturned the judgment and echoed Meiklejohn's philosophy by emphasizing the need for public discussion of public issues.[55]

Justice Brennan, writing for the majority, reviewed the history of libel and sedition in America and found "a profound national commitment" to the principle of "uninhibited, robust, and wide-open" debate on public issues.[56] Such debate, he wrote, "may well include vehement, caustic, and sometimes unpleasantly sharp attacks on government and public officials," but this debate was nonetheless crucial "to the end that government may be responsive to the will of the people and that changes may be obtained by lawful means."[57] The statement at issue in *New York Times Co.* v. *Sullivan* concerned civil rights, a topic of major controversy, and thus deserved First Amendment protection: "The present advertisement, as an expression of grievance and protest on one of the major public issues of our times, would seem clearly to qualify for the constitutional protection."[58] To emphasize the necessity of public debate, the Court acknowledged that even error merits some constitutional protection. Justice Brennan wrote that "erroneous statement is inevitable in free debate" and insisted that "it must be protected if the freedoms of expression are to have the 'breathing space' that they 'need to survive.'"[59] A rule of absolute truth in public debate "dampens the vigor and limits the variety of public debate."[60]

The Court was unwilling to accept all error, however, and excluded deliberately or recklessly false statements from constitutional protection.[61] The marketplace of ideas was not completely free from control.

Significantly, Justice Brennan valued free speech and press not as individual rights of self-expression but as contributions to proper governance. The *New York Times* advertisement "communicated information, expressed opinion, recited grievances, protested claimed abuses, and sought financial support on behalf of a movement whose existence and objectives were matters of the *highest public interest and concern.* [Emphasis added.]"[62] And Justice Brennan contended, "The general proposition that freedom of expression upon *public questions* is secured by the First Amendment has long been settled by our decisions . . . 'to assure unfettered interchange of ideas for the bringing about of political and social changes desired by the people.' [Emphasis added.]"[63] As Brennan stressed, the *"protection of the public* [emphasis added]" required full discussion and information.[64]

Three aspects of the *New York Times* case would figure prominently in the future. First, although only the speaker received special legal protection, the majority opinion acknowledged that listener interests constituted a vital ingredient in public debate; "free" speech, of necessity, thus included the listener as well as the speaker. Second, the Court introduced a new fault requirement: public officials (the obvious targets of criticism in public debate) must show that the press acted with knowledge of falsity or reckless disregard of the truth.[65] Some error could be tolerated, but lying and reckless reporting would threaten the integrity of the debate and thus the listener would not receive information vital to good governance. Such a provision would necessitate scrutiny of the behavior of individual journalists and thus entail examination of the news process. The attempt to impose a measure of purity on the public debate added controls far more stringent than those of Meiklejohn, but the new fault standard was a logical development due to the Court's concern for the listener. Listeners had no need for—indeed, they would be harmed by—irresponsible speakers. Third, the words *public debate* were not self-defining. Was the public debate in the *New York Times* case acceptable because the justices sympathized with the civil rights movement?[66] And, most important, what did the listener need to know to assure proper governance?

The progeny of *New York Times Co.* v. *Sullivan* follow the same basic commitment to freedom of speech and press as part of a larger goal of proper governance. Speech and press are weighed and valued according to their ability to promote that goal, and the parties in libel suits are categorized according to the degrees and nature of their involvement in public debate.[67]

This process of weighing speech with societal interest in good government led to an increasing involvement of the Court in the operations of the press, as demonstrated in 1966 by *Curtis Publishing Co.* v. *Butts* and its companion case, *Associated Press* v. *Walker*.[68] The major issue in these cases was defining public officials or public figures, but the added dimension of particular importance here derives from the Court's attention to the fault standard first devised in *New York Times.*

In *Curtis Publishing Co.* v. *Butts*, the *Saturday Evening Post* had accused University of Georgia athletic director Wally Butts of fixing a Georgia-Alabama football game; in *Associated Press* v. *Walker*, the Associated Press carried stories indicating that Walker had led segregationist rioters.[69] In reviewing both cases, the Court analyzed the process involved in news gathering.

Writing for a plurality of four, Justice Harlan cited impermissible any "extreme departure from the standards of investigation and reporting ordinarily adhered to by responsible publishers."[70] What followed was nothing less than a wholesale critique of the *Post*'s news process. According to Justice Harlan, the Butts story "was in no sense 'hot news,'" elementary precautions and important sources had been ignored, the *Post* writer did not know enough about football, and the magazine's attitude was poor.[71] On the other hand, the Associated Press reporter in *Walker* apparently suffered from no such character failings; by judicial fiat the stories were "hot news" which was presented in good faith and thus served the listener well. Chief Justice Warren, although disagreeing with the plurality's "extreme departure" standard, upheld the examination of the news process by endorsing the "reckless disregard" standard from *New York Times*.[72] A majority clearly favored scrutiny of the news process to guarantee the purity of the public debate.

Such excursions into the newsroom and into the thoughts, knowledge, or attitude of individual reporters are fraught with problems. Almost a half century earlier Justice Brandeis argued, "Courts are ill-equipped to make the investigations which should precede a determination of the limitations which should be set upon any property right in news or of the circumstances under which news gathered by a private agency should be deemed affected with a public interest."[73] Justice Brandeis wanted the Court to eschew such involvement in the news process and argued that the courts would be "powerless" to create adequate standards or to create the "machinery required for enforcement of such regulations." He urged judicial restraint: "Considerations such as these should lead us to decline to establish a new rule of law in the effort to redress a newly disclosed wrong, although the propriety of some remedy appears to be clear."[74] Justice Black's dissent in *Curtis* and *Walker* echoes the Brandeis concern that courts should not meddle in the news process:

> If this precedent is followed, it means that we must in all libel cases hereafter weigh the facts and hold that all papers and magazines guilty of gross writing or reporting are constitutionally liable, while they are not if the quality of the reporting is approved by the majority of us. . . .
> It strikes me that the Court is getting itself in the same quagmire in the field of libel in which it is now helplessly struggling in the field of obscenity. . . . In fact, the Court is suggesting various experimental expedients in libel cases, all of which boil down to a determination of how offensive to this Court a particular libel judgment may be, either because of its immense size or because the Court does not like the way an alleged libelee was treated.[75]

In the 1970s, the Court followed the basic patterns established in the 1960s cases, although disputes arose over the definition of public debate. Just how much information—and on what topics—did the informed listener need? In *Rosenbloom* v. *Metromedia, Inc.*, a plurality of the Court provided the broadest definition of acceptable public debate.[76] That breadth evaporated three years later, in *Gertz* v. *Robert Welch, Inc.*,[77] when the Court turned away from the expanding Meiklejohnian concept of definition of public issues and instead endorsed a truncated Meiklejohnian view reminiscent of that expressed in *Curtis* and *Walker.* Justice Powell, writing for the Court, narrowed the definition of public figure:

> Hypothetically, it may be possible for someone to become a public figure through no purposeful action of his own, but the instances of truly involuntary public figures must be exceedingly rare. For the most part, those who attain this status have assumed roles of especial prominence in the affairs of society. Some occupy positions of such persuasive power and influence that they are deemed public figures for all purposes. More commonly, those classed as public figures have thrust themselves to the forefront of particular public controversies in order to influence the resolution of the issues involved. In either event, they invite attention and comment.[78]

The Supreme Court has followed the *Gertz* decision in three cases.[79] These cases provide no new discussion on the Debate Model itself and generally provide no new criteria for status of public figure other than what can be found in *Gertz.* Their significance is in their narrow construction of public concern; in all three cases, libel plaintiffs were construed by the Court to be private figures. The public had no need for information about them.

In one late 1970s case, the Court returned to an examination of the news process. *Herbert* v. *Lando*[80] grew out of a libel suit by Lt. Col. Anthony Herbert against CBS, for a report of "Sixty Minutes," and Barry Lando, the show's producer, for an *Atlantic Monthly* magazine article.

Herbert sought extensive pretrial discovery to ascertain whether the defendants had acted with actual malice. In so doing, he asked a large number of questions regarding the news process. Defendants sought to shut off the discovery process, arguing for a limited constitutional protection of the news process from invasion.[81]

The *Herbert* majority rejected the defendants' argument and ruled that state of mind and other aspects of the news process always had been involved in the fault standard of *New York Times.*[82] That case based the press right to print not on the individual speaker's First Amendment rights, but on the good of society and public debate. Well-behaved reporters were just one ingredient of a well-run public debate; society would lose much, the Court implied, from misbehavior.

In *Herbert* v. *Lando,* Justice White argued that the investigation into the editorial process would only aid the reporter in pointing out good behavior when it occurred.[83] Such rosy views aside, the ruling allows courts to make judgments about the reasonableness of the editorial process.

Four important assumptions underlie the Court's attitudes in the defamation cases. First, the Court majority has assumed that generally the people (listeners) can make proper decisions based on wide-ranging, conflicting, and even false information. The actual malice rule excludes lies from the marketplace, but honest error can be tolerated. By allowing debate and concomitant error, the Court has signaled some belief in the public's ability to differentiate between truth and error. Second, the Court consistently has viewed free speech and press not as a separate entity deserving nurturing, but as part of a larger process; Justice Brennan and others clearly see free speech and press as contributing to good government. Third, although the listener has no legal rights, his presence is quite clear. Indeed, since the *raison d'etre* of free speech and press is an informed listener, expression unrelated to government is entitled to only limited protection. But the very difficulty in arriving at workable definitions of public speech—necessitated by such concern for the listener—compounds a difficult situation. Justice Brennan, invoking Meiklejohn, writes, "Education in all its phases, the achievement of philosophy and the sciences, literature and the arts, all fall within the subjects of 'governing importance' that the first amendment absolutely protects from abridgement."[84] But the Court has construed public speech much more narrowly than would Justice Brennan, especially since *Gertz*. In comparing *Rosenbloom* v. *Metromedia, Inc.*[85] with *Hutchinson* v. *Proxmire*[86] and *Wolston* v. *Reader's Digest Association*,[87] the great latitude the Court possesses in defining public speech becomes quite clear. In reality, the protection for the speaker behind the actual malice defense may be deep, but it is nonetheless quite narrow. Fourth, the actual malice standard may be a Pandora's box; the malice standard appears at first to protect a speaker's rights, but it also invites close scrutiny and evaluation of the speaker's behavior and attitude by the courts.

The Right-to-Know Model

The second model of free speech and press differs greatly from the Debate Model. While the Debate Model, under Meiklejohn's influence, indirectly recognized that listeners had needs and particular interests and some type of vaguely defined nonlegal "rights," only in the Right-to-Know Model are the listener's rights legally binding and the rights of the speaker circumscribed. A problem arises, however, in adjudicating the new-found legal status of listener vis-à-vis speaker. Here the marketplace is invaded by a third party with additional interests: the governmental agency.

Broadcasting. Five years after *New York Times*, the Supreme Court dealt with broadcast regulation in reviewing the FCC's fairness doctrine in the landmark case *Red Lion Broadcasting Co.* v. *FCC*.[88] As in *New York Times*, the Court stressed the importance of wide-ranging debate on public issues. Justice White, for the majority, wrote that the goal of the First Amendment was "producing an informed public capable of conducting its own affairs."[89] "Vigorous debate of controversial issues of importance and concern to the public" was central to the public interest.[90] Justice White also invoked the theme of the marketplace of ideas: "It is the purpose of the First Amendment to preserve an uninhibited marketplace of ideas in which truth will ultimately prevail."[91]

Despite these pious assertions of commitment to public discussion and to the marketplace of ideas, the majority in *Red Lion* departed from the philosophy of *New York Times*. Justice White gave paramount importance not to the speaker, but to the listener; he reduced the freedom of the speaker dramatically and cast doubt on the existence and value of the traditional concept of the marketplace of ideas. In *Red Lion*, the Court wrote into law the long-standing interests of the audience and gave these interests not equality, but preeminence over those of the speaker:

> But the people as a whole retain their interest in free speech by radio and their collective right to have the medium function consistently with the ends and purposes of the First Amendment. *It is the right of the viewers and listeners, not the right of the broadcasters, which is paramount.* [Emphasis added.][92]

The interests of the listeners were, of course, considered and valued in *New York Times*, its progeny, and even in 1940s thought. None of these, however, elevated the listener to legal dominance. *Red Lion* magnified the listener's rights while concomitantly diminishing those of the speakers. Justice White noted that broadcasters had only the "temporary privilege" of using designated frequencies and that even then there was little latitude for action.[93] A licensee, he wrote, was nothing more than "a proxy or fiduciary with obligations to present those views and voices which are representative of his community."[94] The renewal of a broadcast license or the granting of a new license depends on the "willingness to present representative community views on controversial issues."[95] The government itself, through the Federal Communications Commission, emerges as the so-called neutral umpire to enforce society's interest in representative and fair programming.[96]

The assumptions in *Red Lion* merit scrutiny, for they reveal the major differences in the assumptions behind the Debate Model and the Right-to-Know Model. In *New York Times* and its progeny, the Court assumed that some sort of a marketplace of ideas (albeit limited) existed and that protection of speakers' rights would help operation of the marketplace. Implicit in the libel cases was a belief that members of the audience were listening and that they were probably intelligent enough to discern right from wrong. Purposeful falsehood was excluded, but honest error could remain. Milton's argument that truth would indeed vanquish falsehood seemed twisted, since the Court insisted that purposeful lies and reckless errors be excluded from the marketplace.[97]

In *Red Lion*, the Court demonstrates little confidence in speakers or in the ability of truth to succeed in its Miltonic battle with falsehood. As the Court sees it, the marketplace of ideas cannot exist without some sort of intervention by some agency such as the Federal Communications Commission. Indeed, as Justice White's majority opinion demonstrates, broadcast regulation (and, in particular, the fairness doctrine) is an attempt to *create* a marketplace where one does not already exist.

As Judge Bazelon argued three years later, the whole theory of regulation of broadcast content was wrongheaded. Dissenting in *Brandywine-Main Line Radio, Inc.* v. *FCC*,[98] Judge Bazelon noted that a controversial right-wing broadcaster, providing a unique (although one-sided, controversial, and venomous) service in a large metropolitan area, was denied a license renewal because the programming at that one small station was not balanced and fair. Never mind that the metropolitan area may have lost those opinions altogether; never mind that another station in that metropolitan area might balance the right-wing station; never mind that enforcement of this artificial marketplace of ideas was actually excluding ideas. Indeed, the FCC insisted that each station be balanced and fair, so that the imaginary and fragile listener who heard only one station would not be misled.

In *Red Lion*, there is no encouragement or belief in a free and unfettered exchange of ideas among thinking and rational persons. Broadcasters are required to be fair and balanced so that they do not deceive the listening public. Such a rule casts doubt upon the ability of the listeners to make their own rational decisions based on the information before them and this is incompatible with classic notions of the marketplace of ideas. Despite the rhetoric of public debate and a marketplace of ideas, the majority in *Red Lion* rejects the concept of a marketplace and, in effect, denies the public's ability to make rational decisions from the information placed before it. Indeed, a third party emerges to referee the debate to assure that all is fair and that the listener is not hurt. Milton's words could best be rephrased: Truth would defeat error in an open contest so long as an umpire was present to require that there was a reasonable balance of opinion disseminated.

Further attacks on the premise of the marketplace of ideas and on the value of information freely exchanged came in *Columbia Broadcasting System, Inc.* v. *Democratic Nat'l Comm.*[99] Again, the Court paid ritualistic attention to the need for public debate and then reiterated the *Red Lion* claim that the rights of the viewers and listeners were paramount, not the rights of the broadcasters.[100] The Court continued to weigh speech issues in favor of the listener; the broadcaster still was a public trustee or proxy who acted not in his own interests but in those of the greater public.[101]

The critical portion of *CBS* v. *DNC*, however, came when the Court dealt with residual issues from *Red Lion*. Justice White's proclamation in *Red Lion* that listeners' rights were paramount sparked some hope for a right of access to broadcasting. The reasoning seemed logical: if listeners' rights were paramount, listeners should have some say in the content of the medium. Nevertheless, in *CBS* v. *DNC*, the Court rejected any such right of access. The Court noted that members of the audience who seek to take messages to other members of the audience were neither the best judges of the value of their own ideas or of the best way to present those ideas.[102]

Chief Justice Burger wrote, in the majority opinion, that broadcasters, not members of the public, should determine which ideas will be broadcast.[103] The opinion was no endorsement of journalistic rights, however. Rather, journalistic discretion was preserved because public access would be chaotic and because listeners just did not have the ability to provide thoughtful or intelligent expression of their own views.

Ironically, Chief Justice Burger invoked the "admonition of Professor Alexander Meiklejohn that 'what is essential is not that everyone shall speak, but that everything worth saying shall be said.'"[104] And so the notion of the marketplace of ideas was further derogated by the Court: members of the audience had no clear idea what was best, even though their interests were legally paramount. Broadcasters, whose interests were subsidiary to those of the listening public, could act as proxies on behalf of the myopic audience. And above these mere mortals was the Federal Communications Commission, insisting that the proxies remain fair and thus not confuse the audience. As the Court noted, "Determining what best serves the public's right to be informed is a task of great delicacy and difficulty."[105] The result—particularly when the Court distrusts the ability of the listener—is that the government becomes an overseer and ultimate arbiter and guardian of the public interest.

In *Red Lion*, the Court ruled that listeners had a right to balanced information, and in *CBS* v. *DNC*, the Court expressed doubts about the ability of the audience to perceive what was right. Five years later, in *FCC* v. *Pacifica Foundation*,[106] the Court displayed a continuing parental, almost condescending view of the audience by ruling that listeners must be protected from words that would shock or offend them. Such protection represented a substantive departure from the philosophy of a free marketplace with rational persons making rational decisions.

In *Pacifica Foundation*, the Court majority denied that persons could discern the value of George Carlin's commentary, "The Filthy Words," as broadcast over a radio station. Justice Stevens argued that the monologue, aired during early afternoon, could be heard by children and even "unsuspecting adults."[107] The Court's duty was to protect these poor, unsullied children and fragile adults from hearing "indecent" words.

Justice Stevens, writing for the majority, issued the ritual claim that "it is a central tenet of the First Amendment that the government must remain neutral in the marketplace of ideas."[108] Then the Court declared the words in Carlin's satire without value and excluded them from the marketplace.[109] As Justice Brennan argued in dissent, the decision "ignores the constitutionally protected interests of those who wish to transmit."[110] The decision marked a profound paternalism on the part of the Court.

Commercial Speech. The same parental guidance from a government agency arises in commercial speech cases, which also protect listeners' rights at the expense of speakers' rights.

In *New York Times Co.* v. *Sullivan*, the Court agreed that ideas were protected by the First Amendment even when they appeared in advertising.[111] The advertisement in question, however, urged social and political action; there was no commercial element in the message.

The distinction between commercial advertising and the communication of political ideas[112] blurred in 1975 when the Court said that the First Amendment also shielded a brief advertisement in a Virginia weekly newspaper.[113] In the advertisement, a New York women's agency offered to counsel women about abortions and to assist in placing them in accredited hospitals and clinics in New York. In *Bigelow* v. *Virginia*, the Court invoked the First Amendment because of the "public interest" element.[114]

"Public interest," however, did not justify protection of advertising if the product or service offered was illegal in the place where it was offered. The Court held that Virginia, whose laws forbade abortions, could not punish for an advertisement of abortion services legally offered in New York. The test of legality had been upheld as a substantial limit on free speech two years earlier in *Pittsburgh Press Co.* v. *Pittsburgh Commission on Human Relations*,[115] a case involving classified employment advertising—"classic examples of commercial speech."[116] The First Amendment, the Court said, does not prevent enforcement of an ordinance barring a newspaper from illegally classifying job ads according to sex.[117] There was no question that the state could regulate the economic activity of employment. But the advertisement of job opportunities had not before been linked so closely with speech protected by the First Amendment. The conjunction augured trouble. In the political arena, the legality or illegality of the object did not remove the speech from the center of First Amendment protection so long as the speech did not transcend advocacy to become incitement.[118] It would have been consistent for the Court to recognize that the legality or illegality of the advertised products or activities should not make a difference for purposes of First Amendment protection. The content of such advertising might well play some role in informing the marketplace of ideas.

The Court, however, appeared dedicated to building a separate level of protection for commercial speech; at that level, no value at all was to be accorded to commercial speech dealing with illegal matters. The result was inconsistent not only with the expansive Meiklejohnian ideal but also with the Court's own endorsement of a robust and error-tolerant debate in *New York Times*.

In 1976, in *Virginia State Board of Pharmacy* v. *Virginia Citizens Consumer Council, Inc.*,[119] the Court struck down a Virginia statute that prohibited pharmacists from advertising prescription drug prices. The case involved no ringing statements on public issues; it was the most fundamental commercial message: "I will sell you the X prescription drug at the Y price."[120]

The opinion by Justice Blackmun, endorsed by five other justices, held that consumers have a right to receive at least a part of the message conveyed by the merchant hawking his wares—that is, the product and the price. "If there is a right to advertise, there is a reciprocal right to receive the advertising."[121] *Virginia Pharmacy* is the most extensive and harmful acceptance thus far of a constitutional idea of a public right to know. Justice Blackmun carried out his extension of the First Amendment in words that rang of the most calculated political rhetoric. Noting and dismissing the advertiser's "purely economic" interest in price information, Justice Blackmun turned to the consumer's interest: "That interest may be as keen, if not keener by far, than his interest in the day's most urgent political debate."[122]

Justice Blackmun's effort to explain the elevation of messages about products to the level of political discourse was strained. Resources are allocated through "numerous private economic decisions," he wrote. Since those private economic decisions have far-reaching implications for the economy, they ought to be "intelligent and well informed."[123] To this point, the justice's reasoning had no application to the First Amendment at all, so he made the forced connection that regulation of the economy, certainly a public issue, depended on those private economic decisions being well informed.[124] Equating information about toothpaste and shampoo with opinions that fueled public decision making was a disservice to the First Amendment. Justice Blackmun credited in a footnote the writings of Alexander Meiklejohn.[125] That the philosopher would have been deeply troubled by that context did not seem to occur to Justice Blackmun. The decision had fused what Meiklejohn eloquently insisted had to be kept separate—public and private speech.[126] Meiklejohn stated that the First Amendment protects speakers absolutely, so long as they discuss public issues. The Court, in *Virginia Pharmacy* and in the other commercial speech cases, asserted that freedom of the press also protects commercial speech but in a restricted form due to the interests of the public and its desire to know about products and services. Commercial speech which advertises illegal matters can be suppressed, and commercial speech which advertises legal matters must be truthful and nondeceptive. Moreover, the Court recalled, it had long been accepted that the state could impose time, place, and manner restrictions on any kind of speech, including advertising. "The First Amendment, as we construe it today, does not prohibit the State from insuring that the stream of commercial information flow cleanly as well as freely."[127] The extent of regulation permissible for this form of speech was further described in a footnote, in which Justice Blackmun noted that commercial messages might be required to appear "in such a form, or include such additional information, warnings, and disclaimers, as are necessary to prevent its being deceptive."[128] Moreover, the hallowed prohibitions against prior restraints of protected speech[129] might be made inapplicable in commercial speech cases.

The *Virginia Pharmacy* decision requires the formulation of a test of deception to decide whether commercial speech enjoys or loses constitutional protection. That burden is passed to Congress, to the administrative agencies such as the politically vulnerable Federal Trade Commission, and, ultimately, to the courts. Yet, such a test may not be easily found. Chief Justice Burger expressed that fear in his concurring opinion: "I doubt that we know enough about evaluating the quality of medical and legal services to know which claims of superiority are 'misleading' and which are justifiable."[130]

In a dissent that referred to "second class First Amendment rights,"[131] Justice Rehnquist suggested the issue was beyond the scope of the First Amendment. The common intercourse between seller and buyer had been elevated to the plane previously reserved "for the free marketplace of ideas."[132]

The problem raised by the case could have been attacked through antitrust, a revision of the state regulations, consumer class actions, or legislation. There is no compelling reason to conclude that the only way to allow pharmacists to divulge their prices is to weaken the First Amendment by stretching it over their commercial enterprise. Moreover, once the rule had been invoked in the case of pharmacists, it would, as Justice Rehnquist warned, have to be extended to other professionals and to other kinds of commercial information. The Court indeed has become enmeshed in those questions, legislating case by case on the kinds of speakers and types of information subject to the new protection.

In 1977, the Court struck down a New York statute that prohibited advertising of contraceptives and argued as it had in *Virginia Pharmacy* that consumer interests required disclosure of information.[133] Then, consistent with Justice Rehnquist's warning in *Virginia Pharmacy*, the Court reviewed the issue of attorney advertising and ruled that the state of Arizona could not prevent newspaper publication of truthful advertising about routine legal services.[134]

By 1980, the Court had turned to a "four-step analysis" as a way of sorting out the kinds of commercial speech which, though protected, would be subject to governmental regulation.

> At the outset, we must determine whether the expression is protected by the First Amendment. For commercial speech to come within that provision, it at least must concern lawful activity and not be misleading. Next, we ask whether the asserted governmental interest is substantial. If both inquiries yield positive answers, we must determine whether the regulation directly advances the governmental interest asserted, and whether it is not more extensive than is necessary to serve that interest.[135]

The Court majority ruled against a state utilities commission ban on utility bill inserts that promoted electrical use, but Justice Powell suggested that the utility commission still might restrict advertising format and content without breaching First Amendment protection. The growing complexity of such matters prompted Justice Blackmun, the author of the *Virginia Pharmacy* opinion, to complain that "no differences between commercial speech and other protected speech justify suppression of commercial speech in order to influence public conduct through manipulation of the availability of information."[136]

In the area of commercial speech, the Court is engaged in an increasingly difficult chore of managing the flow of information that serves the nation's commerce. Having accorded "second class rights" to advertising, it necessarily must determine how to distinguish such speech from that which the First Amendment had traditionally protected. The inevitable tests lead to the inevitable result that the speech the Court purports to protect is subject to the shifting interpretations of the justices. The mushiness of the Court's handling of commercial speech threatens to spread to the realm of political speech.

If advertising of products were treated as a form of speech beyond First Amendment protection, the right to speak, at least, would retain some of its original vitality. The First Amendment interest in vigorous discussion, in virulent debate so animated that error is its by-product, has no bearing on product promotion.

Conclusions

A survey of the shifting meanings of press freedom in recent years could range beyond the three substantive areas explored in this paper. Evidence of deserting basic First Amendment concepts emerges in a variety of cases involving media rights.

In cases involving press demands for special access to public institutions, such as courts and prisons, the Supreme Court has framed the issue not in terms of the press's (speaker's) right to inform itself so it could speak, but heavily on the public's right to know. Oddly, that right to know has not, in recent cases, implied the right of the press to gather news, but only the right of the government to determine to what extent its prisons, courts, and public agencies should be revealed to the public, so greatly in need of information. The right to hear implies little more than a governmental right to restrict.[137]

In the past few decades, then, two new models of free speech and press have emerged, both purportedly embodying First Amendment principles; yet they are incompatible with one another. Their very differences demonstrate a growing elasticity or variability in the fundamental meaning of the First Amendment.

This society has long placed its faith in individuals, whose motivation to speak and act has maintained the political compact so eloquently described by Meiklejohn. Our trust has been that the society would prosper as long as the individual was free to act on his conscience. It was no idle interest in selfish communication; we always have understood the fundamental linkage between individual freedom and a healthy, self-governing society. Free speech is precisely that: a right to speak. The rights of the many hearers are important but derivative. Those who devised the Debate Model tinkered with the basic philosophy of free speech and press. In the Debate Model, the speaker is still protected but the value of speech is weighed by its contribution to public good or welfare. Although the Supreme Court has provided some important protections for speakers in the area of libel, the philosophy of the Debate Model ensures only very narrow protection for speech and press. Meiklejohn wanted to protect all public speech absolutely; yet the Court never has adopted his broad definition of "public" and has, indeed, even narrowed its view, beginning with *Gertz* v. *Robert Welch, Inc.* Additionally, the actual malice rule lays bare the editorial process of the media under the guise of pretrial discovery.

Of more serious consequence, however, is the Right-to-Know Model. At best, the "right to know" is sloganeering; at worst, it is a pernicious constitutional doctrine which is destructive of First Amendment rights. The problem is complex.

First, reporters, judges, and others have succumbed to the siren song of this right to know because it sounds good. One scholar, John C. Merrill, explains the fascination with the term: "Defenders of press freedom have appropriated the expression (from where, nobody is quite sure) because it sounds more democratic than the simple term 'freedom of the press' and shifts the theoretical emphasis from a private and restricted institution (the press) to a much broader and popular base (the citizenry)."[138] As Oregon Supreme Court Justice Hans Linde notes, the "right to know" is a "wishy-washy" slogan designed to make the press seem "noble," while accomplishing nothing.[139] The press, he says, has the *constitutional* right to print many things that the public has no *constitutional* right to know.[140]

Second, the right to know, as referred to here, is passive. It relies not on a positive search for truth but on passive reception from others. At best, it is a derivative "right" which depends upon the imagination, wisdom, or strength of others, and thus it is no more than a second-class "right." As Thomas I. Emerson explains, "It is the speaker who is more directly affected, is more highly motivated to secure his right, will press harder to achieve it, and may have more power to succeed. To focus on the more indirect and diffuse rights of the listener would likewise tend to weaken the system."[141]

Third, the concept, as these cases demonstrate, is vague. Walter Gellhorn has noted: "The 'right to know' principle is itself so broadly and vaguely phrased that it cannot decide cases. Judges must still decide the cases."[142] Judges must and will rely on their own opinions in determining the public's need to know. Such an unpredictable *constitutional* standard may be of little value, because unpredictability in the application of First Amendment doctrine encourages self-censorship.

Fourth, the "right to know" must be defined by someone or some group, independent of the listener. As Merrill notes:

> Somebody or some group, of course, must decide what is "public business" or necessary information for the people to govern themselves. It is exactly at this point that such a "right to know" dissolves—if it ever had substance—for when it is agreed that somebody or some group must determine what the people shall or shall not know, the mythical nature of such a "right" becomes very clear.[143]

Fifth, the "right to know" is pernicious because it derogates the right of speakers. Limitations on freedom of commercial or broadcast speech may come to haunt political speech. In cases involving the "right to know," it is significant that the rights of the speaker have been consistently subordinated to listener rights and thus often curtailed.

And sixth, any determination of what the public has a right to know involves as well a determination of what the public has no right to know and thus involves censorship.

There are no easy solutions to the complex problems of free speech in society; indeed, the hodgepodge created by the Court should convince us of the lack of easy answers. In a perfect world, we could easily sound a clarion call for absolute free speech. Yet, our philosophers and institutions weigh heavily against so fundamental or absolute a system.

At the very minimum, democratic society needs information to function. In his widest expressions, Meiklejohn provided a workable system for speech which still gave great latitude to individual belief and thought. As Justice Brennan wrote, Meiklejohn envisioned a wide ideal of public speech: "Education in all its phases, the achievements of philosophy and the sciences, literature and the arts, all fall within the subjects of 'governing importance' that the First Amendment absolutely protects from abridgement."[144] Unlike Meiklejohn, however, we must not elevate the listener unduly, for to do so is to jeopardize the basics of free speech and press.

The great need for public information necessitates deregulation of broadcasting. Regulation of content not only invites but assures the interference of a third party as filter, arbiter, and censor.[145]

Lastly, it is easy to deceive ourselves in First Amendment rhetoric, and so it is essential to note that the extensive regulation of purely commercial speech indicates the clear absence of First Amendment rights. The claim that commercial speech is protected under the First Amendment is at best a sleight of hand. Further, commercial speech merits no such protection under Meiklejohn's scheme, for it is not public speech, but speech incidental to economic activity.

Notes

1. Evidence of the decline of press rights can be found in other areas of press law as well. These three areas, however, show particularly well how Court views of the First Amendment have changed. See pp. 70–80.
2. Harold L. Nelson described the Hughes Court decisions on freedom of the press as "clearly libertarian in spirit and effect." Harold L. Nelson, ed., *Freedom of the Press from Hamilton to the Warren Court* (Indianapolis: Bobbs-Merrill Co., 1967), p. xxxvii.

   Zechariah Chafee, Jr., considered the 1920s and 1930s central to the building of a framework for freedom of the press. Of the Court's work in those years, he wrote: "It is not just a question of particular situations. Through them all runs a new philosophy of the importance of open discussion in American life, which stems from the great dissent of Justice Holmes in *Abrams* v. *United States*." Zechariah Chafee, Jr., Free Speech in the United States (Cambridge, Mass: Harvard University Press, 1941), p. 437. Paul L. Murphy termed 1931, the year of the *Near* v. *Minnesota* decision,

   > the quiet and subtle beachhead of a new era. In fact, 1931 was a major turning point toward a new type of judicial instrumentalism in civil liberties in which the judiciary came to take the lead in opening up new federally guaranteed channels to assure formerly helpless Americans a new opportunity to utilize their constitutionally guaranteed rights.

   Paul L. Murphy, *The Meaning of Freedom of Speech* (Westport, Conn.: Greenwood Publishing Co., 1972), p. 8.
3. Near v. Minnesota ex rel. Olson, 283 U.S. 697 (1931).

4. Lovell v. Griffin, 303 U.S. 444 (1938).
5. Ibid. at 450–51.
6. Grosjean v. American Press Co., 297 U.S. 233 (1936).
7. 268 U.S. 652 (1925).
8. Chafee, *Free Speech in the United States*, p. 50, citing Masses Publishing Co. v. Patten, 246 F. 24, 39 (2d Cir. 1917).
9. Nelson, *Freedom of the Press*, p. xxv.
10. 249 U.S. 47, 52 (1919).
11. See Chafee, *Free Speech in the United States*, pp. 36–354, for a detailed history of state and federal prosecutions of political dissent during the war and in the years shortly after.
12. 268 U.S. at 668.
13. Whitney v. California, 274 U.S. 357, 375 (1927) (Brandeis, J., joined by Holmes, J., concurring).
14. Ibid. at 377.
15. Ibid. at 375–76 (footnotes omitted).
16. Commission on Freedom of the Press, *A Free and Responsible Press* (Chicago: University of Chicago Press, 1947).
17. Alexander Meiklejohn, *Free Speech and Its Relation to Self-Government*, reprinted in *Political Freedom* (New York: Harper & Row, Publishers, 1960).
18. Commission on Freedom of the Press, *A Free and Responsible Press*, p. 81.
19. William E. Hocking, *Freedom of the Press: A Framework of Principle* (Chicago: University of Chicago Press, 1947).
20. Ibid., p. 18.
21. Ibid., p. 96.
22. Zechariah Chafee, Jr., *Government and Mass Communications*, 2 vols. (Chicago: University of Chicago Press, 1947), 1:26–27.
23. Commission on Freedom of the Press, *A Free and Responsible Press*, p. 6.
24. Ibid., p. 112.
25. Hocking, *Freedom of the Press*, p. 169.
26. 326 U.S. 1 (1945).
27. Hocking, *Freedom of the Press*, pp. 52–53.
28. Ibid., p. 172.
29. Meiklejohn, *Political Freedom*, p. 57.
30. Ibid., p. 26.
31. Ibid.
32. Ibid., p. 27.
33. Ibid., p. 55.
34. Ibid.
35. Ibid.
36. Ibid., p. 37.
37. Harry Kalven, Jr., "Metaphysics of the Law of Obscenity," in *Supreme Court Review 1960*, ed. Philip B. Kurland (Chicago: University of Chicago Press, 1960), pp. 15–16.
38. Alexander Meiklejohn, "The First Amendment Is an Absolute," in *Supreme Court Review 1961*, ed. Philip B. Kurland (Chicago: University of Chicago Press, 1961), p. 263.
39. In re Editorializing by Broadcast Licensees, 13 F.C.C. 1246, 1257–58 (1949).
40. U.S., *Statutes at Large*, Radio Act of 1927, vol. 44, p. 1162 (1927) (repealed in 1934).
41. Ibid. at 1248 n. 1.
42. Ibid. at 1247.
43. Meiklejohn, *Political Freedom*, p. 87.
44. 319 U.S. 141 (1943).
45. Ibid. at 143.
46. 326 U.S. 501, 505 (1945).
47. See also Stanley v. Georgia, 394 U.S. 557, 568 (1969) (state cannot make "mere private possession of obscene material a crime"); Lamont v. Postmaster General of United States, 381 U.S. 301 (1965) (statute permitting the government to require addressee's affirmative request for "communist propaganda" held unconstitutional). Both cases recognized a right to receive information, but neither cast the right in terms of a control on the content of the communication.

48. Thomas v. Collins, 323 U.S. 516 (1944).
49. Ibid. at 534.
50. Ibid. at 545–46.
51. CBS, Inc. v. Democratic Nat'l Comm., 412 U.S. 94, 145 (1973) (Stewart, J., concurring).
52. 376 U.S. 254 (1964).
53. William J. Brennan, Jr., "The Supreme Court and the Meiklejohn Interpretation of the First Amendment," *Harvard Law Review* 79 (November 1965): 17, citing Harry Kalven, Jr., "The New York Times Case: A Note on 'The Central Meaning of the First Amendment,'" in *Supreme Court Review 1964*, ed. Philip B. Kurland (Chicago: University of Chicago Press, 1964), p. 221 n. 125.
54. 376 U.S. at 256.
55. Ibid. at 270, 292.
56. Ibid. at 270.
57. Ibid. at 269–70.
58. Ibid. at 271.
59. Ibid. at 271–72, quoting NAACP v. Button, 371 U.S. 415, 433 (1963).
60. Ibid. at 279.
61. Ibid. at 279–80. The actual malice rule required that public officials prove knowledge of falsity or reckless disregard of the truth.
62. Ibid. at 266.
63. Ibid. at 269, quoting Roth v. United States, 354 U.S. 476, 484 (1957).
64. Ibid. at 272, quoting Sweeney v. Patterson, 128 F.2d 457, 458 (D.C. Cir. 1942).
65. Justice Hugo Black assailed the new fault requirement:

> "Malice," even as defined by the Court, is an elusive, abstract concept, hard to prove and hard to disprove. The requirement that malice be proved provides at best an evanescent protection for the right critically to discuss public affairs and certainly does not measure up to the sturdy safeguard embodied in the First Amendment.

376 U.S. at 293 (1964) (Black, J., concurring).
66. There were political overtones to the case, as Harry Kalven, Jr., noted. "Alabama somehow pounced on this opportunity to punish the *Times* for its role in supporting the civil rights movement in the South." Kalven, "The New York Times Case: A Note on 'The Central Meaning of the First Amendment,'" p. 200. The Court, sympathetic to the civil rights struggle and desirous of helping the *Times* in face of financial ruin, sought a pro-press decision and thus had to derive a rationale for it. "One problem among the many that the Court faces in cases of this kind is attributable to the fact that it cannot, like the man in the street, simply state the result it likes." Ibid.

    At least seventeen civil libel actions by public officials of the Southern states were pending against the media in April 1964. Nelson, *Freedom of the Press*, p. 98.

    Compare New York Times Co. v. Sullivan, 376 U.S. 254 (1964), with cases in which the Court has denied protection to political expression with which it did not sympathize, e.g., Wolston v. Reader's Digest Ass'n, 443 U.S. 157 (1979) (plaintiff accused of being a Soviet agent); Gertz v. Robert Welch, Inc., 418 U.S. 323 (1974) (John Birch Society publication accused lawyer of being a "Leninist" and a "Communist-fronter").
67. Public officials include public employees who "have, or appear to the public to have, substantial responsibility for or control over the conduct of governmental affairs." Rosenblatt v. Baer, 383 U.S. 75, 85 (1966). In *Curtis Publishing Co.* v. *Butts* and its companion case, *Associated Press* v. *Walker*, the Court applied the higher fault standard to public "figures," that is, those who by their "purposeful activity" thrust themselves into the "'vortex' of an important public controversy." Public figures, like public officials, "had sufficient access to the means of counterargument to be able 'to expose through discussion the falsehood and fallacies' of the defamatory statements." 388 U.S. 130, 155 (1967). See generally Comment, "Defamation and the First Amendment: Protecting Speech on Public Issues," *Washington Law Review* 56 (December 1980): 75–97.

    The Court consistently stressed the importance of debate in informing the public. In *Curtis Publishing Co.* v. *Butts*, Justice Harlan declared that free speech "is as much a guarantee to individuals of their personal right to make their thoughts public and put them before the community . . . as it is a social necessity required for the 'maintenance of our political system and an open society.'" 388 U.S. 130, 149 (1967). See also Greenbelt Cooperative

Publishing Ass'n v. Bresler, 398 U.S. 6, 11–12 (1970), and St. Amant v. Thompson, 390 U.S. 727, 731–32 (1968).
68. 388 U.S. 130 (1967).
69. Ibid. at 135–40.
70. Ibid. at 155.
71. See ibid. at 157–58.
72. Ibid. at 164 (Warren, C. J., concurring).
73. International News Service v. Associated Press, 248 U.S. 215, 267 (1918) (Brandeis, J., dissenting).
74. Ibid.
75. 388 U.S. at 171–72 (Black, J., dissenting).

Attorney James C. Goodale, at one time vice president of the *New York Times*, has written:

> If the courts recognize the right to know, however, they will begin to perform the function of gathering information. They will also act as editors, since only the courts can apply the qualifications inherent in the right to know. Editing will require judgments about what information to release to the public and what to withhold. The right to communicate will thus be affected, since one cannot communicate what has been withheld.

James C. Goodale, "Legal Pitfalls in the Right to Know," *Washington University Law Quarterly* 1976 (Winter 1976): 32.
76. 403 U.S. 29, 42 (1971). The plurality would have expanded the defense provided to speakers by allowing them to erect the actual malice defense against all persons involved in issues of great concern or controversy to the listener. Ibid. at 43.
77. 418 U.S. 323 (1974).
78. Ibid. at 345. The end of strict liability was not a particular protection for the press; rather, it was a device to protect and nurture public debate. As Justice Powell wrote, "The First Amendment requires that we protect some falsehood in order to protect speech that matters." Ibid. at 341.
79. See Wolston v. Reader's Digest Ass'n, 443 U.S. 157 (1979); Hutchinson v. Proxmire, 443 U.S. 111 (1979); Time, Inc. v. Firestone, 424 U.S. 448 (1976).

In *Time, Inc.* v. *Firestone*, the Court ruled that a sensational divorce case was not a public controversy as envisioned in the concept of public debate. Justice Rehnquist wrote, for the majority, that the "details of many, if not most, courtroom battles would add almost nothing toward advancing the uninhibited debate on public issues thought to provide principal support for the decision in *New York Times*." 424 U.S. at 457. This sweeping statement differed greatly from recent precedents by the Court and pointed out the great variability—and thus, instability—in definitions of what constituted acceptable topics for public debate.

Only one year before *Time, Inc.* v. *Firestone*, Cox Broadcasting Corp. v. Cohn, 420 U.S. 469 (1976), held that court records were of interest to the public:

> In the first place, in a society in which each individual has but limited time and resources with which to observe at first hand the operations of his government, he relies necessarily upon the press to bring to him in convenient form the facts of those operations. Great responsibility is accordingly placed upon the news media to report fully and accurately the proceedings of government, and official records and documents open to the public are the basic data of governmental operations. Without the information provided by the press, most of us and many of our representatives would be unable to vote intelligently or to register opinions on the administration of government generally. With respect to judicial proceedings in particular, the function of the press serves to guarantee the fairness of trials and to bring to bear the beneficial effects of public scrutiny upon the administration of justice.

420 U.S. at 491–92.

Cox Broadcasting Corp. v. *Cohn* dealt with reporting of a criminal case, and *Time, Inc.* v. *Firestone* was a civil case. But are only criminal cases of public concern? Could not civil libel suits, such as those against the *New York Times* in the early 1960s, demonstrate the attempts of some to bankrupt one of the nation's leading papers because it supported the civil rights movement? Obviously, such a suit would be part of a bona fide public debate. The point is not that the gossip reported in *Time, Inc.* v. *Firestone* merits protection; rather, the point is that the yardstick by which the Court measures bona fide public issues and events is invisible; it is as likely to rest on a personal whim as on philosophy.

80. 441 U.S. 153 (1979).
81. Ibid. at 157–58.
82. Ibid. at 160. Jerome A. Barron has written:

> In short, it seems apparent that the workings of the *New York Times* actual malice test always assumed the availability of inquiry into the state of mind on the part of the media defendant. If that is true, then all that the *Lando* decision has done is to clarify the law on this point.

Jerome A. Barron, "The Rise and Fall of a Doctrine of Editorial Privilege: Reflections on *Herbert v. Lando*," *George Washington Law Review* 47 (August 1979): 1016.

83. 441 U.S. at 172–73.
84. Brennan, "The Supreme Court and the Meiklejohn Interpretation," p. 13.
85. 403 U.S. 29 (1971). See note 76 and accompanying text supra.
86. 443 U.S. 111 (1979). See note 79 and accompanying text supra.
87. 443 U.S. 157 (1979). See note 79 and accompanying text supra.
88. 395 U.S. 367 (1969).
89. Ibid. at 392.
90. Ibid. at 385.
91. Ibid. at 390.
92. Ibid.
93. Ibid. at 394.
94. Ibid. at 389.
95. Ibid. at 394.
96. Ibid. at 389.
97. John Milton, "Areopagitica," in *The Works of John Milton*, ed. Frank A. Patterson, 18 vols. (New York: Columbia University Press, 1931–38), 4: 347:

> And though all the windes of doctrin were let loose to play upon the earth, so Truth be in the field, we do injuriously by licensing and prohibiting to misdoubt her strength. Let her and Falsehood grapple; who ever knew Truth put to the wors, in a free and open encounter.

98. 473 F.2d 16, 63 (D.C. Cir. 1972) (Bazelon, J., dissenting).
99. 412 U.S. 94 (1973).
100. Ibid. at 102, quoting Red Lion Broadcasting Co. v. FCC, 395 U.S. at 390.
101. Ibid. at 135.
102. Ibid. at 124.
103. Burger said:

> For better or worse, editing is what editors are for; and editing is selection and choice of material. That editors—newspaper or broadcast—can and do abuse this power is beyond doubt, but that is no reason to deny the discretion Congress provided. Calculated risks of abuse are taken in order to preserve higher values.

Ibid. at 124–25.

104. Ibid. at 122, quoting Meiklejohn, *Political Freedom*, p. 26.
105. Ibid. at 102.
106. 438 U.S. 726 (1978).
107. Ibid. at 748–49.
108. Ibid. at 745–46.
109. "Patently offensive, indecent material presented over the airwaves confronts the citizen, not only in public, but also in the privacy of the home, where the individual's right to be left alone plainly outweighs the First Amendment rights of an intruder." Ibid. at 748. In its paternalism, the majority of the Court imposed its own narrow view of acceptable speech upon both speaker (broadcaster) and listener.
110. Ibid. at 764. Justice Brennan further noted the "depressing inability" of the Court "to appreciate that in our land of cultural pluralism, there are many who think, act, and talk differently from the members of this Court, and who do not share their fragile sensibilities. It

is only an acute ethnocentric myopia that enables the Court to approve the censorship of communications solely because of the words they contain." Ibid. at 775 (Brennan, J., dissenting).

111. An advertisement on behalf of the Rev. Dr. Martin Luther King, Jr., "communicated information, expressed opinion, recited grievances, protested claimed abuses, and sought financial support on behalf of a movement whose existence and objectives are matters of the highest public interest and concern." New York Times Co. v. Sullivan, 376 U.S. at 266.

112. Valentine v. Chrestensen, 316 U.S. 52 (1942). For a history of deceptive advertising as an element in First Amendment protection of commercial speech, see Melinda Sue Lockett-John, "Commercial Speech and the First Amendment: An Historical Inquiry" (M.A. thesis, University of Washington, 1980).

113. Bigelow v. Virginia, 421 U.S. 809 (1975).

114. Ibid. at 822.

115. 413 U.S. 376 (1973).

116. Ibid. at 385.

117. Justice Powell, who wrote the opinion, said:

> Sex discrimination in nonexempt employment has been declared illegal.... Any First Amendment interest which might be served by advertising an ordinary commercial proposal and which might arguably outweigh the governmental interest supporting the regulation is altogether absent when the commercial activity itself is illegal and the restriction on advertising is incidental to a valid limitation on economic activity.

Ibid. at 388–89.

118. See Brandenburg v. Ohio, 395 U.S. 444 (1969).

119. 425 U.S. 748 (1976).

120. Ibid. at 761.

121. Ibid. at 757.

122. Ibid. at 763.

123. Ibid. at 765.

124. Justice Blackmun said:

> And if it is indispensable to the proper allocation of resources in a free enterprise system, it is also indispensable to the formation of intelligent opinions as to how that system ought to be regulated or altered. Therefore, even if the First Amendment were thought to be primarily an instrument to enlighten public decision-making in a democracy, we could not say that the free flow of information does not serve that goal.

Ibid. (footnotes omitted).

125. Ibid. at 765 n. 19.

126. Meiklejohn said:

> If men are engaged, as we so commonly are, in argument, or inquiry, or advocacy, or incitement which is directed toward our private interests, private privileges, private possessions, we are, of course, entitled to "due process" protection of those activities. But the First Amendment has no concern over such protection. That pronouncement remains forever confused and unintelligible unless we draw sharply and clearly the line which separates the public welfare of the community from the private goods of an individual citizen or group of citizens.

Meiklejohn, *Political Freedom*, pp. 79–80.

127. 425 U.S. at 771–72.

128. Ibid. at 771 n. 24.

129. See Near v. Minnesota ex rel. Olson, 283 U.S. 697 (1931).

130. 425 U.S. at 775 (Burger, C. J., concurring).

131. Ibid. at 786 (Rehnquist, J., dissenting).

132. Ibid. at 781 (Rehnquist, J., dissenting).

133. Carey v. Population Services Int'l, 431 U.S. 678 (1977).

134. Bates v. State Bar of Arizona, 433 U.S. 350 (1977).

Attorney solicitation of business, traditionally prohibited by bar association rules, failed to gain First Amendment sanction when the Court reviewed the case of a lawyer who had visited a young woman in her hospital room to offer his services for a personal injury suit.

Speech, in this case, did not serve her need to deliberate about the suit. Ohralik v. Ohio State Bar Ass'n, 436 U.S. 447 (1978). Cf. In re Primus, 436 U.S. 412 (1978) (solicitation by civil rights attorney for purposes of political expression cannot be prohibited).

135. Central Hudson Gas & Elec. Corp. v. Public Serv. Comm'n, 447 U.S. 557, 566 (1980).

136. Ibid. at 578 (Blackmun, J., concurring).

137. See, e.g., Gannett Co. v. DePasquale, 443 U.S. 368 (1979) (judges have discretion to close pretrial hearings); Houchins v. KQED, Inc., 438 U.S. 1 (1978) (media have no First Amendment right to information about conditions of jails); Saxbe v. Washington Post Co., 417 U.S. 843 (1974) (prison regulations prohibiting face-to-face interviews of inmates by newsmen did not violate the First Amendment).

138. John C. Merrill, "The 'People's Right to Know' Myth," *New York State Bar Journal* 45 (November 1973): 461.

139. Hans Linde, "Free Trials and Press Freedom—Two Rights Against the State," *Willamette Law Journal* 13 (Spring 1977): 218.

140. Ibid.

141. Thomas I. Emerson, "Legal Foundations of the Right to Know," *Washington University Law Quarterly* 1976 (Winter 1976): 4–5.

142. Walter Gellhorn, "The Right to Know: First Amendment Overbreadth?" *Washington University Law Quarterly* 1976 (Winter 1976): 26.

143. Merrill, "The 'People's Right to Know' Myth," p. 464.

144. Brennan, "The Supreme Court and the Meiklejohn Interpretation," p. 13.

145. Deceptive advertising would still be subject to regulation by the Federal Trade Commission and appropriate state authorities.

CHAPTER 3

Safeguarding Speech and Press Guarantees: Preferred Position Postulate Reexamined

Harry W. Stonecipher*

At the First Amendment Congress held in Philadelphia in January 1980, more than 250 delegates from both the news media and the public engaged in a lively two-day debate on the role of the press in America. The major themes emerging from the congress were that First Amendment rights belong to everyone—not just to the press—and that the news media must do a better job explaining these rights to the public.[1] Nearly two centuries earlier, Alexander Hamilton, writing in *The Federalist*, had opposed including in the Constitution a guarantee for liberty of the press because, he argued, the safeguarding of free expression was dependent upon public opinion and "the general spirit of the people and the government."[2] Although the First Amendment eventually became part of the Constitution, Hamilton's point should be considered carefully. Many times in the last 200 years the government has been able to suppress speech because of a lack of resolve on the part of the people.[3] And there is reason to be concerned in the 1980s about the public's perception of press freedom.

For example, during the First Amendment Congress, George Gallup, Jr., reported the results of a national public opinion survey that indicated an atti-

---

*Harry W. Stonecipher is head of the News-Editorial Faculty of the School of Journalism at Southern Illinois University at Carbondale. His teaching specialties include journalism law, legal research, editorial writing, and news writing and reporting.

Among his research interests are First Amendment interpretation, attitude change and persuasive communications, and press criticism and performance. His many articles for scholarly and professional journals include "Protection for the Editorial Function," "Judicial Gag Orders: An Unresolved Dilemma," "The Impact of *Gertz* on the Law of Libel," all in *Journalism Quarterly*, and "The Impact of *Gertz* on the Law of Libel in Illinois" in *Southern Illinois University Law Journal*. He has also written three books: *Electronic Age News Editing* (with Douglas Anderson and Edward Nicholls), *Editorial and Persuasive Writing: Opinion Functions of the News Media*, and *The Mass Media and the Law in Illinois* (with Robert Trager).

Stonecipher earned a doctorate in journalism from Southern Illinois University in 1971. He holds bachelor's and master's degrees in journalism from the University of Missouri, where he was awarded the Sigma Delta Chi Citation for Outstanding Male Graduate of 1953. His scholarship in enriched by his more than twenty years of journalism experience, including ten years as editor and publisher of the *Arcola* (Ill.) *Record-Herald*.

Stonecipher has served as a member of the Legislative and Freedom of Information Committee of the Illinois Press Association and as a member of both the Editorial Awards Committee and the Education Committee of the National Conference of Editorial Writers.

tude of increasing indifference, as well as some hostility, to the cause of press freedom. The poll findings indicated, for example, that 3 of 4 adults did not know what the First Amendment was or what it dealt with. In response to another question about legal controls on the press, 37 percent of the national sample said stricter curbs were desirable, while 17 percent said current controls were too strict. Another 32 percent said controls were "about right," and 14 percent did not express an opinion.[4] Indeed, those favoring stricter press controls combined with those favoring retention of the current level of controls outnumbered those who thought controls were too strict by almost 2 to 1.

These findings came at a time many journalists felt that freedom to report information and discuss issues of general and public concern was being seriously impaired by a hostile and imperial judiciary.[5] Jack C. Landau, executive director of the Reporters Committee for Freedom of the Press, told a group of journalists a few days after the Philadelphia congress that in the face of seemingly hostile court actions, the press had "no choice, as uncomfortable as this may be for many journalists, but to fight back with every tool at our disposal."[6] Gallup had recommended to media delegates to the First Amendment Congress that they embark on a program "to raise the level of consciousness of the American public regarding their basic freedoms."[7]

How can journalists, faced with courts that seemingly ignore the fine distinctions safeguarding First Amendment freedoms and a public that apparently has little understanding or interest in such distinctions, mount an effective campaign toward public enlightenment and support? One aspect of such an effort, without doubt, is a rethinking and reexamination by journalists of First Amendment values and the various judicial and theoretical approaches to First Amendment interpretation. If the speech and press clauses, for example, are not to be read literally ("Congress shall make no law . . . abridging the freedom of speech, or of the press"[8]), then what is the journalist's, as well as the public's, best means of safeguarding freedom of expression? It is clear that the balancing of interests approach as utilized by the Burger Court during the past decade has tended to allow speech and press freedoms to be eroded, some say seriously eroded.[9] Looking toward the future, how can the 'firstness" of the First Amendment, to borrow the phrase of one legal commentator,[10] be most effectively articulated to the public and to the courts? What approach to the First Amendment will sufficiently protect free expression and, at the same time, be understood and philosophically palatable to the public and to the courts?

It will be argued in the pages that follow that there is a "preference for freedom" for both speech and press[11] which is deeply rooted in the political and legal history of the United States.[12] Such a preferred position postulate regarding freedom of expression, though grounded in eighteenth-century political history, was articulated as a constitutional theory by the Supreme Court during the 1940s and the 1950s,[13] and aspects of the theory have been used by a majority of the justices who have served on the Court since then.[14] The doctrine generally holds that freedom of expression, being so essential to the exercise of other basic freedoms, needs to be weighted by the "judicial thumb" in the balancing of interests process.[15] This may be accomplished by taking a "presumption of invalidity" approach, an approach the Court has used in cases involving prior restraints upon expression, or by narrowing the scope for operation of a "presumption of constitutionality" approach, thereby making legislation threatening expression guarantees subject "to more exacting judicial scrutiny." Both these approaches will be discussed below, but it is important to note at the outset the purpose of such judicial weighting. It is not to free the press as an institution from all government restraint but to ensure that the function of those who engage in information dissemination is adequately protected in the interest of free public discussion of government affairs.

Maintenance of such a system of freedom of expression, according to Thomas I. Emerson, a prominent First Amendment scholar, is necessary for four basic reasons: (1) to assure individual self-fulfillment, (2) to attain truth, (3) to secure participation by members of the society in social, including political, decision making, and (4) to maintain the proper balance between stability and change in the society.[16] Support for freedom of expression, though neither unanimous nor complete, is part of the fundamental philosophical tradition of this country. The role the preferred position doctrine can play in the 1980s in maintaining a viable system of freedom of expression as envisioned by Emerson is better understood after a brief examination of the historical precepts of free speech and free press and the judicial doctrines involved in First Amendment interpretation.

Interpreting the First Amendment

Historical Perspective

When the First Congress convened in the spring of 1789, James Madison, who had been a delegate to the Continental Congress and a signatory to the new Constitution, assembled from the states the numerous bill of rights proposals, organized them into some rational order, and guided them through the Congress. During the previous year, Thomas Jefferson, then representing the United States in France, had often exchanged views with Madison about the need for a bill of rights, which was opposed by Hamilton and others. In a letter responding to Madison's own misgivings, Jefferson wrote:

> Experience proves the inefficacy of a bill of rights. True. But tho it is not absolutely efficacious under all circumstances, it is of great potency always, and rarely inefficacious. A brace the more will often keep up the building which would have fallen with that brace the less. There is a remarkable difference between the characters of the Inconveniences which attend a Declaration of rights, and those which attend the want of it. The inconveniences of the Declaration are that it may cramp government in its useful exertions. But the evil of this is shortlived, moderate, and reparable. The inconveniences of the want of a Declaration are permanent, afflicting and irreparable: they are in constant progression from bad to worse.[17]

Of all the framers of the Constitution, Jefferson has been depicted as the foremost apostle of freedom of speech, press, and religion. In an often-quoted letter written from Paris to a friend in Virginia, Jefferson said of press freedom:

> The basis of our government being the opinion of the people, the very first object should be to keep that right; and were it left to me to decide whether we should have a government without newspapers, or newspapers without a government, I should not hesitate a moment to prefer the latter.[18]

Such freedom was not viewed as an end in itself, however. Jefferson concluded, in a sentence which is often ignored by journalists, "But I should mean that every man should receive those papers and be capable of reading them."[19]

Historian Leonard W. Levy, however, has found a "darker side" in Jefferson's public performance, which he terms the "reality of the rhetoric." Levy noted:

> Jefferson was more the democrat than the libertarian, and his libertarianism, except in the field of religious freedom, was scarcely profound, consistent, or courageous. And he had his darker side, a streak of antilibertarianism, that reflected itself in significant breaches between his principles and his practice. In the long run, happily, his pen has proved mightier than his practice, for his rhetoric helped to create an American creed that we pridefully venerate.[20]

Madison's original recommendation to the House of Representatives in regard to speech and press provided that "the people shall not be deprived or abridged of their right to speak, to write, or to publish their sentiments; and the freedom of the press, as one of the great bulwarks of liberty, shall be inviolable."[21] Of the twelve amendments finally submitted to the states for ratification, the third provided that "Congress shall make no law respecting an establishment of religion, or prohibiting the free exercise thereof, or abridging the freedom of speech, or of the press, or the rights of the people peaceably to assemble and to petition the government for a redress of grievances."[22] This concise article of faith in basic civil liberties was to lead off the Bill of Rights after the first two of the twelve proposed articles were rejected by the states.[23]

Any argument boosting the "firstness" of the First Amendment must obviously be based upon evidence other than its position in the Bill of Rights. Are there eighteenth-century precedents to sanction the *grading* of various Bill of Rights guarantees by modern libertarians? Edmond Cahn, a professor of law, after examining the correspondence of Jefferson and Madison and the debates in the First Congress regarding the Bill of Rights, saw both a willingness to classify and grade the various provisions and a firm conviction on the part of the framers that the "freedoms embodied in the First Amendment must always secure paramountcy."[24] Historical interpretation regarding the scope of the First Amendment, the intention of the framers, or the meaning of its language, however, is far more complex and tentative than this one study seems to suggest.

Judicial and Theoretical Approaches

Interpretation and theorizing about the speech and press clauses of the First Amendment have been both divergent and confusing. It should be noted that during the first 120 years following ratification of the Bill of Rights, no cases based squarely upon First Amendment issues reached the Supreme Court. The constitutionality of the Alien and Sedition Acts of 1798, for example, was never tested in the courts, although the attack upon their validity is said to have "carried the day in the court of history."[25] It was not until 1925 in the landmark *Gitlow* v. *New York* decision that the Supreme Court said the guarantees of the First Amendment were applicable to the states through the due process clause of the Fourteenth Amendment.[26] One of the first doctrines used by members of the Court to interpret the First Amendment was the "free trade of ideas" concept articulated by Justice Oliver Wendell Holmes, Jr., in 1919. Holmes, joined by Justice Louis D. Brandeis in dissent in *Abrams* v. *United States*, said, "The best test of truth is the power of the thought to get itself accepted in the competition of the market."[27] This *marketplace of ideas* theory views the First Amendment as protecting the freedom for public discussion of competing ideas, a freedom essential if truth is to emerge. However, as one commentary has noted, such a general theory or principle does not resolve "hard cases." The Court, through the years, has quested for "operative or functional tests permitting reasonably consistent decisions."[28]

Legal scholars, as well as members of the Supreme Court, make frequent references to the historical meaning of the language of the speech and press clauses of the First Amendment, each drawing interpretations compatible with the writer's legal philosophy.[29] Alexander Meiklejohn, philosopher-educator and eminent First Amendment scholar, took an "absolutist" view. In 1948 he wrote:

> No one who reads with care the text of the First Amendment can fail to be startled by its absoluteness. The phrase, "Congress shall make no law...abridging freedom of speech," is unqualified. It admits of no exceptions. To say that no laws of a given type shall be made means that no laws of that type shall, under any circumstances, be made. That prohibition holds good in war as in peace, in danger as in security.[30]

Justice Hugo L. Black, sometimes joined by Justice William O. Douglas, expressed a similar view of the First Amendment.[31] The absolutist interpretation, however, has never been adopted by a majority of the Supreme Court. Even Meiklejohn distinguished between public expression concerned with matters of general public interest, for which he said absolute protection was essential, and private speech, which he said could be subject to some regulation.[32]

Many legal scholars interpret the First Amendment as affording sufficient latitude for a careful balancing of speech and press rights with other governmental interests.[33] Zechariah Chafee, Jr., former Harvard Law School dean and an influential exponent of the balancing of interests approach, said, however, that the theory of balancing did not mean that freedom of expression should not be weighted. In his classic work, *Free Speech in the United States*, he wrote in 1941:

> The true meaning of freedom of speech seems to be this. One of the most important purposes of society and government is the discovery and spread of truth on subjects of general concern. This is possible only through absolutely unlimited discussion.... Nevertheless, there are other purposes of government, such as... protection against external aggression. Unlimited discussion sometimes interferes with these purposes, which must then be balanced against freedom of speech, but freedom of speech ought to weigh very heavily in the scale. The First Amendment gives binding force to this principle of political wisdom.[34]

The problem often arises, however, that the social interest in speech to which Chafee would give greater weight may never even be put on the scales or the courts may balance an individual's interest in speech against the whole nation's interest in safety. Indeed, this occurred during what I. F. Stone called "the haunted fifties" when the anti-Communist plague infected both the Congress and the Supreme Court.[35] While the essential precept of balancing is the objective weighing of all the facts, in practice the balancing doctrine also "opens a broad door through which the judge's personal prejudices and misconceptions pass along with his legitimate and constitutional concerns."[36]

It is also important that First Amendment theory should make a careful distinction between *expression* and *action* and the degree of social control allowed over each, according to Emerson. In his authoritative book, *The System of Freedom of Expression*, Emerson is critical of the balancing approach, even as applied by the more liberally oriented Warren Court during the 1960s. He noted that the Court's efforts to deal with novel or complex problems of First Amendment law "often foundered for lack of a satisfactory theory." Failure to develop a comprehensive theory of the First Amendment, Emerson argued, has left the Court "without satisfactory tools to deal with many new developments that are emerging in the system of freedom of expression." This has, in turn, resulted in a constant shifting of positions, leaving the lower courts, public officials, and private citizens "in a state of confusion over the applicable rules."[37] Emerson said in conclusion:

> No system of freedom of expression can succeed in the end unless the ideas which underlie it become part of the life of the people. There must be a real understanding of the root concepts, a full acceptance of the guiding principles, and a deep resolve to make the system work. This state of affairs can be reached only if we succeed in building a comprehensible structure of doctrine and practice that is meaningful to all and meets the needs of a free society. The task remains largely unfulfilled.[38]

Ten years after the publication of Emerson's scholarly treatise expressing his liberal faith in freedom of expression, that task still "remains largely unfulfilled."

There can be little question that the absolutist position, which failed to win the endorsement of the majority of even the Warren Court, must be ruled out as an approach to First Amendment interpretation in the 1980s. If the Warren Court with its core of liberal justices failed to develop a balancing of interests approach which adequately protected First Amendment values, as Emerson argued, the more conservative Burger Court could hardly be expected to do so.[39] Indeed, it is in part because of the many unfavorable Burger Court decisions in the First Amendment area[40] during the 1970s that reexamination of the preferred position postulate is required.

The Preference for Freedom

Up from a Footnote

The preferred position postulate is usually attributed to a footnote in an opinion written by Justice Harlan F. Stone in a 1938 Supreme Court case, *United States* v. *Carolene Products*, which stated in part:

> There may be narrower scope for operation of the presumption of constitutionality when legislation appears on its face to be within a specific prohibition of the Constitution, such as those of the first ten Amendments, which are deemed equally specific when held to be embraced within the Fourteenth.[41]

The footnote did not refer specifically to the freedoms of speech and press. Indeed, the note, appended to an opinion which dealt with the application of a congressional act prohibiting transportation of certain types of compounded milk products in interstate commerce, was an admittedly tentative and qualified pronouncement of special judicial scrutiny—even as applied to the Bill of Rights generally.[42] Justice Felix Frankfurter was later to argue that preferred position was a "mischievous phrase" and that the footnote "hardly seems to be an appropriate way of announcing a new constitutional doctrine."[43]

What Justice Stone was attempting to refute in his *Carolene* footnote was the so-called "reasonable man theory," which, critics charged, allowed legislatures to have their own way so long as "a reasonable man" could have reached the same conclusion as the legislature. Or as Justice Stone wrote:

> The existence of facts supporting the legislative judgment is to be presumed, for regulatory legislation affecting ordinary commercial transactions is not to be pronounced unconstitutional unless in the light of the facts made known or generally assumed it is of such a character as to preclude the assumption that it rests upon some rational basis within the knowledge and experience of the legislators.[44]

It was at this point in the opinion that the footnote appeared. Although the note undoubtedly provided the catalyst for the later articulation of the preferred position doctrine, the footnote itself did not contain that phrase nor was it used in any Court opinion until four years later.

It was eighteen months after *Carolene* before Justice Stone's "tentative and qualified pronouncement," as one source has noted, "leaped from the footnotes" to become the explicit First Amendment doctrine of the Supreme Court.[45] Justice Owen J. Roberts, writing for an almost unanimous Court in *Schneider* v. *Irvington*, said:

> In every case...where legislative abridgement of the right [to freedom of speech and press] is asserted, the courts should be astute to examine the effect of the challenged legislation. Mere legislative preferences or beliefs respecting matters of public convenience may well support regulation directed at other personal activities, but be insufficient to justify such as diminishes the exercise of rights so vital to the maintenance of democratic institutions. And so, as cases arise, the delicate and difficult task falls upon the courts to weigh the circumstances and to appraise the substantiality of the reasons advanced in support of the regulation of the free enjoyment of the rights.[46]

Like Justice Stone in the *Carolene* footnote, Justice Roberts did not use the term *preferred position*, but he did adopt the essence of the preferred position theory, that legislation restricting the political freedoms—in this case the right to distribute handbills—should be exposed to a more searching and exacting judicial review than other legislation.

The term *preferred position* was first used in a Supreme Court opinion four years after *Carolene*, in a dissenting opinion written by Stone himself, then the chief justice. He wrote: "The First Amendment is not confined to safeguarding freedom of speech and freedom of religion against discriminatory attempts to wipe them out. On the contrary, the Constitution, by virtue of the First and Fourteenth Amendments, has put those freedoms in a preferred position."[47] A year later, Justice Douglas restated the chief justice's position, this time for the Court's majority:

> A license tax certainly does not acquire constitutional validity because it classifies the privileges protected by the First Amendment along with the wares and merchandise of hucksters and peddlers and treats them all alike. Such equality in treatment does not save the ordinance. Freedom of press, freedom of speech, freedom of religion are in a *preferred position.* [Emphasis added.][48]

The preferred position concept can be found in a number of other opinions during the 1940s and the 1950s, most expressing the views of individual justices but some representing the views of the majority.[49] Justice Wiley B. Rutledge offered perhaps the strongest statement of the preferred position doctrine, writing for the majority in *Thomas* v. *Collins* in 1945:

> The rational connection between the remedy provided and the evil to be curbed, which in other contexts might support legislation... will not suffice. These rights rest on firmer foundation.... Only the gravest abuses, endangering paramount interests, give occasion for permissible limitation... where the usual presumption supporting legislation is balanced by the preferred place given in our scheme to the great, the indispensable democratic freedoms secured by the First Amendment. ... That priority gives these liberties a sanctity and sanction not permitting dubious intrusions.[50]

Justice Rutledge stopped short of the extreme view that any legislation touching freedom of expression is infected with presumptive invalidity. He left little doubt, however, that because First Amendment values are so essential to a free society, legislative action infringing such values must be shown to be not only "reasonably" adapted to the attaining of valid social goals but justified by overwhelmingly conclusive considerations.[51]

Criticism of the Presumptive Invalidity Approach

The preferred position doctrine was used by Justices Stone, Rutledge, Douglas, Black, Frank Murphy, and Stanley F. Reed during the 1940s and the early 1950s as an alternative to the "legislative reasonableness" approach more generally used by the majority of the Court. The doctrine's chief critic, particularly in regard to the presumptive invalidity interpretation of the postulate, was Justice Frankfurter. In a lengthy concurring opinion in *Kovacs* v. *Cooper*, Frankfurter denounced the preferred position doctrine employed by Justice Reed in the majority opinion, as a phrase which "radiates a constitutional doctrine without avowing it."[52] As to the claim that "any legislation is presumptively unconstitutional which touches the field of the First Amendment," Justice Frankfurter said that such a doctrine "has never commended itself to a majority of this Court."[53]

Justice Frankfurter, a strong advocate of the balancing of interests approach, also objected to the preferred position doctrine because he felt its use would result in a "mechanical jurisprudence" arrived at through the use of "oversimplified formulas."[54] Justice Robert H. Jackson had earlier expressed a similar view, warning that the use of such "formulistic solutions" would bring about the same fate for civil liberties as had been brought about for liberty of contract, "which was discredited by being overdone."[55] Both Justices Frankfurter and Jackson, rightly or wrongly, were convinced that preferred position was merely a label for "a novel, iron constitutional doctrine, clearly the views of Meiklejohn."[56]

In explicitly rejecting the concept of presumptive invalidity as a means of safeguarding the primacy of the First Amendment, however, Justice Frankfurter concluded his review of preferred position cases with a statement which may be viewed as "one of the most eloquent testimonials to the vitality of the preferred position concept."[57] Justice Frankfurter wrote:

> Without freedom of expression, thought becomes checked and atrophied. Therefore, in considering what interests are so fundamental as to be enshrined in the Due Process Clause, those liberties of the individual which history has attested as the indispensable conditions of an open as against a closed society come to this Court with a momentum for respect lacking when appeal is made to liberties which derive merely from shifting economic arrangements.[58]

In response, Justice Rutledge wrote; "I think my brother Frankfurter demonstrates the conclusion opposite to that which he draws, namely, that the First Amendment guaranties of the freedoms of speech, press, assembly, and religion occupy preferred position not only in the Bill of Rights but also in the repeated decisions of this Court."[59]

Although the majority of the Supreme Court justices during the 1940s and the 1950s had, in one opinion or another, endorsed one or more of the general premises of preferred position,[60] Justice Frankfurter's attack on presumptive invalidity in *Kovacs* in 1949 and the deaths of Justices Murphy and Rutledge that same year, foreshadowed a decline in use of the doctrine by the Supreme Court. One commentator has noted that after *Kovacs*, the Court's more general approach came to be a "studious avoidance" of the phrase.[61]

Utility of the Preferred Position Postulate

In the 1960s and the 1970s, the Supreme Court has generally denied, as did Justice Frankfurter, that the Court in *Carolene Products* intended to assert "a presumption of invalidity against *all* [emphasis added] legislation touching matters related to liberties protected by the Bill of Rights and the Fourteenth Amendment" as a constitutional doctrine.[62] However, the footnote in *Carolene* has, as Justice Frankfurter noted, "stirred inquiry" as to whether there may be a "narrower scope for operation of the presumption of constitutionality," making legislation falling within this scope subject "to more exacting judicial scrutiny."[63] Although Justice Frankfurter made it clear he would resist such inquiries, the preferred position postulate has proved to have great utilitarian and theoretical value in First Amendment interpretation.

When used in conjunction with the Court's balancing of interests approach, the essence of the preferred position theory is that legislation restricting freedom of expression, particularly political speech, should be exposed to a more searching and exacting judicial review than other legislation. In other words, in the metaphor of balancing, in the weighing of one interest or array of interests against another as on scales, the preferred position doctrine assumes that speech and press guarantees, being so basic and vital to the exercise of all political freedoms protected by the First Amendment, should be weighted in the balancing process by placing the legislation in question under a "more exacting judicial scrutiny" than might be done with legislation in less vital areas.[64] Such a judicial weighing process can be, and has been, accomplished short of taking a presumptive invalidity approach. Even the *Carolene* footnote suggested only a "narrower scope for operation of the presumption of constitutionality," not presumptive invalidity per se.

One legal scholar has noted that much of the confusion over the priority to be accorded freedom of speech and press might have been avoided had the expressive phrase *preferred position* been given its natural and literal meaning instead of the various judicial interpretations that have resulted from the *Carolene* footnote.[65] In any case, the preferred position approach need not be rejected because the concept of presumptive invalidity is unacceptable in some or even all circumstances. There are a number of judicial approaches, tests, and procedural safeguards employed by the Supreme Court through the years which, although not originally stated as part of the preferred position doctrine, reflect its essence. Used separately or in combination, they would enable the Court to protect a constitutionally mandated preference for freedom of expression. These include (1) rejecting prior restraint, except under narrowly defined circumstances, as the Court has done in recent years when it has consistently treated prior restraints as presumptively invalid and has placed a heavy burden of proof on those seeking to overcome that presumption, (2) utilizing the clear and present danger test, in which the Court and not the legislature ultimately determines the presence of the danger, (3) using the *New York Times Co.* v. *Sullivan* "actual malice" rule to protect "uninhibited, robust, and wide-open" debate about matters of general and public concern against defamation actions, and (4) maintaining careful scrutiny of procedural due process safeguards when basic speech and press freedoms are involved. The Supreme Court's treatment of these protections, particularly in recent decisions of the Burger Court, will be examined in the following section.

Application of the Preferred Position Approach

Rejecting Prior Restraints

Freedom from government-imposed censorship of a communication prior to its publication has long been held to be protected by the First Amendment.[66] Although the Supreme Court has said not every prior restraint of expression necessarily violates the First Amendment,[67] the Court generally tends to view freedom of expression in a preferred light by placing such restraints under a more searching judicial inquiry. In its per curiam decision in the Pentagon Papers case, for example, the Supreme Court, quoting *Bantam Books, Inc.* v. *Sullivan*,[68] noted that "any system of prior restraints of expression comes to this Court bearing a heavy presumption against its constitutional validity."[69] In addition, quoting *Organization for a Better Austin* v. *Keefe*,[70] which had been decided a few weeks earlier, the Court concluded that the "government 'thus carries a heavy burden of showing justification for the imposition of such a restraint.'" This, the Court held in the Pentagon Papers case, the government had failed to do.[71]

The different treatment of prior restraint as opposed to subsequent punishment reflects the legal rationale that prior restraint, historically imposed by administrative tribunals, is a power readily abused. Administrative systems of prior restraint have been viewed as "more immediately subject to First Amendment attack" than judicial restraining orders because of the fear that administrative tribunals are "more susceptible to acts of suppression."[72] Administrative systems of prior restraint are generally found unconstitutional by the Court unless narrowly drawn procedural safeguards are adhered to.[73] However, the distinction between administrative and judicial prior restraint appears no longer to be significant to the Court, and it has applied the presumptive invalidity doctrine to judicially imposed restraints in all recent cases.[74]

Presumptive invalidity has brought favorable results for freedom of expression interests in a number of prior restraint cases during the 1970s. For example, in *Nebraska Press Association* v. *Stuart*, which dealt with a restraining order issued by a judge in a murder case, the Supreme Court held that "prior restraints on speech and publication are the most serious and least tolerable infringement on First Amendment rights."[75] Chief Justice Warren E. Burger, writing for the Court, said the judge's order prohibiting the reporting of material presented at the open preliminary hearing violated the settled principle that what transpires in an open courtroom cannot be subject to prior restraint.[76] In regard to the restraint imposed by the judge's order on the reporting of other information related to the case, the chief justice wrote that the burden of proof needed to overcome the presumption that the prior restraint was invalid had not been met.[77] Chief Justice Burger said the judge had not adequately assessed (1) whether the nature and extent of pretrial news coverage had seriously threatened the defendant's ability to get a fair trial, (2) whether other measures would have been effective in mitigating the effects of unrestrained pretrial publicity, and (3) whether the restraining order would have been effective in protecting the defendant's right to a fair trial in spite of publicity which had already occurred.[78] The judge had not, to the satisfaction of the Supreme Court, demonstrated "in advance of trial, that without prior restraint a fair trial [would have been] ... denied."[79] The Court viewed prior restraint on speech and publication as "the most serious and least tolerable infringement" because, in contrast to a criminal penalty, a prior restraint "has an immediate and irreversible sanction." The Court noted that while it may be said that a threat of criminal or civil sanctions after publication "chills" speech, prior restraint "freezes" it. The Court also noted, "The damage can be particularly great when the prior restraint falls upon the communication of news and commentary on current events."[80] *Nebraska Press Association* serves as a strong warning to lower courts of the difficulty of persuading the Supreme Court that judicial censorship of the press is constitutional.

The media can point to other victories. An Oklahoma court injunction prohibiting the news media from publishing the name or photograph of an eleven-year-old boy who was being tried before a juvenile court was struck down because the information was accurate and had been "obtained at court proceedings ... open to the public."[81] In addition, a West Virginia statute that made it a crime for a newspaper to publish the names of juveniles in connection with judicial proceedings without a written order of the court was ruled unconstitutional even though it was not a "classic" prior restraint case.[82]

Even in the area of prior restraint, however, the presumption of invalidity does not guarantee that freedom of expression interests will always be upheld. It was six months, for example, before *Progressive* magazine was allowed to publish an article that the government argued contained secret information critical to the construction of a hydrogen bomb. The magazine was freed from the restraining order only because another publication released essentially the same information.[83] In addition, the Supreme Court, without hearing oral arguments, held in *Snepp* v. *United States*,[84] that an agreement by a former CIA agent to submit any proposed publication concerning the CIA for prior review was an entirely appropriate exercise of the CIA director's statutory mandate to protect intelligence sources and methods from unauthorized disclosure. The government did not contend that any classified information had been revealed in Snepp's book, *Decent Interval*, which was based upon the author's experiences as a CIA agent in South Vietnam. Snepp's argument that enforcement of his agreement would, under such circumstances, constitute a prior restraint on speech protected by the First Amendment was rejected by the Court in a footnote.[85]

Also, the Court sometimes disagrees on whether or not an action limiting expression constitutes a prior restraint. In *Pittsburgh Press Co.* v. *Pittsburgh Commission on Human Relations*,[86] for instance, the Court upheld an ordinance forbidding newspapers from carrying "help wanted" classified ads in sex-designated columns. In so doing, the Court's majority rejected Chief Justice Burger's dissenting view that the commission's cease and desist order constituted an unconstitutional prior restraint.[87] Despite these unfavorable rulings, the preferred position postulate is well served by the Court's continuing commitment to the principle that administrative, legislative, and even judicial prior restraint should be treated as presumptively invalid.

Utilizing the Clear and Present Danger Test

The first Supreme Court formulation of a standard for determining when speech may be criminally prosecuted was presented in *Schenck* v. *United States* in 1919. Justice Holmes, writing for the Court, presented an embryonic definition of the clear and present danger test: "The question in every case is whether the words used are used in such circumstances and are of such a nature as to create a clear and present danger that they will bring about the substantive evil that Congress has a right to prevent."[88] As emphasized in subsequent cases, the clear and present danger test was to displace the evil tendency approach being used in the lower courts, which held that if speech had a tendency to produce an evil or if the evil was a natural and probable consequence of the speech, then the speech could be abridged. In a dissent in *Abrams* v. *United States*, Holmes stressed that "it is only the present danger of immediate evil or an intent to bring it about that warrants Congress in setting a limit to expression of opinion where private rights are concerned."[89] In a concurring opinion in *Whitney* v. *California*, Justice Brandeis, joined by Justice Holmes, stressed that the danger must be both "imminent" and serious and that it should be the Court which ultimately determines whether the clear and present danger doctrine should be applied.[90]

Although the clear and present danger test has had a long and checkered judicial history, it played an important role during the period 1937–1951. The test was specifically relied upon to uphold freedom of expression during this period in at least nine cases,[91] although First Amendment rights were upheld in a substantial number of cases in which the danger test might have been applied but was not. Because the clear and present danger test emphasizes the seriousness and imminence of the danger, it affords more protection for freedom of expression than did the historic evil tendency test or the legislative reasonableness approach against which the preferred position postulate was posited. Also, in contrast to the balancing test, which often emphasizes legislative reasonableness through the exercise of judicial restraint, the clear and present danger test posits an active judiciary.

In 1951, however, the Supreme Court all but destroyed the effectiveness of the clear and present danger test by recasting the elements to be taken into account in a way that drastically lessened the emphasis upon the immediacy of the danger. In *Dennis* v. *United States*, Chief Justice Fred M. Vinson adopted language used by Judge Learned Hand in his Second Circuit *Dennis* opinion, which held that in each case the courts must determine "whether the gravity of the 'evil,' discounted by its improbability, justifies such invasion of free speech as is necessary to avoid the danger."[92] The chief justice's plurality opinion, in effect, turned the clear and present danger test into a clear and "probable" danger test.[93]

Six years after *Dennis*, however, the Court seemed to resurrect the criterion of imminence that it had discarded in *Dennis* by subscribing to an "incitement test" that focused more on the substance of expression rather than the circumstances under which it was communicated.[94] Then, twelve years later in *Brandenburg* v. *Ohio*, the Court joined the incitement test to the clear and present danger doctrine. In a per curiam opinion overturning Ohio's syndicalism statute, the Court held that "the constitutional guarantees of free speech and free press do not permit violation except where such advocacy is directed to inciting or producing imminent lawless action and is likely to incite or produce such actions."[95] The courts, in other words, are to focus on both the character of the defendant's expression as well as on the circumstances under which it was made.[96]

Despite the troubled history of the clear and present danger test and despite predictions that the test has been or will be abandoned by the Court,[97] clear and present danger still appears to be a viable First Amendment doctrine. One legal commentator suggested a decade ago that before the clear and present danger test was discarded, its usefulness in developing a more sensitive approach to First Amendment freedom should be considered. He suggested a significant role for the test within the "definitional" balancing approach.[98] The test, he said, could be used to weight the balance in favor of freedom of expression, to "force governmental respect for the protected civil interests of the individual."[99] The clear and present danger test was viewed as playing a role in determining how much of a nexus must exist between legitimate governmental purpose and the sweep of the legislative scheme proposed to implement such a purpose.[100] There is some evidence that the clear and present danger test is being used in such a balancing process.

The danger test has long been used in determining the validity of the contempt power as a sanction against the press intended to safeguard the Sixth Amendment rights of criminal defendants. In 1941, in *Bridges* v. *California*, the power of judges to punish publication was severely limited by a holding that the contempt power could be used against out-of-court comment only when such comment created a clear and present danger that justice would be impaired.[101] Since that time, the danger test has been relied upon to resolve a variety of First Amendment issues arising from press coverage of judicial proceedings.[102] In 1978, in *Landmark Communications, Inc.* v. *Virginia*, the Supreme Court questioned the relevance of the test to the case but reaffirmed the essential, independent role of the courts in applying it. In that case, the Supreme Court reversed the conviction of a newspaper found guilty under a Virginia statute which declared, as a matter of *legislative* judgment, that divulgence of the confidential proceedings of the state's judicial disciplinary commission would create a clear and present danger to the orderly administration of justice. Chief Justice Burger, writing for the Court, combined the test with a balancing approach: "Properly applied, the test requires a court to make its own inquiry into the imminence and magnitude of the danger said to flow from the particular utterance and then to balance the character of the evil as well as its likelihood, against the need for free and unfettered expression."[103]

Earlier, in his *Nebraska Press* opinion, however, the chief justice used Judge Learned Hand's "gravity of the evil" concept as set out in the *Dennis* definition of clear and present danger,[104] leaving some doubt as to how the danger test might be used by the Court in the future. Nevertheless, the fact remains that the Supreme Court is still using the danger test as espoused by Justice Holmes and Brandeis or the more contemporary incitement test of *Brandenburg* in various First Amendment cases.[105] The lower courts are also using these tests.[106] Both weight the judicial balancing scales in favor of more freedom for both speech and the press.

Using the Times *Actual Malice Rule*

In 1964 the Supreme Court, in an effort to encourage "uninhibited, robust, and wide-open" debate on public issues, ruled in *New York Times Co.* v. *Sullivan*:

> The constitutional guarantees require, we think, a federal rule that prohibits a public official from recovering damages from a defamatory falsehood relating to his official conduct unless he proves that the statement was made with "actual malice"—that is, with knowledge that it was false or with reckless disregard of whether it was false or not.[107]

This federal rule was extended to include *public figures* three years later[108] and then, in a plurality opinion of the Court, to include *private persons* if the defamatory statements concerned matters of general or public interest.[109] This constitutional libel privilege affords increased protection for both the citizen critic and the journalist[110] by limiting strict liability under the common law for publication of defamatory falsehoods. In addition, rather than accepting the "preponderance of evidence" standard, the usual burden of proof in civil litigation, the *Sullivan* Court held that the actual malice rule required a standard of "convincing clarity," a heavier burden of proof for the plaintiff.[111]

In 1974, however, a decade after the *Sullivan* case, the Supreme Court, in *Gertz* v. *Robert Welch, Inc.*,[112] made at least two important changes in the constitutional libel privilege that have eroded the broad protection afforded by the *Sullivan* case and its progeny. First, it narrowed the definition of *public figure* under the constitutional privilege.[113] Second, the *Gertz* Court said, contrary to the plurality opinion in *Rosenbloom*, the Constitution did not require the use of the actual malice standard in cases brought for the recovery of damages for actual injury by private plaintiffs involved in matters of general or public concern. The states were allowed to establish liability under a less demanding standard for such persons but were prohibited from imposing liability without fault. The Court left little doubt that the proper standard of liability for awarding general damages should be negligence, not actual malice.[114] It should be noted that the rejection of strict liability for the defendant in cases brought by any category of plaintiff added to the media's protection and that all plaintiffs, as a consequence of *Gertz*, are required to prove actual malice—knowing or reckless falsehood—in order to recover punitive damages. Some states, too, under the discretion offered in the *Gertz* ruling, have not imposed a negligence standard as the *Gertz* Court suggested but have adopted standards more protective of the press.[115] In at least three libel cases reaching the Supreme Court since the *Gertz* decision, the plaintiffs, each of whom probably would have been categorized as a private figure involved in a public issue if the standard of the *Rosenbloom* plurality opinion had been used,[116] were ruled to be private individuals and therefore subject to the lesser fault standard permitted by the *Gertz* decision.[117]

A more substantial threat to the freedom provided by the constitutional libel privilege for those engaging in the debate on public issues, however, may be the reversal by the Supreme Court in *Herbert* v. *Lando*[118] of a U.S. Court of Appeals, Second Circuit, holding that recognized a First Amendment–based editorial privilege. The privilege protected a journalist, during pretrial discovery proceedings in a *Sullivan*-type libel case, from having to disclose how he had formulated his judgments on what to publish or what not to publish.[119] Justice White, writing for a six-member majority in *Herbert*, took a balancing approach. He said the actual malice standard itself, by requiring public officials and public figures to prove knowing or reckless falsehood in order to be able to collect damages, provided an adequate balance between a libel plaintiff's reputational interest and the First Amendment's guarantee of a free press.[120] In other words, the denial of a special editorial privilege to media defendants in a *Sullivan*-type libel action is the other side of the coin: if a public person must prove knowing and reckless falsehood to collect damages to his reputation, he must have the opportunity to meet that burden of proof, even if that means asking "state of mind" questions that may intrude into the editorial process. Any preferred position argument by the press, or other libel defendants, under such circumstances must necessarily give way to a balancing of interests approach.

Despite the *Gertz* modifications and the denial of an editorial privilege in *Herbert*, the constitutional privilege formulated by the Supreme Court in *Sullivan* still affords considerable protection for media defendants. It is indisput-

able that the overall effect of the constitutional libel privilege formulated by
the *Sullivan* Court has placed the press, as well as the citizen critic,[121] in a
preferred position by protecting even misstatements of facts about the public
lives of public officials or public figures so long as such publication is not
made knowingly or recklessly.[122] Clearly, the Supreme Court since 1964 has
given added protection to political expression in the interest of a more robust
debate. This preference for a free press needs to be carefully safeguarded.

The Maintenance of Procedural Safeguards

In examining the premise that freedom of expression should be placed in a
preferred position in any judicial balancing of interests, procedural as well as
substantive considerations are important. Application of the preferred position doctrine requires that generally higher standards of procedural due process be maintained where basic speech and press freedoms may be in jeopar-
dy. Likewise, the narrowing of the presumption of constitutionality—a basic
premise in the historical development of the preferred position postulate—
requires the careful application of constitutional doctrines such as vagueness
and overbreadth, a relaxation of requirements in order to allow third parties
standing to sue where the citizen critic or members of the press have tangible
First Amendment interests at stake, and more emphasis upon procedural due
process safeguards, particularly the right to a hearing before First Amendment rights are abridged or threatened.[123]

A statute is said to be defectively overbroad when it proscribes activities
that are constitutionally protected—for example, speech and press activities—as well as activities that are not, such as the conduct aspects of
picketing.[124] The vagueness doctrine, which has its roots in the notice requirements of procedural due process, holds that a statute must be drawn
with enough clarity and specificity that people will be sufficiently apprised of
what is expected of them. It can be argued that, "in a sense, the First
Amendment concern to prevent restraints which inhibit freedom of expression
and the concern for fairness which is implemented by the constitutional doctrine of procedural due process coalesce in the vagueness doctrine."[125]
Though the Court often uses the terms together, an overbroad statute need
not be vague, or vice versa.

Censorship of sexually oriented expression is one area of First Amendment litigation plagued with the vagueness problem. One prong of the
Court's *Miller* v. *California* redefinition of obscenity in 1973 stressed that state
laws making it a crime to engage in the dissemination of pornography must
"specifically" define such sexual expression or conduct.[126] Justice William J.
Brennan, Jr., dissenting from another obscenity decision handed down at the
same time, observed:

> After 16 years of experimentation and debate I am reluctantly forced to the conclu-
> sion that none of the available formulas, including the one announced today, can
> reduce the vagueness to a tolerable level while at the same time striking an accept-
> able balance between the protections of the First and Fourteenth Amendments, on
> the one hand, and on the other, the asserted state interest in regulating the dis-
> semination of certain sexually oriented materials.[127]

Though such definitiveness has defied judicial efforts, specificity is required of obscenity statutes because what is defined as obscene is criminal and falls outside the protection of the First Amendment.[128]

Overbreadth as a First Amendment doctrine provides substantive protection, focusing as it does on the language of the law itself. A law is void, the Court has held, if it "does not aim specifically at evils in the allowable area of state control, but ... sweeps within its ambit other activities that constitute an exercise of freedom of speech or of the press."[129] In deciding such First Amendment cases, the Court often applies the phrase "less drastic means," finding that governmental action, even though legitimate insofar as it regulates conduct, is unconstitutional in that it unduly inhibits expression, belief, or association rights protected under the First Amendment. In a speech case involving Communists, for example, the Supreme Court, while refusing to consider whether a federal statute totally banning Communists from employment in certain defense plants was in fact the best of several alternatives to prevent sabotage, held that "when legitimate legislative concerns are at stake ... Congress must achieve its goal by means which have a 'less drastic' impact on the continued vitality of First Amendment freedoms."[130] The concept of less drastic means, when placed in the judicial balancing scales, tends to safeguard expression interests, particularly where speech is linked with activities such as picketing, the distribution of handbills, and other forms of conduct.

In the First Amendment context, in contrast to other areas of law, the Supreme Court has permitted attacks on overbroad statutes without requiring that the person making the attack demonstrate that, in fact, his specific conduct was protected.[131] The reason for the special rule in the First Amendment area, according to the Court, is that an overbroad statute might serve to chill "fragile" First Amendment interests.[132] In addition, the Court has noted, "The use of overbreadth analysis reflects the conclusion that the possible harm to society from allowing unprotected speech to go unpunished is outweighed by the possibility that protected speech will be muted."[133] Justice John Paul Stevens, writing for the Court in *Young* v. *American Mini Theatres, Inc.*,[134] noted that this "exception from traditional rules of standing to raise constitutional issues has reflected the Court's judgment that the very existence of some statutes may cause persons not before the Court to refrain from engaging in constitutionally protected speech or expression.[135] Despite this view, Justice Stevens presented justification in his plurality opinion for validating a Detroit ordinance regulating the exhibition of sexually oriented materials falling within the scope of First Amendment protection. He judged such materials, like commercial advertising, to be in the category of second-class speech.[136]

Media representatives not parties to the litigation have also been granted standing in some jurisdictions to contest judicial restrictive orders directed toward nonmedia sources. The U.S. Court of Appeals, Sixth Circuit, for example, ruled that Columbia Broadcasting System had standing where the gag order, at least arguably, impaired rights guaranteed to the journalist by the First Amendment.[137] Under review was an order restricting news gathering related to the trial generated by the Kent State confrontation between

National Guardsmen and students in which four students were killed. The court said the protected right to publish the news would be of little value in the absence of sources from which to obtain it. Such a clearing away of procedural barriers, one commentator has noted, is "preferred position at its best."[138]

In other areas where First Amendment guarantees are threatened, procedural due process often lacks the exacting measure which such preferred freedoms would seem to require. Myron Farber, a *New York Times* reporter, for example, was sentenced to six months in jail and fined $1,000 without a hearing after he refused to submit material subpoenaed for *in camera* inspection. The journalist, relying upon the New Jersey shield law, sought a hearing on the issues of relevance, materiality, and overbreadth of the subpoena, which sought thousands of documents used in preparing an investigative story, documents which he and his newspaper had reason to believe were protected under the statute. The New Jersey Supreme Court, while acknowledging that the appellants were entitled to a hearing on the issues of relevance, materiality, and overbreadth of the subpoena, held that they had aborted their right by refusing to submit the subpoenaed materials for an *in camera* inspection.[139] However, the court said, "Those who in the future may be similarly situated... are entitled to a preliminary determination before being compelled to submit the subpoenaed material to a trial judge for inspection."[140]

The search of a newsroom for information relevant to criminal investigations, even though the news organization and its personnel are innocent parties to the matters under investigation, poses another news-gathering problem and raises procedural due process questions. The Supreme Court, in *Zurcher* v. *Stanford Daily*,[141] answering arguments that a surprise search of a newsroom would seriously interfere with the ability of the press to gather, analyze, and disseminate news, ruled that neither the Fourth Amendment nor the First gave the press or journalists special protection from valid search warrants. Justice White, writing for the majority, said the framers "did not require special showings that subpoenas would be impracticable, and did not insist that the owner of the place to be searched, if connected with the press, must be shown to be implicated in the offense being investigated."[142] The Court pointed out, however, that the Fourth Amendment did not prevent legislatures from establishing nonconstitutional protections against such searches,[143] and within two years the Congress[144] and seven states had passed such limitations.[145] While the Supreme Court clearly favored Fourth Amendment guarantees over those of the First in the context of criminal investigation as set out in *Zurcher*, ironically it was the Congress, barred by the First Amendment from abridging expression guarantees, which acted to safeguard those rights.

In *Reporters Committee* v. *American Telephone & Telegraph Co.*, the issue was whether the government should be permitted to subpoena the telephone records of a news organization or a journalist without giving the media representative prior notice and the opportunity to oppose the subpoena in court. The U.S. Court of Appeals, District of Columbia Circuit, said no notice was required,[146] and the Supreme Court denied certiorari.[147] The Court of Appeals reasoned that so long as the inspection of journalists' telephone toll-call records, which were released by the telephone company without prior notice to journalists, was in good faith, the First Amendment was not violated. The court said any First Amendment news-gathering right was subject to those general and incidental burdens that arise from good faith enforcement of valid civil and criminal laws.[148]

Even the rule of civil procedure allowing any party to a civil action, including a journalist, to move for summary judgment when the party believes that there is no genuine issue of material fact has been brought into question. This rule of law, which has proved beneficial to media libel defendants, was questioned by Chief Justice Burger, writing for the Court's majority in *Hutchinson* v. *Proxmire*.[149] The District Court had ruled that in determining whether a plaintiff had made an adequate showing of actual malice, summary judgment might well be "the rule rather than the exception."[150] The Chief Justice, however, noting "the nuances of the issues" involved, wrote, "The proof of 'actual malice' calls a defendant's state of mind into question . . . and does not readily lend itself to summary disposition."[151]

One commentator has noted that in the concentration on substantive rights in regard to freedom of expression, it has been a common mistake to disregard the procedural connotations.[152] It is clear that in matters regarding speech and press freedoms, the careful judicial scrutiny emphasized by the preferred position doctrine for substantive due process must also be applied in the procedural areas noted above if these basic freedoms are to be safeguarded in the ongoing process of judicial balancing.

Implications of the Speech-Press Clause Debate

Protection for the Institutional Press?

Justice Potter Stewart, in a 1974 address at Yale Law School, stated that the First Amendment explicitly and purposively provides for the press protection that is independent from that provided to others under the speech clause. He explained:

> The Free Press guarantee is, in essence, a *structural* provision of the Constitution. Most of the other provisions in the Bill of Rights protect specific liberties or specific rights of individuals: freedom of speech, freedom of worship, the right to counsel, the privilege against compulsory self-incrimination, to name a few. In contrast, the Free Press Clause extends protection to an institution. The publishing business is, in short, the only organized private business that is given explicit constitutional protection.[153]

Justice Stewart observed that cases coming to the Supreme Court during the first fifty years after the First Amendment had been extended to the states dealt primarily with "the rights of the soapbox orator, the nonconformist pamphleteer, the religious evangelist," but seldom with the rights, privileges, or responsibilities of the organized press.[154] More recently, however, cases involving the established, institutional press have reached the Court—cases dealing with public libel, the right to protect confidential sources, the right to publish government documents without prior restraint, and questions of access to print and broadcast media.

The Court's approach to these questions, Justice Stewart said, has been based upon the assumption that the press as an institution has constitutional protection. He explained:

> This basic understanding is essential, I think, to avoid an elementary error of constitutional law. It is tempting to suggest that freedom of the press means only that newspaper publishers are guaranteed freedom of expression. They *are* guaranteed that freedom, to be sure, but so are we all, because of the Free Speech Clause. If the Free Press guarantee meant no more than freedom of expression, it would be a constitutional redundancy.[155]

In his view, the unifying principle underlying recent Supreme Court decisions dealing with the press was the understanding that the First Amendment protects the institutional autonomy of the press. The press clause's primary purpose, Stewart said, was to create "a fourth institution outside the Government as an additional check on the three official branches."[156]

The speech-press clause debate has spawned numerous law review articles and commentary, both pro and con.[157] One commentator has attempted to demonstrate that Justice Stewart's judicial opinions, both before and after the Yale address, have consistently stated similar themes.[158] Chief Justice Burger, however, in a concurring opinion in *First National Bank of Boston* v. *Bellotti*,[159] took the occasion to caution the press that it had no special First Amendment rights. He said he did not believe there was a historical basis for making a distinction between the speech and press clause guarantees.[160] The chief justice also saw a fundamental problem with defining that part of the press to be afforded special protection. He viewed the task of including some entities within the "institutional press" while excluding others as contrary to the Court's approach in the past. In short, the chief justice concluded, "The First Amendment does not 'belong' to any definable category of persons or entities: it belongs to all who exercise its freedoms."[161]

A few days after his *Bellotti* concurrence, the chief justice wrote the opinion for a unanimous Court in *Landmark Communications, Inc.* v. *Virginia*,[162] holding that the state may not penalize the press for reporting facts concerning a confidential judicial commission investigation since the publication Virginia sought to punish "lies near the core of the First Amendment." Indeed, the chief justice pointed out, "The article published by Landmark provided factual information about a legislatively authorized inquiry pending before the Judicial Inquiry Commission and in so doing clearly served those interests in public scrutiny and discussion of governmental affairs which the First Amendment was adopted to protect."[163] The chief justice made clear that the First Amendment forbade criminal punishment of "third persons who are strangers to an inquiry, including the news media," although the state could punish participants in the proceedings for breach of the statute.[164]

Justice Stewart, in a four-paragraph concurring opinion in *Landmark*, took the opportunity to reiterate his Yale Law School theme that the press does have greater First Amendment rights than others. He wrote:

> If the constitutional protection of a free press means anything, it means that government cannot take it upon itself to decide what a newspaper may and may not publish. Though government may deny access to information and punish its theft, government may not prohibit or punish the publication of that information once it falls into the hands of the press, unless the need for secrecy is manifestly overwhelming.[165]

Justice Stewart was clearly focusing upon the press as an institution, but the chief justice's opinion for the Court applied the holding not just to the press but to "any strangers to an inquiry" exercising their freedom under the First Amendment. Indeed, Chief Justice Burger acknowledged in a *Bellotti* footnote that some cases decided by the Court during the 1970s may be read as suggesting that the press clause has no independent scope while others tend to suggest just the opposite conclusion. The Court, he said, had "not yet squarely resolved" the question.[166]

Implications of Special Privilege for the Press

The question of the interrelatedness of the speech and press clauses arising from Justice Stewart's claim for special protection for the press as an institution has numerous legal implications for the preferred position doctrine. While it may be true that "freedom of the press as a right recognizably distinct from that of freedom of speech is an idea whose time is past due,"[167] what effect might such an approach have on protection for freedom of expression overall? While many aspects of the speech-press debate go beyond the scope of this study, a number of problem areas do have preferred position implications.

Even assuming the efficacy of special constitutional protection for the press as an institution, a problem clearly exists in providing historical documentation for such a press clause claim. For example, a *New York Times* reporter and syndicated columnist with considerable expertise in press law took issue with Justice Stewart's conclusion that the eighteenth-century concept of freedom of the press applied exclusively to the institutional press. While acknowledging that the precise motives of those who drafted the speech and press clauses were unlikely to be discovered, he concluded:

> The most natural explanation seems the most probable: The framers wanted to protect expression whether in unprinted or printed form. Freedom of the press was more often mentioned in colonial and state bills of rights than freedom of speech; at the time of the first amendment ten state constitutions protected the former while only two the latter. . . . But the two phrases were used interchangeably, then as now, to mean freedom of expression.[168]

Chief Justice Burger has likewise argued that "the history of the [Press] Clause does not suggest that the authors contemplated a 'special' or 'institutional' privilege."[169] Indeed, the chief justice found substantial authority for the proposition that the framers used freedom of speech and freedom of the press synonymously.[170] Burger's analysis prompted one media attorney to respond:

> Whatever other conclusions may be drawn—and disputes engaged in—from the history of the adoption of the press clause of the first amendment, one thing is clear: The press clause of the first amendment was no afterthought, no mere appendage to the speech clause. The press clause was *not*, the views of Chief Justice Burger to the contrary, merely "complementary to and a natural extension of Speech Clause liberty."[171]

However, as another participant in the speech-press clause debate has observed, "The Framers have left us language in the first amendment which justifies the present debate—language which, under almost any view one takes, is less than clear."[172]

If the claim of Justice Stewart for a constitutional protection of the press as an institution is dismissed, there still remains the question of whether the journalist, under certain circumstances, can or should seek special First Amendment privileges not afforded to members of the public generally. Many journalists, stressing "the extraordinary importance of their function of gathering and distributing the information required by a self-governing people," have argued that such a preference for press freedom is essential.[173] As has been noted, however, such efforts have been largely unsuccessful with the Court.[174]

Treating the press as an institution or affording it special constitutional privileges may also tend to arouse uneasy feelings on the part of the general public, it has been argued. Powerful newspapers and broadcast networks are not universally beloved as it is, and critics often point to "the arrogance of the media." To the degree that free press rights depend upon public understanding and support, as suggested by Hamilton in *The Federalist*, claims for special press rights may only serve to separate further the professional press from the public it represents.[175] It is also true that institutions are often subject to external check and regulation in the American system, as the result of both public opinion and governmental action. Special privilege itself may be viewed as imposing various obligations upon the press. Chief Justice Burger, for example, has observed, "The extraordinary protections afforded by the First Amendment carry with them something in the nature of a fiduciary duty to exercise the protected rights responsibly—a duty widely acknowledged but not always observed by editors and publishers."[176] Justice Stewart, of course, argued that "the public's interest in knowing about its government" would best be protected by an "autonomous press" free from governmental restraints.[177]

The First Amendment need not, indeed should not, be read to grant special rights only to those engaged in institutionalized communication. One media attorney has argued:

> What it should protect is not the *institution*, but the *role* of the press: To afford a vehicle of information and opinion, to inform and educate the public, to offer criticism, to provide a forum for discussion and debate, and to act as a surrogate to obtain for readers news and information that individual citizens could not or would not gather on their own. A special guarantee for freedom of the press should apply not simply to those whom a court might label "press" but to whomever, of whatever size, by whatever means, regularly undertakes to fulfill the press function.[178]

Indeed, a more persuasive argument can be made for a preferred position for both speech and press freedoms.

Robert H. Bork, a former solicitor general of the United States, has observed that the "preferred position rests upon grounds so strong that they could properly have been inferred by judges from the structure of the entire Constitution, even if no First Amendment had ever been adopted." He noted, "[The preferred position] theory requires great freedom for both speech and press."[179] Bork, however, would apparently accord such preference only to "speech that is explicitly political."[180]

Justice Brennan would likewise afford "more or less" absolute First Amendment protection for political expression to all "individuals who wish to speak out and broadly disseminate their views." He noted that his *speech* model drew "its considerable power...from the abiding commitment we all feel to the right of self-expression." This speech model, which he applied to the press as well as to that "collection of individuals" who wish to speak out on governmental affairs, was characterized as readily lending itself to "the heady rhetoric of absolutism."[181]

The growing body of literature touching on the speech and press clause debate, while it may illuminate some aspects of First Amendment interpretation, does little to clarify or to strengthen the preferred position postulate. As a constitutional principle, Justice Stewart's institutional press claim is clearly unacceptable to a majority of the Supreme Court. Even if it were acceptable, there is evidence the press may gain greater benefit from bracing its rights within those of the public[182] than from arguing for a special privilege for itself, even though that privilege is to be used to serve the public's interest.[183] It is also possible that any argument for a preference for free expression will have more force in the area of political expression than in the various areas of private speech, a distinction clearly significant for the press.

Implications of Preferred Position in the Access Context

One court has noted that the day-to-day operation of the press is tripartite in nature: reporters must have the means of acquiring information, the information must be edited and processed, and the information must be disseminated.[184] The third part, however, has received more First Amendment protection than the first two, and the second more than the first. The dissemination of the news has long been accorded constitutional protection.[185] Numerous decisions by the Supreme Court have reiterated that the right to publish truthful information of general public interest and concern, which has been legally acquired, is within the scope of the protection afforded by the First Amendment.[186] The Court has also explicitly upheld First Amendment protection for the editorial function of newspapers and broadcast journalists upon at least two occasions during the 1970s,[187] although it rejected such protection in the specific circumstances of another case.[188] The protection for news gathering, however, has been, at best, qualified.[189]

Does the claim of a First Amendment right for the institutional press, as argued by Justice Stewart in his Yale Law School address, offer a doctrinal approach which would enhance the press's access claim to governmental facilities and proceedings as surrogate for the general public? Alternatively, would such access arguments be aided by acknowledging that the First Amendment should be read as guaranteeing a personal freedom to publish belonging to every individual? A number of Supreme Court cases during the late 1970s dealing with access to governmental facilities and to judicial proceedings may give an insight into the conflicting claims of speech and press clause advocates.

Access to Governmental Facilities

Justice White, writing to deny newsmen a First Amendment–based testimonial privilege in *Branzburg* v. *Hayes* in 1972, provided a dictum which was utilized by the Court in determining later access questions. White wrote that "it has generally been held that the First Amendment does not guarantee the press a constitutional right of special access to information not available to the public generally."[190] Two years later, in *Pell* v. *Procunier*[191] and *Saxbe* v. *Washington Post Co.*,[192] the press attempted to establish a First Amendment right to gather news within state and federal prisons. Justice Stewart, writing for the *Pell* Court, cited Justice White's *Branzburg* dictum and held that "newsmen have no constitutional right of access to [state] prisons or their inmates beyond that afforded the general public."[193] Relying on *Pell*, the *Saxbe* Court held that a similar policy of the federal prison system which permitted press interviews only with individually designated inmates in minimum security facilities did not abridge press freedom.[194]

As a matter of fact, in both *Pell* and *Saxbe*, as the Supreme Court pointed out, the press had been granted substantial access beyond that afforded the general public,[195] and there was no evidence in either case that officials had attempted to conceal information about prison conditions.[196] Four years later, in *Houchins* v. *KQED, Inc.*,[197] the Court had the opportunity to rule in a case in which the press had been absolutely barred by informal administrative policy from investigating conditions at a California county jail where a prisoner had committed suicide. A badly divided Court, however, in a decision participated in by only seven justices who wrote three separate opinions, once again denied access to journalists. The denial was again linked to the question of how much access had been provided to the public generally.[198]

Chief Justice Burger, in an opinion joined only by Justices White and Rehnquist, acknowledged that prison conditions were a matter "of great public importance" and that the press had traditionally played a powerful role in informing the public about the operation of public institutions. However, he argued, these facts afforded no basis "for reading into the Constitution a right of the public or the media to enter these institutions, with camera equipment, and take moving and still pictures of inmates for broadcast purposes. This Court has never intimated a First Amendment guarantee of a right of access to all sources of information within government control."[199] Justice Stewart, concurring, disagreed with the rationale of the plurality opinion. Like the chief justice, Stewart did not question the application of *Pell* and *Saxbe*, but he argued that the concept of equal access must be accorded more flexibility. Noting that the chief justice appeared to view "equal access" as meaning access that was identical in all respects, Justice Stewart said, "I believe that the concept of equal access must be accorded more flexibility in order to accommodate the practical distinctions between the press and the general public."[200] Justice Stevens, in a strong dissent joined by Justices Brennan and Lewis F. Powell, Jr., argued that *Pell* and *Saxbe* should not be controlling because those decisions dealt with situations in which the press had been granted substantial access. He also noted that Sheriff Houchins had arbitrarily prohibited all press and public access at the time KQED filed its action. Like Chief Justice Burger, Justice Stevens would have granted the press no greater right of access than that given the public, but Stevens would have given press and public alike more than Sheriff Houchins's once-a-month tours.[201]

The lack of consensus among the majority of the seven justices taking part in the *Houchins* opinion leaves the issue of constitutional protection for news gathering in governmental facilities in some question. There is not much question, however, that a majority of the Court has been reluctant to grant members of the press First Amendment–based access privileges which go beyond those granted to the public generally.

Journalists have met with the same lack of success in seeking access to view, record, and make eyewitness reports of executions in state prisons. The Fifth Circuit, for example, overturned an order requiring Texas prison authorities to permit the filming for broadcast of an execution. Relying upon *Pell*, the court emphasized that members of the press were afforded no greater access to state executions than members of the public.[202] The press was similarly unsuccessful in a First Amendment challenge of a Utah statute that specifically denied the general public access to executions.[203]

The requirements of news gathering may indeed demand a preference for the institutional press, as argued by Justice Stewart. A strong argument can certainly be made that more flexibility in prison access regulations is needed to accommodate the essential function of news gathering. While such arguments have been singularly unsuccessful in the past, the issue of access to judicial proceedings may offer some evidence that the Court is shifting toward a more liberal stance on access to governmental facilities generally.

Access to Judicial Proceedings

Conflict between First Amendment free speech and free press guarantees and Sixth Amendment fair trial guarantees has had a long history. The Supreme Court, in a series of decisions beginning in 1941, had placed strict limits on contempt as a sanction against out-of-court publications dealing with judicial proceedings.[204] While the Court, on occasion, has appeared to base its decisions upholding press freedom on the rationale that "judges are supposed to be men of fortitude, able to thrive in a hardy climate,"[205] one observer has noted that "it seems more likely that the Court determined that the value of free discussion of this aspect of government outweighs the cost in actual or apparent extrajudicial influence upon the administration of justice."[206] In any event, with the privilege to publish generally secured under the First Amendment,[207] interest during the late 1970s in gaining access to judicial proceedings intensified.

The first Supreme Court test of the right of trial judges to close judicial proceedings to both the public and members of the press came in 1979. In that decision, *Gannett Co.* v. *DePasquale*,[208] the Court virtually ignored First Amendment interests in upholding the barring of the press and the public from pretrial hearings. Justice Stewart, writing for the Court, held that the language of the Sixth Amendment—"the accused shall enjoy the right to a speedy and public trial"—afforded no right of access to the public or the press;[209] nor would the phrase, "public trial," support the claim of access to public pretrial hearings.[210] Although the decision was based primarily upon Sixth Amendment grounds, not on whether the press had a right to attend trials under the First Amendment,[211] the decision played havoc with press efforts to inform the public about judicial proceedings. Within a year, at least ten states had relied on *Gannett* in approving either trial or pretrial secrecy.[212] Some trial courts even closed trials to the press but not to the public.[213]

Justice Blackmun, in a lengthy dissent joined by Justices Brennan, White, and Marshall, argued in *Gannett* that a public right to open judicial proceedings was acknowledged and that public trials were the custom at the time the Constitution was adopted. He stated that open trials at both federal and state levels have "always been recognized as a safeguard against any attempt to employ our courts as instruments of persecution."[214] His reasoning, however, obviously fell short of demonstrating to a majority of the Court that the public right of access was to be secured by the Sixth Amendment.

A year later, in *Richmond Newspapers, Inc.* v. *Virginia*,[215] a case dealing with a state trial judge's closing of a criminal trial on the basis of *Gannett*, the Supreme Court reversed both the trial court and the Virginia Supreme Court, holding that "absent an overriding interest articulated in findings," the First Amendment required that "the trial of a criminal case must be open to the public."[216] Noting that the question before the Court in *Gannett* dealt with the narrow question of access to a pretrial proceeding, Chief Justice Burger, writing for the Court's plurality,[217] said:

> But here for the first time the Court is asked to decide whether a criminal trial itself may be closed to the public upon the unopposed request of the defendant, without any demonstration that closure is required to protect the defendant's superior right to a fair trial, or that some other overriding consideration requires closure.[218]

The chief justice then launched into a lengthy historical review of criminal trials, beginning with the Norman Conquest,[219] a review which Justice Harry A. Blackmun, concurring, said he found "gratifying" because he had taken "great pains in assembling" such historical material in his *Gannett* dissent.[220]

Justice Stevens, in a concurring opinion, labeled *Richmond Newspapers* a "watershed case."[221] He viewed the decision as reading a right of access into the First Amendment and wrote, "Until today the Court has accorded virtually absolute protection to the dissemination of information or ideas, but never before has it squarely held that the acquisition of newsworthy matter is entitled to any constitutional protection whatsoever."[222] One commentator has noted that Justice Stevens's observation may be "wishful thinking" or an effort to persuade lower courts to so interpret the *Richmond Newspapers* decision.[223] There is little doubt that the decision clarified the badly fragmented *Gannett* decision in regard to the scope of that Court's ruling. The question as to whether the First Amendment grants the press and public a right of access to information about governmental activities or access to governmental facilities is far more complex. Yet, recognition of a right of access may well be essential if the First Amendment is to continue to serve the basic function of keeping the public informed about the increasingly complex activities of its government.[224]

It is clear that for the issue of access to judicial proceedings, tying speech and press rights together has served the interest of press access claims. Chief Justice Burger, in the historical analysis supporting the Court's decision in *Richmond Newspapers*, noted that the "evidence demonstrates conclusively that at the time our organic laws were adopted, criminal trials both here and in England had long been presumptively open."[225] He viewed the question before the Court as one dealing with the access right of both the public and the press.[226] If the opinions of the various justices in the case support Justice Stevens's conclusion that *Richmond Newspapers* is a watershed access case, then the press may benefit in limited areas of news gathering, for example, in gaining access to governmental facilities. The Court's 1981 decision in *Chandler* v. *Florida*[227] upholding a state's right to provide for radio, television, and still photographic coverage of a criminal trial for public broadcast over the objection of the accused consistent with constitutional guarantees of a fair trial is encouraging.[228]

Conclusions

If the Supreme Court is to exercise its historic role as guardian of the fundamental freedoms flowing from the speech and press clauses of the First Amendment, it is imperative that those basic freedoms be carefully safeguarded in the balancing of interests approach being employed by the Court. One writer, noting the governmental barriers to press freedom being erected, borrowed a metaphor from Thomas Erskine's speech in defense of Thomas Paine's *Rights of Man* and characterized the present Court as "a constitutional sentry fallen asleep."[229] There is some evidence that "sentries" in the private sector may also have fallen asleep to the dangerous erosion of their basic freedoms.

While public apathy, even hostility, toward the press may be indicated by the opinion poll announced in conjunction with the First Amendment Congress meeting in Philadelphia in January 1980, there is little reason to believe that public concern was any greater in regard to press freedom in 1789 when the First Congress met to consider adoption of a bill of rights. It should also be noted that less than a decade after ratification of the Bill of Rights, an aroused public opinion contributed to the demise of the Alien and Sedition Acts, the first serious statutory threat to freedom of political expression. There is little reason to doubt that an aroused public would act any differently today to a serious threat of governmental censorship.

Anyone espousing a preferred position for speech and press freedoms must acknowledge that, under some circumstances, balancing of interests is inescapable. However, even under such circumstances when unlimited discussion may interfere with other governmental purposes, freedom of speech ought to weigh very heavily in the scale. The weighting of the scale can be accomplished in a number of ways. One obvious way is to take more care with what is placed on the scale, as noted by Justice Black and other libertarians. Individual freedom of expression, for example, need not be balanced against the overall interest of an ordered society. Another way is to place governmental strictures which threaten freedom of expression under a "more searching judicial inquiry" than might be done when nonspeech interests are at stake. Or, in terms of the *Carolene* footnote, when basic expression guarantees are threatened, there should be "a narrower scope for operation of the presumption of constitutionality."[230] This approach would fall short of presumptive invalidity which strikes press critics as absolutism.

In any case, the preferred position doctrine need not be rejected because the concept of presumptive invalidity is unacceptable. A preference for freedom has been enhanced and may continue to be enhanced by: rejecting prior restraints on expression, except under narrowly defined circumstances, as the Court has done in recent years when it has consistently treated prior restraints as presumptively invalid and has placed a heavy burden of proof on those seeking to overcome that presumption; utilizing the clear and present danger test, in which the Court and not the legislature ultimately determines the presence of danger; using the *New York Times Co.* v. *Sullivan* "actual malice" rule to protect "uninhibited, robust, and wide-open" debate about matters of general and public concern against defamation actions; and maintaining careful scrutiny and procedural due process safeguards when basic speech and press freedoms are involved.

Further claims by the press for special privilege as an institution, despite Justice Stewart's interpretation of the press clause, are unlikely to advance the cause of press freedom. In most areas involving freedom of expression—for example, in gaining access to judicial proceedings—espousal of the historical interrelatedness of speech and press rights may afford a better judicial approach. In special problem areas, such as news gathering and protection for the editorial process, where at least a limited privilege is consistent with the function of communication, a claim for special privilege is more likely to succeed. Such claims, however, should not be for the press alone, but for all those who seek to serve as a vehicle of information and opinion to inform and educate the public. This, by necessity, would include authors, researchers, pamphleteers, and others engaged in public communication, as well as members of the institutional press. But, as Justice Stewart has also noted, "The public's interest in knowing about its government is protected by the guarantee of a Free Press, but the protection is indirect." For some information, he pointed out, the press must rely on "the tug and pull of the political forces in American Society." While the "press is free to do battle against secrecy and deception in government," he noted, "the Constitution . . . establishes the contest, not its resolution."[231]

In most areas touching upon free speech and free press, however, the preferred position approach to First Amendment interpretation has utility, not only as a safeguard for freedom of expression guarantees in judicial balancing but also as a statement of faith in the democratic process.[232] Freedom of speech and press, as articles of faith, are so vital to the maintenance of a free society that their primacy must be recognized by both the courts and the general public. While press responsibility is not mandated by the First Amendment, the successful espousal of a preferred position must ultimately depend upon a press performance which merits such a doctrinal approach and an editorial vigilance sufficient to maintain a healthy and free marketplace of ideas without which the democratic process would flounder.

Notes

1. Lenora Williamson, "Philadelphia Congress Sparks Lively Debate," *Editor & Publisher* 113 (26 January 1980): 15, 48.
2. Roy P. Fairfield, ed., *The Federalist Papers*, 2d ed. (Garden City, N.Y.: Doubleday, Anchor Books, 1966), pp. 263–64.
3. See, e.g., Zechariah Chafee, Jr., *Free Speech in the United States* (Cambridge, Mass.: Harvard University Press, 1941).
4. *The Gallup Opinion Index*, no. 174 (January 1980): 23–27. By way of comparison, in a similar 1958 Gallup poll, 21 percent answered a comparable question by saying they would approve of placing greater curbs on what newspapers print, 58 percent said they would disapprove, while another 21 percent did not express an opinion. George Gallup, Jr., "Americans Favor Tougher Controls on the Press," *Editor & Publisher* 113 (19 January 1980): 7. In a more recent national public opinion survey conducted by the Public Agenda Foundation and funded by the Markle Foundation, the majority of those polled favored more governmental controls, including application of the fairness and equal time doctrines of broadcasting to newspapers. On the other hand, the poll indicated that the public rejects—by a margin of 2 to 1—laws which place curbs on what the media may print or broadcast. See "Public Favors Fairness Law to Regulate Newspapers," *Editor & Publisher* 113 (1 November 1980): 14.
5. See, e.g., Floyd Abrams, "Judges and Journalists: Who Decides What?" *Nieman Reports* 28 (Winter 1974): 34–41; Walter Cronkite, "Is the Free Press in America under Attack? The Public's Right to Know," *Vital Speeches* 45 (15 March 1979): 331–34; Jack C. Landau, "The

State of the First Amendment," *Nieman Reports* 33 (Spring 1979): 18–25; Eugene H. Methvin, "Journalists versus Justices: Supreme Court Decisions," *Vital Speeches* 46 (1 December 1979): 120–23; Allen H. Neuharth, "Future Directions in American Newspapers: The Dangers of an Imperial Judiciary," *Vital Speech* 45 (1 February 1979): 253–55.

    Among the troubling cases were Gannett Co. v. DePasquale, 443 U.S. 368 (1979) (no guaranteed constitutional right under the Sixth Amendment for press or public to attend pretrial hearings); Herbert v. Lando, 441 U.S. 153 (1979) (denying journalists editorial privilege to safeguard against "state of mind" questions during pretrial discovery); Wolston v. Reader's Digest Ass'n, 443 U.S. 157 (1979) (narrowing the definition of "public figure" libel plaintiff); FCC v. Pacifica Foundation, 438 U.S. 726 (1978) (limiting "indecent" speech in broadcasting); Houchins v. KQED, Inc., 438 U.S. 1 (1978) (rejecting claims of a First Amendment right of access to governmental facilities); Nixon v. Warner Communications, Inc., 435 U.S. 589 (1978) (denying right to copy tapes previously presented in evidence in a criminal trial); Zurcher v. Stanford Daily, 436 U.S. 547 (1978) (upholding the search of a newsroom conducted under the authority of a warrant); Zacchini v. Scripps-Howard Broadcasting Co., 433 U.S. 562 (1977) (denying newsworthiness as a privacy defense in a "right of publicity" context); Time, Inc. v. Firestone, 424 U.S. 448 (1976) (narrowing the definition of "public figure" libel plaintiff); Young v. American Mini Theatres, Inc., 427 U.S. 50 (1976) (upholding a zoning ordinance regulating the location of certain businesses, even though some of the businesses engaged in speech falling within the scope of First Amendment protection).

6. Commenting upon numerous joint press-bar efforts during the 1970s to foster a better understanding by both press and bar about press law problems, Landau lamented:

> And what has been the result of all this reasonableness and moderation and discussion? They [the courts] have jailed our reporters. They have held our editors in contempt. They have fined our publishers. They have allowed our confidential investigative records to be seized en masse. They have permitted police in our newsrooms. They have allowed the secret seizure of our telephone calls. They have forced us to disclose our internal newsroom discussions and private thoughts. They have destroyed our journalist shield laws and our libel law protections. And at the same time, they have been trying to prohibit information about themselves from being made freely available to the public.

Jack C. Landau, "The State of the First Amendment—1980," speech to the Mid-America Press Institute, St. Louis, Mo., January 25, 1980.

    For a jurist's critique of press criticism, see William J. Brennan, Jr., "Address," *Rutgers Law Review* 32 (1979): 173–83.

7. Gallup, "Americans Favor Tougher Controls on the Press," p. 7.

    A second First Amendment Congress held in Williamsburg, Va., in March 1980 adopted a series of resolutions outlining broad-based concerns regarding the exercise of First Amendment rights and proposing ways in which the press and the public might work together to ensure the preservation of all constitutionally protected freedoms. Andrew Radolf, "First Congress Adopts 12 'Action' Measures," *Editor & Publisher* 113 (22 March 1980): 11, 16.

    A 1976 study of the interdependence of the media and the courts found ironic overtones in the dispute between the press and the judiciary. It was pointed out, for example, that judges, as well as journalists, depend on "moral suasion for effective institutional survival." Also, the study noted:

> The central foundation of support for the rulings of the judiciary is the people. That support can be most effectively achieved through the media. . . . Such a condition might be thought to lead to a level of cooperation between those in the courtroom who interpret the law and those in the newsroom who write about the conduct of the public business.

Howard Simons and Joseph A. Califano, Jr., eds., *The Media and the Law* (New York: Praeger Publishers, 1976), p. 2.

8. It has generally been held that freedom of speech and press are not absolute rights and, despite the efforts of Justices Hugo L. Black and William O. Douglas, that the language of the First Amendment was never intended to be strictly construed. Justice Black, concurring in Smith v. California, 361 U.S. 147, 157–59 (1959), said of his absolutist position:

> I read "no law abridging" to mean *no law abridging*. The First Amendment, which is the supreme law of the land, has thus fixed its own value on freedom of speech and press by putting these freedoms wholly "beyond the reach" of *federal* power to abridge. No other provision of the Constitution purports to dilute the scope of these unequivocal commands of the First Amendment. Consequently, I do not believe that any federal agencies, including Congress and this Court, have power or authority to subordinate speech and press to what they think are "more important interests."

More recently Justice Harry A. Blackmun, dissenting in the Pentagon Papers case, said: "Each provision of the Constitution is important, and I cannot subscribe to a doctrine of unlimited absolutism for the First Amendment at the cost of downgrading other provisions. First Amendment absolutism has never commanded a majority of this Court." New York Times Co. v. United States, 403 U.S. 713, 761 (1971).

9. Refer to note 5 supra. For an evaluation of the Burger Court, see Archibald Cox, "Foreword: Freedom of Expression in the Burger Court," *Harvard Law Review* 94 (November 1980): 1–73; Thomas I. Emerson, "First Amendment Doctrine and the Burger Court," *California Law Review* 68 (May 1980): 422–81; Philip R. Higdon, "The Burger Court and the Media: A Ten Year Perspective," *Western New England Law Review* 2 (Spring 1980): 593–680.

10. Edmond Cahn, "The Firstness of the First Amendment," *Yale Law Journal* 65 (February 1956): 464–81.

11. The phrase is from Robert B. McKay, "The Preference for Freedom," *New York University Law Review* 34 (November 1959): 1182–227.

12. In an often-quoted review, one legal scholar observed that the framers probably had "no very clear idea as to what they meant by 'freedom of speech or of the press.'" Zechariah Chafee, Jr., review of *Free Speech and Its Relation to Self-Government* by Alexander Meiklejohn, *Harvard Law Review* 62 (March 1949): 898. For a similar view, see Leonard W. Levy, *Legacy of Suppression: Freedom of Speech and Press in Early American History* (Cambridge, Mass.: Belknap Press of Harvard University Press, 1960): xii, 247–48. Levy strongly disagreed with Chafee, however, in regard to the premise that it was the intention of the framers of the First Amendment to "wipe out the common law of sedition, and make further prosecutions for criticism of the government, without any incitement to law-breaking, forever impossible in the United States of America." Chafee, *Free Speech in the United States*, p. 21. In the preface to his *Legacy of Suppression*, p. vii, Levy stated:

> I find that libertarian theory from the time of Milton to the ratification of the First Amendment substantially accepted the right of the state to suppress seditious libel. . . . The evidence drawn particularly from the period 1776 to 1791 indicates that the generation that framed the first state declarations of rights and the First Amendment was hardly as libertarian as we have traditionally assumed. They did not intend to give free rein to criticism of the government that might be deemed seditious libel, although the concept of seditious libel was—and still is—the principal basis of muzzling political dissent.

13. Despite this fact, most mass communications law textbooks give scant attention to the preferred position doctrine. See, e.g., William E. Francois, *Mass Media Law and Regulation*, 2d ed. (Columbus, Ohio: Grid, Inc., 1978), pp. 27, 32, 47, 87, 263–64; Marc A. Franklin, *Mass Media Law* (Mineola, N.Y.: Foundation Press, 1977), pp. 50, 51, 122, 448; Donald M. Gillmor and Jerome A. Barron, *Mass Communications Law*, 3d ed. (St. Paul, Minn.: West Publishing Co., 1979), pp. 27–34, 81, 172; Harold L. Nelson and Dwight L. Teeter, Jr., *Law of Mass Communications*, 3d ed. (Mineola, N.Y.: Foundation Press, 1978), p. 11. One other textbook, Don R. Pember, *Mass Media Law*, 2d ed. (Dubuque, Iowa: Wm. C. Brown Co. Publishers, 1981), and a speech-press handbook for lawyers, Jerome A. Barron and C. Thomas Dienes, *Handbook of Free Speech and Free Press* (Boston: Little, Brown, 1979), make no mention of the preferred position doctrine.

14. One legal commentator wrote in 1959 that "every member of the Court since 1919 has concurred in one or many of the collective expressions of preference for the first amendment." McKay, "The Preference for Freedom," p. 1190. Support by members of the Burger Court for various judicial approaches, tests, and procedural safeguards tending to enhance the preferred position doctrine is discussed in the text accompanying notes 66–152 infra.

15. This metaphor is used by McKay, "The Preference for Freedom," p. 34.

16. Thomas I. Emerson, *Toward a General Theory of the First Amendment* (New York: Random House, Vintage Books, 1966), p. 3. The Court, as well as individual justices, has also recognized a so-called "societal function" of the First Amendment, a function aimed toward the preservation of free public discussion of governmental affairs. See, e.g., Saxbe v. Washington Post Co., 417 U.S. 843, 862–63 (1974); Houchins v. KQED, Inc., 438 U.S. at 31 (Stevens, J., dissenting). Two authorities often cited by the Supreme Court in enunciating the theory that self-government assumes an informed citizenry are James Madison and Alexander Meiklejohn. Madison addressed the general assumption: "A popular Government without popular information or the means of acquiring it, is but a Prologue to a Farce or a Tragedy; or, perhaps both. Knowledge will forever govern ignorance: And a people who mean to be their own Governors, must arm themselves with the power which knowledge gives." "To W.T. Barry, August 4, 1822," in *Writings of James Madison*, ed. Gaillard Hunt, 9 vols. (New York: G.P. Putnam's Sons, 1900–10), 9: 103, cited in Houchins v. KQED, Inc. 438 U.S. at 31–32 (Stevens, J., dissenting). Meiklejohn tied the societal function to the First Amendment:

> Just as far as . . . the citizens who are to decide an issue are denied acquaintance with information or opinion or doubt or disbelief or criticism which is relevant to that issue, just so far the result must be ill-considered, ill-balanced planning for the general good. It is that mutilation of the thinking process of the community against which the First Amendment of the Constitution is directed.

Alexander Meiklejohn, *Free Speech and Its Relation to Self-Government* (New York: Harper & Brothers, 1948), p. 26.

17. "To James Madison, March 15, 1789," in *The Papers of Thomas Jefferson*, ed. Julian P. Boyd, 19 vols. to date (Princeton, N.J.: Princeton University Press, 1950–), 14: 660–61. (Inconsistencies in spelling have been corrected.)

18. "To Edward Carrington, January 16, 1787," *The Papers of Thomas Jefferson*, 11: 49.

19. Ibid.

20. Leonard W. Levy, *Freedom of the Press from Zenger to Jefferson* (Indianapolis: Bobbs-Merrill, 1966), p. 327.

21. U.S., Congress, House, *Annals of Congress*, 1st Cong., 1st sess., 1789, 1: 434.

22. U.S., Congress, *Annals of Congress*, 1st Cong., 1789–1791, 2, appendix: 1984.

23. For a further discussion of the origins and meaning of the First Amendment, see George Anastaplo, *The Constitutionalist: Notes on the First Amendment* (Dallas: Southern Methodist Press, 1971); Irving Brant, *The Bill of Rights: Its Origins and Meaning* (Indianapolis: Bobbs-Merrill, 1965); Edward G. Hudon, *Freedom of Speech and Press in America* (Washington, D.C.: Public Affairs Press, 1963); Leonard W. Levy, *Legacy of Suppression: Freedom of Speech and Press in Early American History* (New York: Harper & Row, 1963); James Madison, *The Virginia Report of 1799–1880* (Richmond, Va.: J. W. Randolph, 1850); Robert A. Rutland, *The Birth of the Bill of Rights, 1776–1791* (Chapel Hill: University of North Carolina Press, 1955); Robert P. Williams, ed., *The First Congress: March 4, 1789–March 3, 1791* (New York: Exposition Press, 1970).

24. Cahn, "The Firstness of the First Amendment," pp. 470–73, set out three dramatic scenes in arguing that the "judicial libertarianism of the American present is securely linked with a very old and genuine tradition." The first tableau, which took place in Paris, involved a letter written by Thomas Paine following a long talk with Thomas Jefferson. The letter concerned Paine's "ideals of natural and civil rights and the distinction between them." Cahn linked Paine's views with John Locke's grading of "qualities" in Locke's *Essay Concerning Human Understanding*. While Paine thought his own classification "novel," Cahn argued that for "the educated men of the Enlightenment, it would be a short leap from Locke's grade of 'primary' and 'inseparable' qualities to Paine's corresponding 'natural right of personal competency.'"

The second tableau, which was set in New York, involved James Madison's role before the First Congress where "far from considering the rights all of one piece, grade and texture, he classifies and re-classifies them like a virtuoso of the taxonomic art." The result of such classification, Cahn argued, placed First Amendment liberties in a position of primacy.

    The third tableau, with Jefferson now in Philadelphia as Secretary of State, involved a letter written to Noah Webster in which Jefferson sought to defend himself for advocating the adoption of a bill of rights. Although in his grading Jefferson placed freedom of the press in a secondary category, which he called "fences against wrong," Cahn argued that "it is not likely that Jefferson intended to derogate from the press's station and dignity as a means of free personal expression." Indeed, Cahn noted, "It is enough to record that like others of his era he did grade the various guarantees and that, in grading them, he awarded primacy to the freedoms of conscience and personal expression." Ibid.

25. New York Times Co. v. Sullivan, 376 U.S. 254, 276 (1964).
26. 268 U.S. 652 (1925).
27. 250 U.S. 616, 624 (1919) (Holmes, J., joined by Brandeis, J., dissenting).
28. Harvey L. Zuckman and Martin J. Gaynes, *Mass Communications Law in a Nutshell* (St. Paul: West Publishing Co., 1977), p. 6.
29. For a discussion of the ongoing debate over the meaning of the speech and press clauses resulting from Justice Potter Stewart's 1974 Yale Law School address (n. 153 infra), see text accompanying notes 153–78 infra.
30. Meiklejohn, *Free Speech*, p. 17.
31. E.g., n. 8 supra, quoting from Smith v. California, 361 U.S. at 157–59 (Black, J., concurring). See generally Edmond Cahn, "Justice Black and First Amendment 'Absolutes': A Public Interview," *New York University Law Review* 37 (June 1962): 549–63.
32. Meiklejohn, *Free Speech*, pp. 34–41. An application of Meiklejohn's contextual approach is evident in the Court's formulation of a constitutional libel defense in New York Times Co. v. Sullivan, 376 U.S.. 254 (1964), and its progeny. Justice Brennan has spoken of two "models of the role of the press . . . that claim the protection of the First Amendment." Under his *speech* model, the press—indeed, anyone—is afforded absolute protection for freedom of expression, for freedom to communicate. Under what he calls the *structural* model, the press is given less than absolute First Amendment protection for the gathering and preparation of information for dissemination. Brennan, "Address," pp. 175–77.
33. For a discussion of *balancing* as opposed to *absolutism*, see Bean Afange, Jr., "The Balancing of Interests in Free Speech Cases: In Defense of an Abused Doctrine," *Law in Transition Quarterly* 2 (Winter 1965): 35–63; Laurent B. Frantz, "The First Amendment in the Balance," *Yale Law Journal* 71 (July 1962): 1424–50; Gerald Gunther, "Learned Hand and the Origins of Modern First Amendment Doctrine: Some Fragments of History," *Stanford Law Review* 27 (February 1975): 719–73; Robert A. Leflar, "The Free-ness of Free Speech," *Vanderbilt Law Review* 15 (October 1962): 1073–84; Wallace Mendelson, "On the Meaning of the First Amendment: Absolutes in the Balance," *California Law Review* 50 (December 1962): 821–28; Melville B. Nimmer, "The Right to Speak from *Times* to *Time*: First Amendment Theory Applied to Libel and Misapplied to Privacy," *California Law Review* 56 (August 1968): 935–67.
34. Chafee, *Free Speech in the United States*, p. 31. Chief Justice Fred M. Vinson defined and applied the balancing test in a 1950 case upholding the validity of a federal statute. He wrote, "When particular conduct is regulated in the interest of public order, and the regulation results in an indirect, conditional, partial abridgment of speech, the duty of the courts is to determine which of these two conflicting interests demands the greater protection under the particular circumstances presented." American Communications Ass'n, CIO v. Douds, 339 U.S. 382, 399 (1950).
35. See, e.g., Dennis v. United States, 341 U.S. 494 (1951); Scales v. United States, 367 U.S. 203 (1961). See also Donald L. Smith, "Zechariah Chafee Jr. and the Positive View of Press Freedom," *Journalism History* 5 (Autumn 1978): 86–92.
36. Note, "The Speech and Press Clause of the First Amendment as Ordinary Language," *Harvard Law Review* 87 (December 1973): 379. The balancing approach raises other questions: for example, who should do the balancing, the legislature or the Court? Chief Justice Vinson, in espousing balancing in American Communications Ass'n, CIO v. Douds, 339 U.S. at 399, viewed the legislature as carrying the primary responsibility. Such a view is associated with the doctrine of judicial restraint: if a statute is reasonable, it should not be overturned. Justice Black disapproved of either the Court or the legislature balancing First Amendment interests. He noted: "Of course the decision to provide a constitutional safeguard for a particular right, such as . . . the right of free speech protection of the First [Amendment], involves a balancing of conflicting interests. . . . I believe, however, that

the Framers themselves did this balancing when they wrote the Constitution and the Bill of Rights." Hugo Black, "The Bill of Rights," *New York University Law Review* 35 (April 1960): 879.

Balancing may also be classified as either definitional or ad hoc. In *definitional* balancing, the interests balanced are said to go beyond the merits of the case at hand. Where the Court focuses on the interests at stake in the individual case, the balancing is said to be *ad hoc*. Definitional balancing is said to make it easier to predict the outcome of the balancing process because of the generalized quality of the decision. One commentator has observed, however, that "the only difference between a balancing first amendment and none at all is that it permits the balance to be struck twice, first by Congress and then again by the courts." Frantz, "The First Amendment in the Balance," p. 1443. For a discussion of definitional balancing, see Emerson, "First Amendment Doctrine and the Burger Court," pp. 438–40; Thomas I. Emerson, "Toward a General Theory of the First Amendment," *Yale Law Journal* 72 (April 1963): 916–18; Gerald Gunther, "In Search of Judicial Quality on a Changing Court: The Case of Justice Powell," *Stanford Law Review* 24 (June 1972): 1026–27; Nimmer, "The Right to Speak from *Times* to *Time*," pp. 935–67.

37. Thomas I. Emerson, *The System of Freedom of Expression* (New York: Random House, 1970), pp. 718–21.
38. Ibid., p. 721.
39. For a critical evaluation of the decade of the 1970s, see Emerson, "First Amendment Doctrine and the Burger Court." Emerson noted: "Broad agreement concerning the basic values that underlie our system of freedom of expression continues to exist. Unfortunately the quest for effective legal doctrine that would translate those values into reality has not been successful." He concluded, "The outcome has been that freedom of expression has by no means received the special protection to which it is theoretically entitled.... A more rigorous doctrinal framework is imperative if the system is to survive the stresses that are likely to come." Ibid., p. 481.
40. Refer to nn. 5, 9 supra.
41. 304 U.S. 144, 152 n. 4 (1938). The rest of the so-called "embattled footnote" reads:

> It is unnecessary to consider now whether legislation which restricts those political processes which can ordinarily be expected to bring about repeal of undesirable legislation, is to be subjected to *more exacting judicial scrutiny* under the general prohibitions of the Fourteenth Amendment than are most other types of legislation.... Nor need we enquire...whether prejudice against discrete and insular minorities may be a special condition, which tends seriously to curtail the operation of those political processes ordinarily to be relied upon to protect minorities, and which may call for a correspondingly *more searching judicial inquiry*. [Citations omitted, emphasis added.]

For a historical analysis of this footnote, see Alpheus T. Mason, *Harlan Fiske Stone: Pillar of the Law* (New York: Viking Press, 1956), pp. 512–16.
42. Of course, had the Court attempted to apply "a more exacting judicial scrutiny" (304 U.S. at 152 n. 4) to each of the first ten constitutional amendments, the test would not have been helpful in resolving conflicts among the amendments themselves—for example, apparent conflicts between the First and Sixth Amendments.
43. Kovacs v. Cooper, 336 U.S. 77, 90–91 (1949).
44. 304 U.S. at 152.
45. C. Hermann Pritchett, *The American Constitution*, 3d ed. (New York: McGraw-Hill, 1977), p. 306.
46. 308 U.S. 147, 161 (1939).
47. Jones v. Opelika, 316 U.S. 584, 608 (1942) (Stone, C. J., dissenting). In using the term, however, the chief justice did not refer to his earlier *Carolene* footnote. One source has suggested that, in reality, the judicial origin of the preferred position concept might be found in Justice Benjamin N. Cardozo's statement in an earlier decision that freedom of speech and thought is "the matrix, the indispensable condition, of nearly every other form of freedom." Palko v. Connecticut, 302 U.S. 319, 327 (1937). A similar position was taken in 1937 in Herndon v. Lowry, 301 U.S. 242, 258–59 (1937).
48. Murdock v. Pennsylvania, 319 U.S. 105, 115 (1943).
49. See, e.g., Poulos v. New Hampshire, 345 U.S. 395, 423 (1953) (Douglas, J., dissenting); United States v. Rumely, 345 U.S. 41, 56–58 (1953) (Douglas, J., concurring); Saia v.

New York, 334 U.S. 558, 562 (1948); Marsh v. Alabama, 326 U.S. 501, 509 (1946); Prince v. Massachusetts, 321 U.S. 158, 164–65 (1944). For an appendix listing preferred position statements in these and other cases, see McKay, "The Preference for Freedom," pp. 1223–27.
50. 323 U.S. 516, 529–30 (1945).
51. The latter Rutledge interpretation, according to Pritchett, is "a more moderate" interpretation of the preferred position. Pritchett, *The American Constitution*, p. 305.
52. 336 U.S. at 90.
53. Ibid. at 94–95. To the extent that the Court's majority in *Schneider* v. *Irvington, Murdock* v. *Pennsylvania*, and *Thomas* v. *Collins* can be said to have adopted the preferred position doctrine, Justice Frankfurter's statement appears to be a misinterpretation of the facts.
54. Ibid. at 96.
55. Douglas v. City of Jeannette, 319 U.S. 158, 181 (1943). In 1959, McKay, "The Preference for Freedom," p. 1182, considered Justice Frankfurter as the only justice to have opposed the preferred position doctrine explicitly.
56. See Samuel Krislov, *The Supreme Court and Political Freedom* (New York: Free Press, 1968), p. 117, citing Craig v. Harney, 331 U.S. 367, 391 (1947).
57. McKay, "The Preference for Freedom," p. 1192.
58. Kovacs v. Cooper, 336 U.S. at 95 (Frankfurter, J., concurring).
59. Ibid. at 106 (Rutledge, J., dissenting).
60. McKay, "The Preference for Freedom," p. 1190, noted "that every member of the Court since 1919 has concurred in one or many of the collected expressions of preference for the first amendment."
61. Krislov, *The Supreme Court*, p. 90.
62. Kovacs v. Cooper, 336 U.S. at 91 (Frankfurter, J., concurring).
63. Ibid. at 91–92.
64. An Alabama antipicketing statute designed to guard against harassment of potential customers by union threats, for example, was held to be overbroad because the law unduly restricted the expression guarantees of those engaged in picketing. Because First Amendment rights were involved, the Court's careful judicial scrutiny determined that the statute proscribed activities which were constitutionally protected as well as activities which were not. Thornhill v. Alabama, 310 U.S. 88 (1940). For a discussion of the careful judicial scrutiny required to maintain procedural due process safeguards for speech and press guarantees, see text accompanying notes 123–52 infra.
65. McKay, "The Preference for Freedom," p. 1183.
66. Patterson v. Colorado ex rel. Attorney General, 205 U.S. 454 (1907).
67. Near v. Minnesota ex rel. Olson, 283 U.S. 697, 716 (1931).
68. 372 U.S. 58, 70 (1963).
69. New York Times Co. v. United States, 403 U.S. at 714.
70. 402 U.S. 415, 419 (1971).
71. New York Times Co. v. United States, 403 U.S. at 714.
72. Barron and Dienes, *Handbook of Free Speech*, p. 37.
73. See, e.g., Southeastern Promotions v. Conrad, 420 U.S. 546, 559 (1975); Freedman v. Maryland, 380 U.S. 51, 59–60 (1965).
74. E.g., Nebraska Press Ass'n v. Stuart, 427 U.S. 539 (1976); New York Times Co. v. United States, 403 U.S. 713 (1971).
75. 427 U.S. at 559.
76. Ibid. at 568.
77. Ibid. at 570.
78. Ibid. at 562–570.
79. Ibid. at 569.
80. Ibid. at 559.
81. Oklahoma Publishing Co. v. Dist. Ct., 430 U.S. 308, 310 (1976).
82. Smith v. Daily Mail Publishing Co., 443 U.S. 97 (1979). The Court was more concerned that the West Virginia statute provided for a penal sanction for publishing lawfully obtained and truthful information. The Court said, "A free press cannot be made to rely solely upon the sufferance of government to supply it with information. . . . If the information is lawfully obtained, as it was here, the state may not punish its publication except

when necessary to further an interest more substantial than is present here." Ibid. at 104.
83. United States v. Progressive, Inc., 486 F. Supp. 5 (W.D. Wis. 1979).
84. 444 U.S. 507 (1980).
85. Ibid. at 509 n. 3.
86. 413 U.S. 376 (1973).
87. Ibid. at 395.
88. 249 U.S. 47, 52 (1919).
89. 250 U.S. at 628 (Holmes, J., dissenting).
90. 274 U.S. 357, 372–80 (1927) (Brandeis, J., concurring).
91. Craig v. Harney, 331 U.S. at 373; Pennekamp v. Florida, 328 U.S. 331, 335 (1946); Thomas v. Collins, 323 U.S. at 530; West Virginia State Bd. of Education v. Barnette, 319 U.S. 624, 633–34 (1943); Taylor v. Mississippi, 319 U.S. 583, 588–90 (1943); Bridges v. California, 314 U.S. 252, 263 (1941); Carlson v. California, 310 U.S. 106, 113 (1940); Thornhill v. Alabama, 310 U.S. 88, 104–05 (1940); Herndon v. Lowry, 301 U.S. at 260. In two other cases, Terminiello v. Chicago, 337 U.S. 1, 4–5 (1949), and Cantwell v. Connecticut, 310 U.S. 296, 308–11 (1940), references to the clear and present danger test appear to be dicta.
92. 341 U.S. at 510, quoting from the lower court opinion at 183 F.2d 201, 212 (2d Cir. 1950). Ironically, the *Dennis* plurality, while recognizing the Holmes-Brandeis emphasis upon the elements of imminence and seriousness had evolved to become a majority view of the Court, refused to apply it to the case at hand. Chief Justice Vinson, writing for the *Dennis* plurality, observed that "although no case subsequent to *Whitney* and *Gitlow* has expressly overruled the majority opinion in those cases, there is little doubt that subsequent opinions have inclined toward the Holmes-Brandeis rationale." 341 U.S. at 507.
93. For a discussion of the impact of the *Dennis* reinterpretation, see McKay, "The Preference for Freedom," pp. 1209–12.
94. Yates v. United States, 354 U.S. 298, 318 (1957).
95. 395 U.S. 444, 447 (1969).
96. For a discussion of the history of the clear and present danger test, see Gerald Gunther, "Learned Hand and the Origins of Modern First Amendment Doctrine: Some Fragments of History," *Stanford Law Review* 27 (February 1975): 719–73.
97. E.g., Edwin S. Corwin, "Bowing Out 'Clear and Present Danger,'" *Notre Dame Lawyer* 27 (Spring 1952): 325–59.
98. For a discussion of "definitional" balancing, see note 36 supra.
99. Frank Strong, "'Clear and Present Danger': From *Schenck* to *Brandenburg*—and Beyond," in *Supreme Court Review 1969*, ed. Philip B. Kurland (Chicago: University of Chicago Press, 1969), p. 64.
100. Ibid., pp. 64–66. For a more critical view of the value of the clear and present danger test, see Emerson, "First Amendment Doctrine and the Burger Court," pp. 435–38.
101. 314 U.S. at 263.
102. See, e.g., Wood v. Georgia, 370 U.S. 375 (1962); Craig v. Harney, 331 U.S. 367 (1947); Pennekamp v. Florida, 328 U.S. 331 (1946).
103. 435 U.S. 829, 842–43 (1978).
104. 427 U.S. at 562. Chief Justice Burger wrote, "We turn now to the record in this case to determine whether, as Learned Hand put it, 'the gravity of the "evil," discounted by its improbability, justifies such invasion of free speech as is necessary to avoid the danger.'" Ibid.
105. See, e.g., Communist Party of Indiana v. Whitcomb, 414 U.S. 441 (1974); Hess v. Indiana, 414 U.S. 105 (1973); Cohen v. California, 403 U.S. 15 (1971).
106. A listing of relevant cases can be found in Barron and Dienes, *Handbook of Free Speech*, pp. 30–31.
107. 376 U.S. at 279–80.
108. Curtis Publishing Co. v. Butts, 388 U.S. 130 (1967).
109. Rosenbloom v. Metromedia, Inc., 403 U.S. 29 (1971) (Brennan, J., plurality opinion).
110. Justice Brennan, writing for the Court in *Sullivan*, referred to "the critic of official conduct." 376 U.S. at 279.
111. Ibid. at 285–86.
112. 418 U.S. 323 (1974).
113. The Court said:

> In some instances an individual may achieve such pervasive fame or notoriety that he becomes a public figure for all purposes and in all contexts. More commonly, an individual voluntarily injects himself or is drawn into a particular public controversy and thereby becomes a public figure for a limited range of issues. In either case such persons assume special prominence in the resolution of public questions.

Ibid. at 351.

114. Ibid. at 348.
115. For a list of state fault standards for private individuals, see John B. McCrory, "Defending the News Media," in *Communications Law 1980*, ed. James C. Goodale, 2 vols. (New York: Practising Law Institute, 1980), 1: 117–20.
116. Rosenbloom v. Metromedia, Inc., 403 U.S. 29 (1971).
117. Hutchinson v. Proxmire, 443 U.S. 111, 134–35 (1979); Wolston v. Reader's Digest Ass'n, 443 U.S. at 166–69; Time, Inc. v. Firestone, 424 U.S. at 453.
118. 441 U.S. 153 (1979).
119. On interlocutory appeal, the Second Circuit had concluded, "If we were to allow selective disclosure of how a journalist formulated his judgments on what to print or not to print, we would be condoning judicial review of the editor's thought processes." 568 F.2d 974, 980 (2d Cir. 1977).
120. 441 U.S. at 169–70.
121. Although the constitutional privilege probably was never meant to be applied to media defendants alone, the defense has been used most frequently by media representatives. The majority opinion in *Gertz*, written by Justice Lewis F. Powell, Jr., as well as at least two other separate opinions, used media terms. 418 U.S. at 332, 341, 347, 350. Only Justice Byron R. White, dissenting, assumed that the Court's holding applied to both media and nonmedia defendants. Ibid. at 392.
122. In one state, North Carolina, the actual malice standard has been applied by statute to contempt law. In order for a judge in a North Carolina state court to find a newspaper in contempt of court for a report of court proceedings, he or she must find that the report is "grossly inaccurate and presents a clear and present danger of imminent and serious threat to the administration of justice, *made with knowledge that it was false or with reckless disregard of whether it was false.* [Emphasis added.]" North Carolina, *General Statutes*, sec. 5A–11.5(5) (1979 Supp.).
123. See generally McKay, "The Preference for Freedom," pp. 1217–22.
124. Thornhill v. Alabama, 310 U.S. at 99–102. See also Erznoznik v. City of Jacksonville, 422 U.S. 205, 210 (1975); Gooding v. Wilson, 405 U.S. 518, 525 (1972); Cohen v. California, 403 U.S. at 26.
125. Gillmor and Barron, *Mass Communication Law*, p. 56.
126. 413 U.S. 15, 24 (1973).
127. Paris Adult Theatre I v. Slaton, 413 U.S. 49, 84 (1973) (Brennan, J., dissenting).
128. Roth v. United States, 354 U.S. at 483.
129. Thornhill v. Alabama, 310 U.S. at 97.
130. United States v. Robel, 389 U.S. 258, 267–68 (1967). See generally Note, "Less Drastic Means and the First Amendment." *Yale Law Journal* 78 (January 1969): 464–74.
131. E.g., Bigelow v. Virginia, 421 U.S. 809, 815–16 (1975); Gooding v. Wilson, 405 U.S. at 521–22; Dombrowski v. Pfister, 380 U.S. 479, 486 (1965).
132. Bates v. State Bar of Arizona, 433 U.S. 350, 380 (1977).
133. Ibid. at 380. The Court noted, however, that "justification for the application of overbreadth analysis applies weakly, if at all, in the ordinary commercial context." The Court said, "Since advertising is linked to commercial well-being it seems unlikely that such speech is particularly susceptible to being crushed by overbroad regulation." Ibid. at 381.
134. 427 U.S. 50 (1976).
135. Ibid. at 59–60.
136. Ibid. at 70–71. See also Justice Stevens's opinion for the Court in FCC v. Pacifica Foundation, 438 U.S. 726 (1978), in which the FCC's regulation of "indecent" forms of expression was upheld despite the First Amendment protection afforded such expression.
137. CBS, Inc. v. Young, 522 F.2d 234, 237 (6th Cir. 1975).
138. McKay, "The Preference for Freedom," p. 1218.
139. Farber v. Jascalevich, 78 N.J. 259, 276, 394 A.2d 330, 337, cert. denied, 439 U.S. 997 (1978).

140. Ibid. at 285, 394 A.2d at 338. This ruling brought a strong dissent from one member of the court who wrote:

> I find it totally unimaginable that the majority can even consider allowing a man to be sent to jail without a full and orderly hearing at which to present his defense. Mr. Farber probably assumed, as did I, that hearings were supposed to be held and finding made *before* a person went to jail and not *afterwards.*

Ibid. at 343 (Pashman, J., dissenting).
The New Jersey shield law was subsequently strengthened to require that (1) a hearing be conducted to determine the relevance of the reporter's notes and (2) a showing that the information in the possession of a reporter cannot be obtained elsewhere. New Jersey, statutes Annotated, sec 2A: 84A–21.1 et seq. The shield law was upheld by the New Jersey Supreme Court in State v. Boiardo, 83 N. J. 350, 416 A.2d 793 (1980), where it was held that the defendants failed to carry the burden, imposed by the shield law, of demonstrating nonavailability of less instrusive sources for the information. Ibid. at 354–55, 416 A.2d at 795.

141. 436 U.S. 547.

142. Ibid. at 565.

143. Ibid. at 567.

144. See Privacy Protection Act of 1980, U.S., *Statutes at Large,* 94: 1879. Section 101(a) limits the use of search warrants by making it unlawful "to search for or seize any work product materials possessed by a person reasonably believed to have a purpose to disseminate to the public a newspaper, book, broadcast, or other similar form of public communication" unless "(1) there is probable cause to believe that the person possessing such materials has committed or is committing the criminal offense to which the materials relate"; or "(2) there is reason to believe that the immediate seizure of such materials is necessary to prevent the death of, or serious bodily injury to, a human being."

145. "State Legislatures Move to Prohibit Most Raids," *The News Media & The Law* 4 (October-November 1980): 4.

146. Reporters Committee v. American Telephone & Telegraph Co., 593 F.2d 1030 (D.C. Cir. 1978).

147. 440 U.S. 949 (1978).

148. 593 F.2d at 1051.

149. 443 U.S. at 120 n. 9.

150. 431 F. Supp. 1311, 1330 (W.D. Wis. 1977).

151. 443 U.S. at 120 n. 9.

152. McKay, "The Preference for Freedom," p. 1218.

153. Potter Stewart, "Or of the Press," *Hastings Law Journal* 26 (January 1975): 633.

154. Ibid., p. 632.

155. Ibid., p. 633.

156. Ibid., p. 634.

157. See, e.g., Floyd Abrams, "The Press *Is* Different: Reflections on Justice Stewart and the Autonomous Press," *Hofstra Law Review* 7 (Spring 1979): 563–93; Randall P. Bezanson, "The New Free Press Guarantee," *Virginia Law Review* 63 (June 1977): 737–87; Margaret A. Blanchard, "The Institutional Press and the First Amendment Privileges," in *Supreme Court Review 1978,* ed. Philip B. Kurland and Gerhard Casper (Chicago: University of Chicago Press, 1978), pp. 225–96; Comment, "Examining the Institutional Interpretation of the Press Clause," *Texas Law Review* 58 (December 1979): 171–96; Comment, "Problem in Defining the Institutional Status of the Press," *University of Richmond Law Review* 11 (Fall 1976): 177–207; Comment, "The Supreme Court and the Not-So Privileged Press," *University of Richmond Law Review* 13 (Winter 1979): 313–29; Comment, "The Supreme Court and the Press: Freedom or Privilege?" *Akron Law Review* 12 (Fall 1978): 261–84; David Lange, "The Speech and Press Clauses," *U.C.L.A. Law Review* 23 (October 1975) 77–119; Anthony Lewis, "A Preferred Position for Journalism?" *Hofstra Law Review* 7 (Spring 1979): 595–627; Melville B. Nimmer, "Introduction—Is Freedom of the Press a Redundancy: What Does It Add to Freedom of Speech?" *Hastings Law Journal* 26 (January 1975): 639–58; L. A. Powe, Jr., "Or of the (Broadcast) Press," *Texas Law Review* 55 (December 1976): 39–66; Robert D. Sack, "Reflections on the Wrong Question: Special Constitutional Privilege for the Institutional Press," *Hofstra Law Review* 7 (Spring 1979): 629–54; William W.

Van Alstyne, "The Hazards to the Press of Claiming a 'Preferred Position,'" Hastings Law Journal 28 (January 1977): 761–70.

158. Abrams, "The Press *Is* Different," pp. 565–67, citing Landmark Communications, Inc. v. Virginia, 435 U.S. at 848 (Stewart, J., concurring); Pittsburgh Press Co. v. Pittsburgh Commission on Human Relations, 413 U.S. at 400 (Stewart, J., dissenting); CBS, Inc. v. Democratic Nat'l Comm., 412 U.S. 94, 133–46 (1973) (Stewart, J., concurring).

159. 435 U.S. 765, 795–902 (1978) (Burger, C. J., concurring).

160. Ibid. at 798–801.

161. Ibid. at 802, citing Lovell v. Griffin, 303 U.S. 444, 450 (1938); Branzburg v. Hayes, 408 U.S. 665, 704–05 (1972); Pennekamp v. Florida, 328 U.S. at 364.

162. 435 U.S. 829 (1978).

163. Ibid. at 839.

164. Ibid. at 837.

165. Ibid. at 849 (Stewart, J., concurring).

166. First Nat'l Bank of Boston v. Bellotti, 435 U.S. at 798 n. 3 (Burger, C. J., concurring). He cited Pell v. Procunier, 417 U.S. 817, 834 (1974), as suggesting that the press has no independent scope, and Bigelow v. Virginia, 421 U.S. at 828, as suggesting the opposite conclusion.

167. Nimmer, "Is Freedom of the Press a Redundancy?" p. 658.

168. Lewis, "A Preferred Position for Journalism?" p. 599.

169. First Nat'l Bank of Boston v. Bellotti, 435 U.S. at 798 (Burger, C. J., concurring).

170. Ibid. at 789–801.

171. Abrams, "The Press *Is* Different," p. 579.

172. Lange, "The Speech and Press Clauses," p. 88.

173. Cox, "Freedom of Expression and the Burger Court," p. 51.

174. Ibid., pp. 51–55. Cox discusses Branzburg v. Hayes, 408 U.S. 665 (1972), in which journalists were denied a testimonial privilege not to disclose sources of information to a grand jury investigating criminal activities; Herbert v. Lando, 441 U.S. 153 (1979), in which the press was denied special exemption from the general rules of pretrial discovery; and Zurcher v. Stanford Daily, 436 U.S. 547 (1978), in which the Court refused to give the press special immunity from search warrants.

175. Lewis, "A Preferred Position for Journalism?" pp. 609, 626.

176. Nebraska Press Ass'n v. Stuart, 427 U.S. at 560. The growing monopolization of the media through group and cross-media ownership also tends to leave the press subject to more governmental regulation. For a discussion of other hazards to the press in seeking special First Amendment privileges, see Van Alstyne, "The Hazards to the Press of Claiming a 'Preferred Position,'" pp. 761–70.

177. Stewart, "Or of the Press," p. 636.

178. Sack, "Reflections on the Wrong Question," p. 633, citing Lovell v. City of Griffin, 303 U.S. at 452; First Nat'l Bank of Boston v. Bellotti, 435 U.S. at 781; Cox Broadcasting Corp. v. Cohn, 420 U.S. 469, 491–92 (1975).

179. Bork, "The First Amendment Does Not Give Greater Freedom to the Press Than to Speech," *The Center Magazine* 12 (March-April 1979): 30.

180. Bork, "Neutral Principles and Some First Amendment Problems," *Indiana Law Journal* 47 (Fall 1971): 20. Such a view is also consistent with several other First Amendment theorists. See, e.g., Alexander M. Bickel, *The Least Dangerous Branch* (Indianapolis: Bobbs-Merrill, 1962), pp. 73–110; Meiklejohn, *Free Speech*, p. 26; Lillian R. BeVier, "The First Amendment and Political Speech: An Inquiry into the Substance and Limits of Principle," *Stanford Law Review* 30 (January 1978): 311.

181. Brennan, "Address," p. 176. Justice Brennan's other model, which he labeled as *structural*, would allow for the balancing of freedom of expression interests, including press interests, with the competing claims of other societal interests. Ibid.

182. See, e.g., Nebraska Press Ass'n v. Stuart, 427 U.S. 539 (1976).

183. See, e.g., Branzburg v. Hayes, 408 U.S. 665 (1972).

184. Herbert v. Lando, 568 F.2d at 976.

185. See, e.g., Organization for a Better Austin v. Keefe, 402 U.S. 415 (1971); Lovell v. Griffin, 303 U.S. 444 (1938); Philadelphia News, Inc. v. Borough Council of Swarthmore, 381 F. Supp. 228 (E.D. Pa. 1974).

186. E.g., Cox Broadcasting Corp. v. Cohn, 420 U.S. 469 (1975); Landmark Communications,

Inc. v. Virginia, 435 U.S. 829 (1978); Oklahoma Publishing Co. v. Dist. Ct., 430 U.S. 308 (1977); Smith v. Daily Mail Publishing Co., 443 U.S. 97 (1979). Contra, Zacchini v. Scripps-Howard Broadcasting Co., 433 U.S. 562 (1977) (right to publish denied by "right to publicity" of a public figure); FCC v. Pacifica Foundation, 438 U.S. 726 (1978) (right to broadcast words considered "indecent" denied).

187. CBS, Inc. v. Democratic Nat'l Comm., 412 U.S. at 124–25; Miami Herald Publishing Co. v. Tornillo, 418 U.S. 241, 258 (1974).
188. Herbert v. Lando, 441 U.S. 153 (1979).
189. See, e.g., Branzburg v. Hayes, 408 U.S. at 681; Zemel v. Rusk, 381 U.S. 1, 17 (1965).
190. 408 U.S. at 684–85.
191. 417 U.S. 817 (1974).
192. 417 U.S. 843 (1974).
193. 417 U.S. at 834.
194. 417 U.S. at 850.
195. 417 U.S. at 830–31; 417 U.S. at 847, 849.
196. 417 U.S. at 830; 417 U.S. at 848.
197. 438 U.S. 1 (1978).
198. Thomas I. Emerson, while noting that the Burger Court has not repudiated the preferred position doctrine, cited *Houchins* as an example in which the Court ignored the doctrine. "First Amendment Doctrine and the Burger Court," pp. 441–43. He listed, among other cases in which the Court disregarded an opportunity to apply the preferred position, Young v. American Mini Theatres, Inc., 427 U.S. 50 (1976), and Gannett Co. v. DePasquale, 443 U.S. 368 (1979).
199. Houchins v. KQED, Inc., 438 U.S. at 9.
200. Ibid. at 16 (Stewart, J., concurring). Justice Stewart would not have required officials to allow the press to go to any parts of the jail not accessible to the general public, but, for example, he would have allowed the press—because of its role as the eyes and ears of the public—to take cameras and recording equipment into areas it was permitted to see. Ibid. at 18–19 (Stewart, J., concurring).
201. Ibid. at 19–40 (Stevens, J., dissenting).
202. Garrett v. Estelle, 556 F.2d 1274 (5th Cir. 1977), cert. denied, 438 U.S. 914 (1979).
203. Kearns-Tribune v. Utah Bd. of Corrections, 2 Med. L. Rptr. 1353 (D. Utah 1977).
204. See, e.g., Wood v. Georgia, 370 U.S. 375 (1962); Pennekamp v. Florida, 328 U.S. 331 (1946); Bridges v. California, 314 U.S. 252 (1941).
205. Craig v. Harney, 331 U.S. at 376. See also Cox v. Louisiana, 379 U.S. 559, 565 (1965); Wood v. Georgia, 370 U.S. at 391 n. 18; Bridges v. California, 314 U.S. at 273.
206. Cox, "Freedom of Expression in the Burger Court," p. 17. For a discussion of the Burger Court and the administration of justice, see ibid., pp. 17–26.
207. See text accompanying notes 181–187 supra.
208. 443 U.S. 368 (1979).
209. Ibid. at 379–84.
210. Ibid. at 384–91.
211. Ibid. at 397 (Powell, J., concurring).
212. For a summary of extensive post-*Gannett* efforts by the lower courts to close both pretrial and trial proceedings, see "Secret Courts: Special Report," *The News Media & The Law* 3 (November-December 1979): 2–24. See also "State Supreme Courts Still Divided," *The News Media & The Law* 4 (August-September 1980): 5.
213. See, e.g., People v. Sullivan, No. 3721–79 (N.Y. Sup. Ct. Aug. 1, 1979); People v. Worth, No. 79–C13 (W. Va. Cir. Ct. July 24, 1979), cited in Cox, "Freedom of Expression in the Burger Court," p. 20 n. 77.
214. 443 U.S. at 419–26 (Blackmun, J., dissenting).
215. 100 S. Ct. 2814 (1980).
216. Ibid. at 2830.
217. Cox, "Freedom of Expression in the Burger Court," p. 21, notes that there was no opinion of the Court in *Richmond Newspapers*, a case which evoked seven opinions from eight justices, six supporting the judgment and one dissenting from it. Gannett had five separate opinions. Cox regards this "insistence upon individual opinions" as a "major fault of the present Justices." Ibid. at 24–25.
218. 100 S. Ct. at 2821.

219. Ibid.
220. Ibid. at 2841 (Blackmun, J., concurring).
221. Ibid. at 2830 (Stevens, J., concurring).
222. Ibid.
223. Cox, "Freedom of Expression in the Burger Court," p. 21.
224. Ibid. at 23.
225. 100 S. Ct. at 2823.
226. Ibid. at 2828.
227. 101 S. Ct. 802 (1981).
228. One commentator, for example, sees *Chandler* as probably hastening the demise of "consent rules" adopted by a number of states, which required that the consent of all parties be obtained before camera coverage is allowed. John L. Huffman, "Analysis," *News Photographer* 36 (March 1981): 28. For a state survey of the status of cameras in the courts prior to *Chandler*, see "Cameras in the Courts," *The News Media & The Law* 4 (June–July 1980): 4–5.
229. Note, "First Amendment Interest Balancing—Behind Bars?" *University of Miami Law Review* 33 (March 1979): 680, 690. Erskine said:

> Let us consider, my lords, that arbitrary power has seldom or never been introduced into any country at once. It must be introduced by slow degrees, and as it were step by step, lest the people should see its approach. The barriers and fences of people's liberty must be plucked up one by one, and some plausible pretenses must be found for removing or hoodwinking one after another, those sentries who are posted by the constitution of a free country for warning the people of their danger.

Edward Walford, *Speeches of Thomas Lord Erskine* (London: Reeves and Turner, 1870), p. 536.
230. 304 U.S. at 152 n. 4.
231. Stewart, "Or of the Press," p. 636.
232. See, e.g., Murray I. Gurfein, "Law of the Press," *New York State Bar Journal* 51 (April 1979): 170–73, 210. Judge Gurfein of the U.S. Court of Appeals, Second Circuit, who as a federal district court judge refused to prohibit publication of the Pentagon Papers, has noted:

> It is a faith that life can be lived better if we do have a free press. And surely, individual life can be lived better if we have free speech. This requires faith, as well however that the newspaper publisher is not only a businessman, but as the Savings Bank advertisements tell us, he is also "People." As one of the people, he is expected to avoid the grossly unfair or the grossly distasteful. The newspaper ethic is a variation of *noblesse oblige*. The fourth estate should acknowledge its contemporary rank as the only order of nobility tolerated in a republic.
>
> My theme is that the free press part of the First Amendment has become an article of faith like Americanism or motherhood. One does not have to prove that Americanism is the best way of life or that mothers are nice ladies.

Ibid., p. 172.

CHAPTER 4

The Burger Court and the First Amendment: Putting a Decade into Perspective[*]

I. A Framework

A. E. Dick Howard[†]

Understanding the U.S. Supreme Court has never been an easy task. The dominant mood of the framers of the Constitution about the role the Court might play in the American system appears to have been one of speculation. Indeed, the very function of judicial review—the Court's power to declare legislation unconstitutional—was not made explicit in the Constitution but was left to be evolved through interpretation from the pen of Chief Justice John Marshall. Presidents have railed at the Court—as Jefferson did at Marshall— and pundits have spilled much ink trying to interpret its decisions.

---

[*]In August 1980, at the national convention of the Association for Education in Journalism, a leading constitutional law scholar—A. E. Dick Howard of the University of Virginia—and a prominent mass media law attorney—Floyd Abrams—discussed the approach of the Supreme Court of the 1970s to the First Amendment. Howard had been asked to provide a general discussion of the Court's treatment of constitutional law as a framework for considering the more specific issue of the Burger Court and the First Amendment. Abrams was asked to provide his interpretation of the Court's treatment of First Amendment issues. The two speakers edited their remarks for publication.

[†]A. E. Dick Howard is the White Burkett Miller Professor of Law and Public Affairs at the University of Virginia. Born and raised in Richmond, Virginia, he is a graduate of the University of Richmond and received his law degree from the University of Virginia. He was a Rhodes Scholar at Oxford University, where he read philosophy, politics, and economics.

After graduating from law school, Professor Howard was a law clerk to Justice Hugo L. Black of the Supreme Court of the United States. He has practiced law in Washington, D.C., and since 1964 has been a member of the law faculty at the University of Virginia.

Active in public affairs, Professor Howard was executive director of the commission that wrote Virginia's new constitution and directed the successful referendum campaign for ratification of that constitution. He has been counsel to the General Assembly of Virginia and a consultant to state and federal bodies, including the United States Senate Judiciary Committee.

Professor Howard has been twice a fellow of the Woodrow Wilson International Center for Scholars in Washington, D.C. His recognitions have included giving the George Mason Lecture at Colonial Williamsburg and having been recently elected as chairman of the Virginia Academy of Laureates.

An authority in constitutional law, Professor Howard is the author of a number of books and monographs. These include *The Road from Runnymede: Magna Carta and Constitutionalism in America* and *Commentaries on the Constitution of Virginia*, which won a Phi Beta Kappa prize. His articles appear frequently in legal and other journals.

With the advent of the "Burger Court" (by convention the Court commonly takes on the name of the chief justice), the effort to capture the Court's essence is no easier. The Burger Court has been in place over a decade, if one counts from the time Warren Burger became chief justice, or at least a decade, if one counts from the time the four Nixon appointees first began to serve together. In any event, the Burger Court has been in existence long enough to begin to analyze its performance. One begins by making some comparisons with the Court that preceded it—the Warren Court of the 1950s and 1960s. The Court in the days of Earl Warren was known above all for its activism— for a willingness to jump in and solve social problems where other branches of government might have been less willing to be involved. Examples include the reapportionment of state legislatures, the use of the Fourteenth Amendment to fasten the provisions of the Bill of Rights upon the states, school prayer cases, desegregation of public schools, and so on.[1] There were not many problems the Warren Court did not appear willing to tackle. Indeed, Philip B. Kurland, a law professor at the University of Chicago, once commented that if the road to hell is paved with good intentions, the Warren Court must be one of the great road builders of all time.[2]

Appraisals of the Warren Court vary enormously, depending upon one's political and philosophical persuasion. In the presidential campaign of 1968, particularly in his "law and order" speeches, Richard Nixon made the Supreme Court a campaign issue. He railed at the justices for turning criminals loose, allowing them to roam the streets and to prey upon victims again. Something had gone terribly wrong, he thought, for the Supreme Court, through an excessive concern for the rights of criminal defendants, to thwart the needs of law enforcement.

It fell Nixon's fortune, not given to many presidents, to put four justices on the Court in about two and a half years.[3] That is not unprecedented in American history, but it certainly has not been very common. I know of no American president who, in making his appointments to the bench, has been as specific as Nixon was in explaining precisely why he picked the people he did. He saw his appointees as sharing his basically conservative political and judicial philosophy.

Those who admired the Warren Court shook in their boots at the idea of what they began to call the "Nixon Court"—the label that people hung on the Court in the early 1970s. News magazines and newspapers, looking for a catch phrase, talked about the "Nixon Court." Today, that phrase appears to have passed.

In the effort to describe the Burger Court, it may be convenient to think of the Court in two phases—the early seventies and the late seventies.

As of the end of the 1975 term—in the summer of 1976—one could begin to paint something of a portrait of the Burger Court. Cases decided that summer included the first decision in forty years drawing on the Tenth Amendment to strike down a federal statute as exceeding Congress's commerce powers, a holding closing the doors of federal courts to large numbers of prisoners seeking to use federal habeas corpus to raise Fourth Amendment (unlawful search-and-seizure) claims, a ruling that assertions of age discrimination required only the minimal judicial scrutiny under the Fourteenth Amendment's equal protection clause, and a decision rejecting the argument that capital punishment is inherently unconstitutional.[4]

As of 1976 one could have described the Burger Court as being—in contrast to the Warren Court—less activist, less aggressive, less egalitarian, more deferential to the country's legislative and political process, and more concerned about the limits of competence of federal judges. In particular, the two Courts differed in their willingness to trust the system. The Warren Court was marked by an inherent distrust of official power. The Burger Court, in contrast, seemed more willing to assume that most of the time the system runs properly and is not abused. Such generalizations were comfortable ones as of 1976.

Several years later, at the outset of the eighties, one must revise rather considerably some of these conclusions. Beginning with the 1976 term, one sees in the Court's decisions evidence of results that are more liberal and techniques that are more activist than the Court's jurisprudence in the period in 1970–1976. The evidence may be found in a number of areas. Even the Fourth Amendment—an area of decidedly conservative character in the early seventies—has been treated more kindly in the last two or three terms.[5] In sex discrimination cases, the Court more often than not has come down on the side of the claim of women's rights.[6]

By the early eighties, the picture of what the Burger Court seems to be doing is mixed. One can pick almost any area of the Court's activity and find something of a split personality. In school desegregation, in some instances it appears as if the Court is about to curb the ability of federal judges to push integration in American education.[7] Yet, in 1979 the Court decided cases from Columbus and Dayton which seem quite generous in upholding remedial decrees fashioned in school desegregation cases.[8] In right-to-counsel cases, the Court has drawn the line on efforts to expand the right of counsel in some areas but extended it in others.[9] Other examples could be cited.

Such mixed results—a pattern so episodic as sometimes to seem random—make generalizations difficult. Nevertheless, one can point to several conclusions about the Burger Court which contrast with the way many observers in the early seventies thought the Court would behave. At that time some bold predictions were being made about the character of the emerging Burger Court. Many of those predictions have proved to be myths or, at the least, have had to be heavily qualified.[10]

First, the "Nixon Court" label has vanished. It is clear that, whatever the justices of the present Court represent, they do not reflect Nixonian policies. Burger Court decisions conflicting with Nixon policies include those recognizing a woman's constitutional right to an abortion, sharply limiting aid to parochial schools, curbing Nixon's efforts to impound funds appropriated by Congress, and—the best example of all—requiring Nixon to hand over the Watergate tapes.[11]

Second, many predicted that the Burger Court would overturn much of what the Warren Court had done. Nixon's justices would be a wrecking crew, hostile to the legacy of the Warren years. Reviewing the actual record of the Burger Court, one finds, in fact, that the modus operandi of this Court is not so much to repeal as it is to qualify, to redefine, to adjust. As a result, the main body of the Warren Court's work remains in place—in school desegregation, reapportionment, and other major areas.[12] At the boundaries, however—where one might stand and look to new issues beyond those explicitly taken on by the Warren Court—in that new terrain, the Burger Court is likely to place the stamp of its own personality.

Third, in the early seventies one might have predicted that the Burger Court would not be an activist bench. To be sure, in some areas the Court has indeed stayed its hand. For example, the Court in 1973 refused to hold that the Fourteenth Amendment's equal protection clause requires states to equalize expenditures among rich and poor school districts.[13] In general, the Burger Court has refused to use the equal protection clause to level economic inequalities.[14] Nevertheless, there is cogent activism in the Burger Court. A paradigm would be the original abortion case, *Roe* v. *Wade*, in 1973.[15] If "activism" means to announce and defend a constitutional right which is not anywhere either explicit or implicit in constitutional text, then *Roe* is unmistakably an activist opinion.[16]

Fourth, at the outset of the Burger Court, some observers supposed that the Court would be given to the use of what I call "avoidance techniques"—lawyers' tools such as standing, ripeness, mootness, and other devices by which to avoid decisions in cases. Without here spelling out all the evidence, I would conclude that there is no indication that the Burger Court has made any more consistent use of avoidance techniques than did the Warren Court. The justices appear, now as then, to use such devices when they please and not to use them when they do not please.[17]

Finally, some Court watchers thought that the Burger Court would somehow constrict the scope and breadth of the Court's business, that the justices would try to curb the opportunities for the uses of judicial power. This is a variation on the judicial activism theme. There are indeed some areas in which the present Court appears to have had no interest at all—for example, "gay rights."[18] The justices appear simply unwilling to take those cases. Consider, however, all the kinds of cases, not on the Court's docket in the 1960s, that in the 1970s became a staple because of the work of the Burger Court—areas such as sex discrimination and capital punishment. Beginning in 1971, with *Reed* v. *Reed*, sex discrimination cases have been conspicuous on the Court's calendar.[19] The Warren Court would not even grant certiorari to consider the constitutionality of the death penalty; the Burger Court, in a line of cases, has sharply limited the states' powers to impose capital punishment.[20]

These trends in the Burger Court reflect what I call the "legalization" or "constitutionalization" of American life. Nothing is more American than the impulse to go to court. Some say that our national motto is, "There ought to be a law." I would strike that and say that the national motto is, "Let's sue." It is shorter and more to the point. One lawyer finds a new gimmick, and every lawyer in the country imitates it. Lee Marvin is sued by his former live-in girlfriend in California, she wins "palimony," and "Marvinizing" comes to the American courtroom. All over the country, jilted roommates want to imitate the Lee Marvin case. Small wonder that this country now leads the world in the number of lawyers per capita. We may get a recession in this country, but not in the law business. Today 574,000 Americans are lawyers—double the number twenty years ago.[21]

Now, to the crux of this portrait of the Burger Court. How may one account for the way this Court runs? How does one explain a track record that is so mixed and so episodic? The Warren Court was much easier to explain. With the Burger Court, it is more difficult to generalize.

Some factors may be suggested in accounting for the Burger Court. One inheres in the personalities of the justices themselves. There may be justices who, as they go to conference, have a shopping list of specific cases which they hope may be the vehicle for making great statements of law. But I think that, by and large, the Burger Court is made up of justices who take the cases as they come. At conference, as they sit around the table and talk about the cases, they take them somewhat in the fashion of practicing lawyers who specialize in whatever kind of case comes through the door that day. This tendency to take the cases as they come is reinforced by pressure of the work load. The Court gets busier year by year. One reads with some amusement accounts of how the Court was thought to be overworked in the thirties, forties, and fifties. The Court then had only a fraction of the cases that it is asked to review now.

Another factor is the lack of the larger-than-life figures of some earlier periods of the Court. Other times have seen a Felix Frankfurter, a Hugo Black, a Benjamin Cardozo, an Oliver Wendell Holmes, or a Louis Brandeis. What the presence of such giants does is to polarize the work of the Court. For example, other justices tended to cluster about Hugo Black and Felix Frankfurter and argue about the meaning of due process, such as Black's argument that the Fourteenth Amendment "incorporated" the guarantees of the Bill of Rights and made them applicable to the states.[22] That was a struggle of titans; everyone else took cover and joined one camp or the other.

Curiously enough, I would submit that the Burger Court is a less ideological place than was the Warren Court. I know that sounds a bit paradoxical because there is a common perception of the Burger Court as, whatever else it might be, a forum for ideology. Yet a fair conclusion seems to be that the Court is less clearly ideological than it was in the sixties.

The present Court also has a distaste for categorical rule making. The kinds of per se rules that one identifies with the Warren Court—such as the *Miranda* doctrine or the exclusionary rule of the Fourth Amendment—are not the kinds of rules this Court likes to fashion.[23] The justices in the 1960s sometimes saw themselves as empire builders—laying down rules for the ages. If so, then some of the present justices must think: Remember Ozymandias, whose broken monument recalls an empire which he, too, thought imperishable. The Burger Court appears to have more modest ambitions.

Another factor in the Burger Court's behavior is the lack of cohesive voting blocs. The Court has a floating voting pattern. On the right are Justice William H. Rehnquist and Chief Justice Burger; on the left are Justices William J. Brennan, Jr., and Thurgood Marshall. The remaining five—Justices Potter Stewart,* Byron R. White, John Paul Stevens, Harry A. Blackmun, and Lewis F. Powell, Jr.—make and unmake majorities. With those five justices lie the center of gravity and the balance of power in the Court. There is no consistent and predictable majority that controls the Court from case to case. It thus

---

* Justice Sandra O'Conner replaced the retired Justice Potter Stewart during the fall of 1981, after the period covered by this article. — Ed.

becomes more difficult to predict where the Court will come out in any given case. Consider the four Nixon appointees. As of about 1975, the four Nixon appointees voted together in two out of three cases—roughly, two-thirds of the time. Two years later that percentage of agreement had dropped to about one case out of three—a dramatic drop. It has continued to be fairly low.

In addition to these factors, one should mention the nature of the issues coming before the Court. The Court's perception of the cases that come before it tends to mirror the way the country looks at issues. Twenty years ago—at the time of the Kennedy inauguration, Camelot, and the New Society—one looked to Washington to solve the great issues. There was, in general, more of a willingness to say, "Yes, we can solve problems." Today the mood of the country seems different. Perhaps that change of mood has affected the justices. They behave as if the Court simply cannot grasp and deal with problems as neatly and simply as it might have tried to do fifteen or twenty years earlier. Contrast, for example, the Court's 1954 decision in *Brown* v. *Board of Education* with its 1979 decision in the *Bakke* case.[24] In *Brown*, a unanimous Court agreed to a short opinion—more of an essay in political theory than in law, a moral judgment, an appeal to the conscience of the country. In the *Bakke* decision six justices wrote 156 pages, yet no one can be sure just what the decision stood for. There is a certain symbolism in the fact that one finds the Court, twenty-five years after *Brown*, dealing with another great moral issue, but this time splitting in several inconclusive directions. I think the issue is clearly more difficult. It seems evident that in *Bakke* the issue of affirmative action was perceived as more difficult—the moral imperatives less clear—than was true of racial segregation in *Brown*.

As we enter the 1980s, we have, therefore, a Court in which no one point of view and no one philosophy prevails on a regular term-to-term, case-to-case basis. It is a Court in which competing forces exist side by side. On the one hand, there is the sort of neoconservativism reflected best of all by Rehnquist and, in a large measure, by the Chief Justice. On the other hand, there are the remnants of the Warren Court majority, represented by Brennan and Marshall. These forces are contending, fighting for the justices in the center; sometimes they win, and sometimes they do not.

It is fascinating that, results aside, the techniques which the Warren Court developed in the 1960s—the techniques of activism—have persisted in the Burger Court. Both camps seem equally willing to use the tools of activism when it suits them. The result, therefore, is a fluid voting pattern, in which neo-Frankfurterian impulses on the one side and neo-Warren impulses on the other compete. It is as if we had ten justices instead of nine, the tenth justice being the German philosopher Hegel. Hegel explained history in terms of the dialectic, the interaction of synthesis and antithesis. It helps to be a nineteenth-century German to understand the dialectic, but Hegel would be very comfortable in this Court. I suspect he would understand the Court better than I do.

Let us turn specifically to the press decisions of the Burger Court. This will serve as an introduction to the analysis of Floyd Abrams, who wrote the book, as far as I am concerned, on press cases. Consider the period of transition from the Warren to the Burger Court, from the sixties to the seventies. First, although Nixon made an issue of the Court in his 1968 campaign, neither the

Warren Court's First Amendment cases generally nor press cases specifically appear to have been an issue. It seems unlikely, therefore, that when Nixon made appointments to the Court he was thinking much about the press and First Amendment cases. Second, as of 1968, although the press was beginning to take on characteristics we now associate with it, the trend was not yet fully obvious. During the Vietnam years—pre-Watergate—the so-called investigative press was only emerging and had not yet come to full flower. The press at that point had not yet become the adversary of government that it would become in the seventies; nor had the press yet become a symbol of power in its own right—power that gives pause to many private citizens. The ability of the press to abuse its power was less obvious in the sixties than it would become in the seventies. Hence, the press issues which the Burger Court has dealt with are issues emerging above all from social and political realities of the seventies, having no obvious precedent in the sixties.

Third, the activism of the Warren Court of which I have been speaking touched a number of areas but did not have much to do with the press. Indeed, it had not as much to do with the First Amendment as one might suppose. The Warren Court never really evolved a comprehensive philosophy of the First Amendment. The cases reflect many theories and ideas, but the First Amendment is very difficult to systematize. I do not think that any of the Warren Court justices succeeded in convincing the majority of their colleagues of a particular view of the First Amendment. In the press area, *New York Times* v. *Sullivan* is one of the few genuine landmark cases of the sixties.[25] Press law, as we will talk about it here, is largely a creature of the seventies. One could teach a course in press law—surely, an adequate course—and confine oneself largely to cases decided since 1970.

Several kinds of questions may be posed about the Burger Court's handling of press cases. The first area has to do with the personalities and the dynamics of the Court. This includes questions such as the following: Are there individual justices who have advanced a consistent philosophy of press cases? Are there leaders in this area (specific attention should be paid to the Chief Justice and to Justice Stewart)? Can one find threads that run through the Burger Court's press cases, or is the ad hocism described earlier also characteristic of press cases? Do the voting patterns tend to be as splintered as those that characterize much of the Court's work?

The second area raises questions about attitudes and philosophies on the Court. Is there evidence of antipress sentiment on the Burger Court? One hears talk about Chief Justice Burger's disliking press people personally. Should such stories be dismissed as being the kind of behind-stairs gossip so popular today? A related question would be: Does the press properly report the Court, or is there an element of overreaction in the hostility evident in much of the editorial comment about the work of the Burger Court? On a more jurisprudential note: Has the Court been activist in the press area? Has it tended to be innovative in creating press law, or has it tended to be more conservative?

Finally, the third major area has to do with technique, with analysis, with doctrine, with the substantive aspect of the Court's work—questions such as the following: Is it possible to find, in the Court's opinions, a model of the press? In many of the criminal cases, the justices proceed from assumptions about the criminal justice process that shape how they react to Fourth Amendment questions, *Miranda* claims, or self-incrimination issues.[26] In press cases, does the Court operate with assumptions about the press that likewise influence the outcome of cases? Looking at the First Amendment, has the Court treated the press clause as being independent of the speech clause? Are the two thought to be hyphenated, like hue-and-cry, and therefore not separable, or are they in fact independent concepts? What analytical techniques does the Court in fact use in these cases? First Amendment cases are full of catch phrases embodying judicial tests—"clear-and-present danger," etc. What test, if any— or which tests, if several—are used in press cases, and how do they operate?

Such questions represent a sampling of the issues raised by the Burger Court's press cases. They are simply meant to stimulate thinking and to serve as a preface to the analysis of Floyd Abrams.

Notes

1. See, e.g., Reynolds v. Sims, 377 U.S. 533 (1964) (requiring reapportionment of state legislatures); Gideon v. Wainwright, 372 U.S. 335 (1963) (requiring appointment of counsel for indigent defendants in state felony trials); Abington School Dist. v. Schempp, 374 U.S. 203 (1963) (forbidding Bible readings and saying the Lord's Prayer in public schools); Brown v. Board of Education, 347 U.S. 483 (1954) (striking down racial segregation in public schools).
2. "Earl Warren, the 'Warren Court,' and the Warren Myths," *Michigan Law Review* 67 (December 1968): 357.
3. Warren Burger became Chief Justice in 1969. Harry A. Blackmun took his seat as an associate justice in 1970, and Lewis F. Powell, Jr., and William H. Rehnquist joined the Court in 1972.
4. National League of Cities v. Usery, 426 U.S. 853 (1976); Stone v. Powell, 428 U.S. 465 (1976); Massachusetts Board of Retirement v. Murgia, 427 U.S. 307 (1976); Gregg v. Georgia, 428 U.S. 153 (1976).
5. See, e.g., Brown v. Texas, 443 U.S. 47 (1979); Delaware v. Prouse, 440 U.S. 648 (1979).
6. See, e.g., Califano v. Westcott, 443 U.S. 76 (1979); Davis v. Passman, 442 U.S. 228 (1979).
7. See, e.g., Milliken v. Bradley, 418 U.S 717 (1974); Pasadena City Board of Education v. Spangler, 427 U.S. 424 (1976).
8. Columbus Board of Education v. Penick, 443 U.S. 449 (1979); Dayton Board of Education v. Brinkman, 443 U.S. 526 (1979).
9. Compare Kirby v. Illinois, 406 U.S. 682 (1972) (refusing defendant's claim that he was entitled to have counsel present at a preindictment police lineup), with Argersinger v. Hamlin, 407 U.S. 25 (1972) (extending to misdemeanor cases the Warren Court's *Gideon* ruling, supra note 1, that a state must appoint counsel in a felony trial for a defendant unable to afford counsel of his own).
10. For a fuller discussion, see A. E. Dick Howard, "The Burger Court: A Judicial Nonet Plays the Enigma Variations," *Law and Contemporary Problems* 43 (Summer 1980): 7–28.
11. Roe v. Wade, 410 U.S. 113 (1973); Lemon v. Kurtzman, 403 U.S. 602 (1971); Train v. City of New York, 420 U.S. 35 (1975); United States v. Nixon, 418 U.S. 683 (1974).
12. See note 1, supra.
13. San Antonio Independent School Dist. v. Rodriguez, 411 U.S. 1 (1973).
14. In addition to *Rodriguez*, see, e.g., United States v. Kras, 409 U.S. 434 (1973) (rejecting an indigent petitioner's argument that he should be allowed to file for bankruptcy without paying $50 in filing fees); Ortwein v. Schwab, 410 U.S. 656 (1973) (rejecting indigents' attack on Oregon's requiring a $25 filing fee as a prerequisite to judicial review of administrative denials of welfare benefits).
15. 410 U.S. 113 (1973) (holding that the Fourteenth Amendment's protection of "liberty" created a "right of privacy" which encompassed a woman's decision whether or not to terminate her pregnancy.)
16. See John Hart Ely, "The Wages of Crying Wolf: A Comment on *Roe* v. *Wade*," *Yale Law Journal* 82 (April 1973): 920–49.

17. For example, compare DeFunis v. Odegaard, 416 U.S. 312 (1974) (in which Marco De-Funis, a white challenger to a law school's affirmative action program, had been admitted pending outcome of litigation; the Court held the case moot because, by the time the case had been heard in the Court, DeFunis was in his final semester and seemed certain to graduate), with Roe v. Wade, 410 U.S. 113 (1973) (in which, despite the fact that by time the Court had heard the case, Ms. Roe had obviously either had a baby or an abortion, the Court held that the case was not moot).

18. See, e.g., Gaylord v. Tacoma School Dist. No. 10, 88 Wash. 2d 286, 559 P.2d 1340, cert. denied, 434 U.S. 879 (1976); Gish v. Board of Education, 145 N.J. Super. 96, 366 A.2d 1337, cert. denied, 434 U.S. 879 (1976) (in which teachers sought to prevent their being fired because of their sexual preference). See also Doe v. Commonwealth's Attorney, 425 U.S. 901 (1976) (summarily affirming a lower court's rejection of male homosexuals' challenge to a state sodomy law).

19. See, e.g., Reed v. Reed, 404 U.S. 71 (1971); Frontiero v. Richardson, 411 U.S. 677 (1973); Craig v. Boren, 429 U.S. 190 (1976); Orr v. Orr, 440 U.S. 268 (1979). See A. E. Dick Howard, "The Sexes and the Law," *The Wilson Quarterly* 6 (Winter 1982): 81–92.

20. See, e.g., Coker v. Georgia, 433 U.S. 584 (1977) (invalidating a state law making the death penalty mandatory for the murder of a policeman on duty); Roberts v. Louisiana, 431 U.S. 633 (1977) (holding capital punishment to be disproportionate as the penalty for rape). See, generally, Margaret Jane Radin, "The Jurisprudence of Death: Evolving Standards for the Cruel and Unusual Punishments Clause," *University of Pennsylvania Law Review* 126 (May 1978): 989–1064.

21. On America's proneness to laws and lawsuits, see A. E. Dick Howard, "A Litigation Society?" *The Wilson Quarterly* 5 (Summer 1981):98–109.

22. Compare Frankfurter's concurrence and Black's dissent in Adamson v. California, 332 U.S. 46 (1947).

23. See Miranda v. Arizona, 384 U.S. 436 (1966); Mapp v. Ohio, 367 U.S. 643 (1961). *Miranda* requires the police to warn a suspect, prior to his interrogation, that he has the right to remain silent, that what he says may be used against him, that he has the right to the presence of a lawyer, and that a lawyer will be appointed for him if he cannot afford one. The exclusionary rule ordains that evidence obtained in violation of the Fourth Amendment may not be introduced into evidence in a criminal proceeding against the person complaining of the constitutional violation.

24. Brown v. Board of Education, 347 U.S. 483 (1954); Regents of the Univ. of California v. Bakke, 438 U.S. 265 (1978).

25. New York Times Co. v. Sullivan, 376 U.S. 254 (1964).

26. See Jerold H. Israel, "Criminal Procedure, the Burger Court, and the Legacy of the Warren Court," *Michigan Law Review* 75 (June 1977): 1319–428; Stephen A. Saltzburg, "Foreword: The Flow and Ebb of Constitutional Criminal Procedure in the Warren and Burger Courts," *Georgetown Law Journal* 69 (December 1980): 151–209.

II. An Analysis

Floyd Abrams*

Assessing the work product of any court over a decade is an intellectually peril-
ous endeavor. It is no less so with the Burger Court, surely no less so with respect to the First Amendment rulings of that Court. "Inconsistency," Professor
Archibald Cox has written, "marks the pronouncements of the Burger
Court."[1] True enough. To which one may add: inconsistency also marks much
of the criticism made of critics of the Burger Court. Particularly when those
critics are journalists.

In recent years, a view has gained widespread acceptance that the press is
not only arrogant (a charge frequently made—sometimes correctly so) but also
more than a bit out of touch, perhaps even a bit balmy. The press is portrayed
in some quarters as overdramatizing its sometimes troubled relationship with
the courts. For example, when some students of mine, themselves journalists,
interviewed a sitting Supreme Court justice, they asked what he thought of the
growing tension between the press and the courts. To which he replied: "What
tension? You've just lost a few."

Still more significant is a growing concern on the part of a number of people who may, without doubt, be fairly characterized as friends of the press.
These people believe that the press has overreacted to losses in recent cases in
a fashion which could well lead to the use of the word *paranoid*. Stanford Law
School Professor Marc Franklin has, for example, characterized the press's
reaction to its loss in the *Herbert* v. *Lando*[2] case as "shrill."[3] The distinguished
and thoughtful journalist Anthony Lewis has written that the press has reacted
"hysterically" to some of its recent losses.[4] So proven a friend of free expression
rights for all as Justice William Brennan has, in a memorable address at the
dedication of the Samuel I. Newhouse Law Center at Rutgers University,

---

*Floyd Abrams is a partner in the New York law firm of Cahill Gordon & Reindel, an
associate in journalism at the Columbia University Graduate School of Journalism, and
a lecturer at the Columbia University Law School. From 1974 to 1980, Abrams was a
visiting lecturer at the Yale Law School. He was graduated from Cornell University in
1956 and the Yale Law School in 1960. In 1967, Abrams was awarded the Ross Essay
Prize of the American Bar Association for his study of the Ninth Amendment of the United States Constitution. In 1978, Abrams was awarded the First Amendment Prize of
the American Jewish Congress.

Throughout the 1970s, Abrams has appeared in a variety of cases on behalf of
newspapers, broadcasters, and journalists. He was co-counsel in the Pentagon Papers
case and has argued in the Supreme Court in cases including *Nebraska Press Association* v. *Stuart, Landmark Communications* v. *Virginia, Smith* v. *Daily Mail, Nixon* v.
Warner Communications, and *Herbert* v. *Lando*, all of which he refers to in the accompanying article. He was counsel to Myron Farber in the litigation arising out of the subpoena served upon Farber in a New Jersey murder case and served as counsel to NBC,
CBS, and ABC in the ABSCAM tapes cases.

Abrams has served as chairman of the Committee on Freedom of Speech and of the
Press of the Individual Rights Section of the American Bar Association. He also has
been chairman of the Committee on Freedom of Expression of the Litigation Section of
the American Bar Association. He has published articles in the *New York Times Magazine, Fortune, Yale Law Journal*, and elsewhere.

138

chided the press for its "vehement, if not violent reactions" to recent Court decisions and warned it against permitting "bitterness [to] cloud its vision [and]
self-righteousness its judgment."[5]

Such individuals are serious. What they say should be seriously considered
by the press—and all who care for it. And, it should be emphasized, those
statements are made by friends.

Yet, there is another side which has not often been proffered. It suggests
that press critics of the Burger Court may not have overreacted, but may, instead, have correctly perceived that the agenda created by the Court has been
a skewed one—and that its rejection of press arguments has too often been
arbitrary, uncompromising, and unyielding. Let me offer three types of Supreme Court cases for your review.

The first type involves the decision by the Supreme Court as to which cases
it will review, often a decision at least as important as any other it makes. By
choosing to review some cases, but not others, the Court sets its agenda—and
ours—for the future. As Yale Law School Professor Fowler Harper and Alan S.
Rosenthal once observed, "When the Court decides a case involving important
matters of public interest, it is making national policy. When it declines to review a case involving important issues, is it not also determining policy?"[6]

My thesis is that by following a practice of reviewing press victories and refusing to review press losses, the Court has too often set its agenda for press
cases in a skewed—and extremely activist—fashion. In addition, by appearing
to "reach" for press cases, or others involving freedom of expression, that the
press has won in lower courts when those cases are ones that the Court would
not otherwise take—even for long-standing procedural reasons—it has seriously compromised its own status as neutral decision maker. For example:

- In *Herbert* v. *Lando*,[7] the Court (by a 6 to 3 vote) reviewed and reversed an
interlocutory discovery ruling* of the U.S. Court of Appeals for the
Second Circuit holding that in libel cases governed by *New York Times Co.*
v. *Sullivan*,[8] the First Amendment barred certain questions to journalists
about their own decision-making process. The decision of the Court of
Appeals was, without question, a significant one. It was, as well, one certainly worthy at some point of Supreme Court review. But why was the
case reviewed by the Supreme Court when it was? The Court rarely reviews discovery rulings and still more rarely reviews them while a case is
pending at the time the discovery ruling is being sought.[9] Review is
available from appellate courts after a party refuses to disclose information
and is held in contempt.[10] Where information has been ordered *not* to be
disclosed, immediate appellate review of the claims of the party seeking
the information is virtually unknown.[11] Still further questions are raised.
Why, for example, was the Court of Appeals opinion reviewed when it was
the *first* case holding that journalists were protected from being forced to
talk about their own decision-making processes? The general rule, of
course, is that the Court, at least as a prudential matter, chooses to await,
even as to constitutional matters, disputes between the circuits.[12] Why, in

---

* This refers to a ruling pertinent to the fact-gathering process preceding a trial which concerned one issue in
the suit, but which did not settle the suit itself.—Ed.

short, did the Court decline to permit the case to proceed to trial, or disposition by motion, to see how the *Herbert* privilege held to exist by the Court of Appeals for the Second Circuit worked in fact? Had the plaintiff lost, the Court could then have reviewed the case. Had the plaintiff won, the Court would not have then reviewed it but, perhaps, then would have been persuaded that there was no need for review. And if there were a need, the Court could surely have found some other relevant final judgment to review—on a factual record demonstrating the effect of what the Court of Appeals had done. But the Supreme Court did not wait.

• In its ruling in *Snepp* v. United States,[13] the Court (also by a 6 to 3 vote) held that a former CIA agent, who had agreed as a condition of his employment to do so, was obliged to submit his manuscripts in advance for CIA prepublication clearance, even when it was admitted that *all* material in the book was unclassified. The court below, the U.S. Court of Appeals for the Fourth Circuit, had held against Snepp but had refused to impose a constructive trust on all of Snepp's profits.* The Court of Appeals held that because Snepp had not, in fact, published any classified material, damages could be nominal only (with the possibility of punitive damages if the government proved tortious conduct at trial).[14] Snepp had petitioned for certiorari. The government, basically content with the judgment below, did not petition for certiorari but filed a conditional cross-petition, seeking more drastic relief against Snepp only if the Court granted his petition for certiorari. The Court decided the case summarily, without argument or briefing. Its decision devoted a single footnote to Snepp's First Amendment claims; the entirety of the opinion was devoted to expanding significantly the remedy granted against Snepp by the court below. But in doing so in this procedural framework, as the dissent of Supreme Court Justice John Paul Stevens pointed out, it acted in an "unprecedented" procedural and substantive manner. The Court was using a petition for certiorari which it did not believe was meritorious as a vehicle to take the case and then overriding the government's own concession that the relief below was "sufficient" to protect its interest.[15]

• In *Nixon* v. *Warner Communications, Inc.*,[16] the Court overturned (by a 7 to 2 vote) a decision in the Court of Appeals for the District of Columbia holding that broadcasters and others were entitled to copy and broadcast the Watergate tapes introduced in evidence at the Watergate cover-up trials. Counsel for petitioner Richard Nixon had urged that the former President had, among other things, a right of privacy in the tapes, notwithstanding their introduction into evidence in the trials—that the tapes obtained by subpoena should still be deemed protected by executive privilege. Opposition to certiorari was based on the unlikelihood of the Nixon situation ever recurring and the fact that the heart of the case—the common law of the District of Columbia—was hardly worthy of review by a supposedly overburdened court. Nixon's counsel did not urge that any act of Congress

---

* The theory behind a constructive trust is that a person who acquires property wrongfully must give up all profits accrued.—Ed.

supported his position. Certiorari was granted, and after argument counsel were asked to brief the question whether the Presidential Recordings and Materials Preservation Act,[17] which sets forth the long-term means of distribution of some tapes to the public, governed this case. Nixon's lawyers candidly conceded it did not. The broadcasters submitted a lengthy brief arguing that the statute related to other tapes and was itself premised on the notion that the tapes introduced in evidence in the Watergate trials *would* quickly be made generally available. The Court, however, disregarded the agreement of counsel and held that the act governed—and that the tapes consequently need not be made generally available at that time.[18]

These cases are cited not for the purpose of demonstrating that the asserted First Amendment position should have triumphed in them. It is, instead, the unusual procedural situations in each of the cases that is of interest: the granting of certiorari from an interlocutory discovery ruling, which laid down for the first time a new substantive First Amendment rule; the granting of a conditional cross-petition for certiorari, which provided the government with more relief than it sought; the rather peremptory disregarding of the conclusions, reached after exhaustive research by all counsel, to the effect that a statute did not govern a particular case. And for responding to such decisions with some heat, the press is said to be paranoid! It is enough to make one so.

Consider, as well, some specific cases the Court decided *not* to consider. Return briefly to the days of Myron Farber's case.[19] Return not to the First Amendment issues in the case, not even to the question whether the subpoena in the case was too broad or whether a hearing should have been held or what sort of hearing it should have been. Consider a simple due process question, and ask whether it was worthy of Supreme Court review. Suppose that a priest were called to testify in a state (such as New Jersey) with a statutory privilege against revealing confidential information "to any court." Suppose the priest had refused, based on the statute, to reveal the information to a court, that he had been ordered to do so, that he had refused and had been held in contempt; and that the supreme court of the state held that his interpretation of the statute had been *correct*—that is to say, that its provisions on their face did, in fact, relieve him of the obligation to tell even the judge, in private, what the confidential information was. Suppose further, however, that the state's highest court said that the statute, otherwise constitutional, had to "yield" to a defendant's Sixth Amendment right to gather evidence.[20] What would be the result? Specifically, would the previous contempt conviction be upheld? Is it not a deprivation of due process to say that an otherwise valid "shield law" relied upon by a witness must "yield" to other interests and to say that *before* it was held that it had to yield, a contempt conviction was lawful? Is this not, at least, a serious due process issue—at least as much an issue requiring immediate judicial review as the cases discussed earlier?

There have been other cases thought unworthy by the Court of review: a case involving a supposed fictionalization of the lives of real people that is generally thought in the publishing industry to threaten significant parts of our current and future literature;[21] a case involving a journalist who did not disclose confidential sources in circumstances in which it was stipulated that others might easily have been approached for the same information;[22] a case involving a libel judgment based upon a most dubious interpretation by the lower court of currently governing law.[23] In each of these cases, the Court denied certiorari. Is this the construct of a paranoid press?

Yet the press is said to be arrogant. It is said to demand absolute protection for itself and to ignore the rights of others. An alternative model is at least as plausible: that it is the Supreme Court, not the press, which has too often acted in an absolutist fashion. Consider the following cases:

In its 1972 ruling in *Branzburg* v. *Hayes*,[24] four members of the Supreme Court (joined, at least to some extent, by Justice Lewis Powell) rejected the view of the four dissenting justices that journalists should not be obliged to testify with respect to information gathered from confidential sources unless the information sought was plainly relevant, not obtainable from alternative sources, and of central import to the proceeding. Justice Powell's critical and determinative concurrence[25] rejected the view of the dissenters that there should be a threshold test before the press should be ordered to provide such testimony, but it supported the proposition that the First Amendment should at least be weighed by the courts when they were considering whether such testimony should be ordered. But four members of the Court would have afforded the press no protection at all.

In its *Zurcher* v. *Stanford Daily* opinion,[26] a majority of the Court rejected the argument of the press that a police search of a newsroom, pursuant to search warrant, may not occur unless there is good reason to believe that a subpoena could not, for one reason or another, serve the same purpose.

In the Court's ruling in *Herbert* v. *Lando*,[27] referred to earlier, questions in a libel suit as to why one statement in a broadcast was made and not another were held proper by a majority of the Court, as were questions as to why one person was interviewed and not another. I will not reargue that case; I simply note that with the exception—once again—of Justice Powell,[28] the majority in *Herbert* did not offer even a word or two of First Amendment solace or guidance for the future.

More recent was the Court's ruling, in *Gannett* v. *DePasquale*,[29] holding that the Sixth Amendment does not afford the public a right to open pretrial (and, perhaps, trial) proceedings when the defendant seeks the closing of those proceedings and the prosecutor and the court acquiesce.

One thing about these cases, and one only, should be emphasized. It is not that the press was necessarily correct in each case in the balance it proposed to strike. It is not even that *all* the cases would have been won by the press with the Court that sat in the 1960s; each is a 5 to 4 or, at worst, a 6 to 3 ruling, which would not have survived the scrutiny of former Justices Hugo Black and William O. Douglas. It is simply that in *none* of the cases did the press demand absolute protection; that in all, the press sought to strike a balance—sought accommodation. And that, except to the extent that Justice Powell's opinions may ultimately carry the day, in all, a slim majority rejected the accommodation sought by the press.

There is another side worthy of more than passing reference. It is that, notwithstanding the above, the American press has never been more free, never been more uninhibited, and—most important—never been better protected by law. The ban on prior restraints is all but absolute.[30] The *Progressive* case,[31] wrongheaded as I believe it was to commence it, would have been unthinkable anywhere else in the world because the editors would have been jailed and not merely the subjects of a failed attempt at an injunction. The ban on requiring the press to print what it chooses not to is nearly absolute.[32] The press may not be punished for publishing almost any information it obtains, even if there were legitimate reasons for keeping the information secret.[33] We may not know what an *opinion* is,[34] but whatever it is, it is absolutely protected.[35] So are truthful statements—and the burden is on the plaintiff to prove lack of truth.[36] In addition, while the definition of *public figure* has been drastically narrowed in recent years (most notably in a case holding that an accused Russian agent was not a public figure, even during his trial for contempt of Congress, because he—in the best tradition of his alleged craft—had not mounted a rostrum and engaged in public debate about espionage),[37] there remains a most significant amount of protection of the press in the libel area.

To go further, I believe that in most areas the war of the 1970s between the press and the courts is over. The battle over prior restraints has been resolved in a manner likely to avoid much serious confrontation in the future.[38] So has the great confrontation over closed courtrooms.[39] The *Zurcher* case,[40] one of the most egregious of the Burger Court, has been overruled by an act of Congress.[41]

The area of confidential sources remains the single one most likely to provoke confrontation in the future. Yet, even there—no thanks to the *Branzburg* ruling[42]—a new mood has often been reflected in lower courts. There, judges have often found some way of avoiding confrontation by holding on non-First Amendment grounds that sources need not be disclosed[43] or vindicating the press position on the basis of a qualified First Amendment privilege.[44] I cannot praise the Burger Court in this area; recent press victories are more in spite of and not because of its rulings. However, in more and more such cases, the press has been prevailing.[45]

To summarize: the dour press perception of the Burger Court has, in good part, been both measured and accurate. In many areas, however, freedom of expression has triumphed under the Burger Court and is likely to again. The war between the press and the courts of the 1970s is ending, if not over, and it is ending on terms with which both the press and the courts can live with surprising comfort. This is, in part, to the credit of the Burger Court and, in part, notwithstanding that Court. In *toto*, it is a surprisingly cheering note upon which to begin the decade of the 1980s.

Notes

1. Arcbibald Cox, "Foreword: Freedom of Expression in the Burger Court," *Harvard Law Review* 94 (November 1980): 31.

2. 441 U.S. 153 (1979).
3. Marc A. Franklin, "Reflections on *Herbert v. Lando*," *Stanford Law Review* 31 (July 1979): 1049.
4. "Amending the Court," *New York Times*, 26 June 1978, p. A–19.
5. "Address by William J. Brennan, Jr.," *Rutgers Law Review* 32 (1979): 182.
6. "What the Supreme Court Did Not Do in the 1949 Term: An Appraisal of Certiorari," *University of Pennsylvania Law Review* 99 (December 1950): 293.
7. 441 U.S. 153 (1979).
8. 376 U.S. 254 (1964).
9. See Robert L. Stern and Eugene Grossman, *Supreme Court Practice*, 5th ed. (Washington, D.C.: Bureau of National Affairs, 1978), p. 300.
10. See, e.g., United States v. Cuthbertson, 630 F.2d 139 (3d Cir. 1980), cert. denied, 101 S.Ct. 945 (1981).
11. See, e.g., United States v. Nixon, 418 U.S. 683, 690–92 (1974); United States v. Ryan, 402 U.S. 530, 532 (1971); Baker v. F & F Investment, 470 F.2d 778, 780 n. 3 (2d Cir. 1972), cert. denied, 411 U.S. 966 (1973).
12. Stern and Grossman, *Supreme Court Practice*, pp. 265–73; Robert L. Stern, "Denial of Certiorari Despite a Conflict," *Harvard Law Review* 66 (January 1953): 465; U.S., Commission on Revision of the Federal Court Appellate System, "Structure and Internal Procedures: Recommendations for Change," *Federal Rules Decisions* 67 (1975): 221–24, 281–82, 298–324.
13. 444 U.S. 507 (1980).
14. United States v. Snepp, 595 F.2d 926 (4th Cir. 1979), rev'd, 444 U.S. 507 (1980).
15. 444 U.S. at 524–26.
16. See Nixon v. Warner Communications, Inc., 435 U.S. 589 (1978).
17. U.S., *Code*, title 44, sec. 2107.
18. 435 U.S. at 603–8.
19. In re Farber, 78 N.J. 259, 394 A.2d 330, cert. denied, 439 U.S. 997 (1978).
20. 78 N.J. at 271–74, 394 A.2d at 336–37.
21. Bindrim v. Mitchell, 92 Cal. App.3d 61, 155 Cal. Rptr. 29 (2d Dist. 1979), cert. denied, 444 U.S. 984 (1979).
22. Kansas v. Sandstrom, 224 Kan. 573, 581 P.2d 812 (S.Ct. Kan. 1978), cert. denied, 440 U.S. 929 (1979).
23. Sprouse v. Clay Communication, Inc., 211 S.E.2d 674 (W.Va. S.Ct. 1975), cert. denied, 423 U.S. 882 (1975).
24. 408 U.S. 665 (1972).
25. Ibid. at 709.
26. 436 U.S. 547 (1978).
27. 441 U.S. 153 (1979).
28. Ibid. at 177.
29. 443 U.S. 368 (1979).
30. New York Times Co. v. United States, 403 U.S. 713 (1971); Nebraska Press Ass'n v. Stuart, 427 U.S. 539 (1976).
31. United States v. The Progressive, Inc., 467 F.Supp. 990 (W.D. Wis. 1979).
32. Miami Herald Publishing Co. v. Tornillo, 418 U.S. 241 (1974).
33. Landmark Communications, Inc. v. Virginia, 435 U.S. 829 (1978); Smith v. Daily Mail Co., 443 U.S. 97 (1979).
34. See American Law Institute, *Restatement of the Law Second; Torts 2d.* (St. Paul, Minn.: American Law Institute Publishers, 1977), vol. 3, sec. 566.
35. Gertz v. Robert Welch, Inc., 418 U.S. 323 (1974).
36. New York Times Co. v. Sullivan, 376 U.S. 254 (1964).
37. Wolston v. Reader's Digest Ass'n, 443 U.S. 157 (1979).
38. See note 30 supra.
39. Compare Gannett v. DePasquale, 443 U.S. 368 (1979), with Richmond Newspapers, Inc. v. Virginia, 448 U.S. 555 (1980).
40. Zurcher v. Stanford Daily, 436 U.S. 547 (1978).
41. U.S., *Code Annotated*, title 42, sec. 2000aa (Privacy Protection Act of 1980).
42. Branzburg v. Hayes, 408 U.S. 665 (1972).

43. See, e.g., United States v. Lance, 5 Med.L.Rptr. 2306 (N.D. Ga. 1979) (reporters' testimony held not relevant).

44. See, e.g., Baker v. F & F Investment, 470 F.2d 778 (2d Cir. 1972), cert. denied, 411 U.S. 966 (1973); Steaks Unlimited, Inc. v. Deaner, 623 F.2d 264 (3d Cir. 1980).

45. See, e.g., State v. St. Peter, 132 Vt. 266, 315 A.2d 254 (S.Ct. Vt. 1974); People v. Bonnakemper, 74 Misc.2d 696, 345 N.Y.S.2d 900 (City Ct., Rochester, N.Y. 1973); Zelenka v. State, 83 Wis.2d 601, 266 N.W.2d 279 (S.Ct. Wis. 1978).

PART III

The First Amendment
in the 1980s

CHAPTER 5

Democracy and Free Speech: A Normative Theory of Society and Government

John L. Hodge*

I. The Need for Free Speech Theory

In a true democracy, what would freedom of speech mean, to what extent would it be valued, and how would it be protected? Would the legal doctrines of free speech in such a society differ from the present doctrines in our own society?

Although the courts in the United States have frequently attempted to resolve disputes involving the free speech and press clause of the First Amendment to the United States Constitution by examining the meaning of free speech in a democratic society, they have done so case by case and by analyzing specific issues without systematic reference to an articulated theory of democracy.

> The Supreme Court has neither embraced a unifying theory of the speech clause of the first amendment nor reached a consensus on appropriate premises for first amendment cases. An abundant first amendment literature has failed to dispel the climate of uncertainty and intellectual disorder that permeates the concept and im-

---

*John L. Hodge, who has been a member of the faculty of the Department of Philosophy at California State University, Hayward, since 1969, spent the 1980–81 academic year as a visiting scholar in the Department of Philosophy at Harvard University. He also taught during that year at Brandeis University in the Legal Studies Program and at the Boston campus of the University of Massachusetts in the Law and Justice Program.

Hodge holds both a Ph.D. in philosophy from Yale University and a Juris Doctor from Boalt Hall at the University of California, Berkeley. His teaching and research interests draw on both disciplines and include jurisprudence, legal reasoning, human rights, social ethics, and contemporary social and political issues (including race relations and feminist philosophy). He earned his undergraduate degree in mathematics at the University of Kansas, where he was named to Phi Beta Kappa. He held a Danforth Fellowship from 1961 to 1968.

The present focus of Hodge's research and writing is jurisprudence and theories of justice, with particular emphasis on law and theories of human rights and on freedom of communication. His book, *Cultural Bases of Racism and Group Oppression* (with D. K. Struckmann and L. D. Trost), was published in 1975.

Hodge has been involved in community and legal work and labor organizations. Among other activities, he served as a draft counselor and peace intern with the American Friends Service Committee in Houston and in Seattle from 1965 to 1968; he was a member and officer of United Professors of California (AFL/CIO) from 1969 to 1976; and since 1980 he has been a member of the Committee on Blacks in Philosophy of the American Philosophical Association. He was admitted to the Massachusetts Bar in 1981 and will serve as law clerk for the Massachusetts Appeals Court for 1982–83.

plementation of freedom of speech . . . . A carefully articulated conception of the basic purposes of the amendment is essential to first amendment adjudication and commentary.[1]

Without a systematic articulation of a theory of free speech, adjudication of free speech issues will remain subject to ad hoc decision making resulting in unclear, uncertain, and sometimes contradictory legal doctrine.

One major and important attempt to remedy this deficiency in legal literature and court opinions was Thomas I. Emerson's extensive work *The System of Freedom of Expression*.[2] Emerson's approach bases a doctrine of free speech on four basic values: (1) individual self-fulfillment through expression, (2) the advancement of knowledge and truth, (3) the participation by all members of the society in the decision-making process, and (4) the achievement of a more adaptable and hence more stable society. These four values serve as the basic assumptions or premises of his theory.[3]

There are two weaknesses in Emerson's approach which should be noted here. One weakness Emerson himself points out. He feels his theory may not be adequate to resolve an increasingly crucial question of our time: "Can the system of freedom of expression survive the shift from the liberal laissez-faire to the mass technological society?"[4] To answer this question, it is necessary to discuss to what extent democratic theory can guide the development of the newly emerging order and to describe in detail the meaning and importance of free speech in a society that is truly democratic.

A second weakness in Emerson's approach is inherent in any theoretical framework based on a plurality of potentially conflicting values with no preferential ordering among the different values. If the several basic values or premises can be shown to be independent and without conflict or contradictions among them, then the system may be consistently developed with the several premises, analogous to a mathematical system based on several axioms, where each axiom is given a weight or value equal to each of the others.[5] However, if the premises do not fulfill this mathematical ideal and instead pull in different or contradictory directions in particular cases, then the premises cannot give adequate rational grounds for resolving those cases. In such a situation of conflict, one must balance the conflicting values and decide on an ad hoc basis which value is to be given greater weight in a particular case.[6]

Such a problem is inherent in Emerson's approach, based as it is on a plurality of values that in some cases pull in opposite directions. For example, when Congress passed the Federal Election Campaign Act of 1971, it apparently placed great value on the need for participation in the decision-making process by all members of society—Emerson's third value. That act, among other things, limited the amount of money a candidate may spend on his or her own election campaign and limited the amount of money a non-candidate may spend in behalf of a candidate. The purpose of the act was to reduce the ability of persons of wealth to affect the decision-making process to the relative exclusion of the less wealthy. The U.S. Supreme Court, however, emphasizing the value of individual expression—Emerson's first value—found these portions of the act to be unconstitutional limitations on the expression of many individuals. (The Court's decision in *Buckley* v. *Valeo* is discussed in more detail below.) Where there is more than one value that is *basic*, there will usually be such unresolvable conflict among them. The mathematical model generally cannot be adequately duplicated in the realm of social and political theory. Another approach is needed.

Emerson's approach is certainly an improvement over the nonsystematic, ad hoc balancing typical of many court decisions. Possibly, the world is sufficiently complex that a free speech theory based on fewer than four basic values would necessarily be inadequate. Perhaps, any adequate theory must contain several conflicting basic premises such that at least some cases must be decided by balancing basic values on an ad hoc basis. However, this should not be assumed in the absence of a theory based on a sounder model. A sounder theretrical model would rest on basic values or assumptions that are ranked, or given different weights in order of their importance. In such a model, one basic value would stand as primary, and fulfillment of any other values would be important only after the primary value had been satisfied. In turn, the remaining basic values would also be ranked. Whether this approach can lead to a theory with adequate practical applications cannot be known until such a theory is developed and examined. In the absence of such theories, the approach of Emerson wins by default.

Alexander Meiklejohn began the development of a theory based on a primary value.[7] His "basic value" was the ideal of democracy (Emerson's third value), which he defined as self-government. This essay will begin where Meiklejohn began and will attempt to develop a democratic theory of free speech. However, this normative theory will take us beyond the paths that Meiklejohn began to travel.

The first step in any theory requires some definition of basic terms. Although the ambiguities inherent in language make absolute precision impossible, precision of usage is nonetheless a desirable and useful goal. Thus, Section II will concern itself with clarification of some of the terminology to be used and some of the underlying concepts upon which the theory rests. Section III will present a normative theory of democracy and a normative theory of free speech based upon it. Section IV will examine some of the applications of the theory to issues that have been decided by the U.S. Supreme Court. Some further clarification of the theory will result from the examination of these issues and from the application of the theory to them.

Before proceeding, however, the reader should be forewarned that this essay will raise more questions than it answers. It is, at best, the beginning of a theory. This beginning, however, may provide a foundation for answering many of the questions raised and left unanswered.

II. Terminology and Definitions

The key terms to be defined in this section are *normative theory*, *free speech*, and *rights*. A definition of *democracy* will be given in Section III.

Normative Theory

This essay presents a normative theory of society, a theory not of existing rules of behavior but of behavior which ought to exist.[8] Thus a normative theory of society must be distinguished from a theory of social or political science. The former concerns questions of values. The latter concerns matters of fact. The procedure appropriate for determining the acceptability of the former is radically different from the procedure appropriate for verifying the latter. The procedure for verifying the latter has been generally accepted to be the method of science. The procedure for determining the acceptability of the former has not been agreed upon or fully understood.[9] For the purposes of this essay, the acceptability of the theory presented may be viewed as dependent upon the extent to which it is soundly based in some generally accepted notions of democracy.

It is important to distinguish carefully the two kinds of theories so that refutations that are appropriate for one are not assumed to be appropriate for the other. A theory concerning matters of fact can be refuted by showing that the facts do not agree with a deduced consequence of the theory. For example, a theory that attempts to explain the underlying basis of the U.S. Supreme Court's decisions in the area of free speech would be a theory dealing with matters of fact. If the theory correctly explains the Court's decisions in all its free speech cases over a specified period of time, then the theory is sound to that extent. However, if the theory purports to explain all the Court's decisions during a specified time period, and someone discovers a decision during that period that is contrary to the decision which would have been made were the theory correct, then the theory has been refuted. A simple fact refutes a theory that predicts the fact should be otherwise.[10]

The refutation of a normative theory, in contrast, depends on its relation to a much broader body of experience, perhaps including sentiment and feeling, and the precise nature of this relation remains the subject of considerable debate. No simple fact can refute a normative theory, because such a theory is a statement of what *ought to be*, not of what is.

> The whole point of a normative social theory is that it is introduced to change the *de facto* situation at least in part, rather than to conform to it. It defines the ideal society at which we are aiming. It does not purport to designate, after the manner of a theory in natural science, the *de facto* state of affairs which we actually have.[11]

As this essay is presenting a normative theory of society and a normative theory of free speech, it is not a refutation of those theories to show that they conflict with an existing fact situation. The only fact that clearly refutes a normative theory is a fact of impossibility. If it can be demonstrated that the ideal society presented by a normative social theory is a complete impossibility, then the fact of impossibility refutes the normative theory.[12] The possibility of this type of refutation is based on the assertion that *ought* implies *can*.[13]

If a normative theory of free speech conflicts with the existing body of law, that in itself is not an adequate basis for rejecting the normative theory. The conflict only raises the question of which is to be preferred, the existing law or what the law would be if the normative theory were fully implemented.

Conflicts between the normative theories presented here and the existing body of law are to be expected. Where such a conflict exists, the question raised is whether there is an alternative normative theory which (1) provides an adequate basis for the existing law and (2) is to be preferred. The current problem with the existing law in the area of free speech is that there seems to be no consistent normative theory underlying or guiding it.[14]

Free Speech

Free speech is used in this essay not to refer specifically to the speech clause of the First Amendment but to refer to the general issue of freedom of communication. It is not necessary for the purposes of this essay to discuss the possibility that the speech clause and the press clause are separable and should be treated differently.[15] The phrase *freedom of communication* is to be preferred over the often-used generic term *freedom of expression*. *Communication* more clearly suggests the involvement of a speaker and a listener. When we speak of a *right of free speech*, we must consider the rights of both the speakers and the listeners. The term *expression*, on the other hand, suggests the primary focus should be on the speakers. What we conclude about the relative rights of speakers and listeners is another matter.[16] We should avoid suggesting by our choice of language a preference for speakers.

The phrase *freedom of communication* also suggests the relevant issues concern the interactions among people, not simply the acts of isolated individuals. The social nature of the issues is directly and correctly implied by this choice of words. That there is a relation between the rights of individuals to engage in communication and the rules and laws governing social interactions need not be mysterious or obscure. Thus in the term *free speech*, *speech* is to be understood in this essay to be synonymous with *communication*.

Freedom and Rights

A considerably more difficult task is to define the other word in the term *free speech*: *free*. What is meant by *freedom*, or *liberty*?

These terms are often used to mean *absence from constraints*.[17] Yet, the contexts in which they often appear negate this meaning. Although the term *freedom of speech* may be used to mean a general absence of constraints on speech, more frequently it is used to mean only an absence of governmental constraints. It is not clear, however, why *freedom* should be used to refer to a situation in which one form of constraint does not exist, while another form, equally constraining, does. For example, under existing law, a private employer (that is, where there is no *state action*) may fire an employee solely because of the latter's political speech.[18] When this is seen as consistent with *freedom of speech*, that freedom does not refer to a general freedom but only to a particular freedom against governmental constaint (and that with qualifications).[19] This loose usage tends to mask the fact that many constraints exist under this form of freedom. More precise usage is necessary to remove this mask.

In this essay, *freedom* will be defined in terms of *rights*, simply because all freedoms in society depend upon legally protected rights.[20] Although there is something common to all rights, it is best to begin by defining two different kinds of rights, *passive* (or *negative*) rights and *active* (or *affirmative*) rights. We must take care not to place value judgments on the terms *active* and *passive*. As the examples below illustrate, an active right is not in itself superior to a passive one, nor vice versa. We must also not assume that the difference between active and passive rights is always clear-cut. Many rights are complex, involving a mixture of active and passive components.

Rights may also be legal or normative. A *legal right* is a right affirmed by law. A *normative right* is a right affirmed by a normative theory. Sometimes normative rights are called *moral rights*. Of course, normative rights and legal rights need not be mutually exclusive, and which normative rights are rights that should also be legally enforced would depend on the particular normative theory. Those normative rights that should be legally enforced will be called *normative legal rights*.

An example of a legal right that is predominantly passive is the right against unreasonable searches and seizures as expressed in the Fourth Amendment. This right requires, among other things, that no governmental agent or unit invade the privacy of one's home without a properly authorized search warrant. This is a right against a particular form of governmental interference in our private lives. It is passive, or negative, in that it requires the government to refrain from acting in a particular manner.[21]

An example of a legal right that is predominantly active is the right to a jury trial in criminal cases as guaranteed by the Sixth Amendment. This right requires the government to act affirmatively to provide a jury trial to a criminal defendant who has not waived that right.

In more precise terms, a person or entity, P_1, has a *passive right* against another person or entity, P_2, to do a particular act, A, whenever P_1 cannot be interfered with by P_2 when P_1 does A. A person or entity, P_3, has an *active right* against another person or entity, P_4, whenever P_4 must do an act B in P_3's behalf after the occurrence of specified conditions, C. The passive right is violated whenever there is interference in A by P_2. The active right is violated whenever there is inaction by P_4 in performing B. The right of P_1 implies a correlative duty of P_2 to refrain from interfering with P_1, and the right of P_3 implies a correlative duty of P_4 to act in behalf of P_3.

These rights are *legal rights* whenever violation of them results in a legal liability on P_2 or P_4. By P's *legal liability* is meant that existing law permits imposing some requirement on P. These rights are *normative* whenever violation ought to result in some form of liability on P_2 or P_4, whether or not they could or should be legally imposed.[22] When a normative theory prescribes that certain legal rights ought to exist, those rights are *normative legal rights*.

By defining rights more abstractly, a common definition may be devised for both active and passive rights: P_1 has a *right* against P_2 that A occur if and only if the nonoccurrence of A due to P_2 would result in P_2's liability.[23] If A is an act which P_1 is permitted to do without interference by P_2, the right is *passive*. If A is an act which P_2 must do, the right is *active*.

With these definitions of the concept of *rights*, it is clear that a right always involves three major components: (1) a party who has the rights; (2) a party against whom the right exists; and (3) an event which should or should not occur because of the acts of the party against whom the right exists. Where one does not hold a right against all other parties in a society (including governmental bodies), rights are limited. The currently existing legal rights implicit in the phrase *freedom of speech* are such limited rights, for this freedom is predominantly a passive right only against governmental interference.[24] This limitation on existing legal rights protecting speech is no longer masked by the general term *freedom* once this freedom is examined in terms of clearly defined rights. In this essay, therefore, we should understand *free speech* to mean a right of communication. The phrase *right of free speech* will be used as a convenient expression to refer to rights of communication.

We now turn to examining normative legal rights of free speech—the legal rights which should exist in a democratic society.

III. The Democracy Principle and the Right of Free Speech

The Democracy Principle

The normative theory presented here is based on the assumption that democracy is the primary goal to be attained. *Democracy*, however, is not a term with a single, unambiguous meaning. To some, it means majority rule; to some, it means a system of minimal government and free enterprise; to some, it means self-government. What democracy *really* is, of course, is subject to debate. In this essay, the essence of democracy is viewed as self-government. The definition of self-government used here is called the *democracy principle*, and it is on this principle that the arguments in this essay are based.

The *democracy principle* is this: the powers of government legitimately exist (1) only insofar as the citizens under that government delegate those powers to it and (2) only when the powers of delegation are equally distributed among the citizens. The two components of this principle, (1) the delegation component and (2) the equal powers component, will be examined below.

Although a normative theory presents what ought to be, not what is or what has been, it is generally helpful to understand the historical background of the theory. A part of that background is the Declaration of Independence. The democracy principle expresses two of the basic components of democracy expressed in that declaration. The delegation component is expressed in the passage "governments are instituted among men, deriving their just powers from the consent of the governed"; and the equal powers component is expressed in the phrase "all men are created equal."[25] The democracy principle does not, however, express all of the points of the declaration, nor does it express the two components in exactly the same way.

Although the democracy principle can be clarified by examining the two components separately, the full meaning of this principle cannot be understood without understanding how the two components interact with and limit each other. Therefore, there must be a third component of the democracy principle which states the principle of how the first two are to be related. This third component in the theory is that the first two components are of equal weight. Neither has priority over the other. The two components limit each other in a clearly defined way, so that it will be unnecessary to resort to ad hoc balancing of them when the democracy principle is applied to particular cases.

The first component establishes the legitimate source of government power and one of the two primary limitations upon that power. The power of government resides in the citizenry, and that power is legitimately sustained only insofar as that power is continually delegated by the citizenry to the government. This may occur by direct citizen participation in the decisions of government or by the direct selection by the citizens of representatives who make those decisions. The limitation on the power of government is that it may not extend beyond what has been delegated to it. The extent to which government exercises powers not delegated to it is the extent to which that government acts illegitimately.

The second component establishes the primary manner in which the delegation component is to be exercised. The powers of delegation are to be equally distributed among the citizenry. This means no citizen has significantly more or significantly less power to determine the decisions of government than any other citizen. This component also establishes the second major limitation on the power of government. Government power may not be legitimately used to give some citizens a greater power of delegation than others. It may not alter the equal distribution of the powers of delegation.

It is reasonable to assume that in a large, complex society the preservation of the equal distribution of delegatory powers can be adequately achieved only through governmental protection of that equality. Thus, as a practical matter, the second component also prescribes to government the responsibility for protecting the equal distribution of the delegatory power. Where the delegatory power is exercised through elections, for example, the government cannot allow one group of citizens to prevent another group from voting. There must be governmental protection of the voting process so that anyone who wishes to vote is not discouraged from doing so. This is one of the ways in which the two components interact.

The second component limits the delegatory power of the citizenry. The citizenry may not delegate to the government the power to unequalize the delegatory powers. If, for example, the first component operates as a practical matter through majority rule, the majority may never take away any of the delegatory power of a minority (not, that is, without making the democracy principle ineffective). The second component thus acts as a limit on the power of the majority.

Another way the components interact is that the scope of essential equality in the second component is limited by the first component. The equality *required* by the democracy principle is not equality in all matters. What must be equally distributed is the power of delegation and, by implication, anything which would directly affect that power. However, additional equalities, although not implied or required, are permitted.

This distinction between essential equalities and additional equalities corresponds to a distinction between basic rights and other rights. When the citizenry delegates power to the government to set up a legal system to preserve the functioning of the democracy principle itslef, the citizenry obtains certain rights against the government that the government correctly carry out its mission. These are the rights of the citizenry against the government that there occur a continued functioning of the democracy principle. These rights are the citizen's *basic rights*.

The citizenry, through the exercise of its delegatory power, may obtain other rights in addition to the basic rights by requiring the government to establish laws providing for them. These additional rights would undoubtedly be deemed by the citizenry to be important ones, so these may be referred to as *important rights* to distinguish them from basic rights.[26]

Although a thorough presentation of the democracy principle and its implications would require discussion of all the basic rights, such a discussion is beyond the scope of this essay. Just two such rights—voting rights and free speech rights—will be discussed to illustrate why such rights must be secured and preserved if the democracy principle is to function.[27]

Voting Rights

Voting rights represent a paradigm of basic rights. Whenever the basic decisions of government or the selection of representatives to legislative bodies is made through an electoral process, the right of each citizen to vote and to have that vote weighed the same as every other vote is basic to the functioning of the democracy principle. Thus the electoral process is a practical means by which the citizens delegate their power to the government, and the principle of *one person, one vote* must be rigorously followed in order that the power of delegation be equally distributed among the citizens. Each citizen has, therefore, a right against the government that everyone within a district where an election is being held not be prevented from voting and that everyone's vote weigh the same as everyone else's.

This right must, if the democracy principle is to be secured, be more than a right that the government not interfere with the act and equal weighing of voting. It must be an active right involving an affirmative duty on the part of government to set up the election machinery and to remove any obstacle, whether from a governmental or from a nongovernmental source, which might interfere with any citizen's desire to vote or which might alter the equal weighing of votes. Thus an employer may not prevent its employees from voting by requiring them to work during all voting hours. There must be a secret ballot, so that no one need fear that anyone would be subject to any injury whatsoever due to the way he or she voted. Where there are legislative representatives elected by geographically determined districts, each district must contain close to the same number of people.

Most of these concepts are not controversial today, but it was only a few years ago, in 1964, when the U.S. Supreme Court held that congressional districts of unequal population were unconstitutional[28] and that the seats of state legislatures must be apportioned on a population basis.[29] Also, a state-imposed obstacle to voting, the poll tax, was not abolished for state elections until 1966.[30] Although there are still areas of controversy—for example, whether felons should have the right to vote—the notions that democracy requires the removal of barriers to voting and the weighing of each vote equally have now been generally accepted.[31]

The Basic Right of Free Speech

The basic right of free speech has two components. The first is the right of the citizenry against the government that there occur no stifling by government of certain communications. The government has the duty not to interfere with communications among the citizens. It is a negative duty, in that the government is obliged to refrain from acting in a way which prevents certain communications from occurring.

The second component is the right of the citizenry against the government that there occur no stifling by any nongovernmental forces of certain communications among the citizens. The government has an affirmative duty to act in a way which enables certain communications among the citizenry to occur.

It is important to clarify the kind of speech which the democracy principle would require to be treated as a basic right and to show how the democracy principle requires both negative and affirmative duties of government.

Since basic rights are those of the citizenry against the government that there occur a continued functioning of the democracy principle, the basic right of free speech would concern only that communication necessary to ensure the continued delegation by the citizens of the power of government and to ensure the equal distribution of that delegatory power among the citizens. In addition, the citizenry may establish important rights of free speech which could extend beyond that considered a basic right.[32]

What distinguishes basic rights from important rights is not necessarily a difference in the nature of the government's duty. An important right might also require a corresponding positive duty on the part of government. What distinguishes them is their source and relative weight. The source of a basic right lies in the conditions necessary for the proper functioning of the democracy principle. The source of an important right lies in the citizenry's decision making and delegatory power exercised while the democracy principle is properly functioning. Because any abridgment or limitation of basic rights is also an abridgment or limitation of the democracy principle itself, any conflict which might arise between basic and important rights should always be resolved in favor of basic rights.

Since this essay will not discuss all basic rights, it is impossible to give a definitive example of what would not be a basic right but might be an important right. It is, however, quite unlikely that further development of the theory in this essay would lead to the conclusion that every citizen has the basic right to an equal income. Yet, such a right might be permitted as an important right, at least as a theoretical possibility. A separate issue is whether every citizen has the basic right to a minimal income. Whether this right would be a required basic right or a permitted important right would have to await development of the theory. In the area of speech, the focus of this essay will be to establish a minimum core of a basic right of free speech, rather than to explore the perimeter where basic rights and important rights may be distinguished.

Because basic rights are necessary conditions for the functioning of the democracy principle, they cannot logically contradict any component or content of that principle. Because the principle requires that the delegatory powers be spread equally among the citizens, basic rights must also be spread equally among the citizens. Basic rights, therefore, are equal rights. Important rights need not be equal rights; but whether equal or unequal, they must not conflict with basic rights.[33] Thus the government's duty is to establish and maintain as an equal right that component of free speech which is a basic right.

Any speech which directly affects the electoral process is at the core of the basic right of free speech. A violation of this basic right occurs when any speech affects the voting process in a way that adversely affects or renders ineffective the equal right of voting. The scenario which follows illustrates the importance of the connection between certain political expression and the electoral process. It presents an extreme case, but its relationship to what we all may have experienced should not seem too obscure.[34]

Scenario

Two candidates, *A* and *B*, are running for the office of mayor of Buttfield, a midwest city of 60,000 and the largest city within 100 miles. The election in April is reserved solely for local candidates and issues. Buttfield is served by strong signals from two television stations and two AM radio stations. The city has one daily newspaper. *C*, a strong supporter of candidate *A* and *A*'s major financial backer, owns a controlling interest (between 35 percent and 45 percent of the shares) in the three separate corporations which own the newspaper, one of the TV stations, and one of the radio stations and owns a controlling interest in a fourth corporation which owns all local billboards. *A* owns a controlling interest (48 percent of the shares) in the two corporations which own the other TV and radio stations. Because the other shares in these corporations are distributed among a relatively large number of people, the controlling interests of *A* and *C* are sufficient to enable them to elect and completely dominate a majority of the boards of directors of their respective corporations.

Local polls have shown that over 90 percent of Buttfield citizens rely on one or more of these local media sources for local and national news. *C*, in order to ensure that candidate *A* gets elected, decides to have "his" newspaper and "his" radio and TV stations, as well as "his" billboard corporation, adopt a policy of refusing to accept any paid political advertisements from any candidate prior to this election. *C* convinces *A* that it is in her interest to require a similar policy for the stations she controls. *C*'s newspaper, however, prints editorials, all approved by *C* prior to publication, which favor *A* and her views on the issues and which are critical of *B* and his views. In addition, all these media outlets print or broadcast news stories which pertain to the issues in the election, but the stories are slanted to favor the views of *A*. For example, *B* favors establishing a committee to examine rapidly increasing rents and to make recommendations to the mayor, but *A* considers such a committee unnecessary and wasteful. News stories present the views of the president of the local real estate association opposing the committee and present no views of those favoring the committee. In addition, *A* creates stories for herself by making frequent press announcements and by having press conferences once a week. *B* also sends out press announcements, but they do not get printed. He tries to hold several press conferences, but only a reporter from a campus newspaper in a small community forty miles away and the editor of the weekly newsheet of a small local Unitarian church show up. *B* considers broadcasting advertisements from the large stations in the metropolitan area over 150 miles away. However, not only are the costs prohibitive, but the signals are often too weak to be received clearly by local residents.

A and *B* have equal access to the mails, however, and both send out numerous fliers to the constituency. *B*'s fliers announce that *A* and her supporter *C* control the local media. However, through news stories and newspaper editorials, the local media appear to refute these claims just before election day by presenting the facts that each media outlet is owned by a different corporation and that each has a different president, none of whom is *A* or *C*, and that no one owns more than 50 percent of the shares of any of them. The constituents, not versed in corporate matters, assume either that the president of a corporation is the one who owns and controls it or that control requires ownership of over 50 percent of the shares. Thus this refutation is effective and makes the constituents skeptical of *B*'s other claims. *B* does not have the time to formulate and distribute a rebuttal by election day.

A wins the election with 69 percent of the total vote.[35]

Now, we would have been surprised indeed if the scenario had ended any other way, but what does this scenario have to do with the basic right of one person, one vote? Generally we assume that the principle of one person, one vote is one thing and the campaign is another. However, the campaign in this scenario so directly affected the voting process that the principle of one person, one vote was rendered ineffective. The democracy principle itself, therefore, was violated. The connection of the scenario to the democracy principle is this: that portion of the constituency which would have voted for *B* had it received more exposure to *B* and *B*'s views has been denied reasons for delegating a portion of its power of government to *B*.

The connection between denying a person the vote and denying a person a reason for voting for a particular candidate (or for a particular issue) can be made if we assume only that a significant percentage of voters requires reasons for voting a particular way in order actually to vote that way. This assumption does not require us to assume that this group of voters who require reasons is motivated solely or even primarily by rational considerations. It requires only that we assume that a reason to vote a particular way has some persuasive value. Even if there are voters who make their voting decisions based primarily on nonrational or unreasonable factors, many of them require some minimal reasonable ground to support their nonrational views. Thus to deny to a constituency any reasons for voting for a particular choice is as effective as reducing the weight of the votes for that choice when the reasons have not been denied. In either case, the principle of one person, one vote has been thrown askew.

The denial of exposure to reasons is effective against the principle of one person, one vote whether or not the outcome of the election, in terms of who (or what) won and lost, would have been altered had the denial not occurred. This effect occurs for two reasons. When a candidate wins in a race between two main contenders by a close margin, that candidate is more likely to look favorably upon the policies advanced by the opposing candidate and may actually act upon some of those policies in order to secure the next election. Second, when the voting public is aware that the losing candidate advanced policies worthy of consideration, that candidate—or a similarly oriented candidate—has a better chance of winning the next election. Where a candidate's supporters, or would-be supporters, have been denied reasons for voting for that candidate, those supporters have less effect in influencing future governmental policies. They have been as effectively denied equal delegatory power as if each of their votes had counted for less than one.

There must exist, then, a basic right of free speech that would enable communications to occur which would protect the principle of one person, one vote. Where that principle has been adversely affected, so too has the democracy principle been adversely affected. There must be sufficient communication concerning the issues and views of candidates in any election to prevent any person eligible to vote from being denied reasons for voting any particular way.[36] This is the core of the basic right of free speech. This core is the basic right of communication within the political arena, a right shared equally by each citizen. The government's negative duty is not to restrict such communication where it occurs. Its positive duty is to make it possible for such communication to occur where it does not. A negative duty alone would be ineffective in the scenario because nongovernmental forces have subverted the functioning of the democracy principle. The positive basic duty of government is to preserve that functioning, because when government does not fulfill its basic duty, the democracy principle cannot be expected to function.

Had government been operating in accordance with the democracy principle in the scenario, it would have prohibited any media outlet from refusing all political advertising and would have required some access to the media for all candidates. (Further discussion of governmental duties is given in section IV.)

The basic right of free speech has several limits, and these limits must be understood so that arguments counter to the democracy principle do not become "straw-man" arguments. [37] The limits of the basic right of political communication can be derived from the purpose of that right. Its purpose is to give each person access to the available reasons for choosing any of the alternatives presented on the ballot.

First, because this is a right belonging to each individual, it is not a right that permits government to substitute its judgment of what is a good reason for that of each individual. It is the role of each citizen, not the role of government, to decide what constitutes a good reason for voting a particular way.

Second, because this is a right to receive communications from candidates or from persons speaking in behalf of issues relevant to the voting process, it is not a right that gives each individual citizen access to the media to voice his or her views.

Third, because this is a right to have exposure to reasons for making a voting choice, the right does not require that each opposing view receive exactly equal coverage. It does require that the available reasons be adequately presented so that no citizen is denied grounds for his or her decision. This means that each available reason must be presented with sufficient coverage so that no citizen who makes a fair effort to hear or read is denied access to that reason. It does not mean that coverage of some issues beyond this minimum should be prohibited. Coverage beyond this minimum would be appropriate as long as coverage of certain sides of the debate does not effectively drown out the alternative views. Thus there is a minimum to be established and a maximum to be established, and in the range between the minimum and the maximum, differences may occur without serious effect on this basic right of political communication.

It should be kept in mind that this core of the basic right of free speech does not determine the outer boundaries. How far this basic right extends beyond narrowly defined ballot issues must remain an unanswered question until the theory is developed further. Additionally, it should be kept in mind that the citizenry may establish important rights that are not in conflict with basic rights and that extend beyond the basic rights. Thus even beyond the outer boundaries of basic rights, rather than an area of no rights, there lies an area in which important rights may be established.

With the theoretical foundation of the democracy principle and the basic right of free speech laid, Section IV will examine some of the practical consequences of this theory by examining three cases decided by the U.S. Supreme Court: *Buckley* v. *Valeo*,[38] *Miami Herald Publishing Co.* v. *Tornillo*,[39] and *Police Department of Chicago* v. *Mosley*.[40] The examination of these cases will reveal flaws and ambiguities in the U.S. Supreme Court's reasoning that must be corrected if any consistent theory is to be applied to First Amendment cases. It will be shown how these cases would have been decided if the democracy principle had been used. Issues involving the discretionary powers of the Federal Communications Commission have been avoided because the relation of these discretionary powers to the democracy principle would require lengthy treatment.[41]

IV.   Applications

Buckley *v.* Valeo *and Campaign Expenditures*

In *Buckley* v. *Valeo*, the Court ruled on the constitutionality of the Federal Election Campaign Act of 1971, as amended in 1974. The purpose of the act was to reduce or prevent the corruption and appearance of corruption resulting from undue influence on any elected officials by those who contribute or spend large sums of money to elect those officials.[42]

There were several key provisions of the act which were at issue, but only one aspect—the expenditure limitations[43]—is considered here. The act (1) limited any individual or group of individuals to an expenditure of $1,000 "relative to a clearly identified candidate,"[44] (2) limited expenditures by candidates from personal or family resources to set amounts which varied from $50,000 for presidential or vice presidential candidates to $25,000 for most candidates for the House of Representatives,[45] and (3) limited overall campaign expenditures to $10 million for presidential candidates seeking nomination and to an additional $20 million for presidential candidates seeking election to office.[46] These expenditure limitations were held by the Court to violate the First Amendment.[47]

The Court's treatment of the limitation on overall campaign expenditures follows from its treatment of the first two limitations, the limitations on individual expenditures by candidates in their own behalf or by others in behalf of candidates. Consequently, the discussion here will focus on these first two limitations on individual expenditures.

The Court viewed the individual expenditure limitations as limitations on the political speech of those individuals who desire and are able to spend above the act's limits in disseminating their views. "The candidate, no less than any other person, has a First Amendment right to engage in the discussion of public issues and vigorously and tirelessly to advocate his own election and the election of other candidates."[48] The Court's view may be summed up in three propositions: (1) effective political speech costs money;[49] (2) a governmental limit on the amount of money an individual may spend to disseminate his or her political speech is a limitation on the amount of that individual's speech;[50] and (3) any governmental limitation on the amount of political speech an individual may make is violative of the First Amendment, unless that limitation can "satisfy the exacting scrutiny applicable to [such] limitations."[51]

These propositions seem straightforward and reasonable. They rest, however, on certain assumptions that are dubious and that are not consistent with the democracy principle. The Court assumes that the freedom protected by the First Amendment is (1) a freedom of individuals considered separately and (2) a freedom which consists of an absence of governmental restrictions.

These two assumptions generally underlie the Court's treatment of free speech issues except in the area of broadcasting. In broadcasting, the Court has held that it is constitutional for Congress to regulate the use of the air waves in the public interest by establishing an administrative agency, the Federal Communications Commission. However, the Court has not allowed its rationale for such regulation to stray beyond the area of broadcasting.[52]

The first of these assumptions, that the First Amendment protects the freedom of speech of individuals considered separately, would lead the Court to conclude that any violation of the First Amendment can be determined by examining the effect of a restriction on any single individual, without examining interactions among individuals. Thus, if a governmental restriction limits the speech of any individual, then that restriction is suspect and subject to strict scrutiny. That the unrestricted speech of individual A might effectively interfere with the speech of individual B, even when reasonable time, place, and manner requirements are adhered to, is irrelevant to the nature of the restrictions, according to the Court. When the argument was presented to the Court that the government has a legitimate interest "in equalizing the relative ability of individuals and groups to influence the outcome of elections,"[53] the Court responded by saying that "the concept that government may restrict the speech of some elements of our society in order to enhance the relative voice of others is wholly foreign to the First Amendment."[54] Thus the Court explicitly rejects the idea that the government may legitimately seek, by means of restricting the speech of A, to maximize the total speech of A and B. Free speech, to the Court, does not mean a maximum possibility of speech for a group of individuals taken together, but only a maximum possibility of speech for any single individual considered separately.

The Court's second assumption, that freedom consists in the absence of governmental restrictions, is implicit in its notion of *the marketplace of ideas*. In this marketplace occurs the "unfettered interchange of ideas for bringing about of political and social change desired by the people."[55] The Court assumes that what makes this interchange "unfettered" is the absence of governmental restraints. The two assumptions taken together produce the view that freedom of speech means a laissez faire system of individual speech enterprise.

The use of the marketplace analogy is curious and misleading. It is an analogy to a laissez faire economic ideal where goods and money are exchanged without externally imposed regulation. This analogy is based on the assumptions (1) that the laissez faire economic model works effectively and is generally acceptable and (2) that speech is sufficiently like economic goods that the model may be accurately applied to speech. Both assumptions are unsound.

That severe weaknesses in the laissez faire economic model have been perceived and frequently accepted is implicit in the extensive existing network of governmental laws and regulations. Regulations in the areas of antitrust, minimum wage, taxation, labor union protection, race and sex discrimination, social welfare, and broadcasting are but a few examples. Although some political leaders wish to reinstate a laissez faire ideal, it is apparent that this ideal has not gone unquestioned in recent times.[56] The questioning does not in itself prove the ideal is fatally flawed, but it does strongly suggest that a laissez faire marketplace has not usually been the generally accepted, prevailing goal of governmental policy.

Even if we assume the laissez faire model is sound as an economic model, it does not follow that it is sound as a model of free speech. Speech and goods are not the same. One critical difference is that speech does not require an exchange. Goods must be purchased to be owned. The buyer must give up something of value to make the purchase, and presumably there is a rough correlation between the value of the goods and the value of the item or money exchanged for the goods. This element of exchange places limits on how many goods an individual may own or sell.

How such an economic model would apply to speech is problematic. In many areas speech may be conveyed without the receiver giving up anything of value. Advertisements on billboards may be read while one drives by on a highway. The number of advertisements and programs that may be viewed on television has no correlation to the cost of the television set. Advertisements in unsolicited mail may be read by one who does nothing but open an envelope. Thus ideas can be communicated whether or not the recipient performs an affirmative act to receive those ideas. Indeed, the recipient who chooses to watch a particular program on a commercial television channel must take affirmative action to *avoid* receiving the ideas conveyed in the advertisements broadcast during the program.[57]

In addition, purchased goods can frequently be tested and evaluated by the consumer. According to the laissez faire ideal, a bad product is less likely to be repurchased and consumer rejection becomes a force which reduces the frequency of production of poor products. Ideas, however, are not so easily tested. Incorrect information may be repeated a thousand times even though few, if any, recipients can determine its falsity. Repetition may, indeed, increase acceptance without proof of truthfulness. Political ideas may be absorbed and believed even though the recipient may not be able to evaluate them critically.

In short, the putative restraints built into a system based on the laissez faire economic model often do not exist in the realm of speech. These economic restraints create the pressures which would improve the quality of goods, according to the laissez faire theory. There is no reason to believe that "free" speech based on the same model would create pressures improving the quality or truthfulness of speech. It is fair to conclude that the application of laissez faire economic theory to freedom of speech is based on a faulty analogy. Speech must be treated separately from notions of the marketplace.[58]

If, instead, we base our theory of free speech on the democracy principle, a different analysis must be used to examine the expenditure limitations in *Buckley*. The democracy principle requires a basic right of free speech, which at its core is the equal right of each citizen to receive communications that express the available reasons for any ballot decision.[59] According to this theory, it is not unsound to limit the speech of some if this can be shown to be necessary to enable the overall communication of the available reasons to reach the level minimally adequate to reach all citizens who desire and make a reasonable effort to know them. What must be examined is not just whether the speech of an individual is limited, but whether a limit on the speech of one individual is effective in increasing the totality of the political communications relevant to ballot decisions. Where the wealth of a few is used to dominate the media with repeated messages so that the fewer messages of the less wealthy are effectively drowned out, the basic right of free speech not only permits the government to correct the imbalance where ballot issues are involved but also places upon government an affirmative duty to correct the imbalance. Correcting the imbalance would require that government set a maximum level of speech for some parties as well as provide for raising the level of speech to a reasonable minimum for those whose participation in the political process is limited by their own lack of resources.[60]

Some aspects of current legal doctrine concerning speech would not change under the democracy principle. For example, the current legal tests involving the use of strict scrutiny and placing limitations on the use of prior restraint and on vagueness and overbreadth would still be appropriate minimal standards for judging the constitutionality of governmental regulation of speech, even though the specific application of those tests could be different.[61]

Whether these tests could have been passed in *Buckley* or not, the basic point is that the democracy principle would require the Court to make a very different analysis from the one it made. If the democracy principle is accepted as our first premise, then the issue in *Buckley* would not be whether the government has restricted the speech of any individual, but whether the provisions of the Federal Election Campaign Act are necessary to increase the overall speech relevant to ballot issues so that wealth concentrated in the hands of a few does not substantially interfere with the speech of the less wealthy.

Thus the Court's assumption that freedom of speech belongs to individuals considered separately but not in their interactions is contrary to the democracy principle, which requires a basic right of free speech equally distributed among the citizens. Additionally, the Court's notion of the marketplace of ideas is based on a faulty analogy, and its idea that the only suppressor of freedom that need be feared is government is contrary to observable facts.[62]

Miami Herald Publishing Co. *v.* Tornillo *and the Right of Reply*

Miami Herald v. *Tornillo* involved the issue of whether "a state statute granting a political candidate a right to equal space to reply to criticism and attacks on his record by a newspaper violates the guarantees of a free press."[63] The U.S. Supreme Court unanimously found that the statute was unconstitutional.

The Court did not ignore the good reasons advanced in favor of the statute; it presented them in a clear and forthright manner. It said, for example, "The First Amendment interest of the public in being informed is said to be in peril because the 'marketplace of ideas' is today a monopoly controlled by the owners of the market."[64] It also stated, albeit in a footnote, another argument favoring access:

> Freedom of the press is a right belonging, like all rights in a democracy, to all the people. As a practical matter, however, it can be exercised only by those who have effective access to the press. Where financial, economic, and technological conditions limit such access to a small minority, the exercise of that right by that minority takes on fiduciary or quasi-fiduciary characteristics.[65]

The Court saw that this argument supports the view that "the only effective way to insure fairness and accuracy and to provide for some accountability is for government to take affirmative action."[66]

The Florida statute at issue in *Miami Herald* was a *right of reply* statute designed to provide a candidate for political office with a remedy if local newspapers refused to give space to the candidate if he or she had been subjected to press criticism. Such a statute, or perhaps an expanded version of it, would be a minimum governmental duty following from the basic right of free speech under the democracy principle, at least in any locality where citizens are served by only one or two daily newspapers or where common ownership reduces the number of independent daily newspapers to one or two—as is true in nearly every city in the United States, including Miami, Florida.[67] Thus a governmental body would not only be permitted to adopt some form of a right of reply statute under the democracy principle but also would be under an affirmative duty to write and enforce such statutes as a way of partially guaranteeing the basic right of free speech. The Florida statute was a step in this direction. Such a step would have been fully compatible with the democracy principle, but the Court found that it was incompatible with its view of the First Amendment.

This incompatibility is the result of the Court's interpreting the First Amendment in basically the same way it was interpreted in *Buckley*. According to the Court's interpretation, an infringement on freedom of speech or press occurs when any individual speaker is required by government to limit his or her expression. In *Miami Herald*, the Court viewed the Florida statute's requirement that an editor publish a reply as a restriction on that editor's speech. In part, this view was based on the argument that if there is not to be an increase in publishing costs, editorial material generally can be added to a newspaper only if something else is omitted.[68] Even if there were no additional publishing costs, according to the Court, government may simply not interfere at all in this area of editorial discretion.[69] "The choice of material to go into a newspaper, and the decisions made as to the limitations on the size and content of the paper, and treatment of public issues and public officials—whether fair or unfair—constitute the exercise of editorial control and judgment."[70] The editorial content of a newspaper, therefore, is individual expression protected by the First Amendment.

This interpretation of the First Amendment, which focuses on expression as primarily a matter of an individual's spoken or printed word, would prevent the Court from requiring any action to correct the control over communication resulting from monopolization of the press. If we accept the Court's reasoning without qualification—and the Court offered no qualification—then a free press exists even if all newspapers, magazines, and book publishers are owned by one person, as long as that person is not a government official or agent. The First Amendment contains no implicit or explicit antitrust provisions. Although antitrust laws which operate to prevent monopolization of the press may be consistent with and therefore permitted by the First Amendment, they are not required by it.[71] Antitrust law depends on Congress, in the Court's view, not on the Constitution. The First Amendment, in this interpretation, is a manifesto of free enterprise in the area of publications, even if that enterprise should over time result in total monopoly.[72]

A more complicated issue is presented by the scenario in Section III. That scenario contains a combination of near-monopoly control and agreement between competing controllers of both the press and broadcast media. In the area of broadcasting, the Court has permitted the Federal Communications Commission to take some steps to reduce monopoly control.[73] Such FCC action, however, has been viewed as only permitted, not required, by the First Amendment.[74]

Even these permitted FCC regulations have not gone very far. A more frightening scenario may be constructed, consistent with current law and FCC regulations, involving nationwide control of the media. An example of such a nationwide scenario would portray one owner of all existing daily newspapers in cities now serviced by a single daily paper or by daily papers now under common ownership, a second owner of all existing daily newspapers not owned by the first, and three additional owners, each of whom owns five major VHF television stations, one in each of the five largest United States cities. These five owners in any combination could also own the major networks (ABC, CBS, NBC), all communication satellites, all magazine publishers, and all book publishers in the United States (not to mention simultaneous control in other countries). Whether such a scenario or something similar to it could lawfully exist in the future would depend on the vicissitudes of Congress and the FCC in establishing new laws and regulations. According to the current doctrine of the U.S. Supreme Court, such a nationwide scenario would not be prohibited by the First Amendment.[75]

In fact, media empires are growing. In 1980, for example, Gannett owned 78 daily newspapers, 7 television stations, and 12 radio stations.[76] NBC, which owned 5 television stations in 5 major cities and served 213 affiliated stations, was in turn owned by RCA, which also owned and operated two communications satellites.[77]

The democracy principle requires a different interpretation of the First Amendment. The basic right of free speech protects certain communications which affect the political process. There cannot be monopolization of the media by a few owners any more than the electoral process can be placed under the control of a few individuals or corporations. Even if increased monopolization of ownership of the media is necessitated by economic forces, the affirmative duty of government under the democracy principle would then be to increasingly separate ownership from control. Where increased monopolization of ownership occurs, control should be increasingly subject to governmental regulation.

Under the democracy principle, political communication is seen as a social, political process, as interactions among people for the purpose of changing or maintaining a social order. The totality of diverse speech in that process is the issue under the democracy principle. A statute or governmental regulation must pass the test of whether it increases that totality. The issue is not, as the Court saw it, primarily a matter of an individual's expression considered in isolation from that totality. Whether or not the Florida statute would adequately meet this test, it was a reasonable attempt to increase the totality of speech by placing a restriction on the discretion of individual newspaper editors or publishers. If the statute failed that test, the remedy under the democracy principle would be either for the legislature to supplement or revise the statute within judicially determined guidelines or for the Court to declare a more effective right of reply as constitutionally required. Instead, the Court declared that all such statutes are unconstitutional.

Thus, the primary focus of the Florida statute was in accord with the democracy principle, but the primary focus of the Court's opinion was not.[78]

Police Department of Chicago v. Mosley *and the Content of Speech*

The choice of *Police Department of Chicago* v. *Mosley* provides a focus for examining some of the U.S. Supreme Court's expressions of the principle that government under the First Amendment must be neutral with respect to the content of speech.

The Court has frequently confused two different forms of the content neutrality principle. In one form, content neutrality means that government may not place restrictions on speech based in any way on its content. In the second form, it means that government may not place restrictions on speech based *solely* on its content—that is, based on its content *alone*. In *Mosley*, these two forms of the content neutrality principle are treated as one. Understanding the difference between neutrality toward content and neutrality toward content alone is the key both to understanding correctly the Court's actual position and to understanding correctly certain consequences of the democracy principle.

In *Mosley*, the Court held that a Chicago ordinance that prohibited all picketing of any school, except when that school is "involved in a labor dispute," violated the equal protection clause of the Fourteenth Amendment.[79] The Court's argument was that the ordinance prohibited some picketing but permitted others, whereby the distinction between the permitted and prohibited picketing was based on the content of the messages being expressed. One holding of *Mosley* is that when a statute treats any two acts differently, where those acts directly involve "First Amendment interests," then that statute must be "carefully scrutinized" under the equal protection clause of the Fourteenth Amendment.[80]

The Court's conclusion that the statute was unconstitutional is not at issue here, for that conclusion is not at odds with the democracy principle. The problem with the Court's opinion lies in its inconsistent statements of content neutrality and in the consequences of such inconsistency for applying any First Amendment theory.

When the Court expressed the content neutrality principle in its first form, it said: "The essence of this forbidden [government] censorship is content control. Any restriction on expressive activity because of its content would completely undercut the 'profound national commitment to the principle that debate on public issues should be uninhibited, robust, and wide-open.'"[81] As expressed in this form, governmental deviation from content-neutral regulations is "never permitted."[82]

When the Court expressed that principle in its second form, it said, "Selective exclusions from a public forum may not be based on content alone, and may not be justified by reference to content alone."[83]

What distinguishes the two forms is that the first defines content neutrality in terms of content, whereas the second form defines content neutrality in terms of content alone. The simple logical distinction between the two is what distinguishes the statement, "When you go to that restaurant, you must not wear your jeans," from the statement, "When you go to that restaurant, you must not wear your jeans alone." The first statement says you *may not* wear your jeans, and the ordinary meaning of the second is that you *may* wear your jeans if you wear them along with something else. Although both are statements of jeans prejudice, they are inconsistent in that both cannot be true at the same time.

The Court's expression of content neutrality in terms of content (not content alone) is overbroad in that it overlaps in an inconsistent manner with Court doctrines which distinguish protected from unprotected speech.[84] The basis for these doctrines was stated in *Chaplinsky* v. *New Hampshire*:

> There are certain well-defined and narrowly limited classes of speech, the prevention and punishment of which have never been thought to raise any Constitutional problem. These include the lewd and obscene, the profane, the libelous, and the insulting or 'fighting' words—those which by their very utterance inflict injury or tend to incite an immediate breach of the peace.[85]

The reason these areas of speech are not given protection in the Court's view is because "such utterances are no essential part of the exposition of ideas, and are of such slight social value as a step to truth that any benefit that may be derived from them is clearly outweighed by the social interest in order and morality."[86]

The issue here is not whether this view is sound, but whether it is consistent with content neutrality. It is impossible to determine what has "slight social value as a step to truth" without examining the content of the speech and without favoring some contents over others. The Court cannot consistently proclaim content neutrality and also maintain that some speech is not protected because of its "slight social value." One way consistency can be achieved is to retreat from the overbroad doctrine of content neutrality to the narrower doctrine of neutrality toward content alone.

How this retreat saves the Court from inconsistency can be seen by examining the Court's obscenity doctrine. According to the Court's doctrine in *Miller* v. *California*, speech cannot be removed from constitutional protection unless it is determined to be obscene according to "the average person, applying contemporary community standards."[87] What makes speech obscene, then, is not its content alone, but its content *plus* the context of its expression.[88] Only when spoken in a context of a community where the "average" person regards it as obscene may it be removed from First Amendment protection.[89] In removing speech from this protection, the Court does not look at its content alone, but it does look at its content plus the context of its expression. Thus the Court's obscenity doctrine is consistent with neutrality toward content alone; it is inconsistent, however, with respect to neutrality toward content whenever content plus a relevant context is present and not simply content alone.

The relevance of the context of speech is shown again in another aspect of the Court's obscenity doctrine. When determining whether material is obscene, a jury may consider the manner in which the material is expressed. "The circumstances of presentation and dissemination of material are equally relevant to determining whether social importance claimed for material...was... pretense or reality...."[90] This means that the jury may consider not only the content of the material in determining whether it is obscene but the content plus the manner in which it is expressed. Here again, the line between protected and unprotected speech is not neutral with respect to content. Because, however, the complete determination of obscenity requires examination not of its content alone, but of its content plus the circumstances of its expression, that dividing line is neutral with respect to content alone.

To argue that content neutrality applies only to protected speech, not to obscenity, which is unprotected, is to beg the question. The question is, where is the line between protected and unprotected speech to be drawn? If drawing that line involves examining and discriminating among the various contents of speech, then some contents will be favored over others.[91] To say that the Court is neutral with respect to protected speech is only to say that the Court favors some contents by shielding them from further content-related regulation. The only way to avoid this inconsistency in the Court's language is to maintain that what the Court really means by its content neutrality doctrine is that it is neutral only with respect to content alone.

The point here is not that the Court's obscenity doctrine is sound or that it is consistent with the democracy principle. The point is that the Court's rhetoric concerning content neutrality is inconsistent with its obscenity doctrine. Although obscenity has been focused on here as an illustration, a similar point could be made concerning the definitions of other areas of speech which are unprotected: defamation, "fighting words," and words presenting a "clear and present danger."[92]

The failure of the Court to distinguish explicitly content from content alone led it, *in Hudgens* v. *NLRB*,[93] to offer unsound grounds for overruling *Amalgamated Food Employees Local 590* v. *Logan Valley Plaza, Inc.*[94] In *Hudgens*, the Court held, *inter alia*, that employees did not have a right under the First Amendment to enter a privately owned shopping center to advertise their strike against an employer that had outlets in the center. In reaching this holding, the Court followed *Lloyd Corp.* v. *Tanner*,[95] which held that persons who peacefully distributed, in a privately owned shopping center, handbills announcing a meeting to protest the draft and the Vietnam war were not protected by the First Amendment. Quoting *Mosley* to support its view, the Court maintained that "the First and Fourteenth Amendments would not permit control of speech within such a center to depend upon the speech's content."[96]

> It conversely follows, therefore, that if the respondents in the *Lloyd* case did not have a First Amendment right to enter that shopping center to distribute handbills concerning Vietnam, then the pickets in the present case did not have a First Amendment right to enter this shopping center for the purpose of advertising their strike against the Butler Shoe Co.[97]

To reach this result, the Court felt it had to overrule *Logan Valley*. *Logan Valley*, decided four years before *Lloyd*, held that members of a union who peacefully picketed a business located in a privately owned shopping center were protected by the First Amendment.[98] In overruling *Logan Valley* in *Hudgens*, the Court maintained that *Logan Valley* and *Lloyd* were inconsistent (and that *Lloyd* should be followed).

The conclusion that *Lloyd* and *Logan Valley* are inconsistent is easy to accept if First Amendment protection is to be neutral with respect to content, as the

Court maintained in *Hudgens*. However, as argued above, the Court's doctrine of content neutrality is overbroad. In its obscenity cases, for example, the Court has, in effect, rejected content neutrality. It is inconsistent of the Court to maintain content neutrality for the purpose of removing First Amendment protection from speech in private shopping centers and to reject content neutrality for the purpose of permitting states to remove First Amendment protection from obscenity.

Just as the Court's treatment of obscenity is actually neutral only with respect to content *alone*, so can a sound distinction between *Lloyd* and *Logan Valley* be neutral with respect to content alone. In *Lloyd*, the Court distinguished *Lloyd* from *Logan Valley* by pointing out that the picketing in *Logan Valley* was "directly related in is purpose to the use to which shopping center property was being put."[99] Thus, a private shopping center is an appropriate forum for advertising a labor dispute against an employer with retail facilities in the center, because the employer, by opening its premises to the public, subjects itself to public criticism concerning the nature of its operation.[100] In *Lloyd*, on the other hand, the political advertisements could have been readily distributed outside the shopping center with no significant loss in the impact of the message.

This is not to say that the *Lloyd* decision was correct, but to say that a principled distinction could have been made between *Lloyd* and *Logan Valley* if the Court had seen that it consistently recognizes only neutrality toward content alone. A principled distinction can be maintained on the ground that although the First Amendment is not concerned with examining content alone, it is concerned with examining the content plus the appropriate context or forum of expression. The definition of *appropriate forum* in private shopping center cases would be based, following *Logan Valley*, on the relationship of the expression to the purposes for the center's existence. The First Amendment would remain neutral with respect to content alone, for the First Amendment protection would not depend on whether the messages were pro-union or anti-union, pro-war or anti-war. In this manner, the distinction between *Lloyd* and *Logan Valley* could be made in a principled way and be consistent with the principle of neutrality based on content alone.[101]

In conclusion, therefore, the Court was inconsistent when it overruled *Logan Valley* on the grounds of neutrality based on content, for the Court's interpretation of the First Amendment is not neutral with respect to content, as the Court's obscenity doctrine illustrates.[102] It is also ironic that the consequence of *Hudgens*, in following the rhetoric of content neutrality in *Mosley*, makes the permission to speak in privately owned shopping centers totally dependent on the owner's view of the content of the speech (except in the few states which have extended protection of speech to these centers).[103]

Continuation of the confusion between content plus and content alone would result in confusion about the meaning and the application of the basic right of free speech under the democracy principle. At its core, this basic right would require that the government *not* be neutral with respect to content in political contexts (although it would undoubtedly require that it be neutral with respect to content alone). Under the democracy principle, the government has an affirmative duty to enable certain political communications to occur. Where there is a situation requiring diversity of expression, such as a discussion in the media of ballot issues, then the government must consider which messages pertinent to the issues are most appropriate for maximizing diversity. Where that diversity has been restricted beyond what is desirable for adequate communication of political issues, it is the affirmative duty of government under the democracy principle to act to remove those restrictions, whether those restrictions are imposed by a governmental agency or by private parties.[104]

Thus, under the democracy principle, the government is not neutral with respect to the content of messages in political contexts. The goal and affirmative duty of government is to regulate political expression where necessary to achieve maximum diversity. Its negative duty is to refrain from reducing diversity by effectively eliminating any ideas from the public forum.

The principle of neutrality underlying this approach, if correctly understood, is not contrary to present Court doctrine as practiced. The Court is not neutral with respect to content, even though in *Mosley* and *Hudgens* it misled itself (and undoubtedly others) to believe that it is. On the issue of neutrality with respect to content *alone*, as well as of nonneutrality with respect to content, the basic right of free speech under the democracy principle does not require departure from the underlying present doctrine actually practiced by the Court. The application of the neutrality doctrine under the democracy principle, however, would vary from present Court doctrine.

Conclusion

Because a theory of free speech concerns individual expression and social communication in a society and because speech, especially political speech, has social and political consequences, such a theory cannot be adequately formulated without reference to a concept of the kind of society for which the theory is intended.

In this essay, the democracy principle has been postulated as the basic premise of a desired society. A society based on this principle must contain a basic right of free speech distributed equally among its citizens. That right is intimately related to the goal that each citizen have an equal right to determine the nature and actions of government. The right is not a mere freedom from governmental interference but is a right against government that government affirmatively act to maximize the diversity of certain political forms of speech. At the core of this right is speech involving political communication relevant to ballot issues. The right is a right to receive information as well as a right of expression. The extent to which government fails to carry out these duties is the extent to which the democracy principle fails to be effective.

The democracy principle and the basic right of free speech have some practical consequences that differ from some of the consequences of the First Amendment doctrine adopted by the U.S. Supreme Court. A theory of society that consistently explains the various Court doctrines has not been formulated. Perhaps, underlying the Court doctrines is another conception of society, perhaps of a society which also could be called a democracy. Until such a conception has been formulated and made explicit, however, it cannot be examined and evaluated.

This essay began with the proposition that it raises more questions than it answers, and that proposition would also make an appropriate ending. The essay was meant to provide a sound basis for a more complete theory. Perhaps, too, it formulates a basis for the development of alternative and competing theories. When such alternative theories are openly discussed and debated, we have a better chance of arriving at a clearer understanding of what kind of society we wish to achieve and of what rights and liberties it is most crucial to protect.

Notes

1. Lillian R. BeVier, "The First Amendment and Political Speech: An Inquiry into the Substance and Limits of Principle," *Stanford Law Review* 30 (January 1978): 299–300.
2. Thomas I. Emerson, *The System of Freedom of Expression* (New York: Random House, 1970). See also Thomas I. Emerson, *Toward a General Theory of the First Amendment* (New York: Random House, 1966).
3. Emerson, *Freedom of Expression*, pp. 6–9.
4. Ibid., p. 728.
5. See Raymond L. Wilder, *Introduction to the Foundations of Mathematics* (New York: John Wiley and Sons, 1952), pp. 3–41.
6. See the discussion of this problem in John Rawls, *A Theory of Justice* (Cambridge, Mass.: Belknap Press of Harvard University Press, 1971), pp. 34–45.
7. Alexander Meiklejohn, *Free Speech and Its Relation to Self-Government* (New York: Harper, 1948).
8. The use of *normative* in this way is quite common in philosophy. A good explanation of this usage is in F. S. C. Northrop, *The Logic of the Sciences and the Humanities* (Cleveland: World Publishing Co., 1959), esp. pp. 19–34. See also Paul W. Taylor, *The Moral Judgment* (Englewood Cliffs, N.J.: Prentice-Hall, 1963), p. xii; Raziel Abelson, ed., *Ethics and Metaethics* (New York: St. Martin's Press, 1963), pp. 6–7; Charles Sanders Peirce, *Collected Papers*, Vol. 5–6, *Pragmatism and Pragmaticism, and Scientific Metaphysics*, ed. Charles Hartshorne and Paul Weiss (Cambridge, Mass.: Belknap Press of Harvard University Press, 1960), sec. 5.130.
9. It is not the purpose of this essay to examine the grounds for the acceptability of normative theories, although this issue is indeed a crucial one. On the disagreements concerning the justification, verification, or refutation of ethical theories, see, e.g., Philippa Foot, ed., *Theories of Ethics* (London: Oxford University Press, 1967), pp. 1–15; Richard B. Brandt, ed., *Value and Obligation* (New York: Harcourt, Brace and World, 1961), pp. 249–431. For a range of views, see Wilfrid Sellars and John Hospers, eds., *Readings in Ethical Theory* (New York: Appleton-Century-Crofts, 1970).
10. Northrop, *Sciences and the Humanities*, pp. 20–21.
11. Ibid., p. 21. A more complete discussion of the use of the term *normative* would distinguish at least three concepts: (1) a *normative theory* is a theory about what normative rules ought to be accepted, (2) a *normative rule* is a rule which prescribes what behavior ought to occur in a particular area of behavior (for example, an existing statute or a rule of common law), and (3) a *social rule* is a general description of what people believe about how people ought to behave. Ronald Dworkin, for example, distinguishes normative from social rules in *Taking Rights Seriously* (Cambridge, Mass.: Harvard University Press, 1978), pp. 19, 48–58, although he sometimes uses *normative theory* to refer to a descriptive (nonnormative) theory about existing normative rules (e.g., ibid., p. 68) and sometimes refers to normative theory with the term *moral theory* (e.g., ibid., p. 149). In this essay, to avoid such difficulties of usage, *normative theory* is used only as defined above.
12. That a normative theory cannot be perfectly fulfilled in actuality is not a relevant objection to it as long as it can be increasingly fulfilled in the long run. For a discussion of the relation of the ideal of knowledge to practical attainment, see Peirce, *Collected Papers*, vol. 5–6, secs. 5.405–5.508, 5.565.
13. For a discussion of this point, see Rawls, *Theory of Justice*, pp. 236–37.
14. For a general treatment of the relevance of normative theory to law, see Dworkin, *Taking Rights Seriously*. For example: "Constitutional law can make no genuine advance until it iso-

lates the problem of rights against the state and makes that problem part of its own agenda. That argues for a fusion of Constitutional law and moral theory, a connection that, incredibly, has yet to take place," Ibid., p. 149.

15. For a discussion of the relationship between these two clauses, see, e.g., First Nat'l. Bank of Boston v. Bellotti, 435 U.S. 765, 797–802 (1978) (Burger, C. J., concurring); Potter Stewart, "Or of the Press," *Hastings Law Journal* 26 (January 1975); 631–37, Margaret A. Blanchard, "The Institutional Press and the First Amendment Privileges," in *Supreme Court Review 1978*, ed. Philip B. Kurland and Gerhard Casper (Chicago: University of Chicago Press, 1978), pp. 225–96; David Lange, "The Speech and Press Clauses," *U.C.L.A. Law Review* 23 (October 1975): 77–119; Melville B. Nimmer, "Introduction—Is Freedom of the Press a Redundancy: What Does It Add to Freedom of Speech?" *Hastings Law Journal* 26 (January 1975): 639–58; and William W. Van Alstyne, "The Hazards to the Press of Claiming a 'Preferred Position,'" *Hastings Law Journal* 28 (January 1977): 761–70.

16. Meiklejohn, for example, discusses the First Amendment in terms of what people hear. *Free Speech*, pp. 24–25.

17. See, e.g., the definition of *liberty* given by Rawls, *Theory of Justice*, p. 202.

18. "It is, of course, a commonplace that the constitutional guarantee of free speech is a guarantee only against abridgment by government, federal or state." Hudgens v. NLRB, 424 U.S. 507, 513 (1976). The *Hudgens* Court did note, however, that action by a company town had been recognized in Marsh v. Alabama, 326 U.S. 501 (1946), as an exception to the rule limiting the prohibitions of the First Amendment to government action.

19. This notion of rights is deeply ingrained in contemporary Western culture.

> In short, the limitations in the interest of the basic freedoms recognized by the Constitution are directed against the government. The Constitution is concerned with constitutional liberties in the classic sense of the Western world, i.e., as liberties of the individual to be safeguarded against the power of the state. It is because the state enjoys the monopoly of lawfully granted coercive power that restraints on its power are recognized under the Constitution as the important condition of liberty. The Constitution, accordingly, is not concerned with direct restraints on the individual in the interest of defining his duties and reciprocal rights of his neighbors.

Paul G. Kauper, *Civil Liberties and the Constitution* (Ann Arbor: University of Michigan Press, 1962), p. 129. See also John T. Wright, "Human Rights in the West: Political Liberties and the Rule of Law," in *Human Rights: Cultural and Ideological Perspectives*, ed. Adamantia Pollis and Peter Schwab (New York: Praeger, 1979), esp. p. 25, and Richard P. Claude, "The Classical Model of Human Rights Development," in *Comparative Human Rights*, ed. Richard P. Claude (Baltimore: Johns Hopkins University Press, 1976), esp. pp. 41–42.

20. Since there are so many definitions of *rights*, many of which are too ambiguous, vague, or circular to be useful here, the attempt at definition in this essay has been started anew, although not without reference to other definitions. Refer to note 23 infra. Roscoe Pound correctly observed, "There is no more ambiguous word in legal and juristic literature than the word right." *Jurisprudence*, 5 vols. (St. Paul: West Publishing Co., 1959), 4: 56.

21. Of course, there are also active components of this right. For example, the government is generally required to procure a search warrant before searching a private home or business. See, e.g., Coolidge v. New Hampshire, 403 U.S. 443 (1971).

22. To what extent legal rights should be determined by reference to normative rights is a separate issue which, although of fundamental importance, need not be discussed here. See generally Dworkin, *Taking Rights Seriously*.

23. This definition of *right* is essentially equivalent to that of Alan D. Cullison, "A Review of Hohfeld's Fundamental Legal Concepts," *Cleveland-Marshall Law Review* 16 (September 1967): 559–73, and Alan D. Cullison, "Logical Analysis of Legal Doctrine: The Normative Structure of Positive Law," *Iowa Law Review* 53 (June 1968): 1209–68. However, it differs somewhat from that of Layman E. Allen, "Formalizing Hohfeldian Analysis to Clarify the Multiple Senses of 'Legal Right': A Powerful Lens for the Electronic Age," *Southern California Law Review* 48 (1974): 428–87. According to Allen's definition, "x has a right that p shall be done by y," p. 439. The qualification that "p shall be done by y" results in a more restricted use of *right*.

24. The area of broadcasting, however, is an exception. See, generally Marc A. Franklin, *The*

First Amendment and the Fourth Estate, 2d ed. (Mineola, N.Y.: Foundation Press, 1981), pp. 496–665.

25. The notions of the *consent of the governed* and of *political equality* lie at the basis of Meiklejohn's theory. *Free Speech*, pp. 10–11, and *Political Freedom* (New York: Harper & Row, Publishers, 1960), pp. 93–94.

26. It should not be assumed that *basic rights* and *important rights*, as distinguished here, correlate with *fundamental rights* and *important rights* as described in various Court opinions. See, e.g., San Antonio Ind. School Dist. v. Rodriguez, 411 U.S. 1 (1973).

27. According to the Declaration of Independence, "[All] are endowed by their Creator with certain inalienable rights.... That, to secure these rights, governments are instituted among men...." In a large society, the democracy principle cannot be preserved unless government seeks to preserve basic rights. Whereas the Declaration of Independence proclaims that the rights to be secured are "inalienable," it is asserted here only that there are basic rights which must be preserved if the democracy principle is to function. Whether the democracy principle itself is endowed upon us by the Creator or by some other source is beyond the scope of this essay.

28. Wesberry v. Sanders, 376 U.S. 1 (1964).

29. Reynolds v. Sims, 377 U.S. 533 (1964).

30. Harper v. Virginia Bd. of Elections, 383 U.S. 663 (1966).

31. However, even in the area of voting, the acceptance of equal rights has not been complete. For example, the Voting Rights Act of 1965, designed to eliminate racial and language discrimination in voting, has apparently not been adequately enforced. U.S., General Accounting Office. *Voting Rights Act—Enforcement Needs Strengthening: Report of the Comptroller General of the United States* (Washington: General Accounting Office, 1978). There also are areas of continuing legal controversy. See, e.g., Salyer Land Co. v. Tulare Lake Basin Water Storage Dist., 410 U.S. 719 (1973).

    The idea that employees should be guaranteed time off to vote without financial penalty has gained acceptance incompletely and very slowly. In 1964 only seventeen states had provisions permitting any eligible voter to take time off to vote in federal elections without being subject to a reduction of normal pay. Only thirty states had any provisions for time off for voting, and in thirteen of these, various restrictions limited the right. U.S., Department of Labor, Bureau of Labor Standards, *Time Off for Voting under State Laws*, Bulletin No. 138 revised (Washington, D.C.: Government Printing Office, 1964).

    The role of governments in conducting elections was recently discussed in Flagg Bros., Inc. v. Brooks, 436 U.S. 149 (1978).

32. The limits of basic rights would be determined by political relevance. However, the democracy principle may require that *political relevance* be interpreted quite broadly. In addition, to avoid infringement on basic rights, all doubts should be resolved in favor of extension of basic rights.

33. There is room to argue, for example, that an affirmative action program giving unequal opportunities to a discriminated-against group concerns important rights so that the unequal distribution does not automatically conflict with the democracy principle. However, the question of whether affirmative action in some cases can be derived from basic rights is left open.

34. Some real-life scenarios which provide factual background for this fictitious one are described in Benno C. Schmidt, Jr., *Freedom of the Press v. Public Access* (New York: Praeger, 1976), pp. 221–24; Jerome Barron, *Freedom of the Press For Whom?* (Bloomington, Ind.: Indiana University Press, 1973), esp. pp. 1–2, 13–15, 22–25, 160–93; and Robert Cirino, *Don't Blame the People* (New York: Random House, 1971), esp. pp. 278–307. Data concerning concentration of ownership of the media nationwide are in Schmidt, *Freedom of the Press*, pp. 37–46. Refer also to notes 64 and 67 infra.

35. The scenario was devised to avoid violation of the multiple ownership regulations of the Federal Communications Commission and the equal opportunities and reasonable access provisions of the amended Communications Act of 1934. U.S., *Code of Federal Regulations*, Title 47, secs. 73.35, 73.240, 73.636; U.S., *Code Annotated*, Title 47, secs. 312 (a)(7), 315; and FCC v. National Citizens Comm. for Broadcasting, 436 U.S. 775 (1978). FCC multiple ownership requirements would have been satisfied in the scenario even without the presence of the second AM station.

36. Some alteration of this idea may be necessary to make it possible to administer it. For ex-

ample, opposing candidates might be required to limit their reasons to a particular space or time, which would be acceptable as long as these restrictions are not too severe or unreasonable.

37. "The fallacy of the straw man consists in attacking (or defending) a position similar to but different from the one your opponent holds (or attacks). [Emphasis omitted.]" Howard Kahane, *Logic and Contemporary Rhetoric* (Belmont, Calif.: Wadsworth Publishing Co., 1971), p. 33. See also Ronald Munson, *The Way of Words* (Boston: Houghton Mifflin Co., 1976), pp. 289–92.
38. 424 U.S. 1 (1976).
39. 418 U.S. 241 (1974).
40. 408 U.S. 92 (1972).
41. For example, not examined are CBS, Inc. v. Democratic Nat'l Comm., 412 U.S. 94 (1973), and FCC v. Midwest Video Corp., 440 U.S. 689 (1979). The complicating issue is whether the discretionary power of the FCC is compatible with the fulfillment of the government's affirmative basic duty of free speech. Some discretionary decisions of the FCC possibly should be required, some permitted, and some prohibited. Treatment of these factors would take us well beyond the confines of this essay.
42. 424 U.S. at 25–26.
43. Ibid. at 39–54.
44. Ibid. at 39.
45. Ibid. at 51.
46. Ibid. at 54.
47. Although *Buckley* was a per curiam opinion, Justices Byron R. White and Thurgood Marshall, in separate opinions, dissented from this part of the Court's opinion.
    The Court upheld certain other provisions which limited the amount a person or group could contribute to a candidate and to campaign committees. These contribution provisions were held to concern association, not speech, so they were subject to a lower test of constitutionality. This broad definition of *association*, by correspondingly narrowing the definition of *pure speech*, reduces the traditional protection afforded to speech. See ibid. at 20–38.
48. Ibid. at 52. Although the Court provided some alternative grounds for its holding, this part of the Court's opinion was crucial to its reasoning.
49. See ibid. at 18–19.
50. See ibid. at 39.
51. Ibid. at 44–45. See also ibid. at 14–16. The Court did not define *exacting scrutiny* in this case, but apparently it used a test which balanced the governmental interests favoring the statute against the statute's "restriction on the quantity of political expression." Ibid. at 55.
52. See, e.g., Red Lion Broadcasting Co. v. FCC, 395 U.S. 367 (1969); FCC v. National Citizens Comm. for Broadcasting, 436 U.S. 775 (1978). See also Franklin, *First Amendment*, pp. 496–530.
    The Court has allowed the FCC to extend regulation imposed on broadcasters to cable television, as well, on the grounds that such regulation is "reasonably ancillary" to the effective supervision of commission broadcast policies. U.S. v. Southwestern Cable, 392 U.S. 157 (1968), and U.S. v. Midwest Video Corp., 406 U.S. 649 (1972).
    The Court has not ruled whether many FCC regulations applied to broadcast licensees are only permitted by the First Amendment or are actually required. However, in *National Citizens Comm.*, the Court overruled a lower court holding that the First Amendment required greater regulation than the FCC had ordered. 436 U.S. at 790–93.
53. Buckley v. Valeo, 424 U.S. at 48.
54. Ibid. at 48–49. See also note 60 infra.
55. Ibid. at 49.
56. Beginning with Nebbia v. New York, 291 U.S. 502 (1934), the U.S. Supreme Court began to eliminate the laissez faire model's barrier to legislation regulating the economy. See also Olsen v. Nebraska ex rel. Western Ref. & Bond Ass'n, 313 U.S. 236 (1941).
57. This led one court to observe:

Written messages are not communicated unless they are read, and reading requires an affirmative act. Broadcast messages, in contrast, are "in the air." In the age of omnipresent radio, there scarcely breathes a citizen who does not know some part of a leading cigarette jingle by heart. Similarly, an ordinary habitual television watcher can *avoid* these commercials only by frequently leaving the room, changing the channel, or doing some other such affirmative act. It is difficult to calculate the subliminal impact of this pervasive propaganda, which may be heard even if not listened to, but it may reasonably be thought greater than the impact of the written word.

Banzhaf v. FCC, 405 F.2d 1082, 1100–01 (D.C. Cir. 1968), cert. denied, 396 U.S. 842 (1969) (footnote omitted). The idea of a captive audience is also discussed in Lehman v. City of Shaker Heights, 418 U.S. 298, 305–08 (1974) (Douglas, J., concurring).

58. Jerome Barron also criticizes the marketplace idea. *Freedom of the Press*, pp. 320–28. David L. Lange's retort that Barron, too, is a "victim of the market-place myth" is not formulated with sufficient clarity to enable a clear response. Lange, "The Role of the Access Doctrine in the Regulation of the Mass Media: A Critical Review and Assessment," *North Carolina Law Review* 52 (1973): 10. The aspect of the marketplace notion that is criticized in this essay (and that Barron also criticizes) is that interchange of diverse ideas will occur only if the government will not interfere. The aspect of the marketplace notion that is accepted here (and that Barron also appears to accept) is that interchange of diverse ideas is desirable and produces the best results in the long run. It is simplistic to accuse one of being a "victim of the market-place myth" if he accepts the latter but rejects the former.

Lange criticized access notions in part on the basis that such notions conflict with what the Founding Fathers intended. Yet, curiously, he also criticizes the founding-father approach as inadequate. Ibid., pp. 12–14. Clearly, one cannot have it both ways. Indeed, the idea that a theory of the First Amendment should rest on what the Founding Fathers intended would not take us very far. See Leonard W. Levy, *Freedom of Speech and Press in Early American History* (New York: Harper and Row, 1963), esp. pp. xiii–xiv, xxi–xxviii and chap. 6, and Zechariah Chafee, Jr., review of *Free Speech: and Its Relation to Self-Government* by Alexander Meiklejohn, *Harvard Law Review* 62 (March 1949): 891–901.

59. Refer to note 36 supra.

60. Not dealt with here is the issue of whether large expenditures in themselves corrupt or appear to corrupt the political process and thereby undermine public confidence in that process. For such a discussion, see Justice White's opinion concurring in part, dissenting in part in Buckley v. Valeo, 424 U.S. at 257–66. This issue goes to the question of whether the government's interest is sufficient to outweigh the Federal Election Campaign Act's restrictions on speech. The analysis based on the democracy principle instead raises the question of whether the act restricts the total realm of speech or enhances it.

61. The doctrine of prior restraint was first enunciated by the Court in Near v. Minnesota ex rel. Olson, 283 U.S. 697 (1931). For a discussion of the Court's doctrines of vagueness and overbreadth, see Note, "The First Amendment Overbreadth Doctrine," *Harvard Law Review* 83 (February 1970): 844–927.

62. In First Nat'l. Bank of Boston v. Bellotti, 435 U.S. 765 (1978), the Court struck down a Massachusetts statute which prohibited any corporation from contributing to political campaigns or issues where the campaigns or issues did not materially affect the property or business assets of the corporation. Much of the Court's reasoning was based on *Buckley*. However, the Court called into question one of the premises of *Buckley*, that it is "wholly foreign to the First Amendment" for government to restrict some voices in order to enhance others. Buckley v. Valeo, 424 U.S at 48–49. Instead, in *First Nat'l. Bank*, the Court found it relevant that "there has been no showing that the relative voice of corporations has been overwhelming or even significant in influencing referenda in Massachusetts." 435 U.S. at 789 (footnote omitted). This suggests, contrary to *Buckley*, that the Court may consider the relative voices to be a factor in determining the validity of a governmental restriction. So far, however, this suggestion amounts to only an implied dictum. Justice White in his dissent (joined by Justices William J. Brennan, Jr., and Thurgood Marshall) distinguishes *Buckley* on the grounds that the unfair advantage of corporations is the result of wealth amassed "as a result of special advantages extended by the State." Ibid. at 809–810. This distinction, however, is shaky, for the relative wealth of various individuals is also largely the result of special advantages (and disadvantages) extended by government through its tax laws.

63. 418 U.S. at 243. For a discussion of the factual background of *Miami Herald*, see Schmidt, *Freedom of the Press*, pp. 219–35.
64. 418 U.S. at 251. This point is amplified in Schmidt, *Freedom of the Press*, pp. 37–46. For example, he says, "Most citizens in the United States experience monopoly newspapers, a small number of television stations that are dominated by network programming, and a larger number of radio stations broadcasting largely interchangeable programs with a minimum of concern for public affairs." Ibid., p. 39.

    As an illustration, in the state of New York, three newspaper chains—the Tribune Company Owned Newspapers (which owns the New York *Daily News*, with one of the largest circulations in the nation, as well as the *Chicago Tribune*), the New York Times Co., and Gannett Newspapers—account for 53 percent of the daily newspaper circulation. In California, seven chains—the Times Mirror Co., the Tribune Co., Hearst Newspapers, McClatchy Newspapers, Copley Newspapers, Knight-Ridder Newspapers, Inc., and Gannett—account for half of the daily circulation. In Florida, five chains—Knight-Ridder, the Tribune Co., Gannett, Media General, Inc., and the New York Times Co.—account for 51 percent of the daily circulation. None of the five chains has its headquarters in Florida. *1979 Editor and Publisher International Year Book* (New York: Editor and Publisher Co., 1979).

    John H. Shenefield has reported that 1,095 of the 1,753 daily newspapers in 1977 were owned by a group that controlled two or more newspapers in different cities. The groups owned an average of 6.5 newspapers. The twenty largest groups were estimated to control about 50 percent of the newspaper circulation. The largest single chain accounted for 6.3 percent of the daily circulation. "Ownership Concentration in Newspapers," *American Bar Association Journal* 65 (September 1979): 1334.
65. 418 U.S. at 251 n. 14.
66. Ibid. at 254.
67. Most communities in the United States are subject to a single local daily newspaper or to local newspapers under common ownership. Miami is an exception to the degree that the two newspapers are under different ownership. Even in Miami, however, the two papers are part of a joint operating agreement. See generally Franklin, *First Amendment*, pp. 199–202. See also Schmidt, *Freedom of the Press*, p. 40, and Bruce M. Owen, *Economics and Freedom of Expression* (Cambridge, Mass.: Ballinger Publishing Co., 1975), pp. 78–79. Refer also to note 64.
68. 418 U.S. at 256–57.
69. Ibid. at 258. Thus the Court's opinion would have remained the same even if the statute provided for reimbursement of additional costs. While such a reimbursement would not change the Court's opinion, it would meet a major objection offered by Lange, "The Role of the Access Doctrine," pp. 70–71. See also note 78 infra.
70. 418 U.S. at 258.
71. Antitrust action has been concerned only with economic effects and not with political and social effects of concentrated economic power. See Ann Watson, "Note: Media Conglomerates, Antitrust Law, and the Marketplace of Ideas," *Memphis State University Law Review* 9 (Winter, 1979): 278–79, and Shenefield, "Ownership Concentration in Newspapers," pp. 1332–35. See also Schmidt, *Freedom of the Press*, pp. 47–51.
72. Justice White, in a concurring opinion in *Miami Herald*, stated:

    > According to our accepted jurisprudence, the First Amendment erects a virtually insurmountable barrier between government and the print media so far as government tampering, in advance of publication, with news and editorial content is concerned.... A newspaper or magazine is not a public utility subject to "reasonable" government regulation in matters affecting the exercise of journalistic judgment as to what shall be printed.

    418 U.S. at 259. This seems to be an accurate reflection of the Court's unanimous view. Such an "insurmountable barrier" would permit, were it not for antitrust laws themselves not required by the First Amendment, not only the concentration of ownership in the hands of the few but the concentration of the control of content in those same hands.
73. See, e.g., FCC v. National Citizens Comm. for Broadcasting, 436 U.S. 775 (1978).
74. See, e.g., ibid., esp. at 790–93. Refer also to note 52, par. 3, supra.
75. See Franklin, *First Amendment*, pp. 521–30.

76. Ibid., p. 530.
77. *Moody's Industrial Manual*, 2 vols. (New York: Moody's Investors Service, 1980), 1:115, 2: 3906–70. Likewise, CBS owned Holt, Rinehart and Winston Publishing Company, Fawcett Publications, part of the assets of Praeger publishers, five television stations (in Chicago, Los Angeles, New York City, Philadelphia, and St. Louis), seven AM and seven FM stations, *Woman's Day* magazine, and *Mechanix Illustrated* (among other properties). Ibid., 1: 796–97. Refer also to note 64 supra.
78. Probably the affirmative duty of government under the democracy principle would require the government to reimburse the additional costs of printing a reply.
79. 408 U.S. at 92–93. *Mosley* was followed in Carvey v. Brown, 447 U.S. 455 (1980), which invalidated an Illinois statute prohibiting picketing of residences or dwellings except at a place of employment involved in a labor dispute.
80. "Because Chicago treats some picketing differently from others, we analyze this ordinance in terms of the Equal Protection Clause of the Fourteenth Amendment. Of course, the equal protection claim in this case is closely intertwined with First Amendment interests." 408 U.S. at 94–95. "Justifications for selective exclusions from the public forum must be carefully scrutinized." Ibid. at 98–99. "The Equal Protection Clause requires that statutes affecting First Amendment interests be narrowly tailored to their legitimate objectives." Ibid. at 101. The Court did not define exactly what it meant by "carefully scrutinized." Presumably, this is either the strict scrutiny test (necessary relation to a compelling state interest), employed for suspect classifications like race, or the intermediate equal protection test, requiring a substantial relation to an important governmental interest. In *Regents of the Univ. of California* v. *Bakke*, Justice Lewis F. Powell, Jr., uses the strict scrutiny test. 438 U.S. 265, 314–15 (1978). Justice Brennan, dissenting, uses the "substantial relation" (intermediate) test. Ibid. at 358–59. The Court's use of the phrase "substantial governmental interests" in Mosley, 408 U.S. at 99, is a confusion of language but suggests, along with the "narrowly tailored" language, the strict scrutiny test. See ibid. at 101.
81. 408 U.S. at 96, quoting New York Times Co. v. Sullivan, 376 U.S. 254, 270 (1964).
82. 408 U.S. at 99.
83. Ibid. at 96. The Court did not further distinguish between the content of the message and its source. Arguably, the Chicago ordinance at issue in *Mosley* distinguishes between different sources of messages by excepting from its prohibition messages directly resulting from a labor dispute (without regard to the position taken in the messages). The same messages in the absence of a labor dispute would not have been subject to the exception. For the analysis here, however, it suffices to accept the Court's view of content as including the source, although a definition of *content alone*, as discussed here, might exclude the source, if the source can be successfully separated from the position taken in the messages.
84. Chief Justice Burger, in his concurring opinion, expressed reservations about the overbreadth of the Court's expressions. Ibid. at 103.
85. 315 U.S. 568, 571–72 (1942) (footnotes omitted).
86. Ibid. at 572.
87. 413 U.S. 15, 24, 36–37 (1973). Other tests that must also be met are "whether the work depicts or describes, in a patently offensive way, sexual conduct specifically defined by the applicable state law" and "whether the work, taken as a whole, lacks serious literary, artistic, political, or scientific value." Ibid. at 24.
88. Arguably, the Court only defers to local determinations based on content alone. However, local standards typically restrict obscenity according to where and to whom it is expressed— i.e., according to the circumstances, or context, of its expression. Note that the Court has rejected the content-alone determination of obscenity whereby, for example, obscenity is determined by the test of "I know it when I see it." Jacobellis v. Ohio, 378 U.S. 184, 194 (1964) (Stewart, J., concurring).
    The distinction between content alone and content plus is conceptually similar to the distinction between speech and speech plus. See, e.g., United States v. O'Brien, 391 U.S. 367 (1968).
89. The other two tests are mentioned in note 87 supra. It does appear that the third test, "whether the work taken as a whole lacks serious literary, artistic, political, or scientific value," 413 U.S. at 24, is a test based on content alone. However, this test does not stand alone under the current *Miller* doctrine, and the first test, based on the context of expression, must also be met.

90. This statement from Ginzburg v. United States, 383 U.S. 463, 470 (1966), was quoted approvingly by the Court in Splawn v. California, 431 U.S. 595, 598 (1977).
91. Only four of the Court's justices seem explicitly to have recognized this point. In Young v. American Mini Theatres, 427 U.S. 50 (1976), the plurality opinion, written by Justice John Paul Stevens (and joined by Chief Justice Burger and Justices White and Rehnquist) said:

    The question of whether speech is, or is not, protected by the First Amendment often depends on the content of the speech. Thus the line between permissible advocacy and impermissible incitation to crime or violence depends, not merely on the setting in which the speech occurs, but also on exactly what the speaker had to say. Similarly, it is the content of the utterance that determines whether it is a protected epithet or an unprotected 'fighting comment.'

    Ibid. at 66. The plurality opinion went on to say that the degree of protection *within protected speech* may also depend on the content. The majority has rejected the latter view (concerning the degree of protection within protected speech). FCC v. Pacifica Foundation, 438 U.S. 726, 761 (1978) (Powell, J. concurring), 762–63 (Brennan, J., dissenting). However, the former view (concerning the separation between protected and unprotected speech) has apparently not been explicitly rejected by any member of the Court. For example, Justice Powell has explicitly repudiated the latter view but not the former. Ibid. at 761; Young v. American Mini Theatres, 427 U.S. at 73 n. 1; and Erznoznik v. Jacksonville, 422 U.S. 205, 208, 212 (1975). Also, Justices Potter Stewart, Brennan, Marshall, and Harry A. Blackmun have accepted the view that content neutrality does not apply "in the limited context of a captive or juvenile audience." Young v. American Mini Theatres, 427 U.S at 86. See also Ginsberg v. New York, 390 U.S. 629, 634, 637–43 (1968). It also appears that Justices Brennan and Marshall have accepted the view that the determination of "fighting words" also requires an examination of content. FCC v. Pacifica Foundation, 438 U.S. at 763, (Brennan, J., dissenting).
92. For a concise treatment of "clear and present danger," see Franklin, *The First Amendment*, pp. 40–46.
93. 424 U.S. 507 (1976).
94. 391 U.S. 308 (1968). The Court also followed *Hudgens* in Flagg Bros., Inc. v. Brooks, 436 U.S. 149, 159 (1978).
95. 407 U.S. 551 (1972).
96. 424 U.S. at 520 (footnote omitted).

    It is ironic that Justice Marshall, who wrote the opinion in *Mosley*, dissented in *Hudgens*. It is also ironic that Chief Justice Burger and Justice Rehnquist, who joined Part IV-B of Justice Stevens's opinion in FCC v. Pacifica Foundation, 438 U.S. 726 (1978), proclaiming that governmental regulation need not be content neutral, joined the Court's opinion in *Hudgens*.
97. 424 U.S. at 520–21 (1976).
98. Justice White, concurring in *Hudgens*, thought that *Logan Valley* need not be overruled to reach the result in *Hudgens*. Ibid. at 524–25.
99. 407 U.S. at 560, quoting Logan Valley, 391 U.S. at 320 n. 9.
100. This is what appears to be the Court's view in Logan Valley, 391 U.S. at 319–20, and Lloyd, 407 U.S. at 562–63, 570.
101. In *Mosley*, the speech occurred on the public sidewalks, so there was no adequate ground for arguing that this forum or context favored some types of speech over others.

    The apparent inconsistency between *Lloyd* and *Mosley* led Kenneth Karst to remark, "A labor-picketing exception in an ordinance is unconstitutional, but in a 'private' shopping center a labor-picketing exception is constitutionally required." "Equality as a Central Principle in the First Amendment," *University of Chicago Law Review* 43 (Fall 1975): 41. A distinction between these two cases can be maintained in a principled way only by discussing the "plus" factor—the nature of the forum or context.
102. This same distinction between content plus and content alone is necessary to make consistent two otherwise inconsistent statements within the *Mosley* opinion. On the one hand, the Court states that government is "never permitted" to describe permissible and impermissible speech in terms of its "subject matter" (i.e., content), 408 U.S. at 99; on the other hand, it says that "conflicting demands on the same place may compel the state to make choices among potential users and uses" (perhaps a reference to Red Lion Broadcasting

Co. v. FCC, 397 U.S. 367 [1969]). 408 U.S. at 98. It is difficult to see how a rational choice among "users and uses" could be made without some reference to the content (or source—refer to note 83 supra) of the messages.

103. See Prune Yard Shopping Center v. Robins, 447 U.S. 74 (1980), holding that the First Amendment permits a state to extend protection of speech to private shopping centers, although the First Amendment does not require such protection.

104. It is not necessary here to determine whether appropriate governmental regulation would maximize diversity in each media outlet considered separately or in all outlets considered together. Which approach would be best would depend on effectiveness, and determining effectiveness would require an extensive factual analysis.

CHAPTER 6

A Major Issue of the 1980s: New Communication Tools*

Douglas R. Watts†

Americans long have staked their political system on the principle of open and hardy debate among informed members of the public. The national commitment to this principle is embodied in the First Amendment. The constitutional recognition and guarantee of the free flow of information among the people is so fundamental to democracy that government cannot abridge it, even if acting for a majority of the people.

The role of information in our society, however, transcends its function as the lifeblood of the American political system; it has become the lifeblood of our economy. Since the turn of the century, the United States has been transformed from a predominantly agrarian nation, to one primarily engaged in industrial production, to one that is now absorbed in the gathering, processing, delivery, and consumption of information.

In an important work published in 1977, *The Information Economy*, Marc Porat determined that 46 percent of the 1967 Gross National Product flowed from "information activity," the resources consumed in creating, processing, and distributing information goods and services.[1] Using his measuring techniques, the percentage of information activity reflected in the Gross National Product now is well over 50 percent. In addition, the percentage of the work force engaged in information activity as an occupation approaches the same percentage. These trends appear to show no signs of slowing.

Major progress in a broad range of technologies has led the nation into the "Information Age." It is not surprising, therefore, that significant attention is beginning to be focused on the implications of this new era for a postindustrial America. The purpose of this chapter is to address some of the more important developments in telecommunications technologies as they may relate to the mass media and to suggest some First Amendment issues that these new technologies are likely to raise.

---

*A member of the legal staff of the American Newspaper Publishers Association, Douglas R. Watts discussed First Amendment implications of new communications technologies in August 1980. He was an invited speaker at a one-day symposium held in connection with the national convention of the Association for Education in Journalism. Watts substantially revised his convention remarks in preparation for publication, partly because of the rapid pace of changes both in the technologies and in the nature of the discussions of proposed government control over the new and changing media.

†Douglas R. Watts was named legislative counsel for the American Newspaper Publishers Association in 1981. He joined the ANPA in 1977 as an assistant manager for government affairs. He was named staff counsel in the newly formed legal department in 1978. Watts received his bachelor's degree in political science from Albion College in Michigan in 1973 and his law degree from the National Law Center at George Washington University in 1976.

The development of the new technologies has already begun to shatter basic assumptions about the media, assumptions which have been the foundation of current law. An example is the impact technology will have on the U.S. Supreme Court's premise that the First Amendment can be applied differently to the various communications media. As late as 1969, Justice Byron R. White said in a major opinion upholding a form of broadcast programming regulation that "differences in the characteristics of new media justify differences in the First Amendment standards applied to them."[2] Justice White was arguing that the distinctions between the print and the broadcast media allowed regulation of the latter that would not be permitted in the case of the former. Yet, in the 1980s, those historical distinctions between the electronic media—such as telephone, radio, and television—and the print media—such as newspapers and magazines—are breaking down and fading away. The technology for gathering and processing information has become essentially the same regardless of how the final product is ultimately delivered. In the field of entertainment programming, for example, movies were once available only to people who made the trip to the local theater. Today, in addition to taking that trip, a person can stay at home and watch that same movie delivered by over-the-air television, cable television, subscription television, Multipoint Distribution Systems (MDS),[3] video cassettes, video discs, and eventually, perhaps, direct broadcast from communications satellites. The movie looks the same to the consumer; only the method of delivery is varied.

Further, technological developments are allowing one medium to adopt and utilize the techniques, processes, and functions of another medium. For example, television stations are beginning to use the new technologies to acquire an important characteristic of the print media—that of providing a message at whatever time is convenient for the consumer. Conventional distinctions between telephone networks and cable television, or between cable television and broadcasting, or between broadcasting and newspapers and magazines no longer have clear meaning. Technological development once created compartments of activity; now that same technological evolution is breaking down those barriers.

The major catalyst for this homogenization of media has been the convergence of computer and communications technologies. The marriage of two of America's most dynamic industries has the potential to affect the public's receipt of information as profoundly as did the projects of Gutenberg and Marconi. The combination of computer and communications technologies now is widely used by both print and electronic media for the gathering and processing of information. This development has already led the various media to use the same kinds of equipment: video display terminals, mainframe computers, satellites and their small-aperture antennae, and a wide variety of other communications devices.

The new technology allows for storage and distribution of greater amounts of information than most media currently provide. As will be discussed later, information provided through these technologies will be gathered, stored in computers, and delivered through video display terminals located in homes and in businesses. The new computer/telecommunications technology will be increasingly employed in the final step of the "information economy's" activity: delivery to the home for consumption by the public. The declining cost of the new technology will make it both easier and less costly to provide information to the public, creating new opportunities for competition and diversity.

The new electronic information services will be hybrid offspring of today's mass media. They will take from today's major media the best characteristics of each, reassemble them as a package, and transmit them over the new medium. It is not just the traditional media that are being changed by this technology; the technology is also shared by computer companies, telephone companies, and satellite carriers as well, drawing the functions and opportunities of all media closer together. The new technology is creating a common denominator among all information providers. The various information providers are becoming more alike in function and will be competing increasingly for the time, attention, and financial resources of the consumer.

The electronic information services will supplement—not replace—existing media services. The existence of the old and the new media side by side will further—and perhaps, finally—erode any meaningful differences between them. This will frustrate Justice White's rationale for applying different First Amendment standards to different media, as it will frustrate other traditional First Amendment analyses. Also, the new combination of media will pose a significant challenge to the enduring national commitment to a free and competitive marketplace of ideas.

Among the panoply of developing communications technologies, two in particular, may produce First Amendment concerns.[4] The first is cable television; the second is videotex. Before addressing the potential implications for the First Amendment in these technologies, it may be useful to discuss how they work.

Cable television, of course, has attained such stature within the last few years that it hardly needs an introduction. Initially, cable television, or CATV (Community Antenna Television), was installed in rural areas where there was poor reception of standard, over-the-air television signals. A CATV operator would erect an antenna sufficient to receive a quality signal—i.e., a good picture—and then take that signal and retransmit it over coaxial cable wired directly into the homes of the system's subscribers. For many years, cable television had difficulty entering urban markets where reception of broadcast signals already was adequate. However, several technological improvements, most notably the advent of alternative programming distributed to cable system operators via satellite, allowed cable television systems to offer a service that went far beyond the mere collection and retransmission of existing signals. Programming such as first-run movies shown uncut and without commercial interruption, live sporting events, and twenty-four-hour news can now be presented over cable television in markets of all sizes, in direct competition with over-the-air broadcasters for the attention of the viewing public.

Videotex is a generic term for several types of systems which provide for electronic, textual display upon command of computer-stored information. The display either may be shown on a video display terminal otherwise used in conjunction with the burgeoning number of home computers or may be shown on any television set equipped with a "black box" that can decode the information from its digital form and present it on the screen. Although there are many variations among videotex systems, essentially they fall into two categories—viewdata and teletext.

Viewdata is a generic term for any videotex system which provides a hard-wire, interactive connection between a reader and a computer-stored data base. This allows the reader to select particular pieces of information for display. The hard-wire connection between the reader and the computer could be the coaxial cable of a CATV system, provided it has sufficient technical capacity, but in the near future, the hard-wire connection will more probably be a telephone line.

Teletext, also a generic term, denotes a system which encodes information on the vertical blanking interval of a standard television broadcast signal. Currently, the portion of a television signal that appears as a picture on a television screen does not fully use the signal transmitted by the broadcaster. The unused portion of the signal may be seen as the black bar that may appear on the screen if the set's vertical control button is adjusted. Up to 800 frames of information per minute can be broadcast in continuous cycle on the vertical blanking interval—and efforts are underway to expand that capacity. With the use of a control keypad, a reader can demand a particular frame of information, which is then "grabbed" as it is broadcast, decoded by a "black box," and displayed in full textual form on a standard television set.

There is even a hybrid teletext-viewdata system that combines telephone access to a computer in connection with a teletext system. Using the telephone connection, a teletext user can demand a particular piece of information, which is then inserted into the broadcast cycle for immediate transmission.[5]

Both teletext and viewdata systems have been developed largely in Europe, Canada, and Japan, where governmental subsidies have played a major role.[6] In the United States, development, which must rely on private enterprise risk capital, has proceeded at a slower pace.[7] Even so, the results of early experimentation indicate that videotex will become an important new medium of mass communications.

As these communications technologies have been developed, public policy has lagged far behind. Part of the problem is that the statutory basis for regulation of the electronic media is the Communications Act of 1934.[8] This law gives the Federal Communications Commission regulatory jurisdiction essentially over two categories: common carriers and broadcasters. In 1934, the common carriers were telegraph and telephone companies; the broadcasters were radio station operators. Thus, the 1934 law, passed before the advent of television, cable television, computers, satellites, and other modern communications technologies, has been strained to its outer limits by attempts to adapt it to today's dynamic environment.

For example, the FCC, administering the 1934 act, has never quite been able to figure out what to do about cable television. The technology simply does not fit neatly into either of the act's categories of jurisdiction. CATV originates and provides to the public video programming, which makes it appear like broadcasting, upon which the FCC imposes certain content regulations. However, unlike broadcasters, who use the public resource of the electromagnetic spectrum to broadcast their signals—and, as such, have been made public trustees through the federal licensing process—cable television system operators use the private resource of their coaxial cables for delivery of their programming. Similarly, CATV operators clearly provide a form of wire communications, which appears a lot like the service provided by the nation's telephone and telegraph companies. Government supervision of common carriers normally includes price regulation and access requirements. Yet, cable does not provide classic common carrier services, e.g., point-to-point personal communication.

Since 1977, Congress has made several efforts to revise and amend—if not completely rewrite—the Communications Act of 1934. While there have been many differing proposals, the thrust of all of them has been removal of governmental involvement in regulation of electronic media. Therefore, any effort made in 1981 to predict the First Amendment implications of new communications technology must include the caveat that the predictions are based on 1981 statutory and case law. Significant revision of the federal law by Congress, bringing it into synchronization with evolving technologies, may render irrelevant any predictions made up to that time.

The potential First Amendment issues raised by the new communications technology, particularly cable television and videotex systems, appear to fall into four general categories: ownership and control of these systems, access to the systems, regulation of the content transmitted over the systems, and privacy.

The issue of media ownership always has the potential of raising First Amendment concerns. A government-imposed limitation on ownership is a government-imposed limitation on speech and, as such, raises the specter of government control over expression.[9]

The cross-ownership of cable and other media companies already has been a controversial issue and probably will be so again now that cable has become a more significant communications medium. The FCC already has limitations on the ownership of cable systems by broadcasters and by telephone companies.[10] In 1970, the FCC began, in tandem with its rulemaking proceeding on newspaper/broadcast cross-ownership,[11] a companion proceeding that examined newspaper/cable cross-ownership. The FCC concluded in 1975 that no regulations were necessary at that time with regard to the common ownership of newspaper and cable, but it suspended its examination of the issue without deciding the matter permanently.[12] Thus, the question could be reconsidered at any time.

Because cable television is subject to two-tiered regulation—control at the state or local level as well as at the federal level—there also are some state prohibitions on forms of cross-ownership. For example, there have been state prohibitions against common ownership of a newspaper and a cable television system within the same market in Massachusetts, Connecticut, and Minnesota.

In 1981, newspapers owned less than 13 percent of the total number of cable television systems in America, a percentage which had remained roughly constant for several years. The instance of common ownership of newspapers and cable television systems within the same market at that time was well under 5 percent. However, as cable has gained prominence as a medium, there have been spectacular bidding wars waged across the country for the right to wire those few major cities that do not yet have cable. This competition has attracted significant public attention. Further, several large multimedia newspaper corporations, e.g., Times-Mirror, Newhouse, Knight-Ridder, and others, have acquired—and probably will continue to acquire in the future—major, multiple cable systems. These high-priced purchases also have attracted significant attention. The kind of public focus now on cable television may well act as a stimulus for federal or local policy makers to reexamine the question of newspaper/cable television cross-ownership.

Another potential ownership issue may occur when teletext is broadcast on the vertical blanking interval of an over-the-air television signal, which is then retransmitted over a cable television system. CATV operators have the capacity to strip from the vertical blanking interval all the information sent out by a broadcaster, so that the information service would never reach the system's subscribers. Additionally, cable operators have the capacity to insert their own teletext services on the vertical blanking interval of the signals they retransmit. The FCC has not resolved the extent of a broadcaster's proprietary or First Amendment rights in the vertical blanking interval portion of its signal. However, developments in communications technologies soon may force it to do so.

Another question that can be raised in connection with this issue is whether a broadcaster can, consistent with his license obligations to operate in the "public interest, convenience, and necessity," lease away the vertical blanking interval. Further, if it can, may it lease the vertical blanking interval to a newspaper so that the newspaper can provide an electronic version of its printed edition? FCC regulations, upheld unanimously by the United States Supreme Court,[13] prospectively prohibit a newspaper from owning a broadcast station in the same market and thereby providing program signals, including the vertical blanking interval. This potential issue serves to demonstrate further the manner in which the convergence of communications technologies may pose difficult and frustrating problems for First Amendment analysis.

The merging technologies also create an interesting paradox from the vantage point of the First Amendment. Services such as videotex and cable television have the capacity to expand diversity of viewpoints flowing to the public far beyond that available through any other medium. However, access to the system is the essential tool by which to achieve diversity. With the new technology, control of the potential diversity is vested in the hands of the entity controlling the delivery technology—in the case of cable, the system's operator, or in the case of viewdata, the telephone company.

The potential for diversity has been demonstrated as local governments have franchised cable television systems with a capacity to provide programming over more than eighty channels. In Dallas, Warner-Amex was awarded a franchise requiring it to provide band width for 120 channels. Clearly, this could present unprecedented opportunity for diversity of programming to the subscribers of that system. Similarly, with a viewdata system, the number of information providers is theoretically limitless. Because the system used for delivery is the switched network of telephone companies, anyone with access to a telephone could become an information provider over the system.

This raises a second potential First Amendment issue. The question of the right of access to a controlled system should not be a problem where the delivery mechanism is a telephone company. Telephone systems are government-regulated monopoly common carriers that must provide access upon reasonable request. Despite the sordid history of this nation's dominant telephone company, AT&T, in denying access to its network,[14] the legal basis for requiring such access is abundantly clear. For cable television, however, from the vantage point of the First Amendment, access requirements are somewhat in doubt. In 1976, the FCC adopted regulations requiring at least four access channels per CATV system with more than 3,500 subscribers and mandating that all unused channels be available for leased access on a nondiscriminatory, first-come, first-served basis. In 1978, the U.S. Court of Appeals for the Eighth Circuit threw out these rules because, among other things, it said, the FCC had exceeded its statutory authority—that is, the rules went beyond the jurisdiction of the commission. The court also discussed at some length the conflict of the regulations with the First Amendment rights of cable operators. Though the court did not specifically rule on the First Amendment question, it did say that 'were it necessary to decide the issue, the present record would render the intrusion represented by the present [access] rules constitutionally impermissible."[15]

The Eighth Circuit relied on an analogy it drew between cable television and newspapers. It took extensive note of *Miami Herald Publishing Co.* v. *Tornillo*,[16] a Supreme Court decision that struck down a state statute requiring access to newspapers under particular circumstances. The Eighth Circuit said:

> Despite the [Supreme] Court's guidance in *Miami Herald*,... the Commission has attempted here to require cable operators, who have invested substantially to create a private electronic "publication"—a means of disseminating information—to open their "publications" for all for use as *they* [those granted access] wish. That governmental interference with the editorial process raises a serious First Amendment issue.[17]

If the Supreme Court were to decide directly the access issue with regard to cable television on the same grounds as discussed by the Eighth Circuit,[18] then cable television system operators could not be constitutionally required to provide access to their systems on demand. They would enjoy First Amendment freedoms more equivalent to those guaranteed the print media—that is, freedom from government-imposed access requirements.[19]

Thus far, however, cable system operators are subject to the same limited access requirements that are imposed upon broadcast licensees. The FCC requires both to adhere to the equal time provision of the 1934 Communications Act and to the personal attack aspect of the fairness doctrine. The equal time provision requires that any broadcast licensee or cable system operator permitting a legally qualified candidate for federal office to use its facilities must afford equal opportunities to all other such candidates for that office at comparable charges.[20] The personal attack rules, adopted by the FCC as regulations in the mid-sixties, provide that if a broadcast licensee or a cable system operator airs an attack on an individual's honesty, character, or integrity during the discussion of a controversial public issue, it must offer that person a reasonable opportunity to respond.[21]

Both broadcasters and cable system operators also are required to adhere to the fairness doctrine in general. The fairness doctrine is an FCC programming policy that requires broadcast licensees, as part of their responsibility to operate in the public interest, to provide programming about controversial issues of public importance and, once an issue is addressed, to provide opposing viewpoints.[22] While cable system operators cannot be required to provide coverage of controversial public issues because they are not required to originate programming, they are bound to offer differing viewpoints once such programming has been aired.[23]

The fairness doctrine and the equal time rule, as government content regulations, raise the third First Amendment issue potentially related to the new communications technologies. Although the U.S. Supreme Court has never directly considered the constitutionality of such program regulations imposed on cable system operators, it has upheld the constitutionality of the fairness doctrine as applied to broadcasters. In *Red Lion Broadcasting Co.* v. *FCC,* Justice White said this diminution of First Amendment rights—clearly such regulations could not constitutionally be imposed on the print media—was justified because broadcasters use a public resource, the electromagnetic spectrum, to deliver their information. Because of the nature of the spectrum, the Court said, frequencies available for broadcasting are limited. Exclusive licenses are granted to broadcasters to operate on a particular frequency so long as that operation is in the public interest, convenience, and necessity. Because there cannot be boundless diversity in the number of people directly allowed to use the spectrum to present viewpoints, the Court reasoned, a licensee given permission to use the airwaves must present a diversity of views.[24]

Because cable television operators do not use the airwaves, the imposition of federal regulations on cable has been limited to that which is considered "reasonably ancillary" to the regulation of broadcasting.[25] The spillover rationale, however, does not overcome the First Amendment implications of government regulation of programming content originated by cable system operators. The imposition of such programming regulations as the fairness doctrine on cable is becoming less and less persuasive as cable systems provide more and more opportunity for diversity. The application, in effect, of a scarcity rationale to justify the content regulation of cable systems with a potential for eighty channels or more of programming would seem illogical.

Indeed, future FCC actions may well reduce the logic of the scarcity rationale even as it is applied to broadcast licensees. Underway are efforts to (1) reduce the spacing between radio station frequencies, thereby increasing the number of potential broadcasters; (2) license for program origination low-power television stations (having broadcast radii much smaller than that of full-service television licensees), in essence creating the potential of thousands of mini-TV stations; and (3) allow direct broadcast from satellites, which could provide several channels of programming directly to homes equipped with small, rooftop satellite signal-receiving dishes.

The convergence of new communications technologies presents a challenge to ensure that all media receive the full guarantees and undiluted freedoms of the First Amendment. Perhaps the greatest challenge will be provided by the viewdata-type videotex services—the hybrid technology that uses telephone or cable lines to deliver newspaper- and magazine-type information for display on a television set. Possibly, more than any other new communications technology, viewdata systems will challenge America's commitment to competition in the marketplace of ideas from a diversity of sources.

For the foreseeable future, viewdata systems will be delivered over the switched network of the nation's telephone companies. That is an extremely important point. Unlike virtually any other medium, entry into the viewdata market will not require an entrant to purchase, erect, and maintain a delivery mechanism for its product. In the case of cable television, over-the-air broadcasters, and newspapers, this delivery cost is a principal—if not paramount—expense, both in the initial investment and in the cost of operation.

The fact that the delivery system—the telephone network—is already in place leads to two results. First, a market entrant need only purchase the "front end" of a system, a device which allows him or her to input into the network. Although there will be costs for the transmission of information, the economic barrier to entry into the new medium will be significantly lower than it is for other media. Quite literally, a home computer plugged into a telephone becomes the functional equivalent of a printing press; and its "newspaper" can be delivered to anyone with a telephone. Further, micro-chip technology continues to drive down the cost of these computers. America could soon witness the resurrection of that favorite child of the First Amendment—the lonely pamphleteer. No longer, however, will the pamphleteer have to stand on a street corner to distribute ideas. He or she will have instant access to a potentially massive audience and will stand figuratively side by side with the *Wall Street Journal*, the *New York Times*, and on down the list. We could have a golden age of diversity.

The second result of this in-place delivery system is somewhat the converse of the first. Viewdata system operators will not need to create and maintain a delivery system for their products, but they *will* be totally dependent upon the delivery system they use. In the case of the nation's telephone companies, that system is a government-granted and government-regulated transmission monopoly that reaches, collectively, more than 90 percent of the American public. One potential market entrant—and only one—has the capacity to achieve an economic competitive advantage in this technology. One potential market entrant—and only one—has the ability to monopolize the market. That potential entrant is the local telephone company. All other potential entrants would have to depend upon the telephone company for the delivery of information.

As FCC Commissioner Joseph Fogarty has pointed out, to allow the telephone company with the local loop of telephone exchange to offer services such as viewdata may give the telephone company what he termed "natural monopoly" economies.[26] Telephone company provision of a viewdata service, in competition with others, would grant solely to the telephone company a level of vertical integration[27] unobtainable by the others. Basic economics would dictate that the economies of scale of vertical integration would work toward monopolization and concentration of information providers, rather than toward promotion of diversity and competition in this emerging market. Fogarty noted that if the resulting economies emerged on a large enough scale, the telephone company would have an "unfair" advantage only in the sense that it might be "inherently unbeatable."[28]

The issue of whether the provider of the transmission lines for a viewdata system should also be allowed to send its own information across those lines is a difficult First Amendment issue. Some have suggested that telephone companies should be precluded from creating a *combination* of information service and monopoly telephone exchange service. Such an approach clearly would eliminate any potential for monopolization and would establish a market structure which would allow for full and fair competition among information providers. It is the purpose of the First Amendment to preserve an uninhibited marketplace of ideas in which the truth ultimately will prevail, rather than to countenance monopolization of that market, whether it be by the government itself or by a private interest.[29] Yet, it could be argued that such a restraint on telephone company participation in this new medium could be considered a prior restraint, presumptively an invalid abridgment of a telephone company's freedom of speech.[30] This issue, being debated in Congress and in other forums, is a First Amendment issue of major proportions that must be resolved soon.

A fourth First Amendment problem potentially raised by viewdata systems is that of the protection against the invasion of privacy. Government oversight or restraint of the operations of any medium of mass communication creates a situation of tension with the freedoms of the First Amendment. Yet, the exercise of these freedoms with viewdata technology creates the potential for intrusion into another fundamental right of the American people—the right to be let alone, or the "penumbral" constitutional right of privacy.[31]

Viewdata systems, whether delivered over telephone lines or by cable, include a capacity—as no medium before has had—for the system operator to monitor system usage by each and every subscriber. That operator can tell what programs are watched or what individual pieces of information are accessed, when, and by whom. The operator can determine what auxillary services, such as at-home shopping, at-home banking, and electronic mail, are used and by whom. Perhaps like no other aspect of new communications technology, these monitoring capabilities conjure up all the fearful images of George Orwell's Big Brother from *1984*.

Former FCC Chairman Charles Ferris has stated well the potential implications of the new media systems:

> The history of repression has been interwoven with the history of technology. There was wire tapping almost as soon as there were telephones to be tapped. But in the future, significant facts about every American could be available by gaining access to just one or two giant computers.
>
> Should our right to be let alone be entrusted solely to the marketplace? Or, should we rely on government to set and enforce standards—to preserve the spirit of the Bill of Rights during an era when our privacy could fall victim to our own inventive genius? These questions demand the very best of our imagination.[32]

The monitoring capacities of viewdata systems may well stimulate a demand by the people for legislative measures that respect their privacies— legislative measures that ultimately must be balanced against the exercise of First Amendment freedoms. A measure of both the effective use and the misuse of First Amendment freedoms will be the extent to which the public continues to trust the media to protect the right of privacy. The level of trust will be reflected by the strength and urgency of any demands for government intervention and by the extent to which those demands challenge fundamental First Amendment values.

In conclusion, it seems clear that the United States soon will witness an explosion in communications services that will dramatically alter the way the American people obtain information and communicate with one another. This explosion will be marked by technological developments that will obscure the differentiating characteristics of the media and that will bring all of us closer than we have ever been before.

New communications technologies present a new, yet familiar, challenge to the freedoms guaranteed by the First Amendment. As technology modifies and adapts existing means of communications, First Amendment analyses and approaches also will have to be modified and adapted in order to ensure vigorous competition among the media that is both a lifeblood of a strong, healthy economy and, at the same time, the essence of a robust marketplace of ideas.

Notes

1. U.S., Department of Commerce, Office of Telecommunications, *The Information Economy: Definition and Measurement*, prepared by Marc Uri Porat, Special Publication 77–12(1) (Washington, D.C.: Office of Telecommunications, 1977), p. 8.
2. Red Lion Broadcasting Co. v. FCC, 395 U.S. 367, 386 (1969).
3. MDS is a specialized broadcast service that allows for receipt of video programming on a targeted contractual basis.
4. As this chapter was being prepared, several proceedings were pending at the Federal Communications Commission concerning new communications technologies which could present additional First Amendment challenges. One of the more important of these is a proposal to allow satellites—currently common carriers—to engage in direct broadcasting to the public. U.S., FCC, "Inquiry into the Development of Regulatory Policy in Regard to Direct Broadcast Satellites for the Period Following the 1983 Regional Administrative Radio Conference," Notice of Inquiry, General Docket No. 80–603, *Federal Register* 45 (3 November 1980): 72719. Another is a proposal to allow low power television translaters (which currently are used mainly in rural areas to relay television signals) to provide programming to the public, potentially creating an opportunity for thousands of new television stations. U.S., FCC, "Inquiry into the Future Role of Low Power Television Broadcasting and Television Translaters in the National Telecommunications System," Notice of Proposed Rulemaking, BC Docket No. 78–253, *Federal Register* 45 (17 October 1980): 69178.
5. This system was developed by Bonneville International and experimented with at station KSL, Salt Lake City, Utah.
6. Significant teletext systems in operation in Europe include CEEFAX and Oracle in Great Britain and Antiope in France. Significant viewdata systems include Prestel in Great Britain, Antiope in France, Teledon in Canada, and Captains in Japan.
7. At publication, no telephone-based viewdata system was widely, commercially available. Several significant experiments were underway, however, including the Knight-Ridder/AT&T Viewtron experiment in Coral Gables, Florida, and the multinewspapered CompuServe experiment in Columbus, Ohio.
8. U.S., *Code*, Title 47, sec. 301 et. seq.
9. This is not to suggest that all government regulation of media as business is unconstitutional. Regulation of business practices such as anticompetitive activity can survive constitutional scrutiny. Indeed, some government limitations on ownership could improve the opportunity for the dissemination of diverse views, an important product of free expression. Such a situation might occur, if, hypothetically, the FCC was faced with a decision among competing applicants for the five standard broadcast stations in a particular area. The FCC would be fostering First Amendment values if it were to insist that five different owners operate the five stations rather than choose one or two owners for all five stations. The hypothetical is an example of competition for a limited resource rather than competition for an unlimited resource. However, government-imposed limitations on ownership must withstand intense constitutional examination. Such government intervention should be the extreme exception rather than the rule.
10. A broadcast licensee cannot own a cable system within its market area. U.S., *Code of Federal Regulations*, Title 47, sec. 76.501. A telephone company cannot own or operate a cable television in the same market in which it owns monopoly transmission facilities. Ibid., sec. 64.601.

192   *The First Amendment in the 1980s*

11. Amendment of sections 73.34, 73.240, and 76.636 of the Commission's Rules Relating to Multiple Ownership of Standard, FM, and Television Broadcast Stations, Second Report and Order, 50 F.C.C.2d 1046 (1975).
12. U.S., FCC, Amendment of Part 76 of the Commission's Rules and Regulations Relative to Diversification of Control of Community Antenna Television Systems; and Inquiry with Respect thereto to Formulate Regulatory Policy and Rulemaking and/or Legislative Proposals, First Report, Docket No. 18891, 52 F.C.C.2d 170 (1975).
13. FCC v. National Citizens Committee for Broadcasting, 436 U.S. 775 (1978).
14. E.g., MCI v. AT&T, Nos. 80–2171, 80–2288 (7th Cir. 1981).
15. Midwest Video Corp. v. FCC, 571 F.2d 1025, 1056–57 (8th Cir. 1978).
16. 418 U.S. 241 (1974).
17. 571 F.2d at 1056.
18. The Supreme Court reviewed the Eighth Circuit's *Midwest Video* decision in 1979 and affirmed it on jurisdictional grounds. FCC v. Midwest Video Corp., 440 U.S. 689 (1979).
19. As it is, the issue is not settled as the lower court's language was dicta and the Supreme Court did not effectively address the issue. The Supreme Court said, in a footnote, that because the decision was based on statutory grounds, "we express no view on [the constitutional] question, save to acknowledge that it is not frivolous and to make clear that the asserted constitutional issue did not determine or sharply influence our construction of the statute." Ibid. at 709.
20. U.S., *Code*, Title 47, sec. 315. Accord, Amendment of Part 74, Subpart K, of the Commission's Rules and Regulations Relative to Community Antenna Television Systems; and Inquiry into the Development of Communications Technology and Services to Formulate Regulatory Policy and Rulemaking and/or Legislative Proposals, First Report and Order, 20 F.C.C.2d 201, 219–20 (1969). Specific exceptions to the equal time requirement include newscasts, news interviews, news documentaries, and on-the-spot coverage of news events involving a candidate. U.S., *Code*, Title 47, sec. 315 (a).
21. See U.S., *Code of Federal Regulations*, Title 47, secs. 73.1920, 73.1930. The regulations also apply to groups attacked during the discussion of a controversial public issue. The regulations require that a broadcast licensee transmit within a week of the attack (1) notification of the date, time, and identification of the broadcast, (2) a script or tape of the attack, and (3) an offer of a reasonable opportunity to respond. Exceptions to the personal attack rule are attacks on foreign groups or public figures; personal attacks made by legally qualified candidates, or those closely associated with them, on other candidates and those associated with them; and newscasts, news interviews, and on-the-spot coverage of news events. A related regulation, adopted at the same time, requires the same kind of notice and opportunity to respond when a licensee broadcasts an editorial endorsing or opposing a legally qualified candidate for public office. The candidate not supported in the editorial must be notified within twenty-four hours. Special provisions are made for such editorials coming within seventy-two hours of a related election. Ibid. These rules are applied to cable system operators by Amendment of Part 74, Subpart K, of the Commission's Rules, 20 F.C.C.2d at 219–20.
22. See, e.g., The Handling of Public Issues Under the Fairness Doctrine and the Public Interest Standards of the Communications Act, Fairness Report, 48 F.C.C.2d 1, 7, 9–21 (1974).
23. Programming origination requirements were dropped with Amendment of Part 76, Subpart G, of the Commission's Rules and Regulations Relative to Program Origination by Cable Television Systems; and Inquiry into the Development of Cablecasting Services to Formulate Regulatory Policy and Rulemaking, Report and Order, 49 F.C.C.2d 1090, 1105–6 (1974). Cable system operators are bound to the fairness doctrine by Amendment of Part 74, Subpart K, of the Commission's Rules, 20 F.C.C.2d at 219–20.
24. Red Lion Broadcasting Co. v. FCC, 395 U.S. at 379–90, 397–400.
25. U.S. v. Southwestern Cable, 392 U.S. 157 (1968), and U.S. v. Midwest Video Corp., 406 U.S. 649 (1972). Accord, Amendment of Part 74, Subpart K, of the Commission's Rules, 20 F.C.C.2d at 219–20.
26. U.S., FCC, "Clarification of the Commission's Report and Order Revising the Processing Policies for Waiver of the Telephone Company–Cable Television 'Cross Ownership Rules,' " Memorandum Opinion and Order (Separate Statement of Commissioner Joseph R. Fogarty), CC Docket No. 78–129, *Federal Register* 45 (17 December 1980): 82952.

27. Vertical integration refers to corporate ownership of businesses that directly relate to the production and delivery of a single product. An example would be a company which owns not only a "widget" manufacturing plant but also companies which produce the raw materials to make widgets, deliver the widgets to retail outlets, and operate retail stores that sell widgets. Vertical integration is contrasted to horizontal integration, the ownership of businesses providing the same service or product—for example, a company which manufactures widgets buys three other companies manufacturing widgets.
28. U.S., FCC, Fogarty Statement, p. 82952.
29. E.g., Associated Press v. United States, 326 U.S. 1 (1945), and New York Times Co. v. Sullivan, 376 U.S. 254 (1964).
30. E.g., Nebraska Press Ass'n v. Stuart, 427 U.S. 539 (1976); New York Times Co. v. United States, 403 U.S. 713 (1971); Near v. Minnesota ex rel. Olson, 283 U.S. 697 (1931).
31. E.g., Griswold v. Connecticut, 381 U.S. 479 (1965). Justice William O. Douglas, who wrote the opinion for the Court, said while a right to privacy is not specifically mentioned in the Bill of Rights, it follows from those guarantees which are mentioned. Ibid. at 482–86. He said that "specific guarantees in the Bill of Rights have penumbras, formed by emanations from those guarantees that help give them life and substance [cite omitted]. Various guarantees create zones of privacy. The right of association contained in the penumbra of the First Amendment is one." Ibid. at 484.
32. "New Technology and the Merging Media: A Time for Imagination," a speech to the Audit Bureau of Circulation's Annual Meeting, New Orleans, La., November 7, 1979.

First Amendment–Related Cases
in State Courts, 1787–1925

Listed below, by chronology within states, are the decisions used by Margaret A. Blanchard in the preparation of the chapter, "Filling in the Void: Speech and Press in State Courts prior to *Gitlow*." The list includes media- and speech-related cases from 1787 to 1925 that contained discussion about the First Amendment or about the role of free speech or a free press in society.

State Reporters

Decisions of state courts have been published since the beginning of the Republic with a greater or lesser degree of regularity and accuracy. The early reporter system was highly individualistic and idiosyncratic, as a look at the names of the volumes in which the court decisions were published shows. Written decisions from the state courts in Pennsylvania, for instance, can be found in volumes named after Dallas, Watts and Sergeant, and Yeates. This practice became very confusing, especially as the number of states multiplied over the years. By the middle of the nineteenth century, many state courts dropped the practice of allowing the court reporter to attach his name to the volumes of decisions issuing from his particular state. Most state courts, however, did not go back through their earlier volumes of printed decisions, as Massachusetts did, to reclassify and retitle them. Consequently, the reader of state court decisions needs some help in figuring out which state court is being cited in a decision from Brev. or Cow. The following is such a guide.

A.D. American Decisions, cases of general value and authority decided in the courts of several states from the earliest issue of the state reports, 1760–1869
A.R. American Reports, cases of general interest decided in the courts of last resort of several states, 1869–1887
Brev. Brevard, South Carolina, 1793–1816
Cow. Cowen's Reports, New York, 1823–1829
Dall. Dallas, Pennsylvania, 1754–1809
Daly Daly's New York Common Pleas Court Reports, 1859–1891
Gray Gray, Massachusetts, 1854–1860
Hill Hill's Reports, New York, 1841–1844
Hun Hun's New York Supreme Court Reporter, 1874–1895
Johns. Johnson's Reports, New York, 1806–1823
Johns. Cas. Johnson's Cases, New York, 1799–1803
Misc. Miscellaneous Reports, New York, 1892–date
N.J.Eq. New Jersey Equity Reports, 1830–1948
N.Y. Common Law Reports New York, cases from Supreme Court and Courts of Errors and Appeals, 1791–1848
N.Y.S. New York Supplement, 1888–date
Nott & McC. Nott & McCord, South Carolina, 1817–1820
Paige Ch. Paige's Chancery Reports, New York, 1828–1845
Pick. Pickering, Massachusetts, 1822–1839
S. & M. Smedes & Marshall, Mississippi, 1843–1850
Scam. Scammon, Illinois, 1832–1844
Watts & Serg. Watts & Sergeant, Pennsylvania, 1841–1845
Wend. Wendell's Reports, New York, 1828–1841
Yeates Pennsylvania, 1791–1808

Private Reporters

In addition to the state court reporter system discussed above, regional reporters prepared by private publishers developed. For many years, in fact most of the years covered by this study after the mid-nineteenth century, state court decisions were published in two places—the original, official reporter of the state and those privately published. The privately published reporters group states into certain regions of the country, as the list below shows. Many of the cases included in the study have two citations following the case name, one to the state reporter and one to the private, regional reporter. Most law libraries carry a fairly complete run of the private, regional reporter system volumes even if their collection of individual state volumes is meager. Although the material in the private reporter system is supposed to follow the original state text verbatim, there are discrepancies between the two versions in spelling, abbreviation, capitalization, and punctuation in the texts of many of the early state court decisions. The citations in Chapter 1 are to the state court reporters only, when they were available. A number of states, however, once the private reporter system got off the ground, decided to stop the publication of individual state volumes in favor of this regional collection. Thus, some of the state court decisions discussed in the chapter contain citations to the regional reporters only.

A list of the regional reporters, with appropriate abbreviations and the states covered by each, follows.

A. Atlantic Reporter, compiled from Connecticut, Delaware, Maine, Maryland, New Jersey, New Hampshire, Pennsylvania, and Vermont
N.E. North Eastern Reporter, compiled from Illinois, Indiana, Massachusetts, New York, Ohio, and Rhode Island
N.W. North Western Reporter, compiled from Iowa, Michigan, Minnesota, Nebraska, North Dakota, South Dakota, and Wisconsin
P. Pacific Reporter, compiled from Alaska, Arizona, California, Colorado, Hawaii, Idaho, Kansas, Montana, Nevada, New Mexico, Oklahoma, Oregon, Utah, Washington, and Wyoming
S.E. South Eastern Reporter, compiled from Georgia, North Carolina, South Carolina, Virginia, and West Virginia
S.W. South Western Reporter, compiled from Arkansas, Kentucky, Missouri, Tennessee, and Texas
So. Southern Reporter, compiled from Alabama, Florida, Louisiana, and Mississippi

List of Cases

Arkansas
State v. Morrill, 16 Ark. 384 (1855), contempt of state supreme court.

Arizona
Hughes v. Territory, 10 Ariz. 119, 85 P. 1058 (1906), contempt.

California
Ex parte Barry, 85 Cal. 603, 25 P. 256 (1980), contempt.
Edwards v. San Jose Printing, 99 Cal. 431, 34 P. 128 (1893), libel in article suggesting purchase of votes in election.
In re Shortridge, 99 Cal. 526, 34 P. 227 (1893), contempt for violating gag order.
Dailey v. Superior Court of City and County of San Francisco, 112 Cal. 94, 44 P. 458 (1896), fair trial involving attempt to halt production of play dealing with pending murder case.

Ex parte Lawrence, 116 Cal. 298, 48 P. 124 (1897), refusal to testify about sources.

Jordahl v. Hayda, 1 Cal. App. 696, 82 P. 1079 (1905), prior restraint of boycott.

In re Hartman, 182 Cal. 447, 188 P. 548 (1920), display of flag symbolic of change held illegal under city ordinance.

Snively v. Record Publishing Co., 185 Cal. 565, 198 P. 1 (1921), libel based on cartoon of police chief which implied the chief was unfit for office.

People v. Steelik, 187 Cal. 361, 203 P. 78 (1921), violation of criminal syndicalism law by International Workers of the World.

People v. Taylor, 187 Cal. 378, 203 P. 85 (1921), violation of criminal syndicalism law by formation of Communist Labor Party.

People v. Whitney, 57 Cal. App. 449, 207 P. 698 (1922), criminal syndicalism.

Ex parte Campbell, 64 Cal. App. 300, 221 P. 952 (1923), distribution of literature favorable to the International Workers of the World in violation of law.

People v. Wagner, 65 Cal. App. 704, 225 P. 464 (1924), advocacy of violence by International Workers of the World.

People v. Cox, 66 Cal. App. 287, 226 P. 14 (1924), right of state to protect itself from advocates of violent change in government.

Colorado

Cooper v. People ex rel. Wyatt, 13 Colo. 337, 22 P. 790 (1889), contempt.

People ex rel. Connor v. Stapleton, 18 Colo. 568, 33 P. 167 (1893), contempt of state supreme court.

People ex rel. Attorney General v. News-Times Publishing Co., 35 Colo. 253, 84 P. 912 (1906), contempt.

Joslyn v. People, 67 Colo. 297, 184 P. 375 (1919), refusal to testify about sources.

People v. U.M.W. Dist. 15, 70 Colo. 269, 201 P. 54 (1921), forbidding incitement to strike is not against free speech.

Connecticut

Stow v. Converse, 3 Conn. 325 (1820), libel of member of state constitutional convention.

Moore v. Stevenson, 27 Conn. 14 (1858), libel.

State v. Sykes, 28 Conn. 224 (1859), claim that laws prohibiting publication of information on lottery violated freedom of the press.

Hotchkiss v. Porter, 30 Conn. 414 (1862), libel.

Arnott v. Standard Association, 57 Conn. 86, 17 A. 361 (1888), libel.

Atwater v. Morning News Co., 67 Conn. 504, 34 A. 865 (1896), libel of public official.

State v. McKee, 73 Conn. 18, 46 A. 409 (1900), publication of crime news.

State v. Howell, 80 Conn. 668, 69 A. 1057 (1908), contempt.

State v. Pape, 90 Conn. 98, 96 A. 313 (1916), libel of public officials.

State v. Sinchuk, 96 Conn. 605, 115 A. 33 (1921), advocacy of freedom of speech for aliens.

Florida

Jones, Varnum and Co. v. Townsend's Adm'x, 21 Fla. 431 (1885), libel of candidate for public office.

In re Hayes, 72 Fla. 558, 73 So. 362 (1916), contempt of state supreme court.

Georgia

Giddens v. Mirk, 4 Ga. 364 (1848), slander.

Pledger v. State, 77 Ga. 242, 3 S.E. 320 (1887), refusal to testify in libel case.

Wallace v. Georgia, C. & N. Rwy., 94 Ga. 732, 22 S.E. 579 (1894), free speech in service letter.

Fitts v. City of Atlanta, 121 Ga. 567, 49 S.E. 793 (1905), freedom to speak in public places.

Pavesich v. New England Life Ins. Co., 122 Ga. 190, 50 S.E. 68 (1905), privacy.

Plunkett v. Hamilton, 136 Ga. 72, 70 S.E. 781 (1911), refusal to testify about sources.

In re Fite, 11 Ga. App. 665, 76 S.E. 397 (1912), contempt of state supreme court by lower court judge.

Idaho

Adams v. Lansdon, 18 Idaho 483, 110 P. 280 (1910), election law requiring divulging of expenses.

McDougall v. Sheridan, 23 Idaho 191, 128 P. 954 (1913), contempt of state supreme court.

Robison v. Hotel and Restaurant Employees Local 782, 35 Idaho 418, 207 P. 132 (1922), right to strike.

Illinois

Stuart v. People, 4 Ill. (3 Scam.) 395 (1842), contempt.

Storey v. Wallace, 60 Ill. 51 (1871), libel by pandering to public's low taste.

People v. Wilson, 64 Ill. 195 (1872), contempt.

Storey v. People, 79 Ill. 45 (1875), libel and contempt.

Rearick v. Wilcox, 81 Ill. 77 (1876), libel of candidate for public office.

Spies v. People, 122 Ill. 1, 12 N.E. 865 (1887), free speech for those involved in Haymarket trial.

City of Chicago v. Trotter, 136 Ill. 430, 26 N.E. 359 (1891), public parades.

Block v. City of Chicago, 239 Ill. 251, 87 N.E. 1011 (1909), movie censorship.

City of Chicago v. Weber, 246 Ill. 304, 92 N.E. 859 (1910), regulation of theaters.

People v. Apfelbaum, 251 Ill. 18, 95 N.E. 995 (1911), revocation of physician's license for advertising.

People ex rel. Guggenheim v. City of Chicago, 209 Ill. App. 582 (1918), movie censorship.

People v. Schuettler, 209 Ill. App. 588 (1918), regulation of movies.

Vitagraph Corp. of America v. City of Chicago, 209 Ill. App. 591 (1918), regulation of movies.

Cooper v. Illinois Publishing and Printing Co., 218 Ill. App. 95 (1920), libel of judge.

City of Chicago v. Tribune Co., 307 Ill. 595, 139 N.E. 86 (1923), libel against city corporation.

Indiana

Cheadle v. State, 110 Ind. 301, 11 N.E. 426 (1887), contempt.

Watters v. City of Indianapolis, 191 Ind. 671, 134 N.E. 482 (1922), symbolic speech by wearing shirt with inscription during labor dispute.

Kilgallen v. State, 192 Ind. 531, 132 N.E. 682 (1922), contempt.

Thomas v. City of Indianapolis, 195 Ind. 440, 145 N.E. 550 (1924), antipicketing statutes.

Iowa

Dunham v. State, 6 Iowa 245 (1858), contempt.

State v. Anderson, 40 Iowa 207 (1875), contempt.

State v. Bair, 92 Iowa 28, 60 N.W. 486 (1894), selling cure-all drugs illegally and false labeling of medicines.

Field v. Thornell, 106 Iowa 7, 75 N.W. 685 (1898), contempt.

Cherry v. Des Moines Leader, 114 Iowa 298, 86 N.W. 323 (1901), libel by criticism of performer.

Morse v. Times-Republican Printing Co., 124 Iowa 707, 100 N.W. 867 (1904), libel of private person.

State v. Gibson, 189 Iowa 1212, 174 N.W. 34 (1919), advocacy.

Salinger v. Cowles, 195 Iowa 873, 191 N.W. 167 (1923), libel by criticism of official acts.

Kansas

Castle v. Houston, 19 Kan. 417 (1877), libel.

State v. Balch, 31 Kan. 465, 2 P. 609 (1884), libel of candidate for county attorney.

In re Banks, 56 Kan. 242, 42 P. 693 (1895), obscene publication.

Coleman v. MacLennan, 78 Kan. 711, 98 P. 281 (1908), libel of candidate for reelection as attorney general.

Atchison, T. & S. F. Ry. v. Brown, 80 Kan. 312, 102 P. 459 (1909), free speech in service letter.

State ex rel. Brewster v. Ross, 101 Kan. 377, 166 P. 505 (1917), regulation of movies.

Mid-West Photo-Play Corp. v. Miller, 102 Kan. 356, 169 P. 1154 (1918), review of films.

State v. Fiske, 117 Kan. 69, 230 P. 88 (1924), advocacy.

Kentucky

Riley v. Lee, 88 Ky. 603, 11 S.W. 713 (1889), libel.

Commonwealth v. Herald Publishing Co., 128 Ky. 424, 108 S.W. 892 (1908), obscenity in publication of details about the Henry Thaw murder trial.

City of Louisville v. Lougher, 209 Ky. 299, 272 S.W. 748 (1925), regulation of speech.

Louisiana

Territory v. Nugent, 1 Mart. 108 (1810), libel.

Denis v. Leclerc, 1 Mart. 297, 5 A.D. 712 (1811), libel.

City of New Orleans v. Crescent Newspaper, 14 La. Ann. 804 (1859), tax upon newspaper.

Perret v. New Orleans Times Newspaper, 25 La. Ann. 170 (1873), libel by publication of paid advertisement critical of judge and police officers.

State ex rel. Liversey v. Judge of Civ. Dist. Ct., 34 La. Ann. 741 (1882), prior restraint of libel.

Stave ex rel. Phelps v. Judge of Civ. Dist. Ct., 45 La. Ann. 1250, 14 So. 310 (1893), contempt.

Fitzpatrick v. Daily States Publishing Co., 48 La. Ann. 1116, 20 So. 173 (1896), libel.

Levert v. Daily States Publishing Co., 123 La. 594, 49 So. 206 (1909), libel.

Schwartz v. Edrington, 133 La. 235, 62 So. 660 (1913), injunction against publication of signed petition.

Pierson v. Times-Picayune Publishing Co., 148 La. 817, 88 So. 77 (1921), libel involving investigation about conditions in insane asylum.

Maine

State v. Mockus, 120 Me. 84, 113 A. 39 (1921), blasphemy.

Maryland

Negley v. Farrow, 60 Md. 158, 45 A.R. 715 (1882), libel of public official.

State v. Loden, 117 Md. 373, 83 A. 564 (1912), movie censorship.

Massachusetts

Commonwealth v. Clap, 4 Mass. 163 (1808), libel of public official.

Commonwealth v. Holmes, 17 Mass. 336 (1821), ban of the *Memoirs of a Woman of Pleasure* because of obscenity.

Commonwealth v. Blanding, 20 Mass. (3 Pick.) 304 (1825), libel.

Commonwealth v. Kneeland, 37 Mass. (20 Pick.) 206 (1838), blasphemy.

Barrows v. Bell, 73 Mass. (7 Gray) 301 (1856), libel.

Gott v. Pulsifer, 122 Mass. 235 (1877), libel by criticism of statute.

Cowley v. Pulsifer, 137 Mass. 392 (1884), reporting material from open court.

Commonwealth v. Davis, 140 Mass. 485, 4 N.E. 577 (1886), public speech on grounds of Boston Common.

Commonwealth v. McCafferty, 145 Mass. 384, 14 N.E. 451 (1888), carrying a placard.

Sherry v. Perkins, 147 Mass. 212, 17 N.E. 307 (1888), injunction to stop use of banners in labor dispute.

Sillars v. Collier, 151 Mass. 50, 23 N.E. 723 (1890), slander of public official.

McAuliffe v. City of New Bedford, 155 Mass. 216, 29 N.E. 517 (1892), expression of political opinion by policeman.

Commonwealth v. Davis, 162 Mass. 510, 39 N.E. 113 (1895), public speech on grounds of Boston Common.

Globe Newspaper Co. v. Commonwealth, 188 Mass. 449, 74 N.E. 682 (1905), contempt.

Commonwealth v. Buckley, 200 Mass. 346, 86 N.E. 910 (1909), obscene publication.

Commonwealth v. McGann, 213 Mass. 213, 100 N.E. 355 (1913), movie censorship.

Commonwealth v. Karvonen, 219 Mass. 30, 106 N.E. 556 (1914), state law that prohibited carrying a red flag.

Commonwealth v. Allison, 227 Mass. 57, 116 N.E. 265 (1917), distribution of obscene literature.

Commonwealth v. Boston Transcript Co., 249 Mass. 477, 144 N.E. 400 (1924), statute requiring newspaper to publish legal advertising at its regular rates.

Michigan

Detroit Daily Post Co. v. McArthur, 16 Mich. 447 (1868), question of damages involving libel.

Foster v. Scripps, 39 Mich. 376 (1878), libel of physician employed by city.

Bronson v. Bruce, 59 Mich. 467, 26 N.W. 671 (1886), libel of candidate for public office.

In re Frazee, 63 Mich. 396, 30 N.W. 72 (1886), public gatherings by Salvation Army.

McAllister v. Detroit Free Press Co., 76 Mich. 338, 43 N.W. 431 (1889), libel.

Belknap v. Ball, 83 Mich. 583, 47 N.W. 674 (1890), libel and slander.

Schmedding v. May, 85 Mich. 1, 48 N.W. 201 (1891), inspection of court files.

Hay v. Reid, 85 Mich. 296, 48 N.W. 507 (1891), libel of town marshal.

Owen v. Dewey, 107 Mich. 67, 65 N.W. 8 (1895), libel.

Beck v. Railway Teamsters' Protective Union, 118 Mich. 497, 77 N.W. 13 (1898), distribution of boycott circulars.

People v. Burman, 154 Mich. 150, 117 N.W. 589 (1908), right to parade with a red flag.

Van Lonkhuyzen v. Daily News Co., 203 Mich. 570, 170 N.W. 93 (1918), libel and fair comment.

People v. Ruthenberg, 229 Mich. 315, 201 N.W. 358 (1924), advocacy.

Minnesota

Aldrich v. Press Printing Co., 9 Minn. 123 (1864), libel of a corporation.

City of Duluth v. Marsh, 71 Minn. 248, 73 N.W. 644 (1898), licensing of theaters.

State v. Pioneer Press Co., 100 Minn. 173, 110 N.W. 867 (1907), publication of account of execution in violation of state law.

Higgins v. LaCroix, 119 Minn. 145, 137 N.W. 417 (1912), licensing of theaters.

State v. Holm, 139 Minn. 267, 166 N.W. 181 (1918), seditious publication discouraging enlistment.

State v. Gilbert, 141 Minn. 263, 169 N.W. 790 (1919), seditious speech discouraging enlistment.

Campbell v. Motion Picture Machine Operators' Local 219, 151 Minn. 220, 186 N.W. 781 (1922), prior restraint of trade publication.

Mississippi

Ex parte Hickey, 12 Miss. (4 S. & M.) 751 (1844), contempt.

Williams v. State, 130 Miss. 827, 94 So. 882 (1922), obscenity.

Missouri

Life Ass'n of America v. Boogher, 3 Mo. App. 173 (1876), prior restraint of libel.

Barber v. St. Louis Dispatch Co., 3 Mo. App. 377 (1877), libel in story based on court proceedings.

Flint v. Hutchinson Smoke Burner Co., 110 Mo. 492, 19 S.W. 804 (1892), prior restraint of libel.

State v. McCabe, 135 Mo. 450, 37 S.W. 123 (1896), libel.

State v. Van Wye, 136 Mo. 227, 37 S.W. 938 (1896), obscene publication by sex-oriented newspaper.

Arnold v. Sayings Co., 76 Mo. App. 159 (1898), libel in garbled story from police reports.

Marx & Haas Jeans Clothing Co. v. Watson, 168 Mo. 133, 67 S.W. 391 (1902), prior restraint of boycott.

State ex inf. Crow v. Shepherd, 177 Mo. 205, 76 S.W. 79 (1903), contempt of state supreme court.

Ex parte Harrison, 212 Mo. 88, 110 S.W. 709 (1908), political speech.

Ex parte Heffron, 179 Mo. App. 639, 162 S.W. 652 (1914), right of assembly for labor unions.

Cheek v. Prudential Ins. of America, 192 S.W. 387 (1916), free speech in service letter.

Hughes v. Kansas City Motion Picture Machine Operators Local 170, 282 Mo. 304, 221 S.W. 95 (1920), picketing.

Cheek v. Prudential Ins. of America, 223 S.W. 754 (1920), free speech in service letter.

Montana

In re Shannon, 11 Mont. 67 (1891), contempt.

In re MacKnight, 11 Mont. 126, 27 P. 336 (1891), contempt.

State ex rel. Haskell v. Faulds, 17 Mont. 140, 42 P. 285 (1895), contempt.

Lindsay & Co. v. Montana Federation of Labor, 37 Mont. 264, 96 P. 127 (1908), prior restraint of boycott.

State ex rel. Metcalf v. Dist. Ct., 52 Mont. 46, 155 P. 278 (1916), contempt.

Empire Theatre Co. v. Cloke, 53 Mont. 183, 163 P. 107 (1917), prior restraint of boycott.

State v. Kahn, 56 Mont. 108, 182 P. 107 (1919), seditious speech.

State v. Smith, 57 Mont. 563, 190 P. 107 (1920), sedition.

Nebraska

State v. Bee Publishing Co., 60 Neb. 282, 83 N.W. 204 (1900), contempt.

State v. Rosewater, 60 Neb. 438, 83 N.W. 353 (1900), contempt.

Bee Pub. Co. v. Shields, 68 Neb. 750, 94 N.W. 1029 (1903), rehearing denied, 99 N.W. 822 (1904), libel of public official.

In re Anderson, 69 Neb. 686, 96 N.W. 149 (1903), distribution of circulars.

State v. Junkin, 85 Neb. 1, 122 N.W. 473 (1909), political rights.
Howell v. Bee Publishing Co., 100 Neb. 39, 158 N.W. 358 (1916), prior restraint.
Bee Publishing Co. v. State, 107 Neb. 74, 185 N.W. 339 (1921), contempt.

New Hampshire
Smart v. Blanchard, 42 N.H. 137 (1860), libel.
Palmer v. City of Concord, 48 N.H. 211 (1868), libel by criticism of Northern soldiers.
Barnes v. Campbell, 59 N.H. 128 (1879), libel.

New Jersey
In re Cheeseman, 49 N.J.L. 115, 6 A. 513 (1886), contempt.
State v. Schmidt, 49 N.J.L. 579, 9 A. 774 (1887), libel of public official.
In re Grunow, 84 N.J.L. 235, 85 A. 1011 (1913), refusal to testify about sources.
State v. Boyd, 86 N.J.L. 75, 91 A. 586 (1914), advocating destruction of private property.
New Yorker Staats-Zeitung v. Nolan, 89 N.J.Eq. 387, 105 A. 72 (1918), prior restraint.
State v. Tachin, 92 N.J.L. 269, 106 A. 145 (1919), opposition to war effort because the war was being run by capitalists.
State v. Gabriel, 95 N.J.L. 337, 112 A. 611 (1921), advocacy of Communist doctrine.
Harwood v. Trembley, 97 N.J.L. 173, 116 A. 430 (1922), use of public streets.

New Mexico
In re Hughes, 8 N.M. 225, 43 P. 692 (1895), contempt.
State v. New Mexican Printing Co., 25 N.M. 102, 177 P. 751 (1918), contempt.
State v. Diamond, 27 N.M. 477, 202 P. 988 (1921), advocacy of government overthrow by International Workers of the World.

New York
People v. Croswell, 3 Johns. Cas. 337, 1 N.Y. Common Law Reports 717 (1804), libel against President Jefferson.
Root v. King, 7 Cow. 613, 9 N.Y. Common Law Reports 239 (1827), libel.
King v. Root, 4 Wend. 113, 21 A.D. 102 (1829), libel of public official.
Brandreth v. Lance, 8 Paige Ch. 24 (1839), prior restraint of libel.
Hotchkiss v. Oliphant, 2 Hill 510, 15 N.Y. Common Law Reports 436 (1842), libel by republication from another paper.
Hunt v. Bennett, 19 N.Y. 173 (1859), libel of person seeking appointed office.
Sanford v. Bennett, 24 N.Y. 20 (1861), libel.
N.Y. Juvenile Guardian Society v. Roosevelt, 7 Daly 188 (1877), prior restraint of libel.
Hart v. People, 26 Hun 396, 33 N.Y. Sup. Ct. 396 (1882), publishing accounts of lotteries.
People v. Muller, 96 N.Y. 408 (1884), obscenity.
Matthews v. Associated Press, 61 Hun 199, 15 N.Y.S. 887 (1891), antitrust.
Matthews v. Associated Press, 136 N.Y. 333, 32 N.E. 981 (1893), AP can forbid members from receiving and printing dispatches from UP.
In re Worthington Co., 30 N.Y.S. 361 (1894), obscenity.
Marlin Firearms Co. v. Shields, 171 N.Y. 384, 64 N.E. 163 (1902), prior restraint.
People v. Most, 171 N.Y. 423, 64 N.E. 175 (1902), seditious publication.
People ex rel. Clifford v. Scannell, 77 N.Y.S. 704 (1902), political speech.
Stuart v. Press Publishing Co., 82 N.Y.S. 401 (1903), libel by publishing papers on divorce action.
Ulster Square Dealer v. Fowler, 111 N.Y.S. 16 (1908), prior restraint.
Fox Amusement Corp. v. McClellan, 114 N.Y.S. 594 (1909), movie licensing.

McKenzie v. McClellan, 116 N.Y.S. 645 (1909), movie licensing.
Barry v. Players, 130 N.Y.S. 701 (1911), free speech and group membership.
Star Co. v. Brush, 170 N.Y.S. 987 (1918), prior restraint.
New Yorker Staats-Zeitung v. Brush, 170 N.Y.S. 993 (1918), prior restraint.
German Herold Pub. Co. v. Brush, 170 N.Y.S. 993 (1918), prior restraint.
Star Co. v. Brush, 172 N.Y.S. 320 (1918), prior restraint.
Star Co. v. Brush, 172 N.Y.S. 661 (1918), prior restraint.
Star Co. v. Brush, 185 A.D. 261, 172 N.Y.S. 851 (1918), prior restraint.
City of Buffalo v. Till, 182 N.Y.S. 418 (1920), street gathering.
In re Lithuanian Workers' Literature Society, 187 N.Y.S. 612 (1921), advocacy of government overthrow.
People v. Johnson, 191 N.Y.S. 750 (1921), distribution of circulars by NAACP.
People ex rel. Doyle v. Atwell, 232 N.Y. 96, 133 N.E. 364 (1921), speech in public streets.
Pathé Exchange, Inc. v. Cobb, 195 N.Y.S. 661 (1922), movie licensing.
People v. Gitlow, 234 N.Y. 132, 136 N.E. 317 (1922), advocacy of government overthrow.
Halsey v. N.Y. Society for the Suppression of Vice, 234 N.Y. 1, 136 N.E. 219 (1922), obscenity.
People v. Seltzer, 203 N.Y.S. 809 (1924), obscenity.

North Carolina
State v. Warren, 113 N.C. 683, 18 S.E. 498 (1893), free speech and use of profane language.
Cowan v. Fairbrother, 118 N.C. 406, 24 S.E. 212 (1896), newspaper business contract.

North Dakota
State v. Nelson, 29 N.D. 155, 150 N.W. 267 (1914), refusal to testify about sources.
Englund v. Townley, 43 N.D. 118, 174 N.W. 755 (1919), libel of state senator.

Ohio
Cincinnati Gazette Co., v. Timberlake, 10 Ohio St. 548, 78 A.D. 285 (1860), libel by publishing charges from police blotter before court has taken action.
Myers v. State, 46 Ohio St. 473, 22 N.E. 43 (1889), contempt.
State v. Babst, 104 Ohio St. 167, 135 N.E. 525 (1922), election laws and anonymous publication.

Oklahoma
Burke v. Territory, 2 Okla. 499, 37 P. 829 (1894), contempt.
Dickinson v. Perry, 75 Okla. 25, 181 P. 504 (1919), free speech in service letter.
Berg v. State, 29 Okla. Crim. 112, 233 P. 497 (1925), advocacy of government overthrow by International Workers of the World.

Oregon
Upton v. Hume, 24 Or. 420, 33 P. 810 (1893), libel of candidate for public office.
State v. Laundy, 103 Or. 443, 204 P. 958 (1922), advocacy of government overthrow by International Workers of the World.

Pennsylvania
Respublica v. Oswald, 1 Dall. 319 (1788), libel.
Runkle v. Meyer, 3 Yeates 518 (1803), libel.
Respublica v. Dennie, 4 Yeates 267 (1805), seditious libel.
Foster v. Commonwealth, 8 Watts & Serg. 77 (1844), libel and contempt.

Barker v. Commonwealth, 19 Pa. 412 (1852), indecent language in public streets.

Barr v. Moore, 87 Pa. 385 (1878), libel of public official.

Rowand v. DeCamp, 96 Pa. 493 (1880), slander by citizen calling a public official a thief.

Briggs v. Garrett, 111 Pa. 404, 2 A. 513 (1886), libel.

Goldman v. Reyburn, 36 Pa. County Ct. 581 (1909), advocacy.

In re Franklin Film Mfg. Corp., 253 Pa. 422, 98 A. 623 (1916), movie censorship.

In re Goldwyn Distributing Corp., 265 Pa. 335, 108 A. 816 (1919), movie censorship.

City of Duquesne v. Fincke, 269 Pa. 112, 112 A. 130 (1920), free speech in public streets.

Spayd v. Ringing Rock Lodge, 270 Pa. 67, 113 A. 70 (1921), bylaws of beneficial association.

Rhode Island

Metcalf v. Times Publishing Co., 20 R.I. 674, 40 A. 864 (1898), libel brought for publishing pleadings in court case.

South Carolina

State v. Lehre, 2 S.C.L. 214, 2 Brev. 446 (1811), libel.

Mayrant v. Richardson, 10 S.C.L. 140, 1 Nott & McC. 347 (1818), libel and slander of candidate for Congress.

In re Jager, 29 S.C. 438, 7 S.E. 605 (1888), newspaper licensing and taxing.

South Dakota

In re Egan, 24 S.D. 301, 123 N.W. 478 (1909), contempt.

Williams v. Black, 24 S.D. 301, 124 N.W. 728 (1910), libel in publication about private affairs of private citizen.

McLean v. Merriman, 42 S.D. 394, 175 N.W. 878 (1920), libel of public person.

Tennessee

Tate v. State ex rel. Raine, 132 Tenn. 131, 177 S.W. 69 (1915), contempt for violating gag order.

In re Hickey, 149 Tenn. 344, 258 S.W. 417 (1923), contempt.

Texas

Morton v. State, 3 Tex. Crim. App. 510 (1878), libel.

Thompson v. State, 17 Tex. Crim. App. 253 (1884), occupational tax against newspaper.

Express Printing Co. v. Copeland, 64 Tex. 354 (1885), libel of candidate for mayor.

Ex parte Neill, 32 Tex. Crim. 275, 22 S.W. 923 (1893), prior restraint.

Ex parte Foster, 44 Tex. Crim. 423, 71 S.W. 593 (1903), contempt for violating gag order.

Mitchell v. Grand Lodge Free & Accepted Masons, 56 Tex. Civ. App. 306, 121 S.W. 178 (1909), prior restraint of libel.

St. Louis Southwestern Ry. v. Hixon, 126 S.W. 338 (1910), free speech in service letter.

St. Louis Southwestern Ry. v. Griffin, 106 Tex. 477 (1914), free speech in service letter.

Ex parte Stout, 82 Tex. Crim. 183, 198 S.W. 967 (1917), picketing.

Ex parte Meckel, 87 Tex. Crim. 120, 220 S.W. 81 (1920), challenge to state disloyalty act.

Cooks', Waiters' & Waitresses' Local Union v. Papageorge, 230 S.W. 1086 (1921), injunction against labor strike.

Strang v. Biggers, 252 S.W. 826 (1923), prior restraint of libel.

Utah
Herald-American Publishing Co. v. Lewis, 42 Utah 188, 129 P. 624 (1913), contempt.

Virginia
Commonwealth v. Morris, 1 Va. Cas. (3 Va.) 176 (1811), libel of public official.
Louthan v. Commonwealth, 79 Va. 196 (1884), political participation by school super-
    intendent.
City of Norfolk v. Norfolk Landmark Publishing Co., 95 Va. 564, 28 S.E. 959 (1898),
    license tax on newspapers.
Burdett v. Commonwealth, 103 Va. 838, 48 S.E. 878 (1904), contempt.
Williams Printing Co. v. Saunders, 113 Va. 156, 73 S.E. 472 (1912), libel.
Boorde v. Commonwealth, 134 Va. 625, 114 S.E. 731 (1922), contempt.

Washington
State v. Tugwell, 19 Wash. 238, 52 P. 1056 (1898), contempt.
State v. Fox, 71 Wash. 185, 127 P. 1111 (1912), publication encouraging crime.
State ex rel. Dorrien v. Hazeltine, 82 Wash. 81, 143 P. 436 (1914), contempt.
State v. Haffer, 94 Wash. 136, 162 P. 45 (1916), libel of dead.

West Virginia
Sweeney v. Baker, 13 W. Va. 158 (1878), libel of candidate for state office.
State v. Frew & Hart, 24 W. Va. 416, 49 A.R. 257 (1884), contempt.

Wisconsin
State ex rel. Attorney General v. Circuit Court of Eau Claire County, 97 Wis. 1, 72
    N.W. 193 (1897), contempt.
Hyde v. State, 159 Wis. 651, 150 N.W. 965 (1915), slander.
State v. Pierce, 163 Wis. 615, 158 N.W. 696 (1916), corrupt practice involving limita-
    tion on amount of money that may be spent on political campaigns.

Case Index

Subject Index

213

gag rules, 39
Gallup Poll, 89–90; 116n. 4
Gellhorn, Walter, 81
Goodale, James C., 85n. 75
"gravity of the evil" concept, 102; 123n. 104

Hamilton, Alexander, 20; 110
  opposition to a bill of rights, 1; 45n. 10;
    89; 91
Hand, Learned, 101; 102
Harlan, John Marshall, 53n. 160; 72; 84n.
  67
Harper, Fowler, 139
Hart, Henry M., Jr., 11n. 19
Hay, George, 2
Hocking, William, 65–66
Hodge, John L., 6–7; 8; 10n. 8; 11n. 19;
  148–180
  biography of, 148
Holmes, Oliver Wendell, Jr., 133
  on clear and present danger, 63; 100; 102
  on libel and contempt, 37
  on marketplace of ideas, 82n. 2; 93
  on political rights and free speech, 57n.
    189
Howard, A.E. Dick, 3; 5; 6; 10n. 8; 129–137
  biography of, 129
Hughes, Charles Evans, 37–38; 57n. 191; 63
Hughes Court, 82n. 2

institutional press, 9; 107–109; 116

Jackson, Robert H., 69; 96–97
Jefferson, Thomas, 20; 91–92

Kalven, Harry, Jr., 83n. 37; 84n. 66
Karst, Kenneth, 179n. 101
Kent, James, 19; 20; 22; 23; 47n. 49; 48nn.
  54; 55; 54n. 166
Kurland, Philip B., 130

Landau, Jack C., 90; 116n. 5; 117n. 6
Lange, David, 176n. 58
Levy, Leonard, 45n. 15; 92; 118n. 12
libel, 85n. 78; 107; 143; 169
  actual malice rule of, 10n. 11; 33; 56n.
    181; 71; 72; 74; 84nn. 61; 67; 85n. 76;
    86n. 82; 98; 102–104; 115
  as related to preferred position doctrine,
    102–104
  impact of on free speech and press
    development, 22; 30–34; 38
  of public officials/public figures, 10n. 6;
    32–34; 52n. 135; 54n. 164; 55n. 181;

70; 71; 73; 84n. 66; 85n. 79; 102–103;
  124n. 113
  and state of mind inquiries, 73
libertarian theory, 2
Linde, Hans, 81

Madison, James, 2; 119n. 16
  on Bill of Rights, 17–18; 45n. 14; 91–92;
marketplace of ideas, 93
  and absence of government interference,
    162
  challenges to, by developing technology,
    182; 188; 190
  compared to laissez faire model, 162–163
  criticism of, 176n. 58
  monopoly of, 164
  presumption of, 75–76
Marshall, John, 43; 59n. 210; 129
Marshall, Thurgood, 133; 134
  on access to judicial proceedings, 113–114
  on campaign spending limits, 175n. 47;
    176n. 62
  on content neutrality, 179nn. 91, 96
McKenna, Joseph, 39; 53n. 160
Meiklejohn, Alexander, 72
  on absolute needs, 66–68; 93; 97
  bases of theory by, 64; 74; 119n. 16; 150;
    173n. 16; 174n. 25
  on need for public debate, 70; 71; 76
  on public versus private speech, 69; 78;
    80–82; 87n. 126; 120n. 32
Merrill, John C., 81
Milton, John, 75; 86n. 97
motion picture regulation, 28; 40; 48n. 66;
  50n. 90
Multipoint Distribution Systems, 182;
  191n. 3
Murphy, Frank, 96; 97
Murphy, Paul L., 82n. 2

Nelson, Harold L., 82n. 2
Nixon, Richard, 134; 140–141
  and "Nixon Court," 130; 134
  and press, 135
  and Warren Court, 130
normative theory, 150–151; 154; 172nn. 11,
  12, 14
  versus ethical theory, 172n. 9
  versus political theory, 150–151

obscenity:
  burdens of proof in, 55n. 179; 178nn.
    87–89
  constitutionality of doctrine of, 49n. 82